KARNAK

The temple of Amun-Re at Karnak is arguably the largest and most complex religious site of the ancient world. Yet despite this, there is no single publication in the English language which deals with its historical development from the early shrine of an obscure local deity to the greatest state temple of ancient Egypt's mighty empire over the course of two millennia. *Karnak* endeavours to fill this gap, describing in detail the contribution of each pharaoh in turn through the centuries until the temple's final closure in the Christian era, over two thousand years later.

The period covered involves some of the most illustrious names associated with ancient Egypt: Hatshepsut, Tuthmosis III, Amenhotep III, Akhenaten, Tutankhamun, Ramesses II – names that have resounded down through history to the present day. It is no exaggeration to say that the entire history of ancient Egypt is outlined in the stones of this spectacular monument.

Elizabeth Blyth provides for the first time in English an in-depth examination of the important temple site at Karnak. Supported by comprehensive maps, plans, illustrations and photographs, *Karnak* will be a crucial guide for Egyptologists, students and those people interested in the architectural and political development of this important complex.

Elizabeth Blyth, formerly of the Department of Egyptology, University College London.

KARNAK

Evolution of a temple

Elizabeth Blyth

Routledge
Taylor & Francis Group

LONDON AND NEW YORK

12 Ramesses II to the End of Dynasty XIX   155
13 Ramesses III and Dynasty XX   171

PART 3
The Late Period   **185**

14 Dynasty XXI, Dynasties XXII–XXIV (Libyan Period) and Dynasty XXV
    (Nubian Period)   187
15 Dynasties XXVI–XXX   209
16 The Final Phase   225
Conclusion   236

Bibliography   *238*
Index   *247*

PLATES

2.1	Example of the fine relief work in the White Chapel of Senusret I.	17
2.2	Block of Senusret I, currently in the Open Air Museum, showing Amun-Kamutef.	22
4.1	Alabaster kiosk of Amenhotep I.	35
5.1	Block from the Chapelle Rouge showing cartouches of Hatshepsut and Tuthmosis III.	56
5.2	Block from the Chapelle Rouge depicting Hatshepsut performing a ritual before the sacred bark in its shrine.	56
6.1	Staircase within Akh-Menu leading to the solar sanctuary.	75
6.2	A relief of a lion flanking Tuthmosis III within a pavilion.	82
7.1	The reconstructed Edifice of Amenhotep II.	96
9.1	Shattered block showing a rare example of the cartouche of Akhenaten at Karnak.	126
13.1	Cartouche of Ramesses IV usurped by Ramesses VI (from the Wadjet Hall).	180
14.1	False door on the façade of the chapel of Osiris Heka-Djet.	193
14.2	The entrance to the so-called 'Nilometer' attached to Taharqa's Edifice of the Lake.	204
16.1	Entrance to the temple of Opet.	230

FIGURES

1 General plan of the temple of Amun at the end of Dynasty XXX (after Aldred, C. et al., *Les Pharaons: L'Empire des Conquérants*: 301).   2

2 The development of the temple between the New Kingdom and Dynasty XXX. (a) The temple at the end of the reign of Tuthmosis III, a. The Akh-Menu, b. Middle Kingdom temple, c. Chapelle Rouge and Palace of Maat, d. Fifth Pylon (Tuthmosis I), e. Obelisks of Hatshepsut, f. Fourth Pylon (Tuthmosis I), g. Obelisks of Tuthmosis I, h. Obelisks of Tuthmosis III, i. Seventh Pylon (Tuthmosis III), j. Eighth Pylon (Hatshepsut). (b) Additions of late Dynasty XVIII and Dynasty XIX: a. Third Pylon (Amenhotep III), b. Hypostyle Hall (Seti I and Ramesses II), c. Second Pylon (Horemheb), d. Ninth Pylon (Horemheb), e. Tenth Pylon (Horemheb). (c) Major additions after Dynasty XIX: a. Triple bark shrine (Seti I), b. Bark station (Ramesses III), c. Khonsu Temple (Ramesses III), d. First Pylon (XXX Dynasty) (after Snape, S., *Egyptian Temples*: 37, 39 and 40). Not to same scale.   3–4

2.1 Plan of the Middle Kingdom temple (after Gabolde, L., *Le 'Grand Château d'Amon' de Sésostris Ier à Karnak*: pl. I).   13

2.2 'The High Lookout of Kheperkare', from the White Chapel of Senusret I (after Lacau, P. and Chevrier, H., *Une Chapelle de Sesostris Ier à Karnak*: 67).   15

2.3 Reconstruction drawing of the bark-shrine of Senusret I found within the Ninth Pylon (after Traunecker, C., in *Cahiers de Karnak VII*: 125).   18

2.4 The black granite naos of Senusret I: (a) North side; (b) South side (after Pillet, M., in *ASAE* 23: 149 and 153).   20–1

2.5 Stela of Senusret I found at Karnak giving the boundary of Nekhen (after Chevrier, H., in *ASAE* 49: 258).   25

4.1 Sketch plan showing the constructions of Senusret I and Amenhotep I (after Aufrère, S. et al., *L'Égypte Restituée*, vol I: 88).   34

4.2 The temple in the time of Amenhotep I. (a) Plan showing the limestone chambers flanking the court of the sanctuary. (b) Reconstruction drawing of the temple (after Graindorge, C. and Martinez, P., in *BSFE* 115, 50).   37–8

4.3 Plan of the temple of Amun in the reign of Tuthmosis I (after Aldred, C. et al., *Les Pharaons: L'Empire des Conquérants*: 302).   41

FIGURES

4.4	The Treasury of Tuthmosis I. (a) Plan of the position of the Treasury (after Jacquet, J., in *Problems and Priorities in Egyptian Archaeology*: 106). (b) Plan of the Treasury (after Aufrère, S. et al., *L'Égypte Restituée*: 119). Not to same scale.	43–4
4.5	Lintel block giving the names of Tuthmosis I and Senusret I (after Brugsch, H., *Histoire d'Égypte*: pl. XVI).	46
4.6	Plan of the Festival Court of Tuthmosis II (after Gabolde, L., in *Cahiers de Karnak IX*: 85).	48
4.7	Hypothetical reconstruction of the southern façade of the Festival Court of Tuthmosis II (after Gabolde, L., in *Cahiers de Karnak IX*: 87).	49
5.1	Plan of central Karnak at the end of the reign of Hatshepsut showing the probable position of the Chapelle Rouge (after Carlotti, J.-F., in *Cahiers de Karnak X*: 163).	58
5.2	Processional route from the temple of Amun to the temple of Mut via the sanctuary of Amun-Kamutef (after Kemp, B.J., *Ancient Egypt: Anatomy of a Civilization*: 187).	61
5.3	Way-station and palace of Hatshepsut. (a) The Way-station as depicted on the Chapelle Rouge (after Leblanc, C., in *BIFAO* 82: 301). (b) Possible siting of Hatshepsut's palace (after O'Connor, D., in *Ancient Egyptian Kingship*: 80, Fig. 7.2).	63
6.1	Plan of the Akh-Menu of Tuthmosis III (after Nelson, H., *Key plans showing locations of Theban temple decorations*: pl. VII).	72
6.2	Plan showing the gold decoration of Tuthmosis III in central Karnak (after Lacau, P., in *ASAE* 53: 251).	80
6.3	The House of Gold of Tuthmosis III. (a) Sketch plan showing its position. (b) Plan of the magazines (after Traunecker, C., in *CRIPEL* 11, 90–1, figs. 1 and 2).	90
7.1	Plan of the position of the Edifice of Amenhotep II (after Lauffray, J., *Karnak d'Égypte*: 138).	95
7.2	The porch of the Fourth Pylon (from the tomb of Amenhotep Si-se) (after Yoyotte, J., *CdE* 55 (1953): 28, fig. 7).	102
8.1	The constructions of Amenhotep III. (a) Sketch plan of the constructions (shown in black). (b) Canal and basin in front of the temple (from the tomb of Neferhotep TT49) (after Aufrère, S. et al., *L'Égypte Restituée*: 98 and 127 respectively).	107
8.2	Artist's impression of Karnak's quay and tribune (after Lauffray, J., *Kemi* XXI: 82).	113
8.3	Sketch plan of the processional routes between the temples of Karnak and Luxor (after Hegazy, E., in *Journal of Ancient Chronology Forum* 3 (1989–90): 82).	116
9.1	Possible siting of the palace of Amenhotep III and Akhenaten (after O'Connor, D., in *Ancient Egyptian Kingship*: 80, fig. 7.3).	122
9.2	The 'Nefertiti pillars' in the Ḥwt-bnbn (after Redford, D., *Akhenaten, the Heretic King*: 77).	124

FIGURES

9.3   Theoretical placement of the chapel of Tutankhamun (more probably an area for the consecration of offerings) (after Sa'ad, R., in *Cahiers de Karnak* V: 107). 131

10.1 The constructions of Horemheb. (a) Sketch plan of the constructions (shown in black) (after Aufrère, S., *L'Égypte Restituée*: 98). (b) Façade of the Second Pylon as depicted on the walls of the temple of Khonsu (after Aldred, C. et al., *Les Pharaons: l'Empire des Conquérants*: 306). 135

10.2 Drawing of the bronze plaque with the cartouches of Horemheb found beneath a flagstaff of the Ninth Pylon. (a) Drawing of the plaque as found. (b) Drawing of the plaque as it would have looked when complete (after Azim, M. et al., *Cahiers de Karnak VII*: 86 and 88 respectively). 138–9

11.1 Plan of the Great Hypostyle Hall showing the extent of the decoration of Seti I (after Brand, P., *The Monuments of Seti I*: Plan I). 148

11.2 Temple model showing the names of Amun and Ipet-Sut. (a) Reconstruction of the front; (b) Reconstruction of the left side; (c) Reconstruction of the right side (after Berg, D., in *SAK* 17: 97 and 99). 153

12.1 Plan of the Eastern Temple of Ramesses II with the additions of Taharqa and the Ptolemies. The single obelisk is at the western end (after Aldred, C. et al., *Les Pharaons: l'Empire des Conquérants*: 306). 159

13.1 Line drawing showing the royal cartouches of Herihor to be seen in the hypostyle halls of the temples of Amun and Khonsu (after *The Temple of Khonsu*, vol. I: pl. 7). 184

14.1 Drawing of Shepenwepet I wearing two double crowns, from the Chapel of Osiris Heka-Djet (after Legrain, G., in *RecTrav* 22: 131). 192

14.2 The constructions of Taharqa. (a) Sketch plan of the constructions (shown in black) (after Aufrère, S. et al., *L'Égypte Restituée*: 106). (b) Plan of the 'kiosk' of Taharqa in the First Court of the Temple of Amun (after Arnold, D., *Temples of the Last Pharaohs*: 53). 198

14.3 Artist's impression of the 'kiosk' of Taharqa in the First Court of the Temple of Amun (after Lauffray, J., *Karnak d'Égypte*: 102). 199

14.4 Example of wooden masts bearing emblems erected before a temple entrance (after Lauffray, J., in *Kemi* XX: 162). 201

14.5 Plan of the subterranean rooms of the Edifice of Taharqa (after Parker, R. et al., *The Edifice of Taharqa*: pl. IA). 205

14.6 Hathor façade to the Chapel of the Divine Adoratrices (after Arnold, D., *Temples of the Last Pharaohs*: 55). 206

14.7 Lintel from the chapel of Osiris-Ptah Neb-Ankh showing Taharqa and Tanutamun (after Fazzini, R., *Egypt, Dynasty XXII–XXV*: pl. XXI.3). 208

15.1 Plan of the storehouse of Psamut (after Traunecker, C., in *RdE* 38: 161). 214

15.2 Plan of the route of consecrated offerings from the storehouse of Psamut via the Chapel of Thoth into the Temple of Amun (after Goyon, J.-C. and Traunecker, C., in *Cahiers de Karnak VII*: 356). 215

15.3	Plan showing the position of the chapel of Hakor in front of the First Pylon (after Lauffray, J., *La Chapelle d'Achôris à Karnak,* vol. I: 15).	216
15.4	Plan showing the movement of the sacred bark into and out of the chapel of Hakor (after Traunecker, C., *La Chapelle d'Achôris à Karnak*, vol. *II*: 94).	217
15.5	Artist's impression of the chapel of Hakor (after Lauffray, J., *La Chapelle d'Achôris à Karnak,* vol. I: 60).	218
15.6	Artist's impression of the First Pylon gateway, with the later Roman temple on the right (after Lauffray, J., in *Kemi* XX: 107).	220
16.1	The temple of Opet under Ptolemy VIII. (a) Plan and section (after Arnold, D., *Temples of the Last Pharaohs*: 165). (b) Plan showing the juxtaposition of the temples of Khonsu and Opet (after Aufrère, S. *et al.*, *L'Égypte Restituée*: 115).	231–2

ACKNOWLEDGEMENTS

The libraries of the Egypt Exploration Society and the Institute of Archaeology, University College London, were central to my researches for this book, and I would like to thank their respective staffs for the help that they offered over many years. I am extremely grateful to Dr Elizabeth Bettles for her kind co-operation and for the expert drawing of all the figures, and also to Ian Blyth for supplying the photographs.

I owe an enormous debt of gratitude to Professor Harry Smith whose constant encouragement and enthusiasm have been a source of inspiration to me. His help and advice, so freely given, were invaluable, and he gave unstintingly of his time to read the manuscript and make many useful suggestions and comments.

For the final production of the completed manuscript, I am deeply indebted to my husband Ian, who gave hours of his time and technical expertise to make it possible. No words can adequately express how much I owe him for his unwavering love and support over the many years it took me to write this book: without his quiet and stalwart presence, it could not have been done. To him, therefore, I dedicate this book with heartfelt gratitude and love.

FOREWORD

Elizabeth Blyth's book is a complete and up-to-date account of the history, development and function of the manifold buildings of the great temple of the god Amun-Re at Karnak, both as they were and as they are now. This temple was the major religious centre of the capital city of Thebes in the period of Egypt's greatest impact on the ancient world in the New Kingdom (c.1570–1070 BC), and continued to function into the Roman imperial period; its ruins still form the largest and most spectacular monumental complex in Egypt today. No recent work on its history is currently available in English, yet over the past fifty years so much has been discovered in the temple and its environs that this book will be a priceless boon, not only to those who visit the temple individually and on tours, but also to all Egyptological students and enthusiasts. Guidebooks, of course, provide a routine description of the ruins, usually confined to a single itinerary through them; but these accounts rarely include recent discoveries and give little idea of the temple's long history. The following paragraphs are confined to offering some summary comments on the temple's status and religious and political functions in Pharaonic Egypt as a background to Elizabeth Blyth's excellent account of the historical development of this extraordinary monument.

The temple was founded in the Middle Kingdom by the second ruler of Dynasty XII, Senusret I (c.1971–1928 BC) to be the religious centre of the recently reunited Egyptian state. The god Amun, whose name means literally 'the Hidden One', was an ancient sky-god of no great prominence, whom this dynasty adopted as the new head of the state pantheon, and associated with the sun-god Re, the ruler of the heavens, whose principal seat was at Heliopolis near Cairo. The temple largely supplanted that of the war-god of Thebes, Montu, under whose banner the Upper Egyptian rulers of Dynasty XI (c.2060–1991 BC) had reunited Upper and Lower Egypt after the period of divided rule generally known as the First Intermediate Period. The pharaohs of Dynasty XII proclaimed themselves to be the progeny of Amun, chosen by him to lead Egypt according to the divinely sanctioned principles of order and right (Egyptian Maat).

The Karnak temple of Amun-Re was thus from its inception not only the residence on earth of the supreme ruler of the universe, but also the central religious institution of the state, where the king offered the worship and thanks of the people for the manifold gifts the god bestowed upon them through his son, the pharaoh: the Nile flood, the copious harvest, peace and unity at home, victory abroad, and, in the all-embracing Egyptian phrase, 'life, prosperity and health'. While virtually nothing remains standing of the Middle Kingdom temple, and there is a consequent dearth of informative contemporary inscriptions, the worship of the god Amun-Re and the major kingship rituals were probably conducted there much as they were in the New Kingdom. After a further period in which separate dynasties ruled Upper and Lower Egypt and the Delta fell under the rule of the foreign 'Hyksos' kings (known as the Second Intermediate Period, c.1782–1570 BC), the accession of Dynasty XVIII (c.1570–1293 BC) marked the reunion of the kingship and inaugurated the most expansive period in the history of the country and of Karnak temple. The pharaohs of Dynasty XVIII depicted the universal sky-god Amun-Re as the physical progenitor of each pharaoh, who fathered him upon the chief queen of his predecessor. This myth, together with the practice of royal brother-and-sister marriage, not only safeguarded the legitimacy and aided the continuity of the dynasty, but portrayed pharaoh as the divine ruler of Egypt in the same way as his father Amun-Re was the divine ruler of the universe. Each pharaoh thus wished to express his thanks to Amun-Re by building for him splendid monuments at Karnak and maintaining his offerings and cult, in return for which the god granted him long life, power and stability.

While the daily cult offered before the golden divine image of Amun-Re in his principal sanctuary at Karnak was similar to that offered before the gods in all the great temples of Egypt, the major ceremonies performed in the temple frequently had political overtones. In Egyptian depictions of temple rituals and ceremonies, the king is always shown as the celebrant, since this was his role as the son of the gods; in practice, the higher priests of each temple deputised for him. At Karnak, however, there is little doubt that the pharaoh himself was often present and officiated in the New Kingdom on great religious occasions like the New Year festival, the seasonal festivals, the Festival of Opet and the Beautiful Feast of the Valley. He also usually celebrated royal festivals, like the anniversaries of his accession and coronation and his sed-festivals, both at Karnak as well as at other major religious centres. On such occasions, the image of the god was, after preliminary censings, offerings and adornment, carried out of the sanctuary on the gilded sacred bark which was borne upon the shoulders of white-robed, shaven and manicured priests into the great hypostyle hall of the temple. There, in addition to the higher priesthood of the temple and the temple choir, the members of the court and high officials would be present, having observed the necessary fasts and purity regulations for a stipulated period. After offerings had been made and hymns sung, the will of the god might be consulted.

The Egyptian pharaohs of the New Kingdom regularly consulted the oracle of Amun-Re on major decisions of state, such as going to war, making expeditions to foreign countries, appointing high-ranking priests, building new temples, and upon matters affecting the kingship and the succession. The question to be put to the god was read out before the divine image by the king or the high priest; the god conveyed his assent or denial through backward or forward movements of his image within the bark. This confirmation by the state god Amun-Re of political decisions was considered essential, otherwise they would be ill-omened and their success impaired. Sometimes the god himself took the initiative; a recorded occasion was at the crisis in the succession at the death of Tuthmosis II, when the god's image sought out the young prince Tuthmosis, who was the son of a minor queen, among the crowd in the hypostyle hall, and indicated his wish that this prince should be the successor.

Such major ceremonies within the temple were attended only by priests and by high officials, who themselves frequently held priestly offices. The general public were not admitted within the temple halls and sanctuaries in order to preserve their purity and sanctity, but may have been allowed within the temple enclosure and even the temple forecourt on certain occasions, whence they could hear the singing of the temple choir, savour the smell of the incense, and experience the awe induced by the ceremonies. But at the Festival of Opet, when the image of Amun-Re was carried in pomp on his bark along the sacred way to his temple at Luxor, the people shared in the celebrations, and could present their own private prayers, petitions and oracle questions for the deity when, for instance, the procession halted at one of the many wayside stations. At the Beautiful Feast of the Valley, the image of Amun-Re was carried to the Karnak temple quay, rowed across the Nile in his river-bark, and then carried in procession to the necropolis to visit the mortuary temples of the kings, thus re-conferring eternal life upon each dead pharaoh. While the image rested at these temples, the mortuary priests of private tomb-owners came to take garlands from the god's bark as symbols of life with which they adorned the dead men's statues, so that they participated with former pharaohs in the revivification which the festival ceremonies were thought to bring about.

Egyptian victories in war were attributed to Amun-Re, and an image of the god was regularly taken on campaign. All booty and prisoners thus belonged to the god, and were regularly dedicated to him by pharaoh at a great triumphal ceremony, which was probably held in the great forecourt of the temple on the return from campaign. The booty, which included gold, silver and precious materials, was stored in the temple treasuries which adjoined the temple sanctuary, and was recorded there in detail as an essential element in the accounts of campaigns, of which a typical example is the famous 'Annals' of Tuthmosis III. The campaigns themselves were recorded in magnificent relief scenes on the outside walls of the temple; the most famous of these illustrate the victories of Seti I and Ramesses II in the Levant.

In giving thanks to Amun-Re, pharaoh dedicated vast areas of land all over Egypt which became part of the estate of Amun; some of this was agricultural land, but it also included mines and quarries, like the 'gold-lands of Amun' in Nubia and the eastern desert. A regular temple bureaucracy administered these lands, from which the temple received a large income in kind. A numerous peasant population tilled the ground and sowed the crops, while skilled craftsmen manned bakeries and breweries, fermented grapes, processed flax and oil. Such workers were all paid in kind, while mining and quarrying gangs were mainly made up of prisoners of war. These were, however, not the only means of boosting the temple's revenues. Its workshops produced quantities of material, both for internal ritual use and for sale: fine linen garments; metal, faience and pottery vessels; and even funerary goods, such as shabti-figures and magical amulets. This was in addition, of course, to the massive production of offerings of all types for the many altars in the temple: meat, fish, fowl, vegetables, flowers for garlands, bread and cakes, incense, oil for lamps and wax-tapers. Most of these workshops are likely to have been sited within and immediately outside the vast enclosure wall which delimits the precinct of Amun, though as they were constructed of mud-brick, little trace has yet been found of them.

Into the interesting but disputed questions of how far the wealth of the great temple of Amun-Re was at the direct disposal of the king, and how far the temple itself was a vital unit in the New Kingdom system of government, we cannot venture at length here. We know, for instance, that government officials with royal warranty could in some circumstances call on the temple's resources for materials and labour; that temples were exempt from certain royal taxes and levies; that the high priests of Amun-Re were royally appointed; and that the royal endowments of land were ceremonially reconfirmed at the beginning of each new reign. These facts, while they do not in themselves demonstrate direct control by the king, show that the temple was not the independent priest-governed institution as is often depicted. Indeed, priestly functions in Egypt were carried out on a rota system, each phyle (group) of priests being on duty for one month in four, so that priests were often pluralists, and the higher priests of Amun in particular frequently held high public offices.

The prosperity and importance of the temple of Amun appears at all times to have depended upon the closeness of its links with the state. Thus its fortunes began to wane from the time when, in Dynasty XXI (c.1070 BC), the principal royal residence and state capital was moved to the Delta. This decline continued down to the conquest of Egypt by Alexander of Macedon in 332 BC, with a brief interlude of prosperity under Dynasty XXV of Nubian kings of Napata, who made their Egyptian capital in Thebes and were traditional worshippers of Amun-Re. From the time when the capital was removed to Alexandria in the late fourth century BC, the temple of Amun at Karnak played no specially significant role.

Because of the status and function of the cult of Amun-Re, nearly every pharaoh added new buildings, or at the very least redecorated existing structures or re-dedicated them, adding inscriptions in his own name. Some of these schemes were so ambitious that existing monuments were partly or wholly demolished to make way for the new buildings, and in such cases the dismantled stonework, whether decorated or not, was generally reused in foundations or the internal fill of pylons and walls. For instance, the Middle Kingdom temple fell into disrepair, probably due to flooding, and its façade and portico were dismantled and replaced with a large offering complex by the female pharaoh Hatshepsut of Dynasty XVIII (c.1498–1483 BC), although the rest of the building remained in use until much later times. Pylons II, IX and X were all constructed, or reconstructed, by Horemheb (c.1321–1293 BC); this enormous operation necessitated the clearance of large areas and, accordingly, the blocks of several Dynasty XVIII temples and shrines were found in the fill of both Pylon II and Pylon IX. Among these were many thousands of small decorated blocks which had formed parts of buildings constructed at Karnak by the religious reformer Akhenaten (c.1350–1334 BC) and his consort and co-ruler, Nefertiti, for the sun-deity Aten whom they worshipped. As Akhenaten had removed the name of Amun from the temple, his buildings were deliberately demolished after his death for religious reasons, and the temple restored to the worship of Amun-Re. Many other minor temples, sanctuaries and way-stations have, however, been found in excavations within the enclosure walls of the temple. Some of these shrines, especially of the later periods, had walls of mud-brick, only their doorways and decorative features being of stone; in these cases, the brickwork has frequently been removed by peasants over the centuries for use as fertiliser, but archaeologists have been able to recover the groundplans and sometimes make partial restorations.

Thus the temple of Amun-Re at Karnak now comprises a vast agglomeration of pylons, courtyards, columned halls, sanctuaries, minor temples, bark-shrines, obelisks and colossal statues, and other buildings constructed over a period of about 2000 years, bearing the cartouches of the majority of Egypt's kings, while within its girdle wall,

FOREWORD

apart from the temples of Khonsu and Ptah (which are not treated in this book), there is the 'Open Air Museum', comprising damaged and re-erected buildings and vast areas containing blocks extracted from pylons and dismantled monuments. The whole is breathtaking, awe-inspiring and beautiful, especially by moonlight; but many visitors, more particularly on a first visit, often feel stunned and bewildered by its complexity, and by their inability from what they have read and heard to grasp the unifying purpose, historical relationship or individual significance of all the wonders they have seen. Even those who are well-read in Egyptological literature and who, like myself, have visited the temple many times, can still find it an extremely frustrating exercise to try and visualise it as it was at various epochs of its history.

Elizabeth Blyth has solved this problem for us. She has read in detail the field reports of excavations and restoration projects at Karnak, and much of the modern academic literature concerning the temple. She has studied the reliefs and hieroglyphic inscriptions, perused the accounts of early travellers, and selected plans, drawings and photographs from the mass of material available with a discriminating eye. She has, moreover, visited the temple many times to observe every visible detail for herself, and to absorb its spirit and unique atmosphere. From this cornucopia of information she has distilled this beautifully clear, systematic and succinct account of the temple's history and development. In its completeness and accuracy of detail, it is a work of true scholarship, yet it is also a joy for anyone to read. This is not only because of the easy flow of the narrative, the lucidity and elegance of Elizabeth Blyth's English prose and her avoidance of abstruse terminology; it is also because her love for Karnak and enthusiastic appreciation of Egyptian art and culture constantly shine through her text. As we read, the temple comes alive before our eyes as it was at its various epochs, and we are taken back into its ancient presence and atmosphere in a way that no guidebook summary or photographic album can achieve. I heartily recommend Elizabeth Blyth's book to all English readers with an enthusiasm for ancient Egypt, and to everyone who plans to visit the temple of Amun-Re at Karnak.

Professor H.S. Smith, D.Lit., FBA
March, 2005

CHRONOLOGY

Even after decades of research, it is not possible to give precise dates for Egyptian kings and dynasties upon which all scholars are in agreement.

Egyptian chronology depends upon a variety of sources: the works of classical historians and chronographers, Egyptian king-lists, Egyptian texts bearing regnal year-dates, recorded and dated astronomical events in Egyptian documents, and synchronisms with other ancient Near Eastern states. These sources have been combined and evaluated by different scholars in different ways, so that various dates appear in their publications. In this book, the dates are taken from the table given in W.J. Murnane, *The Penguin Guide to Ancient Egypt*, Harmondsworth, 1983 (reproduced here in part), which represents a fairly general consensus of opinion.

The Middle Kingdom (*c.*2040–1782 BC)

Amenemhet (Ammenemes) I	1991–1962
Senusret (Sesostris) I	1971–1928

Second Intermediate Period (*c.*1782–1570 BC)

Kamose	1573–1570

The New Kingdom (*c.*1570–1070 BC)

Dynasty XVIII

Ahmose (Amosis)	1570–1546
Amenhotep (Amenophis) I	1551–1524
Tuthmosis (Thutmose) I	1524–1518
Tuthmosis II	1518–1504
Tuthmosis III	1504–1450
Hatshepsut	1498–1483
Amenhotep II	1453–1419
Tuthmosis IV	1419–1386
Amenhotep III	1386–1349
Amenhotep IV (Akhenaten)	1350–1334
Smenkhkare	1336–1334

Tutankhamun	1334–1325
Ay	1325–1321
Horemheb	1321–1293

Dynasty XIX

Ramesses I	1293–1291
Seti (Sethos) I	1291–1278
Ramesses II	1279–1212
Merenptah	1212–1202
Amenmesse	1202–1199
Seti II	1199–1193
Siptah	1193–1187
Tauseret	1187–1185

Dynasty XX

Setnakht	1185–1182
Ramesses III	1182–1151
Ramesses IV	1151–1145
Ramesses V	1145–1141
Ramesses VI	1141–1133
Ramesses VII–XI	1133–1070
Herihor	1080–1072

Third Intermediate Period (*c.*1069–525 BC)

Dynasties XXI–XXIV (c.1069–712 BC)

Smendes (Nesubanebdjed)	1069–1063
Pinedjem I [at Thebes]	1070–1026
Sheshonk I	945–924

Dynasty XXV

Piye (Piankhy)	753–713
Shabaka	713–698
Taharqa	690–664

Dynasties XXVI–XXXI (c. 664–332 BC)

Psamtik (Psammetichus) I	664–610
Apries (Wahibre)	589–570
Ahmose (Amasis) II	570–526

Late Period (*c.*525–332 BC)

First Persian Period	525–404
Hakor (Achoris)	393–380
Nectanebo I (Nakhtnebef)	380–362
Teos (Djedhor)	362–360
Nectanebo II (Nakhthorheb)	360–342
Second Persian Period	342–332

Graeco-Roman Period (332 BC–AD 323)
Byzantine Period (c.AD 323-642)
Constantine	AD 323–337
Theodosius	AD 379–395

INTRODUCTION

The temples of Karnak at the height of Egypt's splendour and power must have been glorious to behold. Towering pylons with great cedar flag-staffs bound in bronze and topped with streaming coloured pennants, provided an entrance of unparalleled grandeur to the sacred precincts within. The pylons and great enclosure walls were painted white with the reliefs and inscriptions picked out in brilliant jewel-like colours, adding to their magnificence. Behind the high walls, glimpses of gold-topped obelisks which pierced the blue sky, shrines, smaller temples, columns and statues, worked with gold, electrum and precious stones such as lapis lazuli, must have shimmered in the dusty golden heat. The whole effect would have been one of mystery and power, which must have inspired awe in no small measure. For these great temples were not places of worship for the people as our churches and temples are today. Only the king and priests could enter the holy places deep within where sacred rituals were constantly performed in dim, incense-laden sanctuaries; while other temple personnel worked to serve the cult of the god in the many affiliated buildings within the encircling walls.

The ancient Egyptians themselves spoke of these holy places with reverence. The temple was 'like heaven, beautiful, pure, glorious and excellent'; the pylons were 'luminous mountain-horizons of heaven'; while the flagstaffs before them 'reached the stars of heaven'. The celestial connection was much emphasised.

Despite the ravages of time, the sight of the ruins of Karnak was still able to evoke a similar sense of awe in visitors throughout its long history. It is well summed up in the words of an early European traveller, C.S. Sonnini de Manoncourt, in 1799:

> It would be difficult to describe the sensations which the sight of buildings so grand, so majestic, raised within me. It was not a simple adoration merely, but an ecstasy which suspended the use of all my faculties. I remained for some time immovable with rapture, and I felt inclined more than once to prostrate myself in token of veneration before monuments, the rearing of which appeared to transcend the strength and genius of man ... (Traunecker and Golvin 1984: 96)

The Temple of Amun at Karnak, as the visitor sees it today, is an overwhelming and bewildering complex, yet nonetheless able, even now, to instil that same sense of awe. It is, in fact, a series of temples built over many centuries. Throughout those centuries, kings endeavoured to glorify Amun, the king of the gods, by undertaking

INTRODUCTION

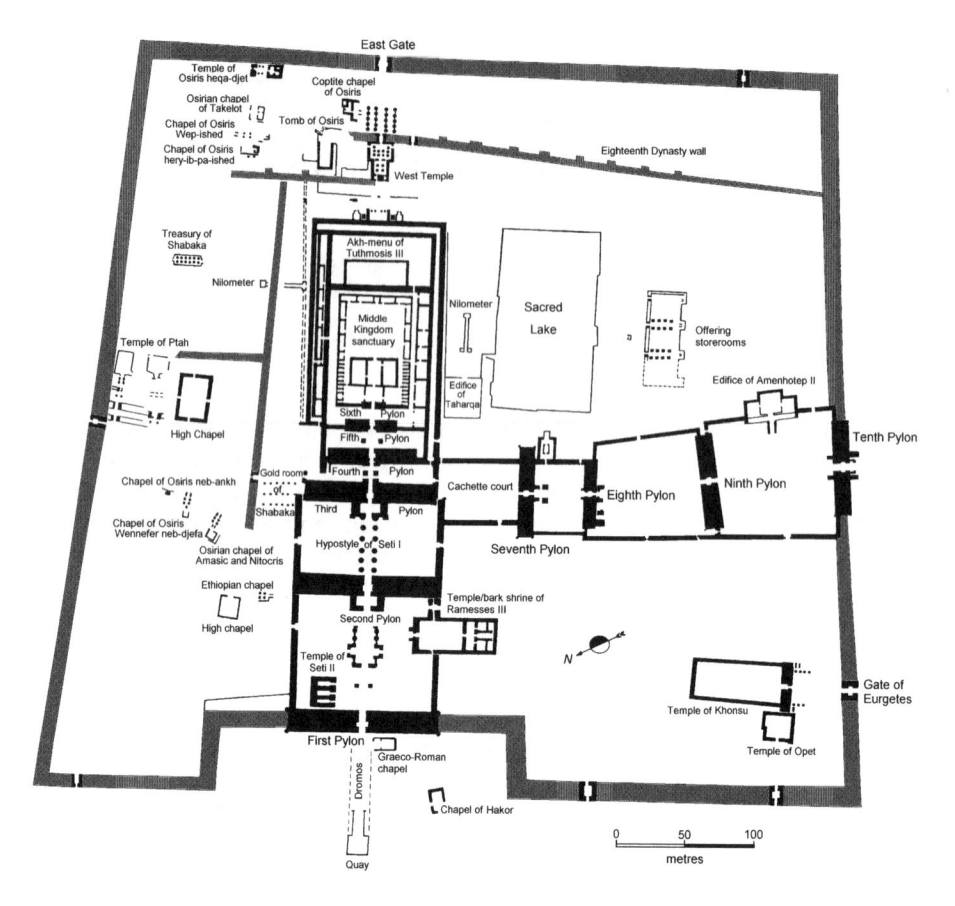

Figure 1 General plan of the temple of Amun at the end of Dynasty XXX (after Aldred, C. *et al.*, *Les Pharaons: L'Empire des Conquérants*: 301).

great building projects, and they also attempted to outdo the magnificence of earlier kings by enlarging, enriching, adorning, replacing, and sometimes simply usurping the monuments which their predecessors had erected. The temple in ancient Egypt was a place of power. Here, celestial and terrestrial combined to form heaven upon earth. Behind the high walls, daily rituals took place to maintain the well-being of Egypt and the equilibrium and harmony of the universe: and the Holy of Holies, the central sanctuary, was the core from which all this power was generated. To honour the gods with rich and costly buildings was to add to this power and to increase the benefits which would flow from the gods to Egypt and its king. This explains the great conglomeration of monuments which accrued over the millennia under countless kings, seemingly without an overall scheme, which makes up Karnak (Fig. 1).

The visitor, on first approaching the temple, ascends a ramp on to a raised quay adorned with two small obelisks of Seti II (Dynasty XIX). The sphinxes lining the avenue ahead are inscribed to Ramesses II (Dynasty XIX) and re-inscribed to Pinedjem

INTRODUCTION

I (Dynasty XXI). To the right is a shrine of Hakor (Dynasty XXIX). Passing through the great First Pylon (Dynasty XXX) and into the court of Sheshonk I (Dynasty XXII), to the left is a tripartite shrine of Seti II and to the right a temple of Ramesses III (Dynasty XX), while ahead are the remains of the huge ten-columned kiosk of Taharqa (Dynasty XXV), behind which rises the Second Pylon of Ramesses I (Dynasty XIX)(Fig. 2).

So far the visitor has only walked a few hundred yards, but might well be excused for feeling somewhat confused since, in this small area alone, a span of some eleven dynasties is represented. As the French scholar Serge Sauneron wrote: 'Karnak is a world in which one can be completely lost' (Posener 1962: 142). There are many excellent guidebooks to the existing temple buildings, but these tend to follow a west-to-east itinerary of the extant buildings and do not in any way give an idea of the temple's evolution through time. The purpose of this book is to endeavour to explain to the visitor the complexities of Karnak's chronological development over more than two thousand years, and to give some idea of what it might have looked like at various great stages of its history, in so far as can be deduced from our current state of knowledge.

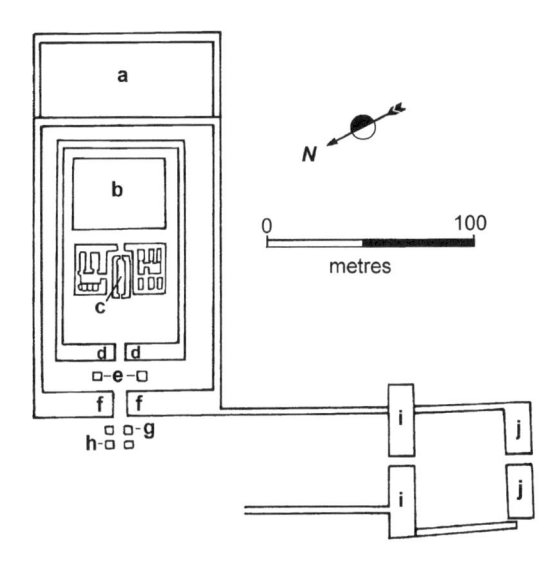

Figure 2 The development of the temple between the New Kingdom and Dynasty XXX. (a) The temple at the end of the reign of Tuthmosis III, a. The Akh-Menu, b. Middle Kingdom temple, c. Chapelle Rouge and Palace of Maat, d. Fifth Pylon (Tuthmosis I), e. Obelisks of Hatshepsut, f. Fourth Pylon (Tuthmosis I), g. Obelisks of Tuthmosis I, h. Obelisks of Tuthmosis III, i. Seventh Pylon (Tuthmosis III), j. Eighth Pylon (Hatshepsut). (b) Additions of late Dynasty XVIII and Dynasty XIX: a. Third Pylon (Amenhotep III), b. Hypostyle Hall (Seti I and Ramesses II), c. Second Pylon (Horemheb), d. Ninth Pylon (Horemheb), e. Tenth Pylon (Horemheb). (c) Major additions after Dynasty XIX: a. Triple bark shrine (Seti I), b. Bark station (Ramesses III), c. Khonsu Temple (Ramesses III), d. First Pylon (Thirtieth Dynasty) (after Snape, S., *Egyptian Temples*: 37, 39 and 40). Not to same scale.

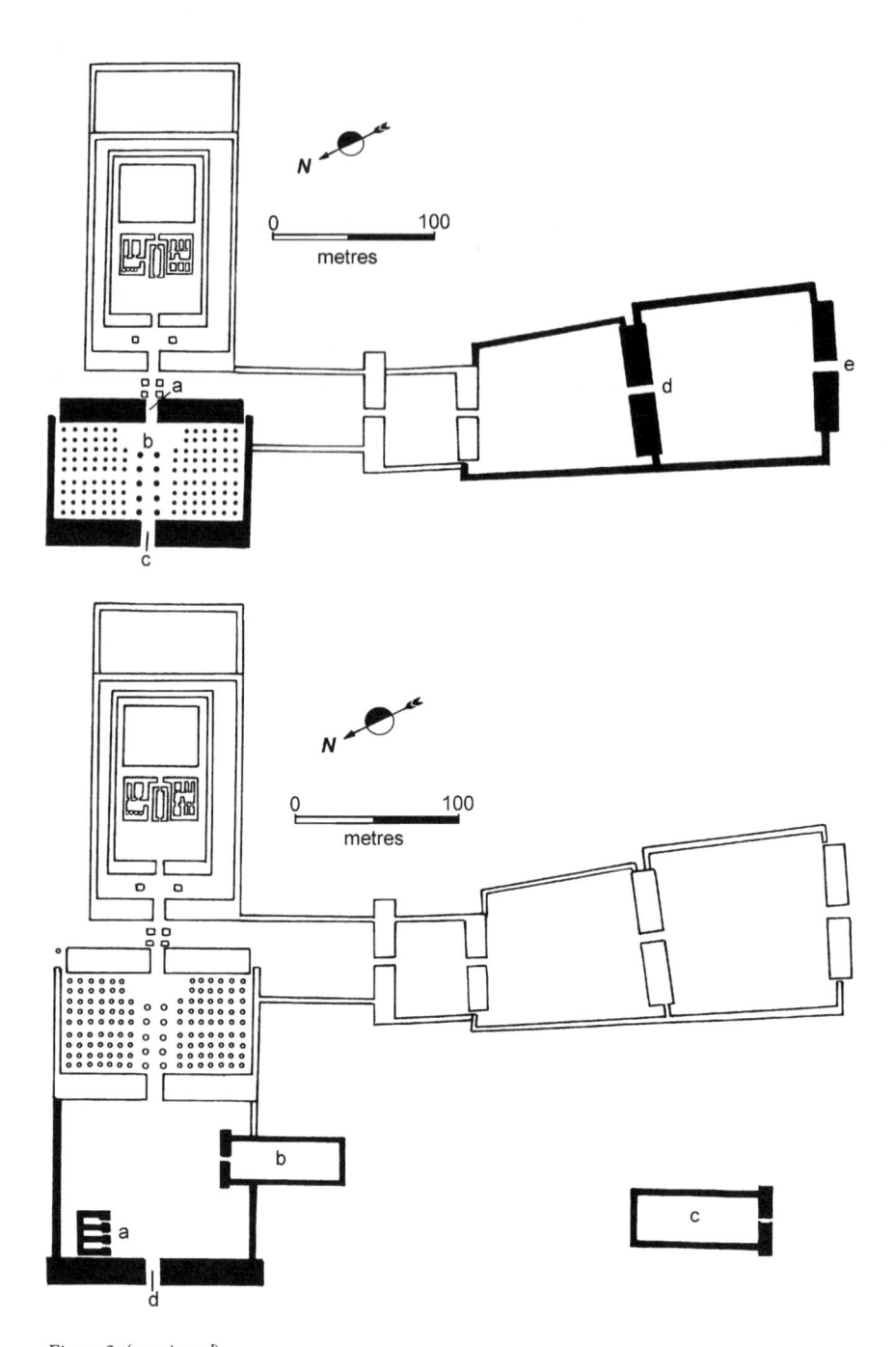

Figure 2 (continued).

Part 1

THE EARLY TEMPLE

1
ORIGINS

Karnak is usually associated in people's minds with the great city of Thebes when it was the capital of the mighty Egyptian Empire, from Dynasty XVIII onwards. But the history of Karnak goes back long before that period to a time when Thebes itself was no more than a small and relatively obscure provincial township on the east bank of the Nile in Upper Egypt. It is not in fact known when the town itself was founded, but very large quantities of palaeolithic flint tools point to an early occupation of this richly cultivatable area. Certainly by the time of the Old Kingdom, evidence is found of tombs on the West Bank opposite Thebes of some very important officials of Dynasties V and VI, indicating a fairly large and well-established settlement area. Even earlier, in Dynasty IV, a deity personifying the Theban nome is represented standing beside the pharaoh Menkaure in one of the famous triad statue-groups from that king's mortuary temple at Giza (Reisner 1931: pls 41–2). Such a representation indicates clearly the considerable importance of Thebes at this early stage.

Although a large hoard of predynastic and archaic antiquities was unearthed at Karnak, this does not necessarily mean that there was a temple there as early as Dynasty I. More probably it indicates that these ancient objects were dedicated to Amun in later times in the belief that his origins were to be found in remote antiquity (Daumas 1967: 204). As to when the temple of Karnak was founded, it is far from certain. Without doubt, the god Montu, the local deity, was worshipped at Thebes and had a temple in the vicinity from an extremely early, though unknown, date; but the founding of a temple to Amun at Karnak is even more shrouded in uncertainty. There are some snippets of evidence which, while not amounting to anything very positive in themselves, are nonetheless worthy of consideration.

The most recent, and concrete, piece of evidence is the unearthing at Karnak of an eight-sided sandstone colonnette of Wah-Ankh Intef II of Dynasty XI with an inscription mentioning Amun-Re and followed by the words: 'he made it as his monument for that god . . .' (Le Saout and Ma'arouf 1987: 294). This is the first known mention of Amun deriving from Karnak itself; it shows no sign at all of any damage or any recarving of the inscription. This must surely imply a temple, or at the very least a shrine, dedicated to Amun at Karnak, particularly since there is a reference to a 'house of Amun' in a tomb at Qurneh dating to the reign of Intef II (Petrie 1909: 17 [8], pl. X). Intef himself left a funerary stela in his pyramid on the West Bank at Thebes on which he had inscribed: 'I filled his temple with august vases . . . I built their temples, wrought their stairways, restored their gates . . .' (BAR I: para. 421). Though whether this particular reference was to Amun or Montu – or even both – is the subject of some debate.

THE EARLY TEMPLE

More tenuous perhaps, but certainly believed by some scholars, is that the Amun temple was more ancient still. In the Festival Hall complex of Tuthmosis III at Karnak there is a small chamber on the south side, named by its excavators the 'Chamber of Ancestors' since it has inscribed on its walls the names of sixty-one kings of former dynasties. The earliest surviving name is that of Snofru (Dynasty IV) – but, intriguingly, there is one which predates Snofru, now sadly destroyed. Since this list appears to be a special selection of names, it is felt that these were probably kings who had endowed and enriched Karnak, and consequently were revered by later rulers. Certain finds in the famous Karnak cache (see p. 231) would seem perhaps to bear this out, although there is no positive proof for the theory. The enormous cache of statues and other temple items, found between 1901 and 1905, was buried beneath the court north of the Seventh Pylon. It contained 751 statues and stelae and 17,000 bronzes: these ranged in date from the very earliest periods of Egyptian history through to the Ptolemaic era. Statues attributed to kings of the Archaic and Old Kingdom periods – Khasekhemui (Dynasty II), Khufu (Dynasty IV) and Neuserre (Dynasty V) – are used to argue the case for there having been some form of sanctuary or temple at Karnak dating back to at least the Old Kingdom, although it is acknowledged that it would have been (and remained for some time) considerably smaller than the then-existing Montu enclosure. And it must be admitted that there is no firm evidence of its being a temple dedicated to Amun, though the likelihood is that it was.

In the Middle Kingdom, Senusret I, whose extensive building programme at Karnak was most certainly in honour of Amun, dedicated much statuary to earlier kings: he honoured amongst others Sahure, Intef, Nebhepetre Montuhotep and Sankhkare Montuhotep, all kings who were commemorated later in Tuthmosis III's Chamber of Ancestors. It is generally agreed that the statues of various Old Kingdom monarchs found in the Karnak cache do not necessarily imply that these actually dated from that period, but were, more probably, the work of later kings wishing to honour their predecessors who, they believed, had founded or contributed to an early sanctuary to Amun. Indeed, as just mentioned, it is acknowledged that Senusret I had dedicated several such statues. However, there is an exception. One statue of Neuserre (Dynasty V) was, according to Bernard Bothmer, a notable authority on statuary, an Old Kingdom statue 'of undisputed date' (Bothmer 1974: 168), which most certainly lends weight to the argument that an earlier temple had existed.

The ancient name for Karnak was Ipet-Sut, translated as 'Most Select of Places', a truly appropriate name for a temple. Strictly speaking, the term Ipet-Sut should only be applied to that central core of Karnak which lies between the Fourth Pylon of Tuthmosis I and the Festival Hall (Akh-Menu) of Tuthmosis III. Inscriptions on some of the later monuments themselves testify to this: the Hypostyle Hall of Seti I/Ramesses II was built 'in front of Ipet-Sut', and the single obelisk of Tuthmosis III, erected by his grandson in the Eastern Temple of Karnak, was described as being 'in the neighbourhood of Ipet-Sut'. The origin and derivation of this name are uncertain, but the earliest known occurrences of it are found on two small monuments of the Middle Kingdom. On the West Bank at Thebes, in the mountains behind Deir el-Bahri, is a small mud-brick temple of Sankhkare Montuhotep of Dynasty XI. This temple, recently re-excavated by a Hungarian team (Vörös and Pudleiner 1997: 37–9), is an interesting little building on several counts: it has the earliest known pylon entrance, which was topped with a limestone crenellation – a unique feature. Within the mud-brick enclosure there was a small chapel made up of a hall and three shrines, from which were recovered the remains of various limestone elements, and amongst whose fragmentary inscriptions can be seen the name Ipet-Sut (Nims 1965: 70). The other Middle Kingdom source for the name occurs on the so-called White Chapel of Senusret I (Dynasty XII) at Karnak (Lacau and Chevrier 1956: 77, para. 185). Although it is not known when the name first came into use, its writing within the White Chapel, using the final hieroglyphic determinative symbol three times to denote the plural, would point to an archaic derivation. Such a rendition to denote the plural is characteristic of archaic literary conventions. Later, plurals were generally rendered by the three plural strokes (|||), though it has to be said that in a religious context the older forms often continued to be used.

If the term Ipet-Sut was being used as early as Dynasty XI, this certainly seems to indicate that a temple to Amun was in existence at that time. The very meagre archaeological evidence of these early periods at Karnak itself could moreover show that there were indeed temples which preceded the sparse Middle Kingdom remains that still exist, as we shall see.

This, I hope, gives a little background to the temple and its possible origins. But, in truth, how little we know about so vast a site, though perhaps this is what gives it some of its appeal: mystery always adds another dimension and speaks to the imagination. French, Egyptian and other archaeological teams have been working for well over a century at Karnak, the central remains of which cover around ninety acres, and Greater Karnak (which includes the temples of Montu and Mut) around 750 acres. The excavation and research these teams undertake is, of necessity, a slow and painstaking business. Nevertheless, thanks to their continuing efforts, it is possible to unravel some of the complexities of the site by studying the remains and attempting to put them in their historical and chronological context, using original textual sources for additional information.

2

THE MIDDLE KINGDOM

The most ancient areas that remain at Karnak are the Middle Kingdom court, the White Chapel of Senusret I, and a large brick ramp which gives access to the Montu precinct on the north-west side, this latter not strictly a part of the temple of Amun. However, although the Middle Kingdom court was once the most sacred area of the temple, we can only guess at its splendour, for, sadly, it is also the most ruinous area. Much other evidence has come to light, as we shall see, giving tantalising glimpses of the early temple.

Senusret I (*c*.1971–1928 BC) must be considered the founder of Dynasty XII temple whose remains are, in some small part, still visible today in the Middle Kingdom court. This king was to place Thebes and Karnak at the centre of state and religious life by building a new temple to Amun under the god's solar aspect – Amun-Re.

Senusret I was a most prolific builder: at least thirty-five sites have yielded monuments or buildings of the king, who also enlarged and enriched almost all the temples in Egypt which were already in existence. On a lintel from one of his many monuments (the temple of Re at Heliopolis) Senusret caused the following words to be inscribed: 'The king dies not, who is mentioned by reason of his achievements' (BAR I: para. 503). It would seem from all that he left behind him that he has been successful in this aim. As to Karnak, it appears that he built upon foundations of earlier temples, which he either pulled down or found in ruins. Several levels of flooring have been found below the existing pavements of the Middle Kingdom court, indicating that more than one temple had previously occupied the site (Lauffray 1980: 20–6; Gabolde 1998: 111).

There is no sure evidence as to which kings had founded these earlier temples. A few odd blocks and other fragments attributed to Nebhepetre Montuhotep have been discovered in various locations around Karnak (Habachi 1963: 35–6), but whether these can be truly dated to Dynasty XI, or whether they are elements dedicated to that great king by later rulers, is uncertain. However, considering the number of fine statues and offering tables of Amenemhet I (the first king of Dynasty XII) that have been unearthed, and also the belief that he may have erected an early shrine to Mut, Amun's consort, he must be considered one likely candidate. It was, after all, Amenemhet I who raised the god Amun at Thebes to become a national deity, and who was the probable founder of the Beautiful Feast of the Valley when Amun of Karnak travelled, amidst great celebration, to the West Bank to visit Nebhepetre Montuhotep's temple at Deir el-Bahri. Moreover, Amenemhet's name was the first king's name to be compounded with that of Amun. However, despite all this, it seems unlikely that Senusret would have pulled down his father's temple and replaced it with one of his own, and it can hardly have been the case that he had found it in ruins. Indeed, it must be admitted that while there are many statues and the like, as mentioned above, of Amenemhet, there is a remarkable lack of architectural elements. Did Amenemhet perhaps, then, merely erect a small shrine or chapel, or did he enrich an already existing temple? Do we indeed have to consider earlier kings as possible founders of the temple to Amun? The evidence of the 'platform' underlying the so-called Middle Kingdom court implies that this perhaps was the case, but again architectural remains are virtually non-existent. In addition, there is nothing to indicate a building programme of Amenemhet I; it is Senusret I whose name is indisputably linked with the founding of the Middle Kingdom temple at Karnak.

It is, therefore, with the extensive, but dispersed, remains of Senusret I's building activities that we can first begin to build up a picture, albeit patchy, of the early Karnak. The Middle Kingdom court, which lies behind the sanctuary of Philip Arrhidaeus, was set on a platform 40 m square; several layers of foundation levels have been identified here, as mentioned above, comprising a mixture of both limestone and sandstone blocks which had been reused from buildings of an earlier period (probably Dynasty XI), and this platform of blocks was itself founded upon an older base of mud-brick, possibly the vestiges of an even more ancient shrine or temple.

Today, there is very little to be seen in the Middle Kingdom court to give any impression of its original design. Three red granite doorsills are still visible in a line along the temple axis; these successive doorways once gave access to three rooms, the rear one assumed to be the sanctuary (Gabolde 1998: 114 and 118). Initially it was thought that in this final chamber must have stood the great alabaster base, whose broken remains have been found; these have been pieced together and the base restored to what was thought to have been its original position (Chevrier 1949: 12–13). It is a square pedestal, approached by a shallow staircase, and upon which several columns of text of Senusret are inscribed, whilst grooves on top of this pedestal indicate where some structure, perhaps a wooden shrine, had once stood. In the same area as these granite sills, remains of sixteen-sided columns in sandstone, bearing the cartouche of Senusret, have been found, as well as elements of a doorway whose inscription mentions a Year 20 of Senusret I, but more of this later.

The Holy of Holies, the deepest and most sacred sanctuary, which once stood in the court of the Middle Kingdom is now completely and totally destroyed. Looking at surviving examples from other temples, it must be assumed that, like them, it was a question of a room of small dimensions containing the naos (usually of granite) in which was housed the god's statue, and in whose image was believed to have rested the great creative force – that divine power which sustained the entire universe. In New Kingdom and later temples, we know that the progress towards this sacred area became ever dimmer as the ground level slowly ascended and the roof level became lower; the doorways opened successively one after another until the king or high priest, the only people who were allowed to approach the god's presence, finally stood before the closed doors of the naos, the very centre of the mystery and power of the ancient Egyptian temple.

From these general observations, one can begin to build up a picture of a typical small, symmetrical Egyptian temple, but until recently it has been almost impossible to say with any degree of certainty what that temple might have looked like and with what courts and chambers it might have been furnished. Whatever the original plan, however, there is no doubt that the Middle Kingdom court had contained the Holy of Holies, which remained in place for many centuries. In fact, it is probable that the entire court remained in use throughout much of the pharaonic period, though its internal arrangements and general environs were obviously adapted and altered.

Little more was known for certain regarding this large blank area of Karnak until very recently, when the publication of in-depth research greatly expanded our knowledge of the Middle Kingdom temple. Thanks to the excavations of the Franco-Egyptian Centre at Karnak, and the work of Luc Gabolde in particular, it is now possible to visualise the very imposing structure that once constituted Senusret I's temple dedicated to Amun-Re (Fig. 2.1).

Although the name of Amun-Re is attested at Karnak as early as the reign of Antef II, it was Senusret who undoubtedly was instrumental in merging the cult of the local god Amun with that of the sun god Re, and thus introducing a Heliopolitan element to the new temple (Gabolde 1998: 117). In later years – from the inception of the New Kingdom in fact – Karnak was often referred to as 'Iwnw-šm', the 'Heliopolis of the south'. This assimilation was to have a profound effect upon the development of Karnak over the centuries, and Senusret himself was greatly revered by later kings.

Senusret's temple stood within a surrounding wall of mud-brick that contained two small stone entrance gateways on the north and south sides, the lintels and jambs of which have been recovered in the area. The foundations of this mud-brick wall have been found exactly around the perimeter of the Middle Kingdom court platform (Gabolde 1998: 114 [185a]). The main entrance gate in the west wall would also have been in stone, but considerably larger in size, and probably flanked by mud-brick pylons. A lintel of Senusret I from just such a monumental gateway has been found, though its original location cannot be ascertained. As mentioned above, pylons were known from the time of Sankhkare Montuhotep (Dynasty XI), and these were already of a fairly impressive size. Indeed, the pylons of Ramesses III's temple (Dynasty XX nearly nine centuries later) at Karnak were no bigger than those of Sankhkare's mountain temple on the West Bank at Thebes, each wing of which had a width of 10 m.

The Middle Kingdom temple itself was constructed of limestone and measured in the region of 40 m square, with walls around 6 m in height. Its façade was preceded by a portico of twelve pillars, each one fronted by a colossus of the king in Osiride form, one of which has been unearthed from the foundations of the Sixth Pylon and is today in the Cairo Museum. Immediately behind the portico a central doorway led into a first court, considerably wider than deep, whose four sides were surrounded by a peristyle of square pillars. For decades, the existence of such a court had been known to Egyptologists, thanks to the discovery of the remains of several of the pillars (Legrain 1903: 12–14). As these were found very largely in the area now termed the Court of the Cachette (or court of the Seventh Pylon), it was assumed that Senusret had erected this peristyle court to the south, just outside the main temple. However, after re-excavation of the Court of the Cachette, which revealed absolutely no foundations or ancient soil levels, and painstaking research undertaken in storage magazines and archives, it has become apparent that Senusret's court was in fact sited within the temple itself. Around the perimeter of this court once stood the limestone pillars, each side of which was carved with fine reliefs of the king, giving his full titulary and showing him worshipping in turn Amun, Atum, Horus and Ptah (Gabolde 1998: 89–93). This emphasised the

■ Remains still in situ

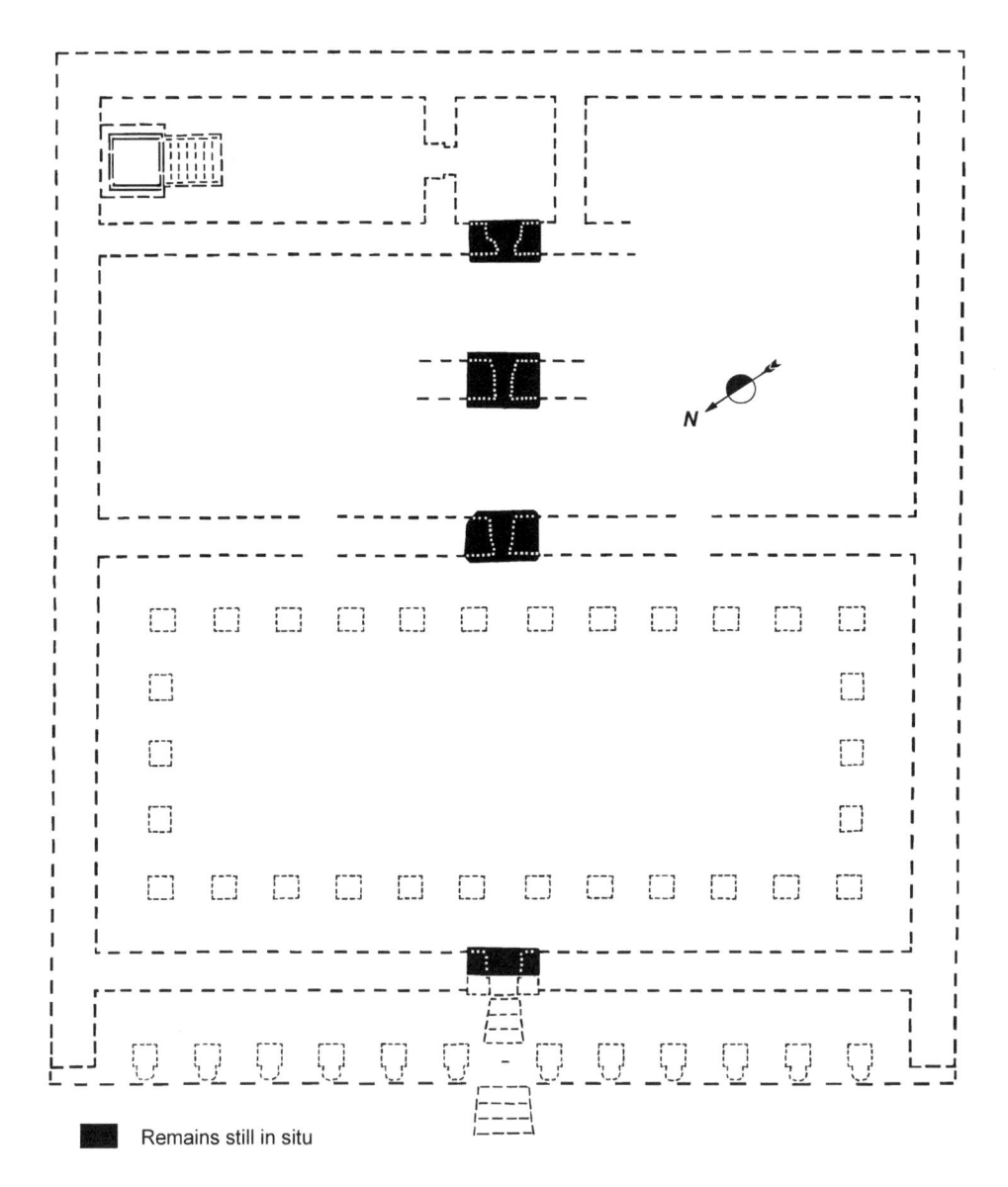

Figure 2.1 Plan of the Middle Kingdom temple (after Gabolde, L., *Le 'Grand Château d'Amon' de Sésostris Ier à Karnak*: pl. I).

king's control over Memphis, Heliopolis and the Delta, as well as Thebes. Could this be an indication that, even at this early date, Karnak should be considered a state temple?

These limestone pillars are not quite as high as those of the portico preceding it, which confirms that Senusret's temple adhered to the age-old tradition of gently rising floor levels and descending roof levels as one progressed through the courts and halls towards the sanctuary.

Behind the main porticoed façade, the temple was divided into two: the western half was, as just outlined, occupied by the peristyle court. A doorway in the rear wall of this court gave access over the first of the three red granite sills, still in place, to a hall – perhaps a narrow hypostyle. From here another door on the axis led into a vestibule of some kind, and a final doorway (over the third sill) opened upon yet another chamber. This last chamber was thought originally to have housed the alabaster altar base mentioned above as still being in place, but subsequent research has shown that this could not have been the case, and that in fact a doorway in the north wall of the chamber gave access to an inner sanctum where a naos, the Holy of Holies, shrouded in mystery, was enshrined upon the alabaster base within the depth of the temple (Gabolde 1995: 253–6).

This, then, was the general layout of the temple of Senusret I dedicated to Amun-Re, which almost certainly remained in use – at least in part – until the end of pharaonic history, though obviously there would have been many adaptations and alterations in both form and function over that time; indeed, the Roman emperor Tiberius left his name on some restoration work there (Legrain 1900a: 63). Amenhotep I, at the start of Dynasty XVIII, was the first king to expand the Middle Kingdom temple substantially, followed by every other New Kingdom ruler, as succeeding chapters will show. Restoration work undoubtedly became necessary from a relatively early date as the limestone, so very vulnerable to water, began to erode. It is probably true to say that the Middle Kingdom temple was already in a state of decay by the time of Hatshepsut/Tuthmosis III. The sixteen-sided sandstone columns found in this area, which are inscribed in Senusret's name, were almost certainly the work of Tuthmosis III, very probably when that latter king found it necessary to replace the decaying limestone pillars of the peristyle court. This can be stated with reasonable certainty since limestone was the material used by Senusret for his temple, whilst Tuthmosis, realising the effect of water erosion on limestone, used sandstone extensively; also, sixteen-sided columns were not in use in Senusret's time, but were common under Tuthmosis III. In addition, it should be noted that the text on these columns is identical to one inscribed under Tuthmosis, which can still be seen today, on the door embrasure leading into the Middle Kingdom court area.

The decoration and relief-work of the Middle Kingdom temple can be admired for its fine quality, as evinced from the scattered remains that survive. The carving, much of it in raised relief, is of the very highest order and makes us all the more aware of the treasures that have been lost. However, one particular relief of Senusret I is well-known today, thanks to the devotion of Tuthmosis III for his great ancestor. It is a copy of a scene which depicted Senusret seated on a throne decorated with the *sm3-t3wy* symbol (the binding of the heraldic plants of Upper and Lower Egypt, symbolising the union of the Two Lands) and flanked by two lions: before the king are the remains of some kind of autobiographical text, most of which, sadly, is missing (Habachi 1985: 350 ff.; Gabolde 1998: 40–3). Part of the text speaks of how Senusret called a meeting of his ministers and courtiers to discuss various important policies – almost certainly, the king's decision to build a temple to Amun. The date of the inscription places this occurrence quite firmly twenty-two weeks after the murder of his father Amenemhet I – the details of which are known from the opening of the story of Sinuhe. Why did Tuthmosis III copy this important historical scene, and where had the original been located in the Middle Kingdom temple? It can be assumed that Tuthmosis found the

Figure 2.2 'The High Lookout of Kheperkare', from the White Chapel of Senusret I (after Lacau, P. and Chevrier, H., *Une Chapelle de Sesostris Ier à Karnak*: 67).

wall containing the original scene in a state of collapse, or possibly he, or Hatshepsut, demolished it in the course of their own building programme. Perhaps by re-inscribing the scene and dedicating it, as he did, to the former king under the title: 'the wall called "Kheperkare (the prenomen of Senusret I) is pure in the temple of Amun"' he was showing his devotion and admiration of his great predecessor. Even more eloquent, perhaps, is the fact that Tuthmosis associated himself on the same wall with Senusret, actually inscribing an identical copy of the scene alongside that of his ancestor, but substituting his own figure and text. Remarkably, yet another version of this scene can be found on the outer southern wall of Akh-Menu.

The reason for Tuthmosis inscribing three copies of this scene is hard to define, but there is no doubt that Senusret was revered by later kings, many of whom imitated his style and incorporated his name into their own monuments. Perhaps by associating themselves with the founder of the temple, they felt they were, in some way, legitimising their claim to the throne which, in certain cases, was a tenuous one.

Despite the paucity of material remains from the Middle Kingdom temple itself, other smaller edifices of Senusret I have fared better. Amongst these, perhaps the most splendid survival is the so-called White Chapel, the blocks of which were found dismantled and buried within the core of the Third Pylon of Amenhotep III. This beautiful little limestone monument, now reconstructed in the Open Air Museum, was built by the king for his first sed-festival (a festival of renewal of power, usually celebrated in the thirtieth year of a king's reign, although often considerably earlier) and was erected in an enclosure called 'The High Lookout of Kheperkare'. Exactly where this enclosure was located is uncertain, but it is unlikely that the shrine would have stood within its own enclosure *inside* the temple walls. Very possibly, it stood in front of the main temple, or else upon the southern way: the fact that almost all of its blocks were placed in the southern flank of the Third Pylon, which was built in this area, adds weight to this theory. However, 'The High Lookout of Kheperkare', which is written in hieroglyphs within a fortified enclosure wall (Lacau and Chevrier 1956: 67), might well denote more than simply the White Chapel, but actually refer to the entire layout of Senusret I at Karnak, not only the temple, but all its ancillary buildings as well, including a royal palace (Kees 1958: 195). The name is certainly inscribed numerous times on the chapel (Fig. 2.2).

The chapel itself is almost square (6.80 m × 6.45 m) and is built upon a platform base approached at each end by a shallow staircase with a central ramp. Sixteen monolithic pillars, ornamented with very fine relief work, support the roof, which is crowned with a cavetto cornice. Square holes, which would have held pegs for the application of gold sheets to some of the reliefs, can be clearly seen. On the external faces of the lower walls and base are some very interesting inscriptions: on the east and west sides are shown Nile personifications bearing on their heads the names of various regions, as well as those of lakes, chapels, temples and fortresses founded by Senusret I; while on the north and south sides is a complete list of the nomes of Upper and Lower Egypt, and also a series of measurements giving heights of the Nile and distances within Egypt (Lacau and Chevrier 1956: 214). Thus the lower part of this architectural gem is full of information of historical and geographical importance. These exceptional scenes seem to emphasise that, even at this early stage in Karnak's development, Amun is being represented as the owner and ruler of the entire land and that he is the one who caused the life-giving inundation with its attendant fertility to all the nomes of Egypt. Already, therefore, we must, as previously suggested, look at Karnak as a 'state' temple in embryo.

There is some disagreement as to the original use of this monument. It was certainly built for the king's first jubilee but not as a bark repository as was first believed (even though perhaps used by later kings for that purpose), since another dismantled shrine of Senusret's has recently come to light which is a much more likely candidate for such a function (see below). The White Chapel was a kiosk designed for special sed-festival rituals, ceremonies which were held in order to rejuvenate the powers and strength of the monarch after thirty years on the throne, and at shorter intervals thereafter. In the centre is an emplacement in the paving slabs for a double throne on which the king would have sat whilst enacting the different ceremonies for Upper Egypt and Lower Egypt wearing either the White or Red Crown as appropriate. The chapel's very name, 'The one who raises the two crowns of Horus', endorses this. There are many representations of such ceremonies dating back to the earliest periods of Egyptian history; indeed, one of the hieroglyphic determinatives for the word 'festival' shows the double throne, and the base of such a one is still to be seen in the Step Pyramid complex at Saqqara. Alternatively, the double throne might have been occupied by two statues of the king, one with the White Crown and one with the Red. Perhaps these statues remained there for the rest of his reign as a visible reminder of the king's rejuvenated powers: a very potent symbol for his people. Around the four central pillars of the chapel are holes in the floor and architrave for wooden posts which would have supported hangings to hide the king, or the divine statues, from the eyes of spectators during parts of the ceremonies. Today the altar in place within the White Chapel is a later one of rose granite inscribed to Amenemhet III and IV, which might possibly be the time when the building was converted into a bark chapel for Amun. Senusret himself caused the following words to be inscribed on the walls of this lovely monument: 'Never did his Majesty find that anything similar had been done in this temple previously'. While it is acknowledged that Egyptian kings nearly always lauded their own achievements, in this particular case, it is hard to imagine his words to have been an idle boast.

The discovery of two monolithic walls and other parts of a shrine of Senusret I, buried within the Ninth Pylon, caused a reassessment of the White Chapel's assumed function as a bark-shrine. The newly found shrine, also built for the king's first sed-festival in fine Tura limestone, is now thought to be the prototype of what was

Plate 2.1 Example of the fine relief work in the White Chapel of Senusret I.

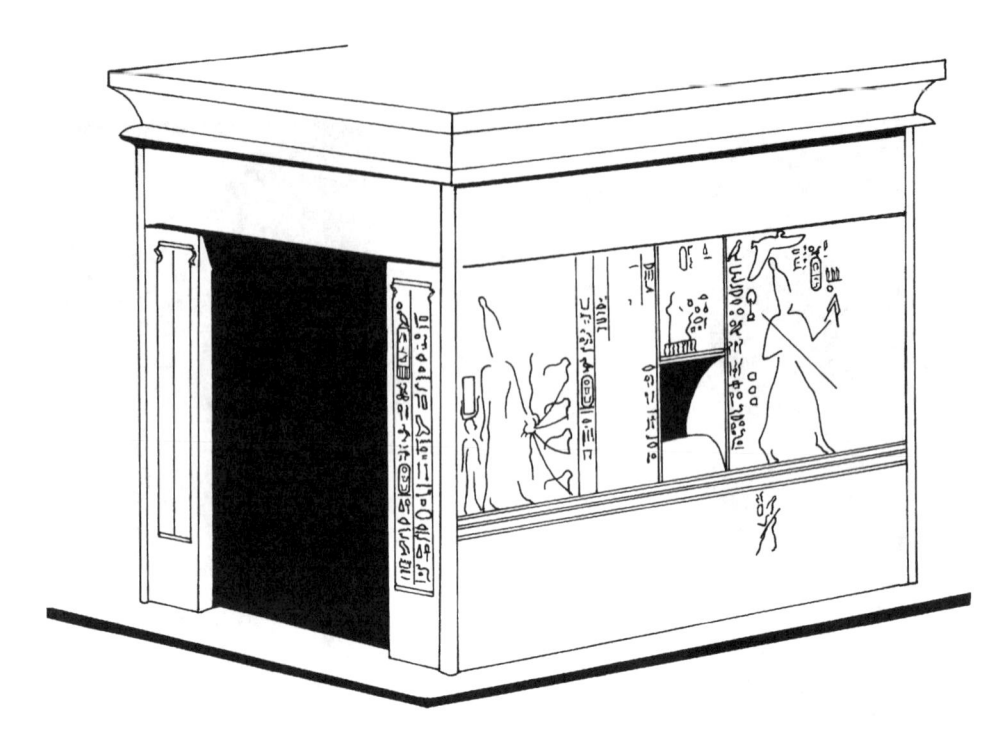

Figure 2.3 Reconstruction drawing of the bark-shrine of Senusret I found within the Ninth Pylon (after Traunecker, C., in *Cahiers de Karnak VII*: 125).

to be the repository chapel for the sacred bark of Amun (Traunecker 1982a: 121). It certainly seems to have been the building upon which Amenhotep I modelled his alabaster bark-shrine (now re-assembled in the Open Air Museum). The design is very similar to those shrines from later times which are known definitely to be bark repositories. One of the scenes decorating the interior of this chapel seems to show the king before the sacred bark: although the bark itself has been hacked out, the shape of the lacuna makes it almost certain. The proportions of the shrine are quite small, measuring externally 4.40 m × 3.20 m and internally only 4 m × 2 m, and comprise a simple oblong room with doors opening at each end. However, this particular shrine of Senusret differs in one marked way from all the others that followed it, in that each of its long side walls is pierced by a small window (60 cm × 80 cm). This is a novel detail, and if the intention was to provide the interior of the shrine with light, then the more obvious choice would surely have been the customary opening in the roof. It has been suggested, therefore, that this unique feature was to allow a view of the bark to people standing outside the chapel – a type of 'window of divine appearances' (Traunecker 1982a: 124). The scenes both internally and externally are those which were to become, with a few minor variations, standard in monuments of a similar type throughout pharaonic history (Cotelle-Michel 2003: 342–53)(Fig. 2.3).

The shrine is known to have continued in use from the time of Senusret I until that of Horemheb, a period of around 650 years. An inscription from the time of Ahmose, found on the base of the north wall, tells of a time when the inundation was so high that the Nile waters reached the chapel (Traunecker 1982a: 121). Later its reliefs were deliberately damaged during the Amarna period, but the scenes have survived well enough to be clearly recognisable. On the inside, only the middle sections of the walls are decorated, while that part which would have been obscured by the folding back of the wooden doors when opened was left blank. There is some evidence to indicate where the shrine once stood. Very recently, the corner of an enclosure wall was unearthed in what is now the courtyard between the Eighth and Ninth Pylons on the southern way. This wall, which is over 6 m thick, is thought to be part of the Middle Kingdom main temple enclosure; adjoining it to the south was a small forecourt and entrance pylon in front of which, west of the axis, was a raised mud-brick platform. The excavators believe that it was upon this platform that Senusret's bark-shrine was originally situated.

Another small, but very impressive monument of Senusret I, which was found buried in the court of the Eighth Pylon, also poses many questions concerning its original siting and, indeed, its function (Pillet 1923a: 143–58). This was a black granite naos dedicated to Amun and, once again, we are looking at a very rich piece: carved from a single block measuring 1.75 m in height, it would have had folding doors of bronze, or possibly of a precious wood with gold panels. Above the door a winged disc was carved, while the names and titles of the king were inscribed down each side: the exterior side walls showed scenes in relief of the king offering to Amun, but the back wall was quite plain with no reliefs at all, indicating that it had stood against a wall. The naos's inscriptions had been defaced, presumably during the Amarna period, and later restored. The restorations were all true to the original with one interesting exception: on the left side one of the figures of Amun had been replaced by Anhur, an unusual substitution (Pillet 1923a: 157). Possibly this was just an error by the ancient restorer, but it is worth noting that on the north face of the Eighth Pylon is an identical representation of Ramesses III offering to Anhur. Is there perhaps a connection, or is it mere coincidence? Since Anhur was a god much associated with the Ramesside kings and the area of their Delta residence, a connection seems the more likely (Fig. 2.4).

Various theories have been advanced as to where this remarkable little monument might have stood. From the direction which the figures of the king face (that is, wearing the Red Crown of the north on the left-hand side of the naos, and the White Crown of the south on the right), it can be deduced that the naos was orientated to the east, and it has been suggested that it was sited on the southern approach, since this was the area in which it was unearthed; however, as it was found in a stratum of very late date, this is uncertain. Its excavator, M. Pillet, believed that it had originally been contained within the Holy of Holies in the Middle Kingdom temple and that it was later reused on the southern approach. There is a third possibility, that has been widely discussed, which is that the naos was dedicated to a cult of the deified king and that it housed, not a statue of the god, but one of Senusret himself (Daressy 1927: 206 and 211). This is argued on the fact that the reliefs all show the king at the rear of the shrine with the god advancing towards him from the shrine's opening – a complete reversal of the customary arrangement. This does not, of course, bring us any closer to knowing the shrine's original location, which remains unknown, as does its true function.

References have already been made to the probable existence at this early date of a southern approach to Karnak, with several small monuments of Senusret I being possible candidates for having once stood upon it. Much depends upon the likelihood of there being a Middle Kingdom shrine or temple at Luxor to which Amun's processional

THE EARLY TEMPLE

statue would have been carried. That such processions took place is shown by a Dynasty XII stela of a priest whose job it was to 'carry upon my shoulder the King of the Gods (Amun) in his bark' (Vernus 1987: 164); the bark-shrine of Senusret, found in the Ninth Pylon must also be considered as evidence for it. And if this shrine had indeed stood upon the southern way, as seems probable, the bark's final destination might well have been a temple at Luxor; certainly the Beautiful Feast of the Valley, with its processions travelling over to the monuments of the West Bank, was thought to have been inaugurated by this time.

Figure 2.4 The black granite naos of Senusret I: (a) North side; (after Pillet, M., in *ASAE* 23: 149 and 153).

Figure 2.4 (*continued*) (b) South side.

Alternatively, another destination could be considered. It is noteworthy that the temple of Amun-Kamutef (built by Hatshepsut) contained the remnants of some Middle Kingdom statues (Gabolde 1998: 122): while no actual mention of Senusret I has been preserved on any of them, there is other evidence which points to the possibility of an early temple to the ithyphallic god – the creative aspect of Amun – having been founded by Senusret. First, there is a block, unearthed once again on the southern way, which shows Senusret being led towards a niche (cut into the thickness of the block) by Amun (Gabolde 1998: 86–8, pl. XXVI; Ma'arouf and Zimmer 1993:

Plate 2.2 Block of Senusret I, currently in the Open Air Museum, showing Amun-Kamutef.

227): one of the inscriptions from the niche refers to 'Amun who presides over his harems' – a designation always associated with Amun-Kamutef. Might this block have derived from, or in the vicinity of, such a temple? (This very interesting block, about which several other theories have been propounded, can today be seen in the Open Air Museum at Karnak.) Second, a block from the Middle Kingdom temple's portico depicts the king standing in a boat which he is navigating towards a stepped dais upon which stands the figure of Amun-Kamutef within his sanctuary (Gabolde 1998: 49–51, pl. IX). But again, where such a sanctuary might have been located is unknown, but that it might have been in the same area as Hatshepsut's later temple seems a reasonable supposition. However, none of this evidence is in any way conclusive.

As so little remains of the Middle Kingdom temple, we often have to rely on later texts and inscriptions for information. Such is the case with the scant remains of buildings lying south and east of what is now the Sacred Lake. These buildings appear to belong to much later periods, but from inscriptions left by priests of Dynasties XIX and XX respectively, we learn of the existence of the High Priest of Amun's dwelling, which was built by Senusret I (Lefèbvre 1929: 60–1). The inscription tells us that the house had become ruinous and Amenhotep, High Priest in the time of Ramesses IX (Dynasty XX), 'found this pure dwelling of the High Priests of Amun of former times, which is in the domain of Amun-Re, fallen into ruin; the construction had been made in the time of Kheperkare, son of Re, Senusret ...'. Amenhotep then goes on to say how he restored the dwelling to its former glory. A little further to the west were the temple kitchens and refectory. These also were found in a ruined state, and it was the High Priest Roy in the reign of Merenptah (Dynasty XIX) who restored these (Lefèbvre 1929: 187). He called upon the 'bakers, mixers, confectioners, makers of cakes and loaves, those who shall enter this refectory daily ...' to praise him for his 'good and great deeds'. Both priests left inscriptions on the east end of the Eighth Pylon concerning their restoration work.

While considering the High Priest's dwelling built by Senusret I, one is left wondering whether the Sacred Lake, beside which the later High Priest Amenhotep tells us this dwelling was sited, was actually in existence in Senusret's day, or was the lake a later construction? We certainly know that the Sacred Lake we see today was initially dug in Dynasty XVIII by Tuthmosis III as he himself informs us, but did it replace or enlarge an earlier one? Depicted on Senusret's White Chapel are two Nile figures, personifications of a Northern and a Southern Lake (Lacau and Chevrier 1956: 209 para. 581; 210 para. 586). They bear their names on their heads, one figure balancing the other on opposing sides of the chapel base, and with a text speaking of 'the one which refreshes the altar of Amun'. Since all priests entering the temple precinct must be purified, it seems logical that a lake or basin would have been situated adjacent to the Middle Kingdom temple.

The descriptions of the temple given above merely put together a possible outline of the pattern and shape of its buildings in the Middle Kingdom period, but to make it come to life, one has to imagine it in all its glory, richly equipped and furnished. Great colossi would have framed gateways, statue-groups of the king with a god or gods would have sat within dim sanctuaries, life-size statues of the king would have lined the courts and processional ways, and offering-tables would have stood laden before altars. Obviously, Senusret I had created a glorious temple to Amun: his buildings were copied, by Ahmose, Amenhotep I, Tuthmosis I and Tuthmosis III;

his name and inscriptions were preserved or reproduced, and statues were dedicated to him. The founder of Amun's temple of Ipet-Sut at Karnak was to be forever remembered.

There is no doubt that yet more is waiting to be discovered. Only recently, for example, Middle Kingdom blocks have been found deriving from the limestone doorway of a storeroom which housed the sacred oils and unguents used in religious ceremonies. The inscribed blocks state that these products came from Asia and, more specifically, from a place that has been tentatively translated as Tyre (Le Saout *et al.* 1987: 330–1). Blocks, lintels and other architectural fragments are all helping the current research which is slowly expanding our knowledge of the Middle Kingdom temple, its associated buildings and its environs.

In addition, there is much fine statuary and a range of beautiful and interesting objects known from Senusret I's reign. An intriguing example is a boundary stela which was found buried in the Middle Kingdom court (Chevrier 1949: 258; Habachi 1975: 33–7). Its inscription marks the north-west boundary of Nekhen (the next nome to the south), but its interest lies first in the fact that only two such stela are known from that period (the other one is of unknown provenance) and, second, poses the question why, since it bears no dedication to Amun, was it to be found at Karnak? Possibly it was made in one of the many temple workshops, and was never taken to its intended destination (Fig. 2.5).

A basalt statue of Senusret with Hathor, found in the Middle Kingdom temple area, raises the question whether there might have been a shrine dedicated to that goddess in Karnak in Dynasty XII, particularly since on the statue Hathor carries the title 'She who is over Thebes' (Gabolde 1998: 115). Another object of some beauty was a limestone offering table in the form of the *hotep* symbol (itself an offering loaf of bread on a table or mat) with its upper surface having circular depressions for the placing of offerings (Chevrier 1949: 258).

Senusret I's successors throughout the rest of the Middle Kingdom seem to have been content to enrich the temple, not with more building projects, but by dedicating many more statues and offering tables to adorn the existing sacred area. Only a fraction of all this richness has been unearthed: possibly there is much more to be discovered.

Apart from the royal statuary, several statues of a noble named Mentuhotep, who was vizier in Senusret's reign, have come to light. At least nine statues of this obviously powerful man are known, five of which came from Karnak: three from the Court of the Cachette, and two of black granite which were found in a specially excavated pit below the platform, or tribune, that stands above Karnak's quay (along with an Osiride statue in painted limestone of Senusret I himself). All of these can now be seen in the Luxor Museum. A series of high titles were inscribed on Mentuhotep's statues, indicating almost certainly that he figured prominently in the planning and construction of the Middle Kingdom temple – one of the reasons why, perhaps, this man was so highly regarded by his king as to be granted the rare privilege of personal statuary at Karnak.

Before leaving Middle Kingdom Karnak, it is worth noting that some interesting excavations took place some years ago on the very ruinous area east of the Sacred Lake, work which became necessary due to the impending seating installations for 'Son et Lumière'. This area was, of course, outside the temple proper in the Middle Kingdom, although we do not know the exact area of the sacred precinct at that time. What has been uncovered is part of the temple enclosure wall built in the reign of Tuthmosis

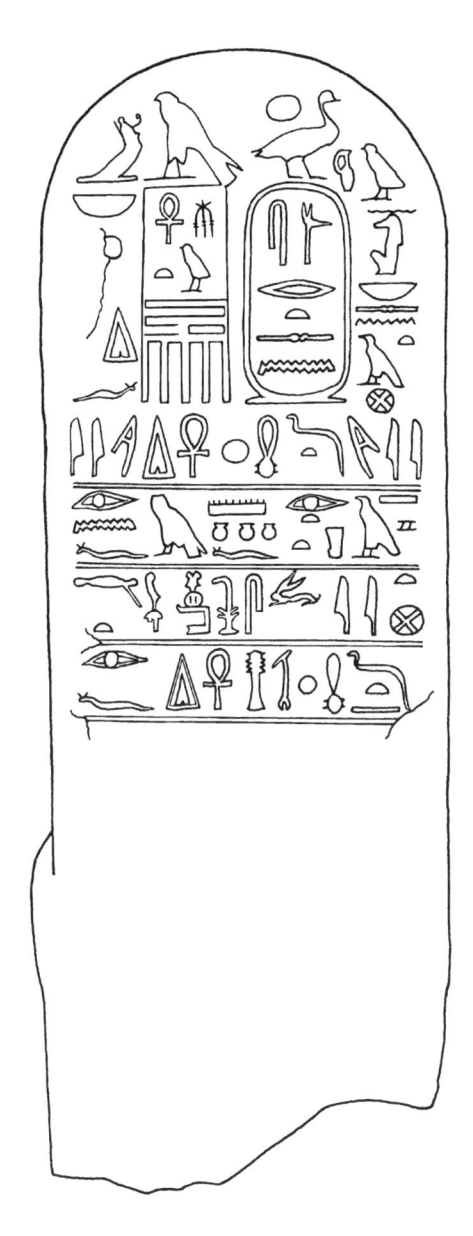

Figure 2.5 Stela of Senusret I found at Karnak giving the boundary of Nekhen (after Chevrier, H., in *ASAE* 49: 258).

III, and to the east of it and partly lying underneath it are several Middle Kingdom and Second Intermediate Period layers of occupation. When these buildings were constructed, they were certainly outside the wall, but nevertheless were thought to have been part of the temple arrangements. Many of the rooms found had limestone column bases, while rooms with silos and kilns were adjoining, and the remnants of some pottery resembling offering-vases were found. For this reason it has been postulated that here were administrative buildings and rooms for the baking and preparation of food offerings (Lauffray *et al.* 1975: 27). Certainly a large number of bread moulds of Middle Kingdom type have been recovered. However, since all these buildings were outside the temple walls, it is more likely that they were, in part, the domestic dwellings of temple personnel, while the columned areas and attached rooms possibly belonged to a palace. Rather intriguingly, a lower stratum still has been uncovered which also featured columned rooms, some containing fragments of Old Kingdom stone vessels (Lauffray *et al.* 1975: 29). Could this be a palace dating back to Dynasty XI (one of Senusret I of Dynasty XII is certainly attested), or even to the Old Kingdom itself? A fascinating thought indeed.

Areas of Middle Kingdom and Second Intermediate Period domestic occupation have also been discovered at various sites around the Karnak complex (Kemp 1989: 160–1): for instance, below the court which lies between the Eighth and Ninth Pylons; underneath the Akhenaten temple remains outside the XXX Dynasty temenos wall; in the region of the 'Treasury' of Tuthmosis I close by the Montu precinct; and below the New Kingdom levels in the Mut enclosure. All this adds up to a sizeable town which probably constituted Middle Kingdom Thebes, since archaeological work has shown that the original town nestled close to the temple walls during that period. However, this Middle Kingdom town appears to have been levelled in Dynasty XVIII in order to provide the area for a vast foundation platform on which the huge stone temples of the New Kingdom were built. The new town that came into being was now at a lower level than the temples on their great platform, which would have dominated the whole area.

There is an interesting postscript that can be considered here. Excavators found that the Middle Kingdom town layout of Thebes was orientated to the points of the compass, whereas the temple constructed by Senusret I was aligned to various great structures on the West Bank, such as the causeway of the great temple of Nebhepetre Montuhotep, an alignment picked up and repeated by subsequent kings. Could this be viewed as the first attempt to link the religious foundations of Thebes into one vast ritual complex – a theme carried to its grandest realisation by Amenhotep III six hundred years later?

Thanks to the continuing research on Middle Kingdom Karnak, we have come to understand more about it, and how it influenced what was to come later: some questions, however, will probably never be answered. It seems possible that Senusret's temple continued to function in some form until the closure of Egypt's great temples in the Christian era. Then, and only then, was the remaining limestone of the Middle Kingdom temple finally removed to the lime-kilns. Senusret I's temple had existed as the 'House of Amun' for over two thousand years.

3

THE SECOND INTERMEDIATE PERIOD

With the decline and final collapse of the Middle Kingdom in around 1782 BC, a period of more than two centuries passed, known today as the Second Intermediate Period, when Egypt split up into different regions. Many little dynasties and kings came and went, holding sway briefly in various areas of the country, many overlapping one another; while in the north, the so-called 'Hyksos' kings – foreign princes who had invaded Egypt – established their capital, Avaris, in the Delta. Many of these ephemeral kings left evidence of some activity at Karnak, including a stela of Sebekhotep IV (PM II 1972: 52) who recorded building works: 'a gate of ten cubits . . . a pure floor . . . a second door . . .'. An inscribed lintel or two, a few stone blocks, some door jambs, are otherwise all that remain to speak of these building programmes; while further stelae, statues, even an obelisk, show that these kings paid homage to Amun by embellishing his temple. Of note, Wegaf (Dynasty XIII) left a throne (PM II 1972: 110), and Ameny-Antef-Amenemhet of the same dynasty dedicated a very large and fine offering-table composed of two sandstone blocks forming a table of the North and a table of the South, each half carved with twenty circular depressions for receiving offerings, and the whole inscribed around its four sides (PM II 1972: 94).

An interesting stela of Dynasty XIII found in the Third Pylon records a flood which occurred during the reign of Sekhemre-Seusertawy-Sebekhotep VIII that was caused by an exceptionally high inundation: 'His Majesty proceeded to the Broad Hall of this temple. Hapy, the great one (the Nile), was seen coming towards his Majesty, the Broad Hall of this temple being full of water. His Majesty waded in it together with the workmen . . .' (Habachi 1974: 210). The Broad Hall in this stela must refer to the peristyle court of the Middle Kingdom temple: it is small wonder, therefore, that the porous limestone from which Senusret I's temple was constructed became, in time, quite badly eroded. High inundations were, generally speaking, much to be desired, as the fertility of the land and its crops depended on the flood waters; but, equally, the inundation could be, on occasion, *too* high and very destructive. Nilometers which measured the height of each year's inundation are known in many temples, Karnak amongst them. A prayer of a king of the Kushite period summed up the ideal: 'May you grant me a great inundation, rich in harvest, a great flood without damage'. But floods and damage, nonetheless, did occur, and apart from the stela of Sebekhotep just mentioned, texts of Ahmose, Tuthmosis III, Merenptah and Taharqa, amongst others, all speak of bad floods.

Towards the end of the Second Intermediate Period, a strong family dynasty came to power in the Theban area, opposing the Hyksos kings who had founded their capital

Avaris in the north: these Theban princes slowly extended their territory and influence. Here are names to conjure with: Seqenenre Tao I, his queen Tetisheri, wife of one king, mother and grandmother of several others: Seqenenre Tao II and his queen Ahhotep, and their sons Kamose and Ahmose. Their protracted struggles and strong leadership led eventually to the reuniting of the Two Lands, the founding of the Eighteenth Dynasty, and the beginning of arguably the greatest period of Egyptian history.

It is from two stelae of Kamose, found at Karnak, that we learn much of the history of this period and of the long drawn out campaign against the Hyksos, which his brother Ahmose brought to a successful conclusion after Kamose's death. The first stela, of which only a few broken fragments were recovered from within the Third Pylon, was discovered in 1935. However, it was the discovery of the second stela in 1954 which caused great excitement among Egyptologists as it was virtually complete and gave much historical information concerning Kamose's exploits, about which little had been previously known. In fact, 1954 was a notable year for Egyptology in which three important discoveries were made which excited much attention: first, the step pyramid of Sekhemkhet at Saqqara; second, Khufu's solar boat beside his pyramid at Giza; and finally, the Kamose stela at Karnak, which concerns us here (Habachi 1972; Smith and Smith 1976: 48–76).

This limestone stela was recovered from the base of a colossal statue of Ramesses II, which now stands in front of the Second Pylon. This stela was carved from a block that had once been a pillar from a monument of Senusret I – the pillared peristyle court comes to mind – and parts of the relief of Senusret before the gods can still be seen down the side. The stela tells of Kamose's struggle against Apophis, the Hyksos ruler, but it is a continuation of the story, thus indicating that it was one half of a double-stela. Things became more complicated at this point. Initially it was thought that the stela fragments found much earlier in the Third Pylon were the remains of the first half of the supposed double-stela, especially as the two texts were obviously complementary. However, it was soon realised that this could not be the case, since the two stela were very different in their design, in the width of the text-lines and the size of the hieroglyphs. It was calculated from the fragments that Stela I had been 2 m in width and could have measured up to 4 m in height, whereas Stela II was considerably smaller. Moreover, if these two stela had indeed been a pair standing side-by-side, then Amenhotep III, when clearing the site – which he did quite ruthlessly – for his own buildings, would surely have broken up both stelae and put them in the filling of the Third Pylon, and not just have removed one and left the other lying about until such time as Ramesses II decided to use it in the base of his statue several centuries later. The solution suggested by Egyptologists to this puzzle is that Stela I (the fragments) and Stela II were entirely different pieces, although containing parts of the same text, and that Stela II originally had a first half to it, now lost, that would have matched it in size and design, which would certainly accord with the ancient Egyptian love of symmetry. But why such a plethora of stelae, all relating the story of Kamose? Perhaps one was placed in a sanctuary to be seen only by the god, while the double-stela might have stood either side of a pylon for more public view. We will probably never know. However, one cannot help feeling that Kamose would have been gratified to know that his stela was being gazed at in the twenty-first century AD, fulfilling his wish, carved by the scribe at the end of the text: 'Let there be set down on a stela everything which my majesty has victoriously accomplished, and let its place remain at Karnak in Thebes for ever and ever.'

Very little else from the reign of Kamose has come to light at Karnak, except for the limestone base of a possible shrine.

Ahmose, his brother, who is considered the first king of Dynasty XVIII, also left little evidence of architectural activity at Karnak, occupied, as he must have been, in the final overthrow of the Hyksos and the establishment of a new order throughout the Two Lands. In fact, the recent discovery of a fine lintel bearing his name is the only actual material evidence to date of this king's architectural programme (Le Saout *et al.* 1987: 306–7), although certain texts from his reign do allude to building works. However, like his brother, he too erected several stelae of some significance. A fine example in limestone, measuring over 2.5 m in height and over 1 m in width, is perhaps from early in his reign since he associates himself on it with his mother, Queen Ahhotep, when he stresses her importance as being second only to himself in the land: 'She is the one who has accomplished the rites and taken care of Egypt. She has watched over her troops and protected them ... She has pacified Upper Egypt and hunted down the rebels' (Legrain 1903: 27–9). It has been suggested that this clearly implies that he came to the throne as a minor and that his mother acted as regent; however, since he was engaged in the final expulsion of the Hyksos, this must surely be unlikely. A more obvious explanation would be that it was the adult king who appointed his mother regent while he was pre-occupied with campaigning.

On this same stela he records how he endowed Karnak and restored the furniture, vessels and sacred utensils for the temple ritual. Had these perhaps been neglected during the chaotic years of the Second Intermediate Period? Certainly his predecessor, Kamose, had attributed his own military success to the power of Amun, but had died before he could achieve final victory; it was left to his successor to do this. With the Hyksos now totally vanquished, Ahmose could now offer his own thanks to Amun in a most concrete form, well summed up in his vivid description:

> Now his majesty commanded to make monuments for his father Amun-Re being: great chaplets of gold with rosettes of genuine lapis-lazuli, seals of gold, large vases of gold, jars and vases of silver, tables of gold, offering-tables of gold and silver, necklaces of gold and silver combined with lapis lazuli and malachite, a drinking vessel for the *ka* of gold, its standard of silver ... a flat dish of gold, jars of pink granite filled with ointment, great pails of silver rimmed with gold, a harp of ebony of gold and silver, sphinxes of silver ... a barge of the 'Beginning of the River' called Userhetamon of new cedar of the best of the terraces, in order to make his voyage therein. I erected columns of cedar likewise ... (BAR II: para. 32)

These words lend a visual dimension to our knowledge of the daily rituals performed in their dim incense-laden sanctuaries, aglow with the richness of precious metals and gems.

Another stela of note from Ahmose's reign is of particular interest as it is, in effect, a legal document. As such it has been compared to a stela known as La Stèle Juridique of Second Intermediate Period date, also found within the Third Pylon. The text of La Stèle Juridique deals with the sale of the office of provincial governor of El Kab, and is not a royal stela at all. One might wonder how it came to be erected in the temple, but it should be recalled that divine approval was a requisite of all legal transactions. The stela of Ahmose records the giving of the religious function of God's Wife of Amun by the king to his wife, Ahmes-Nefertari, and an endowment to maintain the 'Domain of the God's Wife' (Harari 1959: 139–201). The whole transaction, carried out in the presence of magistrates of the city and temple personnel, is shown as a 'sale' for which the 'price' or endowment was paid by the king himself in gold, silver, bronze, unguents, clothing, grain and land. It seems a high price, but it was one that Ahmose himself fixed, apparently for two reasons: first, to ensure that the queen's right to it could never be contested, and second, in order that there might be some 'capital' for the exercise of the office: an office which was to develop into an immensely powerful one at Karnak through most of Egypt's history, but particularly during the Late Period.

A third stela, yet again from the core of the Third Pylon, is of an unusual design in that the identical text is inscribed on both sides; on one face the hieroglyphs are coloured blue with the horizontal lines between in red, while on the other side there is no trace at all of colour. While stelae inscribed on both faces are well attested, this is the only one known to carry the same text on *both* sides, even to the extent of having the identical rare writing of certain words. A possible explanation is that Ahmose set it up in an open space to be easily seen by all. The stela tells of a voyage to Thebes and of a violent storm which struck south of Dendereh (Vandersleyen 1967: 123–59). This tale bears all the hallmarks of a genuine meteorological incident, with vivid descriptions of the devastation caused to the ancient cemetery at Thinis and to all the surrounding area. Ahmose immediately ordered repairs to be carried out and sent help to the afflicted people. Once again, this seems a strange stela to have erected in the temple, but the king seemed to feel that the storm was some kind of divine judgement and he wished to prove to the gods that he had acted swiftly and efficiently to restore the sacred monuments and to alleviate suffering. The king was, after all, responsible to the gods for the well-being of the land and its people, just as he was responsible to the people for maintaining the benevolence of the gods and the harmony of the universe. Swift action on his part was certainly necessary.

Part 2

THE NEW KINGDOM

4

AMENHOTEP I, TUTHMOSIS I AND TUTHMOSIS II

The New Kingdom

It was during the course of the New Kingdom, from *c*.1570 BC, that Karnak evolved into the great state temple whose visible remains still overawe us today. With the Egyptian Empire growing in wealth and strength, Amun became immensely powerful, and all the New Kingdom pharaohs strove to show their piety and their gratitude for the benefits showered upon them by the supreme deity. But Karnak as a religious and state institution encompassed very much more than just the vast and impressive central temple areas: its New Kingdom development was largely dictated by religious ideology and ritual. This lay in two distinct branches of the cult of Amun. First the solemn daily ritual performed for the god within the Holy of Holies from whence emanated the divine power which protected the king, Egypt and the entire universe from the forces of chaos. The second cultic ritual revolved about the bark sanctuary containing Amun's portable bark, a gilded wooden boat on which rested a small naos housing the statue of the god which was carried out of the bark sanctuary around the sacred precincts of Karnak for certain ceremonies, or when the god issued forth from the temple itself in various festival processions. For these great festivals, huge effort and resources were poured into the layout of magnificent processional ways, paved with stone and lined with sphinxes, statues and wayside shrines, or even small temples, where the god could 'rest' on his journeys. One route led through the main temple gateway to a quay from whence a canal led down to the river. This was used for water-borne processions. A second route developed along the southern approach, which was further enhanced by subsequent pharaohs to become the main sacred Processional Way between the temples of Karnak and Luxor, linking up *en route* with the precinct of Mut and possibly that of Khonsu (Amun's wife and son). Looking further afield, the Domain of Amun stretched across the Nile to the West Bank and the great mortuary temples there (Kemp 1989: 203 fig. 71) which were visited annually during the Beautiful Feast of the Valley.

Amenhotep I

With the great Dynasty XVIII now established, Amenhotep I, who followed Ahmose on the throne, consolidated and built upon the success of his predecessor. A military officer named Ahmose, son of Ebana, who served under several kings including Amenhotep I, declared that Amenhotep campaigned to 'broaden the boundaries of Egypt'. Although concrete evidence for this is somewhat thin, by the time of Amenhotep's death, Egypt was flourishing: its stability and wealth enabled his successors to begin a policy of imperial expansion which was to bring the New Kingdom to its full flowering.

Amenhotep himself made no major alterations to the layout of Karnak – that task was left to his successor, Tuthmosis I – but he extended the front by building a large court in advance of the portico of Senusret I's temple to provide a new and imposing entrance, decorating it in identical style to that of the Middle Kingdom – as he did with other monuments of his at Karnak. More than eight hundred blocks of stone, and five hundred fragments, of Amenhotep's temple have been recovered and from these it has been ascertained that the temple façade was decorated in the traditional way showing the king massacring his enemies. Almost undoubtedly a monumental gateway would have stood in this façade and, indeed, one block of stone mentions great flagstaffs (Graindorge and Martinez 1989: 38)(Fig. 4.1).

Apart from this, the king provided the existing temple with many beautiful additions. Most notably today we think of his alabaster kiosk, re-assembled in the Open Air Museum from blocks found largely in the core of the Third Pylon. His own words describe it: 'He made it as his monument for his father Amun … in alabaster of Hatnub. The leaves of the doors are in Asiatic copper of a single piece, and the figures which are on those doors are of gold.' This was a shrine for the sacred bark of Amun, now open at both ends, but once closed by doors of wood overlaid with copper; inside the ceiling is scattered with stars and the opposing walls are each decorated with two registers of scenes. These scenes are of particular interest as they bear the first surviving representation of the sacred bark (bearing in mind that the relief in Senusret I's bark shrine had been hacked out, mentioned above). On the outside, one scene only occupies each wall; the southern exterior face was completed by his successor, Tuthmosis I, which has led to speculation that the two kings perhaps shared a short co-regency at the end of Amenhotep's life. But it is equally possible that the decoration of the shrine was not finished by the time Amenhotep died, and that it was completed by his successor.

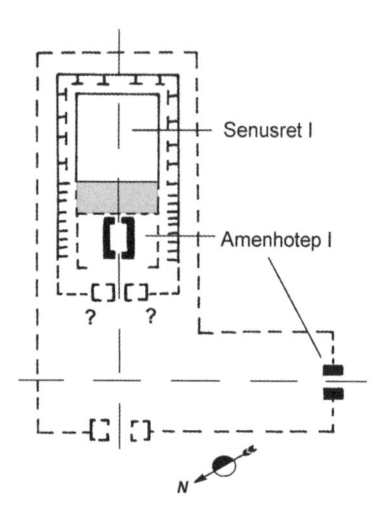

Figure 4.1 Sketch plan showing the constructions of Senusret I and Amenhotep I (after Aufrère, S. et al., *L'Égypte Restituée*, vol I: 88).

Plate 4.1 Alabaster kiosk of Amenhotep I.

Originally this beautiful shrine had parallel screening walls enclosing it either side (Graindorge and Martinez 1989: 42), one of which had reliefs of certain coronation rites, a theme that was to recur on the subsequent shrines of Hatshepsut, Tuthmosis III and Philip Arrhidaeus. An interesting point to note is that Amenhotep's shrine is represented in both name and image on Hatshepsut's Chapelle Rouge (her bark-sanctuary) where the queen (as Pharaoh) is shown performing ritual acts before Amenhotep's shrine. This seems to indicate that it was still standing during her reign. But where was it situated? Several theories have been put forward. One suggestion places it close to the Seventh Pylon (not, of course, in existence at that time), west of the Sacred Lake, an idea that is based on the fact that a bark shrine of Tuthmosis III, which now stands there, bears an identical name to that of Amenhotep's, 'Amun, Enduring of Monuments'. It, too, was constructed of alabaster to virtually identical dimensions (Nims 1955: 113). Because of these facts, it has also been suggested that Amenhotep's shrine was originally surrounded by a peristyle, similar to that of Tuthmosis III, but if so, it is lost, only the screen walls mentioned above are known to us. However, the excavator of Amenhotep's shrine, M. Pillet, believed it once stood where the sanctuary of Philip Arrhidaeus stands today (Pillet 1923b: 116). Recent research endorses this view and suggests that Hatshepsut removed Amenhotep's shrine and other buildings of his in the vicinity in order to construct her own bark shrine and its associated offering rooms (Gabolde 1998: 138). It is known that Hatshepsut did not construct her own shrine before Year 17 of her reign, so it must be assumed that Amenhotep's alabaster shrine stood in its original position until that time. Is it possible that Hatshepsut might have dismantled Amenhotep's shrine and re-erected it in the area of the Seventh Pylon (as suggested above), particularly considering that she took the trouble to show it on her own bark-shrine – surely a rather pointless gesture if she had demolished her ancestor's building? It should be remembered, too, that she was at that time developing and enhancing the temple's southern approach route: the beautiful alabaster shrine would surely have been considered an asset.

This shrine aside, not much of Amenhotep I's work is left standing today, but the remnants of several buildings are known from their excavated remains. Limestone blocks from a monumental gateway, which had once stood over thirty feet in height, were found buried in the Court of the Cachette (Legrain 1903: 14). These were carved with reliefs of the king's first heb-sed festival, some in sunk relief on the angled face of the gateway (therefore the outside), the others in raised relief on the perpendicular face (the inside). The gateway is thought to have formed the southern entrance to Karnak, particularly since a building inscription relating to the gate refers to it as the 'southern (*rsy*) gateway'. Moreover, a large limestone statue of Amenhotep I, found in this area and now in front of the Eighth Pylon, very probably stood outside his monumental gate. The architect of the gateway (and possibly also of the alabaster kiosk) is known to have been Ineni, of whom more will be heard in the reign of Tuthmosis I.

Recent work in the area between the Eighth and Ninth Pylons has uncovered a southern pylon which has been tentatively dated to Amenhotep I (Giddy 2002 [Spring]: 32). Was this the 'Southern Pylon of mud-brick' which Tuthmosis III claimed to have rebuilt in stone? It has long been assumed that Tuthmosis' inscription referred to the Seventh Pylon. Interestingly, this New Kingdom pylon has been discovered to stand upon the mud-brick foundations of a massive Middle Kingdom pylon and great enclosure wall that runs beneath the western flank of the Eighth Pylon, giving us some insight into the size of Amun's temple during the Middle Kingdom. This seeming plethora of gates, pylons and remains of pylons is somewhat bewildering. Further research may find some answers to the many fascinating questions.

Also found buried within the Court of the Cachette were some limestone blocks which had once formed part of two rows of small chambers which had flanked the court either side of the bark sanctuary (Graindorge and Martinez 1989: 45–7). These chambers of Amenhotep I were later to be replaced by Tuthmosis III with ones of his own, built of sandstone but otherwise more or less similar. These were small chapels in each of which was placed a statue of the king to receive offerings. In Tuthmosis III's words they were 'chapels of stone with doors of real cedar to bring the statues of My Majesty there, together with the statues of my fathers, the Kings of Upper and Lower Egypt'. On the walls Tuthmosis III always featured Amenhotep I in the reliefs. The reason for the emphasis on representations of Amenhotep I probably lay in the fact that some time after his death, Amenhotep I was deified and, in the words of Alan Gardiner, enjoyed 'extraordinary prominence' at Karnak (Nelson 1949: 202). Evidence of this can be seen on the north half of the east wall of the Hypostyle Hall where Seti I inscribed a series of reliefs known as the Ritual of Amenhotep I. As versions of this Ritual are known from other temples and papyri, it is thought they probably all drew

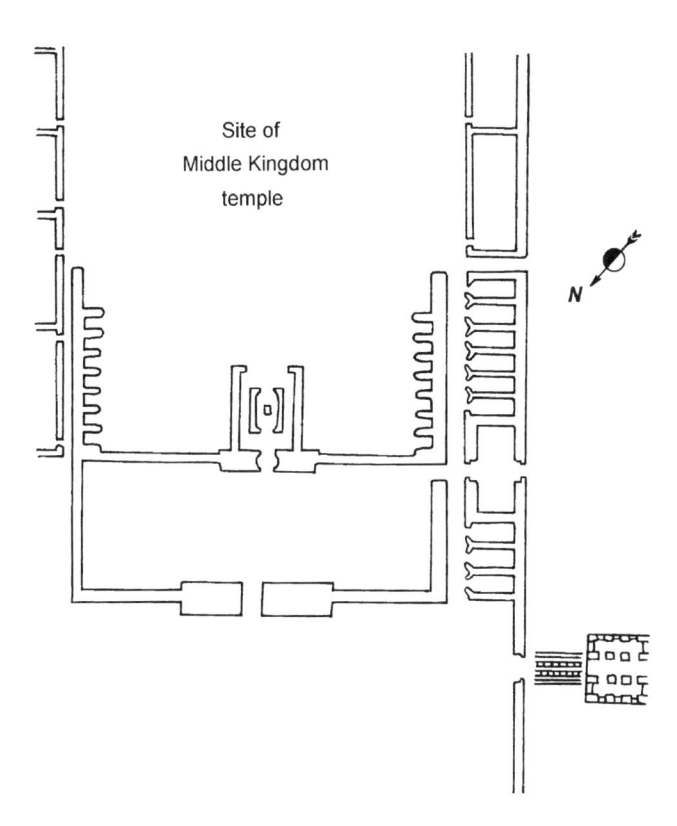

Figure 4.2 The temple in the time of Amenhotep I. (a) Plan showing the limestone chambers flanking the court of the sanctuary (after Graindorge, C. and Martinez, P., in *BSFE* 115, 50).

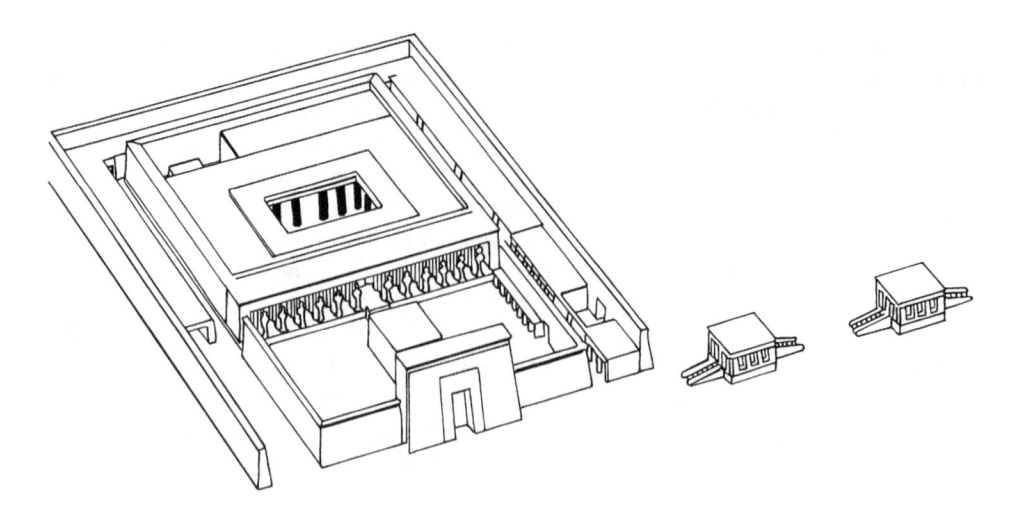

Figure 4.2 (*continued*) (b) Reconstruction drawing of the temple.

from a common source, originating from an earlier date (Nelson 1949: 201ff.). This ritual continued to be observed at Karnak certainly until the Ramesside Period at least.

At Deir el-Medina, the tomb-workers' village on the West Bank, where the deified Amenhotep I and his mother Ahmes-Nefertari are perhaps best known as the patron deities of the community, a statuette of Amenhotep was the object of cult worship, and this was probably a copy of an original colossus of the king at Karnak.

Finally, mention must be made of a limestone copy that Amenhotep I had made of Senusret I's White Chapel (Graindorge and Martinez 1989: 47). One must assume that Amenhotep greatly revered his ancestor and probably also greatly admired (as we do today) the beautiful shrine of Senusret, because the dimensions, style and decoration of Amenhotep's copy were almost identical to those of Senusret's original. Such similarity could surely have been achieved only if the architects of Amenhotep I had the original to copy: so the conclusion would therefore seem to be that Senusret's chapel was still standing in the reign of Amenhotep I. But, as with Senusret's, the siting of Amenhotep's chapel is unknown to us. It seems that Senusret I was not the only ancestor revered by Amenhotep I, who erected a small building in front of Karnak, that was later demolished by Amenhotep III to make way for the Third Pylon. This chapel seems to have been some type of forerunner of Tuthmosis III's celebrated Chamber of Ancestors, for it apparently contained offerings lists of kings of Dynasties XI and XII (Redford 1986: 29 and 171). Amenhotep I was, of course, by no means the only king to revere the memory of his predecessors and indeed, as already mentioned, he himself became the object of a cult in later times. Doubtless he was deified because he was viewed as the founder of the New Kingdom temple of Amun at Karnak, the successor to Senusret I, the founder of the Middle Kingdom temple. Thus he was considered the restorer of *m3't*, or harmony, to the land after the chaos of the Second Intermediate Period. The king-lists, which occurred in various forms throughout pharaonic history, were designed always to show the current monarch as the legitimate successor to the temple's founder and a true 'son of Amun'.

A final, rather intriguing, point: Amenhotep I made extensive use of limestone at Karnak, as well as elsewhere in Egypt, yet there are no obvious signs of his work or of his name at the limestone quarries. It *is* known, however, from the sandstone quarries of Schatt el-Rigal – but no sandstone monuments of his at Karnak are known (Bjorkman 1971: 59). This seems particularly strange, since sandstone monuments in general have survived quite well, while limestone was always susceptible to the activities of the lime-kilns.

Although Amenhotep had obviously been quite active at Karnak, he did not make significant changes to the temple's layout, which continued to look much as it had done in Senusret I's time. It was left to his successor, Tuthmosis I, to alter and enlarge Karnak quite dramatically.

Tuthmosis I

Tuthmosis I was not the son of Amenhotep I; in all probability he belonged to a collateral branch of the family, although the line of inheritance early in Dynasty XVIII is somewhat obscure. However, he had served as a military commander under Amenhotep and must obviously have been very close to the king. His mother was a commoner, Seniseneb, but it is believed that by marrying Ahmes, daughter of one king (Ahmose) and sister of another (Amenhotep), he was attempting to bolster his claim to the throne. (Ahmes was a common name at this time and it is disputed whether these royal connections actually do apply to his queen (Grajetzki 2005: 52)). Scholars give a length of reign for Tuthmosis that varies between six and eighteen years. Whatever the correct figure, his achievements certainly were impressive, and it was he and his successors of Dynasty XVIII who began to build the power-base that was to lead to the great New Kingdom Empire. This they did by exerting a firm control over all areas of the administration, including a considerably enlarged army, the police, law courts and judiciary, and even the priesthood – a very influential body of men. The king's wishes were imposed upon every area of governmental activity by a large number of extremely powerful officials, all answerable to their monarch: these were headed by two viziers (one for Upper and one for Lower Egypt), two treasurers, and a Viceroy of Nubia (known as the King's Son of Kush). Thus no single person had power beyond his own sphere of activity: only the king had jurisdiction over the entire empire.

Tuthmosis I inherited a stable kingdom which enabled him to commence a policy of imperial expansion – though, to be realistic, one must assume that he built upon territorial gains already achieved under Amenhotep I, since Tuthmosis claimed as early as Year 2 of his reign that his empire stretched from the Euphrates in the north to the fourth cataract of the Nile in Nubia to the south. Of course, if one accepts the theory of a co-regency of the two kings in the later years of Amenhotep's reign, then it is perfectly possible for Tuthmosis to have accomplished so much by the second year of his own reign. Whatever the truth, Tuthmosis I was without doubt a great warrior king who campaigned widely and successfully throughout his sole occupancy of the Double Throne. As a consequence, rich tribute flooded into Egypt bringing unprecedented wealth into the coffers of the state and the temples, and Tuthmosis initiated a great building programme at Karnak to honour the god he felt had granted Egypt and its king such notable victories. This work was directed by Ineni, an inspired architect, who had already undertaken works at Karnak for Amenhotep I, and whose titles give some indication of his power and influence in the re-designing of Amun's temple: 'Hereditary prince, count, chief of all works in Karnak; the double silver-house was under his charge, the double gold-house was on his seal; sealer of all contracts in the House of Amun' (BAR II: para. 43). This famous man is perhaps best remembered for his oft-quoted words concerning the secret construction of Tuthmosis I's tomb in the Valley of the Kings 'no-one seeing, no-one hearing . . .', but he also wrote in his autobiography in his own tomb: 'I supervised the great monuments that he (the king) caused to be made at Karnak'. Great monuments indeed, for they were to prove immensely influential for centuries to come, because Karnak was laid out in a style that was destined to be the model for the great state temples of the New Kingdom onwards: the sanctuary enclosed within screen walls, the colonnaded courtyard, the great hypostyle reception hall of the god, the monumental entrance with its pylon and flagstaffs, fronted by towering obelisks (Fig. 43).

Tuthmosis began by enclosing the entire Middle Kingdom temple at Karnak, and a large area in front of it, within a sandstone girdle wall across the front of which he built what is now termed the Fifth Pylon. The open court which was thus formed was called 'the august colonnade which makes the Two Lands festive with its beauty', for it had a columned portico round the inner face of the four walls formed by sixteen-sided columns, between which were placed statues of the king in Osiride form. It must be assumed that within this spacious court was sited a bark-shrine, probably that of Amenhotep I which Tuthmosis was known to have completed, as well as offering chambers. Virtually nothing can now be detected to give any idea of the layout, since the whole area was reworked and almost completely transformed first by Hatshepsut and then by Tuthmosis III.

Later in his reign, Tuthmosis I extended the main east–west axial way by constructing another and much larger pylon (the Fourth) which, despite additions by his son Tuthmosis II, was to remain the main entrance to the temple proper until the reign of Amenhotep III, more than a century-and-a-half later. The court which was formed between the Fourth and Fifth Pylons was thus the main court of the temple and was designated 'an august pillared hall with papyriform columns' (the Wadjet Hall). It was here that Tuthmosis III as a young boy was named as the future king by Amun, who was in procession in his bark. Originally this court had a wooden ceiling supported by five papyrus columns of cedar-wood, some alabaster bases of which can still be seen.

Although the court was constructed by Tuthmosis I, it was much reworked, altered, decorated and inscribed by later kings. Only recently, the remains of niches in the east face of both wings of the pylon have been discovered (Carlotti and Gabolde 2003: 258–61). These niches, part of the original construction before its alteration under Tuthmosis III, were found to contain Osiride statues, some of which were inscribed to Tuthmosis I by his daughter Hatshepsut. Similarly, niches with folding door-leaves have been found in the south wing of the same pylon; the statues that stood in these, however, were uninscribed and cannot, therefore, be positively dated. All this was later buried behind the new façade that Tuthmosis III built against the pylon's eastern face.

The wooden ceiling of this hall was removed by Hatshepsut in order to accommodate her two obelisks, and later Tuthmosis III installed a sandstone ceiling and columns, a fact that we learn from the text he had inscribed on one of the columns, describing how rain was entering the temple and having to be baled out (*URK* IV: 839).

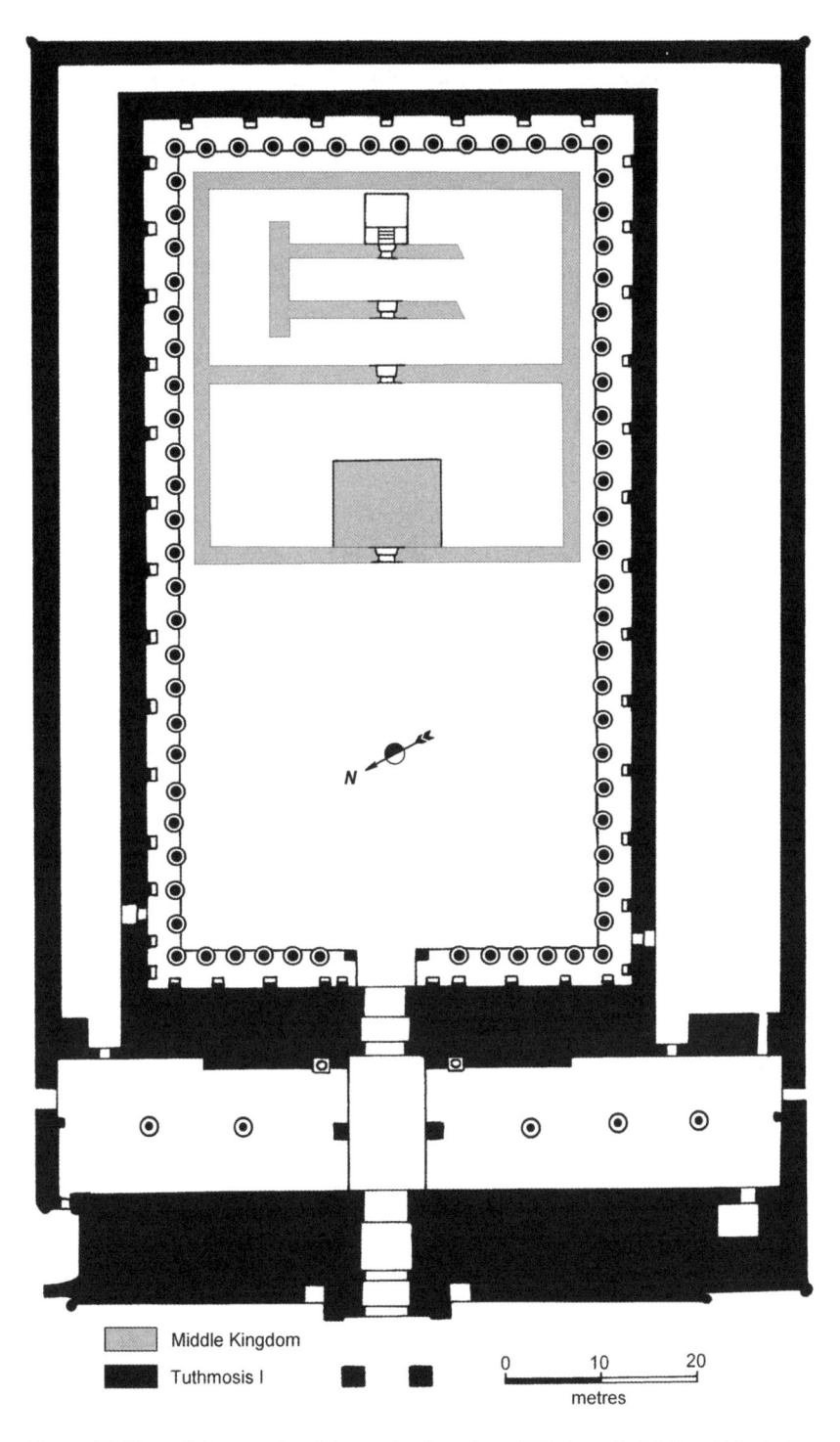

Figure 4.3 Plan of the temple of Amun in the reign of Tuthmosis I (after Aldred, C. *et al.*, *Les Pharaons: L'Empire des Conquérants*: 302).

The statues of Tuthmosis I which now stand in this hall are those which originally stood in the second colonnade behind the Fifth Pylon, but which were removed by Tuthmosis III when he began his own building programme. The statues, which wear the Red Crown in the northern part of the court and the White Crown in the southern, today seem to be somewhat out of proportion in such an enclosed area, and stand rather close to each other in niches which were created by Tuthmosis III when he lined the walls with a skin of masonry to support his stone ceiling.

Commencing at the northern end of the Fourth Pylon, Tuthmosis I now built another great encircling wall which surrounded all of Ipet-Sut. This second wall formed, with the first, an ambulatory corridor around the entire sacred precinct.

The two pylons which Tuthmosis I erected (the Fourth and Fifth) were stated by Ineni to be 'of fine limestone'. In fact they were of sandstone but faced with limestone blocks (Barguet 1962: 87). At the Fourth Pylon were four 'august flagstaffs ... of new cedar ... their tops were of electrum'. The Fifth Pylon had also once boasted two flagstaffs and their bases of pink granite still remain: it is to be supposed that they were no longer used after the Fourth Pylon had been erected. To add to the magnificent impression was the great pylon gateway into the temple: it was named ' "Amun, Mighty of Prestige", its huge door was of Asiatic copper whereon was the Divine Shadow inlaid with gold'. The 'shadow' of the god in this context was a representation of the deity inlaid on to the copper lining of the door as if coming out of his temple. The text was written giving the determinative of an ithyphallic god at the end of the word for 'shadow': undoubtedly a depiction of Amun-Kamutef, the creative aspect of Amun.

Finally, before the Fourth Pylon, stood Tuthmosis I's two obelisks of which only one remains standing today. These are of particular note since they were the first pair of great obelisks to be erected at Thebes (Habachi 1984: 57). They were 22 m in height, of red granite and, we are told, they too had their pinnacles encased in electrum or gold. These were erected for the king's sed-festival, which seems surprising since Tuthmosis I's reign was a comparatively short one, even if one accepts the theory of a co-regency with Amenhotep I. Each obelisk weighed an estimated 130 tonnes, and Ineni informs us that they were floated downstream from Aswan on an 'august' barge which measured 68 m in length and 20 m in width.

The Fourth Pylon was massive enough to accommodate two chambers in its thickness, as well as the customary staircase giving access to its summit. The chamber in the north-west thickness is quite small, but the one in the south-west is larger and has two niches at the back which once closed with wooden doors. Is it possible that these chambers correspond to the library and the room for sacred and ritual vessels, or possibly for robing, which have been found in such late temples as Edfu?

The two pylons bear the names 'Amun-Re, Mighty of Prestige' (Fourth Pylon) and 'Amun, Great of Prestige' (Fifth Pylon) (Barguet 1962: 89 n. 1). An interesting point here is that the word 'prestige' was a homonym of the word for 'ram's head', the ram being sacred to Amun. This appears to be one of the plays on words so much beloved of the ancient Egyptians: $šfyt$ = prestige, majesty: $šft$ = ram-headed figure of Amun. As a small postscript to this, the Sixth Pylon which was built later by Tuthmosis III bore the name 'Amun, Senior of Prestige': seemingly, that king, too, carried on the word-play theme.

It is worth adding a small aside to this account, though it is a view that has not gained general acceptance. It involves a theory which proposes that the Fourth Pylon was not the work of Tuthmosis I but, in fact, was constructed by Tuthmosis III: Tuthmosis I, it is argued, had merely erected an open colonnade in front of the Fifth Pylon. This being the case, the theory continues, it would explain the positioning of Hatshepsut's obelisks which would thus, in this scenario, have been erected by her in front of the temple's main entrance (Wallet-Lebrun 1982: 335–62 and 1984: 331). This obviously would have removed much of the technical difficulty – so often puzzled over – of their erection within so narrow a court.

Outside the sacred enclosure of Ipet-Sut there are the remains of a fascinating small monument of Tuthmosis I. Even today it lies outside the Amun and Montu precincts, but in Dynasty XVIII, when central Karnak comprised only that area occupied by the Middle Kingdom temple, plus the Fourth and Fifth Pylons and their courts, it was a considerable distance away in an area that seems to have been an administrative quarter,

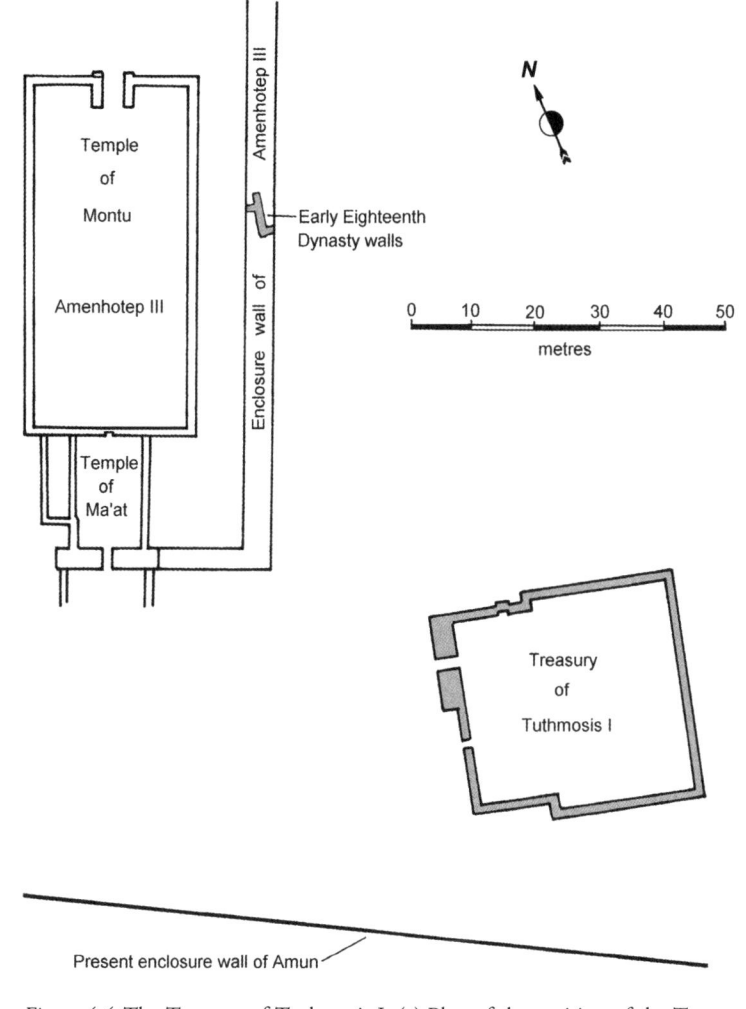

Figure 4.4 The Treasury of Tuthmosis I. (a) Plan of the position of the Treasury (after Jacquet, J., in *Problems and Priorities in Egyptian Archaeology*: 106).

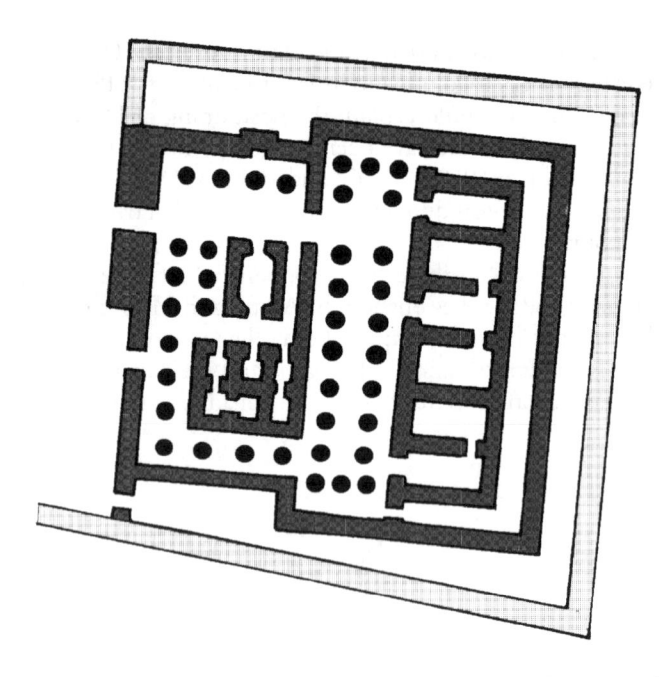

Figure 4.4 (continued) (b) Plan of the Treasury (after Aufrère, S. *et al.*, *L'Égypte Restituée*: 119). Not to same scale.

which fits in well with what has come to light concerning its unique function. Initially it was thought to be a small temple until the discovery of the inscription *pr ḥḏ*, literally the White House, but translated as the Treasury, and sometimes referred to by the ancient Egyptians as the Treasury of the Head of the South (i.e. Upper Egypt). Earlier dynasties make mention of a parallel *pr dšr*, Red House, which obviously pertained to Lower Egypt. Although built in the administrative quarter well outside the sacred precinct, it is easy to understand how this monument was initially mistaken for a small temple, for within its enclosure wall the Treasury was divided clearly into two parts: the first comprising a bark-shrine and multi-roomed sanctuary, which was obviously the domain of the god and his cult. The second part was a series of magazines fronted by a stone-paved colonnade; this area belonged to the king and his activities which were carried out under the benevolent eye of the divinity. Thus, although the complex had religious associations, it was not a temple and was never designated the Treasury of the *God*, but always the Treasury of the *King*. In fact, it is the only known example of its kind. Other Treasuries (such as the one of Shabaka, or the one illustrated in the tomb of Rekhmire) were attached to the temple proper and were specifically religious buildings, while that of Tuthmosis I was of a civil nature (Jacquet 1983: 138). It certainly must have been viewed as a building of considerable importance, small though it was, as later kings embellished it: most notably Hatshepsut and Tuthmosis III, while Seti I restored much of the relief-work after the depredations of Akhenaten's iconoclasts.

Excavation has shown that the site was originally occupied by a small shrine of Ahmose (Jacquet 1983: 97) and, although Tuthmosis I demolished this, it is interesting that he made a point of reusing a few of Ahmose's blocks, carefully retaining their cartouches (Jacquet-Gordon 1988: 92). This deliberate action must surely be seen as an act of piety or mark of respect for one of his predecessors, another example of which we will see later.

The buildings themselves were constructed of rich materials: limestone, granite and alabaster, while the abundance and quality of the decoration, both religious and secular, was of the highest order. Tuthmosis I began by creating a cult place orientated north–south, consisting of the bark-shrine and sanctuary with associated peristyle court. On a door-jamb of this shrine, as on his obelisks, the king tells us that he built it for his first sed-festival (Jacquet-Gordon 1987: 116). Second he added a monumental gateway, colonnaded court and magazines, all within an enclosure wall. We are ignorant as to what the magazines contained, but the presence of workshops and bakeries in the area outside the Treasury's enclosure wall indicate a fairly utilitarian purpose. All the scenes in the magazine area of the complex are standard, showing offerings of food and incense, and certainly the *pr ḥḏ*, and the corresponding *pr dšr*, were known in earlier dynasties to deal with the produce of the land. Perhaps therein lies an indication of its function: particularly as it seems to be reinforced by a Karnak stela of Tuthmosis III that specifically mentions offerings of bread 'made in the bakeries of the Treasury' (Jacquet 1987: 108). Another clue might be found in documents from a later date which state that the community of workmen at Deir el-Medina on the West Bank at Thebes, who prepared and decorated the royal tombs in the Valley of the Kings, were often paid from the 'Treasury of Pharaoh'. As ancient Egypt was not a monetarist society, these 'wages' would have consisted of bread, meat, vegetables, beer, linen and such like – exactly what the *pr ḥḏ* seems to have administered. However, it would be logical to assume that many of the sacred images and vessels used in the temple rituals were manufactured in the veritable village of ateliers and workshops that existed in the vicinity. Therefore, by extension, it seems probable that precious metals, woods, gums and resins were also housed within the Treasury magazines.

In addition to informing us about the offering loaves produced by the Treasury's bakeries, the religious aspect of that building is also highlighted by a stela of Tuthmosis III from the Ptah Temple at Karnak which tells of the procession of Amun in his sacred bark, which took place on certain feast days, passing in front of the Ptah temple on its way to the Treasury (Jacquet-Gordon 1988: 230). This particular procession was also referred to by Amenhotep II in his own bark-shrine at North Karnak, thus intimating that the god halted there also before proceeding to the Treasury, though the purpose of the halt at the Treasury itself is not vouchsafed. These are fascinating pieces of information telling us, as they do, of a hitherto unknown procession of the god Amun, and even supplying the date of the festivities: the twenty-sixth day of the first month of the Inundation (BAR II: para. 621). Perhaps one can assume that it was Tuthmosis I who inaugurated this ritual so closely connected with his Treasury.

The fragments of rich decoration which have been recovered from the Treasury are very badly shattered, but amongst the more obvious standard scenes that can be made out are some of especial interest; in particular, a representation of the sacred *persea* (*išd*)-tree. This scene usually shows the two deities associated with writing, Thoth and Seshat, inscribing the leaves of the tree with the king's names and the number of his regnal years. However, in this earliest-known example of the scene, the tree is in the centre with Amun on one side and Tuthmosis I on the other, but the most curious feature is that some of the leaves contain the name of Senusret I – an event totally without parallel (Jacquet-Gordon 1988: 214). What can be the meaning of this

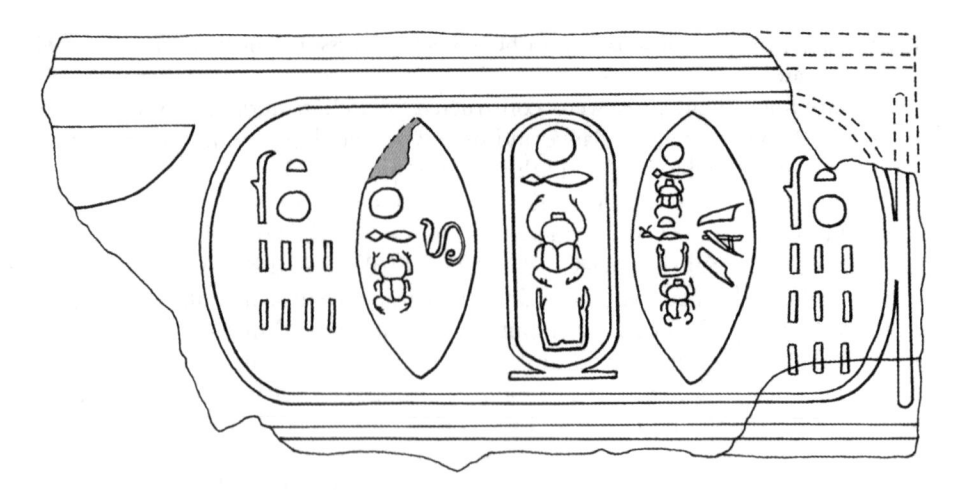

Figure 4.5 Lintel block giving the names of Tuthmosis I and Senusret I (after Brugsch, H., *Histoire d'Égypte*: pl. XVI).

unprecedented fact? Could it be that Tuthmosis I hoped that by associating himself with his revered predecessor, who had built the Middle Kingdom temple at Karnak, he was strengthening his claim to the throne? He was not, after all, the son of the previous king Amenhotep I. Was there any connection with his careful retention of the cartouche of Ahmose, mentioned above? Whatever interpretation one might put on this, there can be no doubt that Tuthmosis I wished to link his name with that of Senusret I, as can be seen even more clearly in a fascinating block found near Tuthmosis' obelisks, in front of the Fourth Pylon, although which building it derived from is uncertain (Petrie 1896: 67). This enigmatic block (Gauthier 1912: 215 [vi] and n. 2), which is dated to Year 8 or 9, has carved upon it a very large horizontal cartouche and within it stands a small vertical cartouche of Aakheperkare (Tuthmosis I). This is flanked on either side by two raised ovals which contain inscriptions that are difficult to interpret, but which appear to state Aakheperkare, beloved of his father Kheperkare (Senusret I) – another of the play on words, this time a visual one, so characteristic of the Egyptians, and another instance of the current ruler linking himself as son and successor to Karnak's illustrious founder (Fig. 4.5).

Tuthmosis II

On the death of Tuthmosis I, the throne passed to his third son since his first two sons, Amenmose and Wadjmose, had predeceased him. The mother of this third son was not Tuthmosis I's chief wife, Ahmes, but was a minor royal wife, Mutnofret. Therefore, in order to strengthen his claim to the throne, Tuthmosis II married his half-sister, Hatshepsut, who was herself the offspring of Tuthmosis I and his Great Royal Wife Ahmes.

Tuthmosis II was quite young upon his succession, and how long he reigned is uncertain. Until recently, it was believed that he had a reign of thirteen years or so, but some research suggests it might have been as little as three years. Whatever length of time his reign might have been, it has – quite understandably – been much overshadowed by the great events of his father's, his wife's and his son's reigns. However, within a short time of ascending the throne, he crushed a revolt in Nubia and later one in Palestine. But it is evident from a stela cut into the rock near Aswan, dated to Year 1, that he did not participate in person in his first campaign – possibly because he was too young. The stela refers to his 'efficacious spirit' accompanying the army in order to guide and protect it (*URK* IV: 137). However, it seems likely that he did go with his army into Palestine on the second campaign. Just how young he was upon his succession is unknown, but he must have been old enough to marry Hatshepsut and beget Neferure and also to have a minor wife Aset who gave birth to the future Tuthmosis III.

Of Tuthmosis II's own building work at Karnak, there is virtually nothing to be seen today, although his names and cartouches are not uncommon on monuments of Hatshepsut, as are those of Tuthmosis III who, after the death or disappearance of Hatshepsut from the scene, removed her cartouches and replaced them with his own or with those of his father Tuthmosis II.

These apart, there is certainly evidence of some structures of Tuthmosis II himself, which had been demolished by later kings. Most notably, recent research has brought to light evidence of a magnificent monument, from which derived the great limestone blocks with large yellow-painted hieroglyphs which had been unearthed from the core of the Third Pylon earlier this century: these are now known to have come from a great festival court which Tuthmosis II erected in front of the Fourth Pylon (Gabolde 1993: 3–65, pls I–XVIII), the main temple entrance at that period. Such a court was customarily built in front of the main entrance, and this one of Tuthmosis would have formed a new forecourt to the temple of his father. More than that, its siting could not have been more symbolic, for the king decided to build this festival court at the crossing point of the two axes of the temple: i.e. where the main east–west processional route crossed that of the north–south southern approach. It was fronted by a great pylon of its own, probably much the same size as the Fourth Pylon which formed the rear wall of the court, while another smaller pylon, surmounted by a cornice and carrying a dedicatory inscription and a winged solar disk, gave access to the court from the south. The court's fourth wall (the northern) was pierced by at least three doorways. These four walls enclosed an area in the region of 73 m by 38 m which was open to the sky. The southern gateway bore the name 'Amun is the one who makes the Two Lands festive' (Bjorkman 1971: 109) – a very appropriate name for an entrance to a festival court.

Tuthmosis II's court was designated a festival court rather than a sed-festival court, and there is certainly nothing in its decoration to indicate that he ever celebrated a sed-festival. In view of the fact that he seems only to have reigned for a span of time variously estimated at between three and thirteen years, this is not altogether surprising; and since the court features frequently in the texts of Hatshepsut (Letellier 1979: 68 and n. 2), it is almost certain that it was she who completed it after her husband's death (Figs. 4.6, 4.7).

What, then, was the function of this imposing court, juxtaposed as it was between the sacred and the profane? Situated inside Karnak's enclosure wall, it formed a 'break', perhaps better described as a 'vacuum', between the most sacred inner areas of the temple and the world outside its entrance pylons, and, as such, served several purposes.

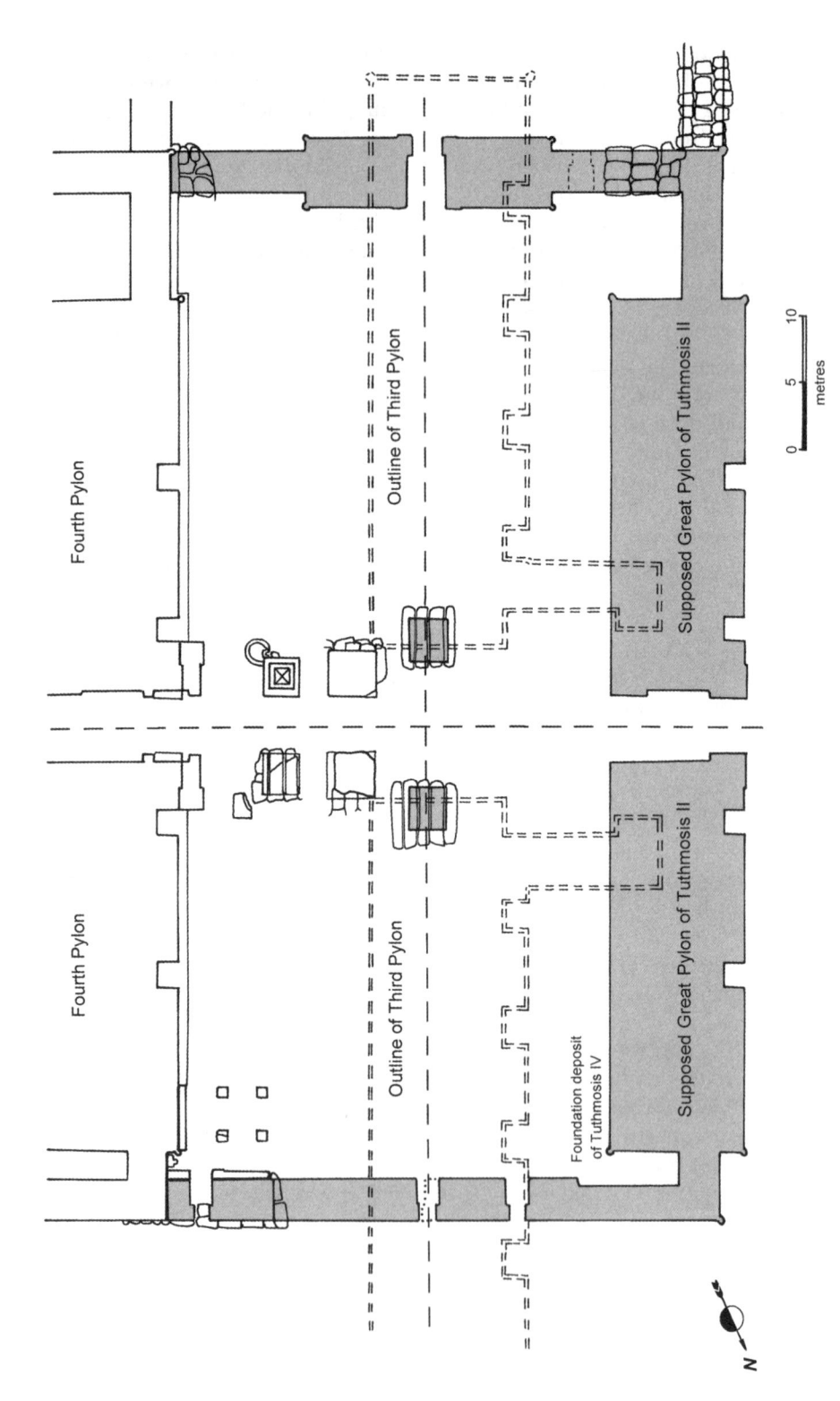

Figure 4.6 Plan of the Festival Court of Tuthmosis II (after Gabolde, L., in *Cahiers de Karnak IX*: 85).

West East

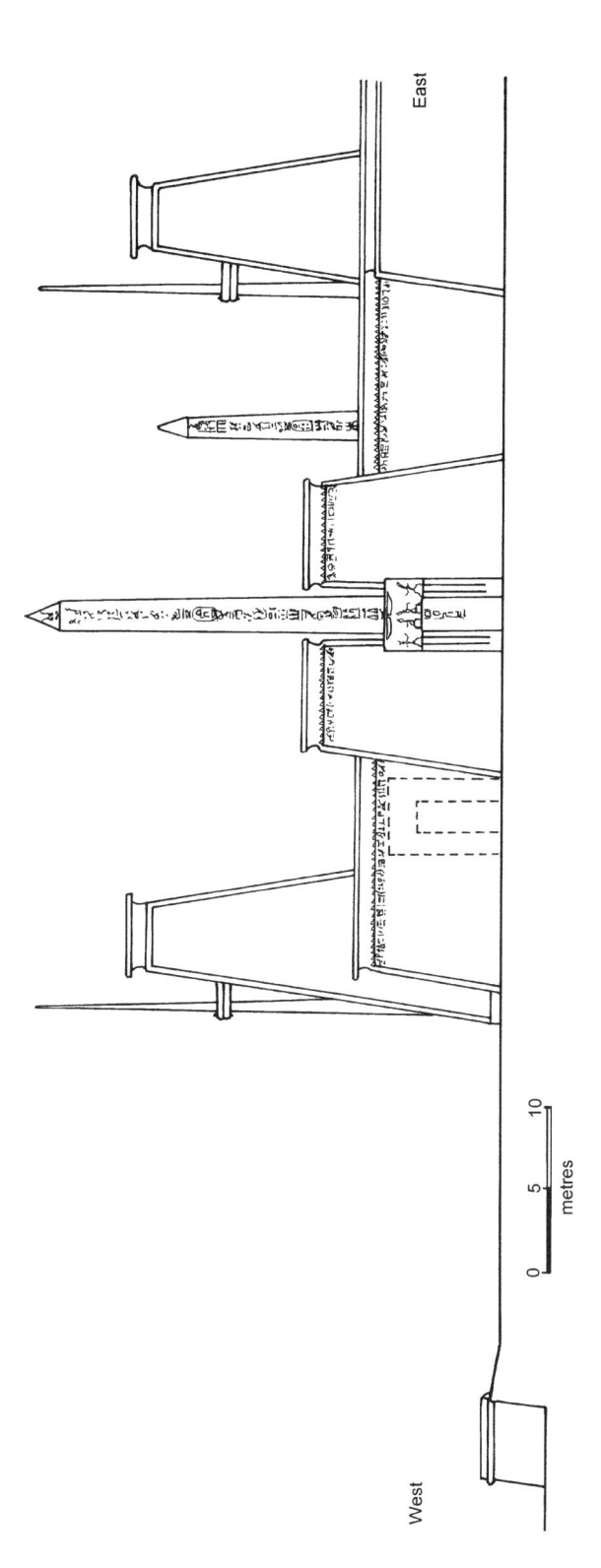

Figure 4.7 Hypothetical reconstruction of the southern façade of the Festival Court of Tuthmosis II (after Gabolde, L., in *Cahiers de Karnak IX*: 87).

First, it was the area where the king and priests were purified before entering the inner abode of the god; second, it was here that the tribute from foreign lands, the products brought home from expeditions, or the spoils of war were presented to Amun, and it seems that altars were erected here for a great show of burnt offerings to the King of the Gods. Here, too, the awarding of the 'gold of recompense' to loyal members of the court or military leaders took place. One of the court's principal functions was to act as the first or last station at which the sacred bark would leave or arrive at Karnak on its processional routes during great festival days. Its role during these great religious festivals was thus very significant, and for this reason it would have been open to special privileged members of the public – perhaps lesser members of the temple hierarchy and certain courtiers, officials and noblemen – who were invited to attend these particular ceremonies. Perhaps, then, its function can best be thought of as one of great pomp and show, of propaganda even, in celebrating some of Karnak's most triumphant ceremonies and solemn rituals in a semi-public environment.

Tuthmosis II also erected obelisks at Karnak, fourteen fragments of which have been discovered: one in red granite bearing his Horus name had been reused in the base of the sanctuary of Philip Arrhidaeus. Where had these obelisks stood? Two socles have been found under the central passageway of the Third Pylon which seem to match the restoration of the obelisks' general design. Thus it would appear that they were erected in the centre of Tuthmosis' festival court aligned exactly on the north–south axis and either side of the main east–west axis. It is generally accepted that Tuthmosis' reign was of too short a duration to have allowed him to complete this major building project, and it was left to Hatshepsut, as ruler, to bring it to fruition.

It should be noted that the relative profusion of obelisks being erected in this area – those of Tuthmosis I, of Hatshepsut, and now of Tuthmosis II (as well as those which were to be added later by Tuthmosis III) – underline the increasingly solar aspect of Amun-Re's temple during the New Kingdom.

A variety of blocks from other dismantled monuments of Tuthmosis II show Hatshepsut associated with him in her role of queen and Great Royal Wife. These blocks were found widely scattered, but the majority were unearthed in the court of the Seventh Pylon. One of these demolished monuments was a limestone bark shrine where the queen (Hatshepsut) is always secondary to her husband (Gabolde 2005: 99–100), while many of the blocks from other buildings have been altered to show Hatshepsut as pharaoh.

Finally, several statues, two still standing at the Eighth Pylon, and three in the Cairo Museum, also testify to Tuthmosis II's work at Karnak. One of the colossal statues in front of the Eighth Pylon has the remains of the statuette of a queen by his leg, thought most probably to be his mother, Mutnofret.

5

HATSHEPSUT

Many aspects of the reigns of Hatshepsut and Tuthmosis III still attract argument and controversy, but what seems certain is that upon the death of Tuthmosis II, his son by a lesser queen ascended the throne as a minor (Tuthmosis III) while the Great Royal Wife (Hatshepsut) became regent for her young stepson. Ineni, the architect whose career began under Tuthmosis I and extended into that of Hatshepsut, wrote in his autobiography:

> He (Tuthmosis II) went forth to heaven and mingled with the gods. His son stood in his place as king of the Two Lands, having become ruler upon the throne of the one who begat him. His sister, the Divine Consort, Hatshepsut, settled the affairs of the Two Lands by reason of her plans . . . . ." (BAR II: para. 341)

However, it appears that within two years, Hatshepsut had elevated herself to the status of joint pharaoh with Tuthmosis III.

Hatshepsut certainly had the most powerful royal credentials, being the daughter of Tuthmosis I and his Great Royal Wife Ahmes, whereas her stepson, Tuthmosis III, could claim only to be the son of Tuthmosis II by a minor wife or concubine named Aset. Whether it was these facts which spurred Hatshepsut on to assume full kingly power, or whether other factors played a part, will probably never be known. It is true that Tuthmosis III was a minor when he came to the throne, but how Hatshepsut managed to install herself and remain as king for so many years is unrecorded, but modern research has gone a long way to dispel the long-held belief that she ruthlessly suppressed her young stepson while he simmered with resentment, powerless until her death, after which he mercilessly hacked out her name and image from all monuments. Today it is accepted that this supposed animosity between them is in some respects a myth (Nims 1966: 100). In various dated inscriptions from her reign, the regnal years given are those of both Hatshepsut and Tuthmosis III; and on many of Hatshepsut's most celebrated monuments, Tuthmosis is regularly shown as pharaoh alongside his stepmother participating in the rituals and celebrations, though, it must be admitted, to a somewhat lesser degree than Hatshepsut who always takes the dominant role.

In the early years of her reign, Hatshepsut appears to have taken part personally in military campaigning and, in addition, there is evidence that Tuthmosis also was undertaking various campaigns on her behalf (Redford 1967: 62). One theory suggests that Hatshepsut put Tuthmosis into the army as a youngster to learn the tactics of warfare so that he could take command of it when he came of age (Redford 1967: 81), while she controlled home affairs, thus, in effect, 'splitting' the role of pharaoh: in other words, she kept him busy abroad whilst continuing to build her own power-base at home. If this theory is indeed correct, there is nothing to indicate that Tuthmosis took any exception to the arrangement, and he certainly campaigned widely during her reign, campaigns which he was to continue with increased vigour when he assumed sole power after her death. Careful study of Hatshepsut's monuments seems to indicate that it was quite late in Tuthmosis' sole reign that any systematic defacement or destruction of his stepmother's buildings began (Hegazy and Martinez 1993: 60–2); *so* late, in fact (van Siclen 1984: 53), that it has even been suggested that it was not until the appointment of Tuthmosis' son, Amenhotep II, as co-regent that the attacks began. Could it be Amenhotep who inaugurated them? Was the reason political or personal?

It would seem that Hatshepsut, throughout her reign, felt it necessary continually to underscore her right to the throne of the Two Lands. On her monuments at Karnak, at Deir el-Bahri and elsewhere she wrote her own 'history': her divine conception and birth, her appointment by Tuthmosis I as his successor, her public selection by Amun and his endorsement of her reign – all 'miraculous' events due to her special relationship with the gods. Amongst her titles she included the all-important ones: 'Hereditary princess, daughter of Geb, heiress of Osiris' – no one was to be left in any doubt concerning her divine descent and consequent rightful inheritance, which she continued to stress time and time again. Even as late as Year 16 of her reign, she inscribed on the obelisks that she erected for her sed-festival: 'He (Amun) caused that I should reign over the Black Land and the Red . . . . I am his daughter in very truth . . .' (BAR II: para. 319).

Her monuments at Karnak, too, emphasised this special relationship. Indeed, Hatshepsut claimed that Amun himself had given her instructions:

> to add to that which existed formerly, to enlarge my (Amun's) treasuries which contain the riches of the Two Banks, to build monuments without stinting on quartzite and black granite . . . and to renew the statues in beautiful white limestone. Embellish the future by that work and surpass the ancient kings on my account, according to the desire of my Majesty (Amun) in doing that which I have ordered to be carried out for me.

Bjorkman points out that Hatshepsut felt it necessary to attribute these words to Amun himself in order to underline divine approval (Bjorkman 1971: 66). This gave her the justification she required to undertake a radical and ambitious scheme of work which was to transform the Karnak complex. In this respect she will have wished to place her monuments in close proximity to the Holy of Holies, the main sanctuary of Karnak situated within the Middle Kingdom temple: she would therefore have had no compunction in demolishing whatever buildings stood in the way of her scheme. There seems no doubt that she did remove or destroy much of Amenhotep I's work at Karnak, some of which was to be restored later by Tuthmosis III. We have already seen that the theory which proposes she had moved Amenhotep's alabaster bark-shrine from its original central position to a place near the Seventh Pylon, west of the Sacred Lake is generally accepted (Nims 1955: 113). And it was almost certainly Hatshepsut who dismantled Senusret I's portico at the same time. The act of removing part of such an ancient and august monument of this revered ancestor could not have been undertaken lightly, or without some danger to her position, as is evident from the many speeches of divine authority with which Hatshepsut hedged herself about. But to be fair, the likelihood was that the Middle Kingdom temple was by this time in partial decay due, in particular, to water erosion at the base of the limestone walls.

Such sweeping schemes extended to the West Bank also, where Hatshepsut demolished a shrine of Amenhotep I and Ahmes-Nefertari which stood in the way of her great Deir el-Bahri temple project. Could her disregard for her illustrious predecessors' monuments, apparently so piously restored in part by Tuthmosis III, be one reason why her own monuments were later attacked?

To understand the meaning of Hatshepsut's monuments, they must be viewed as one entity: a scheme both grand and coherent. Although separate buildings, their functions were religiously all interconnected. Before the very heart of Karnak – its most sacred area – she built her sanctuary of the bark, which she named most appropriately 'The Place of the Heart of Amun' or 'The Favourite Place of Amun' (known today by its French name, the Chapelle Rouge). This contained the god's sacred bark wherein was housed his image within a veiled naos, and it stood before a unique complex of offering rooms called the Great House, or Palace, of Maat (Maat being the goddess of truth, justice and universal order). On festival days, Amun's bark was borne out of the shrine on the shoulders of priests in order to participate in various rites and ceremonies, the most important of which was the Festival of Opet. This great event was possibly inaugurated during Hatshepsut's reign or, at the very least, it was she who raised it to an occasion of the highest significance in the religious calendar (Robins 1997: 132; Graindorge 1993: 46). Although over the centuries, its meaning and its rituals altered somewhat, its initial purpose was to celebrate the sexual union between the god Amun and the mother of the reigning king. This was a belief that Hatshepsut would particularly wish to emphasise since it once again stressed her divine birth, a concept she so graphically illustrated on the walls of her Deir el-Bahri temple. This particular festival, so close to Hatshepsut's heart, necessitated the sacred bark containing the god's image leaving Karnak in order to visit the temple of Luxor. So that she might add greater splendour to the event, she developed a formal southern approach to Karnak, making a paved ceremonial way that linked Karnak to the temples of Mut and Luxor (Kemp 1989: 206). She erected a great pylon (the Eighth) on this southern side through which the sacred bark was carried out of the temple precinct; at intervals along the route she built a series of six way-stations between Karnak and Luxor, at each of which the procession would stop in turn and the bark would be placed within the shrine (a very necessary rest for the priests who were bearing it on their shoulders) while various rites took place.

Hatshepsut gathered about herself an entourage of powerful and loyal ministers: perhaps the most famous of them being her steward Senenmut 'the greatest of the great in the entire land'. A statue of this influential man, which was unearthed at Karnak, bore the inscription:

> An order was given to the Chief Steward Senenmut to control every work of the king at Karnak in the Southern Heliopolis (Thebes), in the temple of Amun *ḏsr-ḏsrw* (Deir el-Bahri), in the temple of Mut in Asher, and in the

Southern Opet (Luxor temple) for satisfying the heart of the majesty of this noble god (Hatshepsut) . . . (BAR II: para. 351)

It is unlikely that Senenmut did in fact oversee all the building projects at Karnak since other names are connected with her works, but it is certain that the first pair of obelisks which the queen had erected were under his charge. From an inscription on the rocks at Elephantine left by Senenmut, we know that these obelisks were cut from the Aswan granite quarries; they were commissioned by the queen after the death of Tuthmosis II while her title was still Great Royal Wife and regent (Habachi 1984: 68). However, by the time they were in place, she had become king. Was she perhaps anticipating the move that was to make her pharaoh? Were these great shafts erected to commemorate her 'accession' – in effect, a type of propaganda?

The obelisks were particularly magnificent, their bases being larger than the ones she was to put up later in her father's Wadjet Hall, and the work that can be seen on the pyramidions and fragments of shafts which have been recovered was very fine. Reputedly they were entirely covered in gold: according to the stela of Djehuti, Hatshepsut's treasurer (Northampton Stela), the obelisks were '108 cubits in height and worked to their length in fine gold, filling the Two Lands with their rays' (Spiegelberg 1900: 118–21). A height of 108 cubits (approximately 62 m) was undoubtedly an exaggeration (something to which the ancient Egyptians were very prone), but that the obelisks were entirely sheathed in gold is perfectly possible.

On the walls of Hatshepsut's temple at Deir el-Bahri is a pictorial account of these obelisks being brought to Thebes by a fleet of ships with troops standing by to unload the great shafts, while priests and court officials look on rejoicing. The final scenes show the obelisks in place and being dedicated.

This pair of obelisks was erected at the eastern end of Karnak, an area that was much reworked by later kings and it is not easy to distinguish what might have stood there in Hatshepsut's time, but that it was of considerable importance is evidenced by the very fact that she erected such magnificent obelisks at that spot. The obelisks stood outside a great stone gateway (later named by the Egyptians, the 'Upper Gateway'), set into the temple enclosure wall, which at that time was of mud-brick. This wall was later demolished by Tuthmosis III when he enlarged Karnak. He built a new enclosure wall of stone slightly further to the east which actually incorporated the bases of Hatshepsut's obelisks: possibly he took down the shafts at the same time.

Why did Hatshepsut erect her most magnificent obelisks at the eastern entrance? It is known that some construction had stood within the temple precinct here, a construction which Tuthmosis III pulled down in order to build his so-called Festival Hall (Akh-Menu). This destroyed building must have been, as already commented, of some importance to merit such obelisks at its entrance and, indeed, the remains of a magnificent great alabaster statue of Hatshepsut enthroned beside Amun was found in this locality (recut in later times to represent Amun-Kamutef beside a 'garden' of lettuces). It had even been suggested that perhaps Hatshepsut had constructed a festival court of her own here, since her treasurer Djehuti makes two references on his stela to a festival court (though not to its locality). But since it seems almost certain that Hatshepsut completed her husband Tuthmosis II's festival court in front of the Fourth Pylon, it is highly improbable that she would have constructed another such court, and so the likelihood is that Djehuti's inscription alludes to the former. It has long been thought probable, as well as particularly apt, that she erected a temple at this eastern end for adoring the rising sun. Her magnificent obelisks, with their solar connection, would be especially appropriate placed here, but excavation and research have uncovered a new possibility, discussed in the next chapter.

Hatshepsut's second pair of obelisks was erected to commemorate her sed-festival in Year 16, and on these she once again claimed her special relationship with the god: 'her father Amun established her great name on the sacred persea (*išd*) tree and her annals in millions of years . . .'. Somewhat strangely, they were set up in her father Tuthmosis I's Wadjet Hall, a relatively narrow court at the best of times. Based on evidence from her coronation inscriptions, it has been suggested that Hatshepsut viewed the Fifth Pylon as the principal entrance to the most sacred inner part of the temple before whose hallowed portals she wished to raise her obelisks. However, since she had to demolish some of the hall's columns, and also its roof, in order to effect this, it seems a strange course of action. Perhaps, more realistically, one should consider that as her husband's (Tuthmosis II) festival court, containing both his and Tuthmosis I's obelisks, now fronted the temple, there was no room to include her obelisks there, causing her to 'squeeze' them in between the Fourth and Fifth Pylons. From a technical point of view, one is left wondering what feat of engineering was required to erect these great shafts, nearly 34 m in height, in so confined an area: in order to accomplish this, she almost certainly demolished the north side of the court.

Each face of Hatshepsut's obelisks carried, as was customary, a central dedicatory band of inscription running down the length of the shaft but, more unusually, these inscriptions were flanked on either side by eight small scenes on the upper half of the shafts, each one containing a figure of Hatshepsut or Tuthmosis III offering to the gods. Here is more evidence to prove that even as late in her reign as Year 16, Hatshepsut was including Tuthmosis as king alongside her on her monuments. The top half of these obelisks was covered in gold and, indeed, holes for affixing the gold plate are still clearly visible on the shaft of the one obelisk which is lying broken on the ground today.

Now to consider Hatshepsut's celebrated Chapelle Rouge, most of whose blocks were found within the Third Pylon, as were those of so many other dismantled monuments. The Chapelle Rouge acquired its modern name from the colour of the red quartzite stone from which it was largely constructed, and its blocks were, for many years, laid out on display in the Open Air Museum at Karnak. However, a remarkable reconstruction has recently been completed, and the full glory of the chapel can now be appreciated.

The Chapelle Rouge and its associated offering rooms should be considered as one ritual complex which was built on a podium in front of the Middle Kingdom temple: the Chapelle Rouge itself stood immediately in advance of the offering rooms and was centred on the main axial way leading directly through to the area of the Holy of Holies, the temple sanctuary. It is an unusual monument in that the blocks were individually assembled, dressed and decorated in the temple stoneyards and workshops prior to construction. It was, in effect, 'prefabricated' and consequently could have been put in position and completed speedily, thus minimising any disruption to the sacred area of the temple where it was to stand. Each block carried a single complete scene: there was no overlapping on to adjacent blocks (Graindorge 1993: 43), but the sequence of events shown make a reconstruction possible.

The shrine was built of red quartzite quarried from Gebel el-Ahmar, the Red

Plate 5.1 Block from the Chapelle Rouge showing cartouches of Hatshepsut and Tuthmosis III.

Plate 5.2 Block from the Chapelle Rouge depicting Hatshepsut performing a ritual before the sacred bark in its shrine.

Mountain (north of Cairo), an exceedingly hard stone and very difficult to work. It was a stone highly prized by the ancient Egyptians for its long-lasting qualities and was normally used only for sarcophagi, statues and small architectural elements, but very rarely for whole monuments on account of the technical problems encountered in working such an intractable material. Possibly this was another reason for carving the blocks individually before assembling them into the completed monument. The fact that the ancient Egyptian word *bi3t*, meaning 'wonder' or 'marvel', was later used to designate this stone is telling.

The monument is spectacular to look at for, while the walls are of the wonderful red quartzite, the base and the cornice, as well as the three doorways, are all of black granite: the contrasting effect is dramatic.

The Chapelle Rouge could not have fitted into the area in the middle of the offering complex, where the shrine of Philip Arrhidaeus stands today, as had originally been assumed. In fact, during its current reconstruction, it has been observed that elements from the roof level show runnels for the collection and evacuation of rainwater (Carlotti 1995: 156) – for which, obviously, there would have been no need had the shrine stood within the Palace of Maat. Modern research believes that it must have stood just in advance of the offering rooms, and at one time it was wondered whether the rear of the shrine might have been keyed into the front of the complex. This might make sense when the arrangement and function of a bark-shrine is considered, but now that the shrine has been reconstructed, it is clear that this was not the case and that the Chapelle Rouge was free-standing. The only other possibility for the shrine's placement is in the centre of Tuthmosis II's festival court, but it would have been very tightly enclosed by the two central obelisks which would have obscured much of the relief work and, indeed, would have left little room to pass around the shrine (Carlotti 1995: 156–7). However, this siting is endorsed by some scholars (Fig. 5.1).

So what were these shrines that figured so prominently in ancient Egyptian temples? Within temples such as Karnak, two statues of the divine image were housed: one was a processional statue that, at certain festivals and special religious occasions, was carried from its shrine and placed within a small veiled naos on the deck of a portable and gilded wooden boat which was then carried out on the shoulders of priests to be seen by the people; while the other statue was the cult image of the god which was so sacred, so holy, that it could never be seen by profane eyes or approached by anyone other than the king or the highest members of the priesthood, and was kept within the deepest and most sacred recesses of the temple.

The Chapelle Rouge could not have been completed before Hatshepsut's Year 17 since on it she commemorated the setting up of her two obelisks in the Wadjet Hall. Its dimensions were about 8 m in height and 17 m in length with a width of 7 m, and it comprised two open-ended rooms: a vestibule followed by a sanctuary in which the bark would have been sited. The main theme of its decoration, both inside and out, stressed the divine connection between Hatshepsut and Amun: her designation for kingship by an oracle of the god, her enthronement at Karnak ['He (Amun) introduces her upon the stairway of the unique lord, he places her upon the Great Seat, he makes her sit upon the dais . . .'], her coronation, the bark processions to the temples of Luxor and Deir el-Bahri, as well as the performance of many rituals and offering ceremonies,

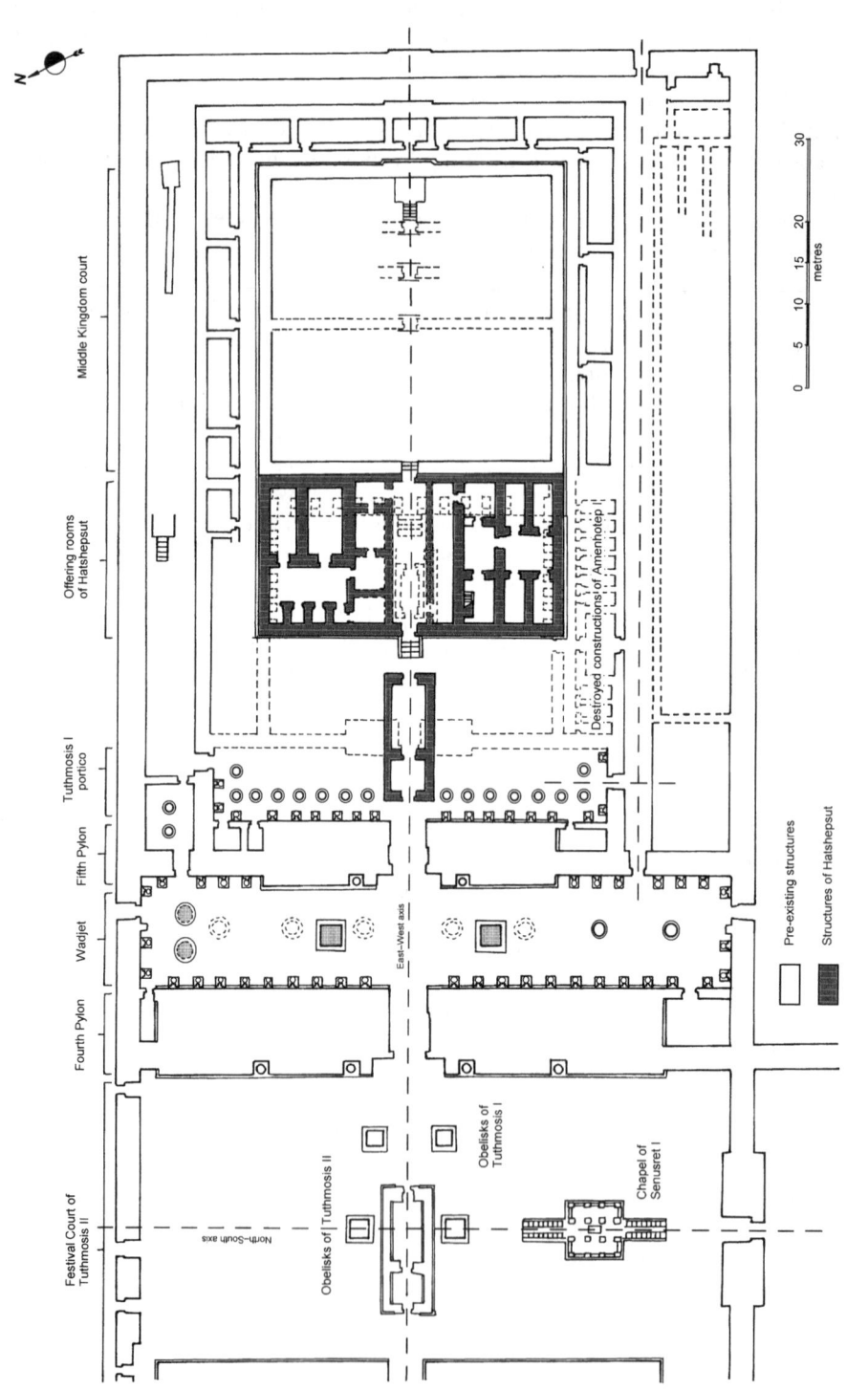

Figure 5.1 Plan of central Karnak at the end of the reign of Hatshepsut showing the probable position of the Chapelle Rouge (after Carlotti, J.-F., in *Cahiers de Karnak* X: 163).

notably a scene of Hatshepsut consecrating great piles of gold to the god (one is tempted here to see her doing this in the festival court of her husband Tuthmosis II). It should be noted that Tuthmosis III, in full royal regalia, is often included in the performance of these rituals. Round the base of the Chapelle Rouge, the lower outer register shows a list of nomes and of various Theban monuments: temples, both state and funerary, with their associated royal canals, shrines, way-stations and palaces. Here is another instance where Hatshepsut acknowledged Tuthmosis III by including several of his monuments, including his funerary temple and royal canal, in the list.

Within the monument itself, the first room, or vestibule, has representations of *rekhyt*-birds round the granite base, indicating that various officials and privileged people probably had access. The inner room, or sanctuary, where the bark would have stood upon a socle, has one ancient paving slab still *in situ* which is decorated with *ankh*, *djed* and *w3s* symbols on a *neb*-basket in shallow raised relief. Since this classic motif can clearly be seen to have continued over all four edges of the slab, it is obvious that the entire floor was once covered in the same design, particularly since the vestibule and chapels on the north side of Hatshepsut's offering complex, the Palace of Maat, also have paving slabs with identical decoration (Giddy 2002 [Autumn]: 28).

Tuthmosis III, after he had appropriated the Chapelle Rouge as his own following Hatshepsut's disappearance from the scene, claimed that he had decorated it inside with 'fine gold'. But was it, in fact, actually so decorated by Hatshepsut herself? And could it perhaps have been with some of the gold that she is depicted as dedicating to the god on the shrine's reliefs? Further, if we look again at the inscription of Hatshepsut's Treasurer, Djehuti, we read 'a large heap of fine gold from the best of foreign countries was in the festival hall'. Might this not indeed be the hall of her husband, Tuthmosis II?

Although today the granite bark-shrine of Philip Arrhidaeus stands in the centre of Hatshepsut's suite of offering rooms, the space it now occupies once contained other chambers of the complex, while the Chapelle Rouge itself is believed to have stood just in advance of them. It is highly improbable that this whole area would have been simply a wide empty space at the time when Hatshepsut undertook her construction work; indeed, as we have seen, it was probably occupied by buildings of Amenhotep I, and perhaps of Tuthmosis I as well. Hatshepsut's offering complex was designated 'the Palace of Maat', and since Tuthmosis I is known to have had offering chambers of an identical name, it has been assumed that these were likely to have been located in the same area, probably fronted by the alabaster bark-shrine of Amenhotep I that Tuthmosis I had completed. These buildings were therefore dismantled by Hatshepsut to make way for her own, which she then constructed right up against what remained of the Middle Kingdom temple façade, having first removed its portico. Today the offering rooms seem divided into two sections, north and south, which was not, of course, the case in Hatshepsut's time. They were a complete entity of ritual significance, as many of the reliefs indicate.

Nowadays there are eight rooms to the south, one containing a staircase which once gave access to an upper floor, now gone. Another room, the largest of the eight, contains a granite altar or possibly a socle for a naos. This room has some interesting, though very damaged reliefs, of two ceremonies which it is possible to recognise since identical scenes have been preserved *in toto* in a later edifice of Taharqa (Barguet 1962: 145–6). One scene shows the celebration of a festival called 'the return of the god' with a solemn procession carrying the statue of

Amun contained within a shrine which, it must be assumed, would have been placed upon the altar/socle of this room. The northern group of rooms also contain important reliefs: one chamber has scenes of Hatshepsut performing sed-festival, or possibly coronation, rites, while another shows the queen/king offering before the nine gods of the Karnak Ennead. All the rooms in the Palace of Maat contained reliefs of Hatshepsut, although many have been completely reworked by Tuthmosis III.

Built up, as the Palace of Maat was, against the Middle Kingdom temple, the main axial way passed on from the Chapelle Rouge through the centre of the offering rooms which gave direct access into Senusret I's peristyle court and then to the main sanctuary, the Holy of Holies – almost certainly still the one which had been constructed by Senusret.

When the sacred bark of Amun was borne out from the Chapelle Rouge for the two greatest festivals of the year, namely the Beautiful Feast of the Valley and the Festival of Opet, it was carried, for the former, to the quay at the temple's main entrance to be placed on the great state barge 'Userhet' in order to cross the Nile to the West Bank; and for the latter, the god's bark processed from Karnak towards Luxor along the southern route between the two temples, a route which Hatshepsut greatly enhanced and developed. It was probably her intention to link the temples of Karnak and Luxor into a processional complex, but on account of the extensive development of this route by later kings, there is little left to give an indication of her plans.

She built a great pylon (the Eighth) of sandstone, which had two special features: one was the large number of royal colossi placed against its façade, and the other, which is thought to be unique, was a low limestone wall which completely encircled it. No other such example exists and its function is not known. Sadly its band of inscription, which might have provided some information, is no longer legible. The texts of Hatshepsut inscribed on the Eighth Pylon were largely obliterated, altered or re-inscribed but, nevertheless, all the texts and reliefs, whether of Hatshepsut, Tuthmosis or later kings, adhered to the same all-important theme of the acceptance of the king by the gods as the legitimate ruler, a theme that Hatshepsut was always particularly careful to emphasise, as we have seen many times. One scene of hers in this genre, which somehow escaped destruction, depicts Tuthmosis I standing before the Theban triad, thanking Amun for placing his daughter, Hatshepsut, upon the throne. Hatshepsut's hand in this piece of propaganda is self-evident.

The pylon's great gateway had, at the base of its inner walls, a spectacular feature: deep grooves can be seen for the inlay of multicoloured faience plaques which would have illumined and glowed within the walls, the surfaces of which may well have been gilded. This sumptuous decoration must have been awe-inspiring to anyone passing through the pylon's great portal, and a worthy entrance for the passage of the god within his divine bark. However, although the Eighth Pylon was Hatshepsut's construction, there is nothing to tell us whether these faience plaques can be attributed to her, particularly since later kings certainly adopted such practices.

Through this great pylon, therefore, the god's image left Karnak's precinct on its way to Luxor temple for the Festival of Opet, stopping along the ceremonial route at the six way-stations which Hatshepsut had positioned to receive the enshrined god on his

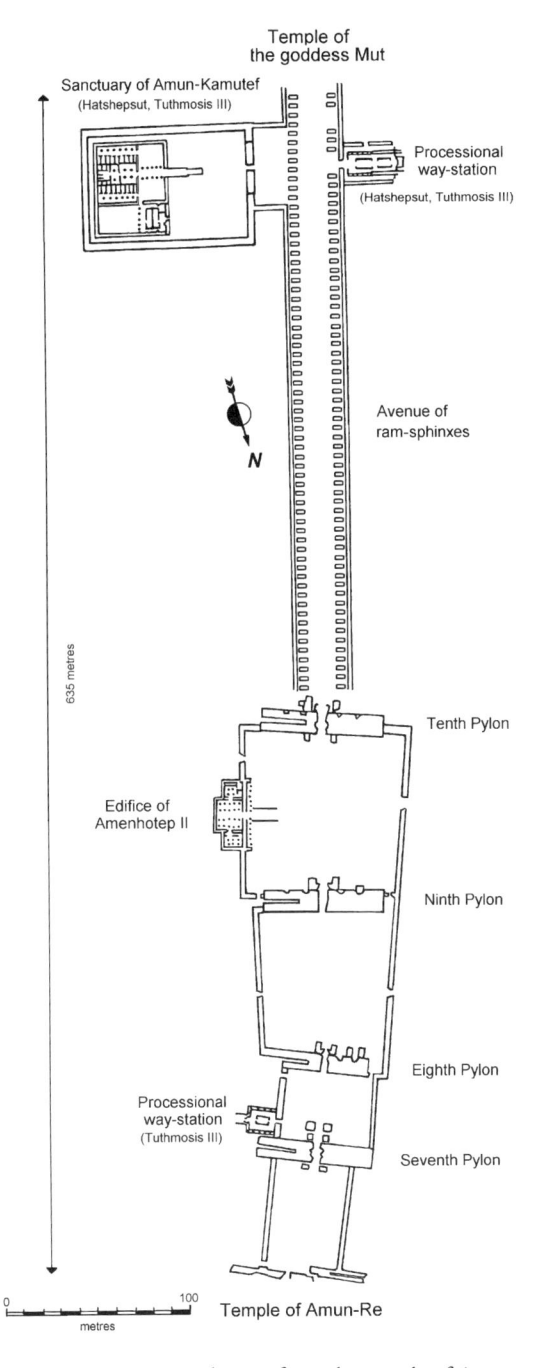

Figure 5.2 Processional route from the temple of Amun to the temple of Mut via the sanctuary of Amun-Kamutef (after Kemp, B.J., *Ancient Egypt: Anatomy of a Civilization*: 187).

journey. In fact, it appears that it was Hatshepsut who first instituted these way-stations, known in ancient Egyptian as 'the place for setting down', when she inaugurated this great processional festival. The route is today lined with sphinxes dating to the reigns of Horemheb (Dynasty XVIII) and Nectanebo (Dynasty XXX), but there is some evidence to show that Hatshepsut had been the first to mark this ceremonial road with sphinxes in her own likeness. This procession is depicted on the Chapelle Rouge where Hatshepsut is shown burning incense before the shrines, each of which is identified with its individual name (Nims 1955: 114). The shrines are shown as being more or less identical although, in truth, this was probably not the case since we have some idea of what the first and the sixth shrines were like. The first shrine of Hatshepsut comprised two rooms – the first, a peripteral chapel, containing a socle on which the bark would have been placed. This bark repository was situated in front of the enclosure wall of the precinct of the goddess Mut, a deity whom Hatshepsut brought to prominence, while on the same axis, but on the other side of the sphinx-lined avenue, was a small temple dedicated to Amun-Kamutef (the ithyphallic aspect of Amun) also constructed by Hatshepsut (Figs. 5.2, 5.3a).

In such close proximity, was there a connection between the temple and the bark-shrine? We know that the shrine was called 'The stairway of Amun in front of *Pr-hn*' (House of the Shrine); we know too that a palace in this area was named 'The palace (called) "Maatkare is beloved of Amun at the head of *Pr-hn*"', and that furthermore, a canal existed in the area 'The canal of Amun at the head of *Hn*'. It would seem reasonable to suppose from this evidence that the temple of Amun-Kamutef here was indeed this 'House of the Shrine'. And since it is known that, in Hatshepsut's time, the procession to Luxor temple for the Opet Festival went along the ceremonial route on its outward journey, but always *returned* by water (Graindorge 1993: 50; Lacau and Chevrier 1977: 154, para. 191), could 'the canal of Amun at the head of *Hn*' be where the return procession left the Nile and approached the Amun-Kamutef temple via the canal before disembarking to re-enter Karnak along the sacred way and through the Eighth Pylon, as it had left? There is no way of knowing, but a study of the Egyptian word *rwty*, meaning 'entrance' is interesting. Most temples had only one main entrance (*rwty*), but at Karnak there were several distinct ones: certainly there was the *rwty wrty*, the great main (western) entrance, but there was also a southern *rwty*, which at one time was Amenhotep I's great limestone gateway, and later became the Eighth Pylon of Hatshepsut as the southern approach developed. Then there was an eastern *rwty*, probably the 'Upper Gateway' outside which Hatshepsut erected her eastern obelisks, and finally there was a western *rwty* which was on the river where Amun landed on his return from Luxor. Where this last was located is not recorded, but it is tempting to think it might have been 'the canal of Amun at the head of *Hn*'. This is a real possibility, since excavation has shown that a quay once existed on the processional way between Karnak and Luxor that was connected to the river by a canal, and recently a possible Nile Gate in the early temple enclosure wall has also been found (Spencer 2004: 29).

The positions of Hatshepsut's four other shrines along the route are unknown, but the sixth and final one was dismantled and some of its elements reused by Ramesses II in his triple shrine in the first court which he added to the front of Luxor temple. The knowledge that six of these way-stations existed must certainly indicate that Hatshepsut had constructed an early sacred way, or embellished an already-existing one, between Karnak and Luxor temples.

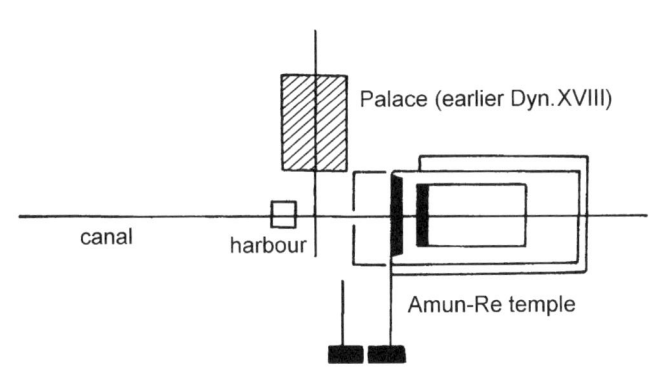

Figure 5.3 Way-station and palace of Hatshepsut. (a) The Way-station as depicted on the Chapelle Rouge (after Leblanc, C., in *BIFAO* 82: 301). (b) Possible siting of Hatshepsut's palace (after O'Connor, D., in *Ancient Egyptian Kingship*: 80, Fig. 7.2).

These, then, are the principal monuments of Hatshepsut left to us today, but that there were other, probably lesser, buildings is certain: blocks, small fragments and, above all, ancient textual sources give proof of this. One fascinating example is given on the black granite jamb of a doorway that bears the legend:

> She (Hatshepsut) made it as a monument for her father Amun-Re, constructing for him an incense room in order to make the pellets (of incense) for each day so that this temple should always be full of the odour of the divine land. (Lacau 1954: 187)

Incense was a vital ingredient in the divine cult, and many kings boasted of sending expeditions to exotic lands to bring back large quantities of this product. The Palermo Stone lists an expedition sent to Punt by Sahure of Dynasty V in order to obtain incense, and an inscription of Dynasty XI date is known in the Wadi Hammamat for a similar purpose. Hatshepsut herself showed on the walls of Deir el-Bahri the incense trees which she brought back from the land of Punt, incense which was primarily intended to be used in the cult of Amun at Karnak. Once again, Hatshepsut's treasurer Djehuti gives a picture: 'Behold there was ordered every fine thing and all the tribute of every foreign land and the most wonderful things of Punt (incense) for Amun, Lord of Karnak . . .' (BAR II: para. 377). Obviously, as the granite jamb shows, Hatshepsut built a magazine or chamber in which to store this precious commodity, though where it stood is unknown. One would assume that all incense, oils and sacred equipment used in the divine cult would have been kept close to the main offering rooms within the heart of the temple, so it is possible that Hatshepsut's incense room was in the vicinity of the Palace of Maat, where incense would undoubtedly have been much in use. Another possibility would place it where the incense was initially dedicated and where so many official ceremonies took place – that is, adjacent to the festival court of her husband Tuthmosis II. But without doubt, every sanctuary, every shrine, every altar within the temple enclosure would have had need of incense: one can imagine that the air of the entire sacred area would have been heavily redolent with its exotic perfume.

An inscription on the walls of Deir el-Bahri concerning the dedication of incense at Karnak is of relevance here, conjuring up, as it does, a public ceremony of dedication by Hatshepsut in the festival court:

> Her Majesty herself put myrrh with her own hands upon all her limbs, her fragrance was like a divine breath, her scent reached as far as Punt. Her skin was of gold, it shone like the stars in the court of festival in view of the whole land. (Gabolde 1993: 59)

It is worth considering for a moment the destination of the incense trees that Hatshepsut said 'were taken up in God's Land (Punt) and set in the ground in Egypt . . . for the kings of the gods'. It is difficult today, whilst wandering amidst the ruined grandeur of Karnak's great stone columns and courts, to visualise them brilliantly painted, plastered and gilded, as they would have been; and to add to the picture, one must also imagine lush gardens of trees, flowers and plants bordering the avenues and gracing the precincts. Some of these gardens were purely ornamental, others were used to provide vegetables, fruit, flowers and possibly incense for the temple's altars and offering tables: examples of both kinds of garden can be seen on the walls of several notable tombs on the West Bank at Thebes.

No temple would have existed without a garden – probably several, some ornamental and some practical. It is an amazing thought that, according to the Great Harris Papyrus, by the time of Ramesses III (Dynasty XX), Amun's temples in the Theban area were adorned by no fewer than 433 gardens (BAR IV: 97). It should be remembered that temples were considered as replicas of heaven upon earth and were beautified accordingly – not only with gold and precious stones, but with flowers, bushes, pools and trees, amongst whose shady groves the god could wander and take his ease. Gardens were therefore always of great importance to the ancient Egyptians, though it is not until the New Kingdom that there is much material or textual evidence for them. So when Hatshepsut states:

> He (Amun) commanded me to establish for him a Punt in his house, to plant the trees of God's Land beside his temple, in his garden . . . . I made for him a Punt in his garden, just as he commanded me, for Thebes. It is large for him, he walks abroad in it . . . (BAR II: para. 295)

was she referring to her funerary temple at Deir el-Bahri or to the temple of Karnak, Amun's house? The likelihood is that this particular text does indeed refer to Karnak, but she would undoubtedly have planted incense trees at both.

The so-called Geographic Procession on the base of the Chapelle Rouge is a great source of information on a variety of buildings constructed by Hatshepsut, of which there is now no trace. Two additional temples are shown – though in all probability these would have been some sort of shrine or chapel – one named 'The temple of Maatkare (called) "Amun is splendid of sanctuary"' (Lacau and Chevrier 1977: 77, para. 124), and another 'The temple (called) "Maatkare is divine of monuments"'. This latter is of some interest since an identically named building was erected by Tuthmosis III merely substituting his name for Maatkare (Lacau and Chevrier 1977: 84, para. 138). As we have seen, Tuthmosis III was quite prepared to take over Hatshepsut's monuments and claim them as his own (as with the Chapelle Rouge itself), but in this case the two buildings were always considered separate since Hatshepsut's was apparently of limestone, while that of Tuthmosis was of sandstone. However, it should be mentioned that the ancient Egyptians themselves were not totally reliable as to the correct identity of various stones.

But now, as mentioned in the last chapter, research has revealed the possible answer to this puzzling duplication. Many blocks from a monument entitled *Ntry-mnw* (Divine-of-Monuments) have been closely studied by Luc Gabolde. These blocks were thought to have come from a dismantled monument of Tuthmosis II, but detailed examination has revealed that the name of that king had been superimposed upon the original cartouches of Menkheperre (Tuthmosis III). The conclusion must be that the building was erected when Hatshepsut was acting as regent for the young Tuthmosis III, and that when she assumed full pharaonic powers, she cut out his cartouches and substituted those of her husband, Tuthmosis II, and herself. This would certainly explain why both she and Tuthmosis III claimed to have erected a temple of the same name.

The emplacement of this temple is unknown, but there is strong evidence that 'Divine-of-Monuments' was indeed the name of Hatshepsut's eastern temple in advance of which she erected her magnificent obelisks (Gabolde 2005: 26). Part of the foundations of an earlier temple (very probably 'Divine-of-Monuments') have been found beneath the floor of Tuthmosis III's Akh-Menu (Carlotti 2001: 23), and blocks from it can be seen re-employed as paving in Akh-Menu's sanctuary.

The names of three palaces feature on the Geographic Procession: one ('Maatkare is beloved of Amun at the head of the House of the Shrine') has been mentioned above. A second palace is of uncertain ownership since most of its name has been destroyed, leaving only the 'Re' element of the cartouche. While the likelihood is that it belonged to Maatka*re* (Hatshepsut), both Aakheperka*re* (Tuthmosis I) or Menkheper*re* (Tuthmosis III) could be possible candidates. However, it is the third palace which is of the greatest interest since this is the one mentioned in Hatshepsut's coronation text:

His Majesty (Amun) entered into the front of the palace of ' "I shall not be far from him" in the Domain of Amun'... The Mistress of the Two Lands came from the interior of the splendours of her palace to meet him and she paid homage to the King of the Gods ... she placed herself upon the ground in his presence ... (Lacau and Chevrier 1977: 103 note n)(Fig. 5.3b).

Textual evidence points to this palace being constructed by Tuthmosis I, but its name (somewhat unusually) does not specify its builder, but alludes instead to the proximity of the palace to the temple of Amun. It was situated in front of Karnak on the north side of the dromos and it had two entrances: the principal one leading out on to the main temple approach close to the quay and basin where water-borne processions would have arrived, and the second entrance was orientated to the west through double doors towards the river (Gitton 1974: 71). This palace, it has been argued, was used for state affairs and above all for temple ceremonial – almost in this respect as an extension of the temple proper with columned courts and rooms, and containing, as the texts tell us, a throne upon a dais. It was not intended primarily as a royal residence: probably *that* function was served by one of the other palaces listed.

It is worth mentioning here that the quay and basin at the temple's main entrance were probably much further to the east than the one that exists today. The T-shaped basin in Hatshepsut's time, therefore, would have been sited more or less in the area where the Third Pylon now stands, and as the temple expanded under later kings, the quay was slowly moved back westwards. In fact the prodigious depth of the foundations of the Second and Third Pylons has been ascribed to the original presence of two successive basins in those areas, although perhaps it should be added here that recent excavations have cast doubt on this assumption (see further Chapter 8). There is no evidence to show that the approach from the quay (wherever it was sited) to the temple was lined by sphinxes at this period: but it would probably have been bordered on either side by walls.

Djehuti, Hatshepsut's treasurer, whose stela has been quoted several times above, listed upon it the works that he undertook at each of Hatshepsut's great foundations in Egypt. Amongst those that he listed for Karnak was: 'a temple built of granite, its firmness is like the pillars of heaven, its work is like a thing of eternity'. It is left to us to wonder which of her buildings this might be: is it one that is still standing, or one that has vanished? The fact that Djehuti stated it was constructed of granite does not necessarily have to be taken literally – the ancient Egyptians were not always very accurate on this point – but Hatshepsut certainly did use granite (the base of the Chapelle Rouge; the upright of the incense-room doorway). Perhaps it refers to one of the unknown temples or shrines of the Geographic Procession list, or even to the demolished edifice at the eastern end of the temple fronted by her first pair of obelisks. One building named by Djehuti is certainly familiar: 'I enlarged the Two Treasuries ... they were filled with tribute to their ceilings ...'. This must surely refer to the Treasury of Tuthmosis I, discussed above, for excavation has shown that these buildings were certainly added to and enlarged in Hatshepsut's reign.

Finally, a tantalising reference to what might have been Karnak's Sacred Lake appears in the Geographic Procession: 'The basin (or lake) of Amun (named) "Cool and pure"' (Lacau and Chevrier 1977: 75 para. 120). Although it was Tuthmosis III who claimed to have dug the Sacred Lake, there can be little doubt that one existed previously.

This reference of Hatshepsut's is particularly intriguing since a very similar name is to be found on the base of Senusret I's White Chapel (Lacau and Chevrier 1956: 210 para. 590). Is this mere coincidence, especially when one considers that the White Chapel bears references to a Northern Lake and a Southern Lake (Lacau and Chevrier 1956: 209 para. 581; 210 para. 586)? Did a Sacred Lake exist therefore in the Middle Kingdom? Almost certainly. Where was it sited? We can only speculate.

6

TUTHMOSIS III

In Year 22 of their joint reign, Hatshepsut disappeared from the scene and Tuthmosis III became sole ruler. There is no reason to suppose that Hatshepsut died from anything other than natural causes, and her monuments were not defaced or dismantled by Tuthmosis until much later in his reign. In this context, it is worth noting that some of the great officials who held office under Hatshepsut were not dismissed but continued to serve under Tuthmosis. None of the tombs and chapels of these men was destroyed, only the queen's name was cut out at a later date. Was the removal of her name a political act? Was Tuthmosis trying to underline his own legitimacy as Hatshepsut had herself once done? Many of her cartouches were replaced by those of Tuthmosis I and Tuthmosis II, the grandfather and father respectively of Tuthmosis III – perhaps again to stress his right to rule. In fact, Tuthmosis III did not replace Hatshepsut's name with his own on the Chapelle Rouge until Year 42 – twenty years after her death. Could, therefore, the instigator of this attack upon Hatshepsut's memory have been Amenhotep II when appointed co-regent at the end of his father's reign, as has already been suggested?

Tuthmosis III's reign was a long one and arguably the greatest and most prestigious in the whole course of Egyptian pharaonic history, and his building programme the length and breadth of the land reflected this: in fact, we still marvel today at his great legacy in stone. Within one year of his independent reign, Tuthmosis had undertaken a military campaign into western Asia, the first of seventeen such campaigns extending over twenty years. It was these foreign campaigns above all that brought huge amounts of wealth flooding into the state coffers, enabling him to channel vast resources into the construction of great monuments. In the temple of Amun at Karnak, Tuthmosis built prolifically in honour of the god to whom he ascribed his victories: his building work there was particularly magnificent, and his use of rich materials and sumptuous decoration was perhaps unparalleled. Every part of the existing temple was to receive his attention. Let us start therefore with the construction linked forever with his name, the so-called Festival Hall.

Akh-Menu

The most impressive of the many buildings Tuthmosis III erected at Ipet-Sut was the magnificent edifice known as the Festival Hall or, more correctly (to use its Egyptian name), Akh-Menu, translated as 'Beneficent-of-Monuments' or 'Brilliant-of-Monuments' – the name always used by Tuthmosis himself. But this imposing structure is also a very enigmatic one and, when reading various accounts of it, quickly becomes apparent that there is no sure consensus as to the original use and function of this complex suite of halls, chambers and sanctuaries. However, it is generally agreed that Akh-Menu was a unique monument, something quite different from the usual cult temple: here were thought to have taken place very particular sacred rites. But of what type and for what reason? Only by studying the layout of the complex closely can one hope to get a glimmering of its sacred purpose. Every part, however, is so thoroughly ruinous that very often only the ground plan and/or the lower courses of walls remain, and it raises as many questions as it answers.

The first thing to note is that it appears to be a totally separate entity: a complete temple built at the eastern end of Karnak, wholly enclosed by its own girdle walls. Tuthmosis claimed that he built Akh-Menu on virgin soil yet, as we know, there had been some building of Hatshepsut's at this eastern end fronted by her mighty obelisks. Tuthmosis demolished this construction, as well as the original mud-brick enclosure wall, when he extended Karnak in order to erect his Akh-Menu, and he incorporated Hatshepsut's obelisk bases into his new sandstone enclosure wall. So can Tuthmosis's claim to have built on virgin soil be a true one? Perhaps a study of his own words gives a clue:

> My Majesty wished to make a monument for my father Amun-Re in Karnak, erecting a dwelling, consecrating a horizon, embellishing Kheft-Her-nebes (Karnak) for him ... the first occasion of erecting a temple in the east of this temple (Karnak). Lo, my Majesty found it encircled by bricks, soil as far as to hide the walls. My Majesty commanded that its soil should be brought away from it in order to extend this temple. I purified it, I removed its dirt, I dispelled its rubble ... I beat flat this place where the encircling wall was in order to build this monument upon it ... I made this as something anew ... I did not work upon the monument of another. (*URK* IV: 833)

What does one make of this statement? The king asserts that he demolished the encircling wall of mud-brick to extend the temple and generally cleared the area for building purposes. But what of his claim that he did not work upon the monument of another, yet at the same time stating here (and in other inscriptions also) that he made the building 'as something anew'? And what of Hatshepsut's structure in the area? The answer to this lies in the fact that Tuthmosis regarded all buildings erected during his joint reign with Hatshepsut as his own – a good example being his assertion that the Chapelle Rouge was his construction. Even more so, therefore, would he have considered the temple *Nṯry-mnw*, built in his name when Hatshepsut was regent (and discussed in the last chapter), as being his own monument and thus not having worked on, or demolished, 'the monument of another'. With such an attitude, he could obviously make such a statement.

But there is another most intriguing facet to the debate: some years ago, excavators at Karnak found a block of limestone from the jamb of a doorway naming an Akh-Menu of Tuthmosis I or II (the cartouche is damaged) (Barguet 1962: 283 n. 5; Letellier 1979: 69). No trace has ever been found of this building, but a structure bearing the name Kheperkare Akh-Menu is known from a red quartzite architrave deriving from a building of Senusret I at Heliopolis (Gabolde 1998: 145). It was Senusret, of course, who had merged Amun with Re at Karnak, bringing the Heliopolitan solar element to the temple. Was Tuthmosis III emulating his illustrious ancestor once again, or could it be that Karnak already housed an Akh-Menu of his father or grandfather which Tuthmosis III pulled down in order to 'make something anew'? There is some compelling evidence to be found in the inscription of a noble named Ouser who acceded to the vizierate in Year 5 of Tuthmosis III's reign (Kruchten 1989: 188–9). On a stela, this official described his initiation into two offices – first, that of vizier and, second, that of Prophet of Amun within a temple at Karnak identified as Akh-Menu. Since Tuthmosis III did not commence the building of his Akh-Menu before Year 23 of his reign, the Akh-Menu spoken of by Ouser, then, can only be an earlier construction of that name. Could it have been, therefore, the building of Tuthmosis I or II? It should be stressed, however, that the siting and, indeed, the existence of an earlier Akh-Menu remains conjectural and, indeed, Luc Gabolde now believes that this particular block derived from the festival court of Tuthmosis II (Gabolde 1993: 42). But let us look at another possibility which has recently gained credence: if it did not exist on the site now occupied by Tuthmosis III's Akh-Menu, could the earlier building of that name possibly have been the general term for the Middle Kingdom complex, upon which design Tuthmosis is thought perhaps to have modelled his own (Gabolde 1998: 141)? There certainly seems to be some similarity between what is known of the Middle Kingdom layout and that of Tuthmosis III's Akh-Menu: the central pillared hall, wider rather than deeper, dominating three consecutive rooms leading to the sanctuary for the portable statue of the god, with another more retired and sacred shrine for the cult image somewhere beyond.

When one considers that many of the limestone constructions of Senusret's Middle Kingdom temple must by this time have been partially in ruin due to the high water-table and occasional flooding, it is natural to suppose that Tuthmosis, who so admired his ancestor, might have wished to reproduce it – in form, if not in function. His restoration work in the Middle Kingdom temple was executed in sandstone – much more resistant to water erosion; now he founded his new monument upon a large sandstone platform: 'I made it for him, raised upon a socle of sandstone, higher and larger, given that the flood ... formerly inundated the temple when Nun arrived in his season' (*URK* IV: 834). One wonders, incidentally, whether this was the reason that New Kingdom monarchs changed from using limestone as the principal building material in favour of sandstone, or was the change influenced by the ease and comparative cheapness of quarrying the latter? Tuthmosis III seems to have reached a practical compromise, using both sandstone and limestone in Akh-Menu (Carlotti 2001: 166 and 255; Daumas 1980: 275 and 277–9).

Today, crowds of tourists walk briefly through the very ruinous so-called 'Festival Hall' of Tuthmosis III, noting its unusual columns, its famous 'Botanical Garden' scenes, and the many decorated but tumbled walls, before passing through to view Karnak's other splendours. But let us pause a while and look at this remarkable building, first at its layout and then at its possible meaning.

That it was a temple of unparalleled richness and beauty there can be no doubt: inscriptions speak of cedar, electrum, gold, silver, lapis lazuli and turquoise used in its decoration, now long vanished; but enough of its halls and shrines survive to instil in us some sense of awe.

The Akh-Menu comprised many individual features, but three main and quite distinct parts can be distinguished: first, a suite of rooms and halls in the south-eastern sector dedicated to Sokar, a Memphite funerary deity; second, to the north and east is a solar complex; and third, there is the 'festival' hall itself or, to be strictly accurate, the *ḥrt-ib* or central hall (lit. 'that which is at the heart of'), a particularly appropriate name, for it was, in effect, the link that joined all parts of the temple together: from this hall there was access to each section of the complex (Fig. 6.1).

At the very start, a strange feature occurs: the only entry to this extensive complex was in the south-west corner (see I in Figure 6.1) through a doorway at the end of a corridor that led straight from the southern court of the Fifth Pylon and which skirted the Middle Kingdom court behind the offering chapels of Amenhotep I. The doorway was approached by a short ramp and was flanked by two Osiride colossi of Tuthmosis III. This extraordinary configuration has never been convincingly accounted for, but the corridor, leading to a building at the rear of Karnak, was known to have been in existence at the time of Tuthmosis I: did it lead to *his* Akh-Menu, or to Hatshepsut's structure perhaps? However, if it is allowed that Tuthmosis III's monument mirrored much of the Middle Kingdom temple, it should be remembered that Senusret's temple had been entered via a portico of Osiride colossi of the king. As Tuthmosis would obviously not have wished to destroy his predecessor's sanctuary by driving an extension of the main east–west axis through the rear wall in order to achieve central access to his new complex, then he would have had no alternative but to have offset the entrance to Akh-Menu, reducing his own version of an Osiride portico to two colossi only.

That this entrance was indeed the main point of entry to Akh-Menu there can be no doubt, and it is worth noting that on one of the walls inside this entrance are the remains of a huge scene of the king massacring a group of prisoners ('a' in Figure 6.1) – the traditional scene usually found on the outer walls of entrance pylons. However, it is difficult to distinguish much of this scene today due to the extensive reworking and recarving of the area by later kings in order to allow the much-enlarged processions of the sacred bark to gain access. The archaeological team currently working on the Akh-Menu complex has recently reported finding traces of an axial door in the west wall of the temple. It must be assumed that this was part of that reworking of the complex by later kings at a time when the sanctuary of Senusret I's temple was no longer in use. (Recently, the existence of these doorway traces has been questioned.)

Ahead of Tuthmosis III's entrance vestibule is a corridor running west to east (II in Figure 6.1); nine chambers open off its southern (right) side, and its northern side is covered almost entirely with sed-festival scenes. A second vestibule (III) has scenes of the sacred barks of Amun, Mut and Khonsu arriving and being placed in their shrines, from whence they would have processed through the central or 'festival' hall to the solar sanctuary at the north end of the temple. It can clearly be seen where later kings enlarged this vestibule, as mentioned above, and also cut away part of the column bases of the hall's central north–south aisle; this was in order to accommodate the increase in size of the sacred barks and the number of priests bearing them.

The second vestibule gives access to the 'festival' hall by means of two doorways; this magnificent hall of sandstone is around 40 m in length and it contains 32 square

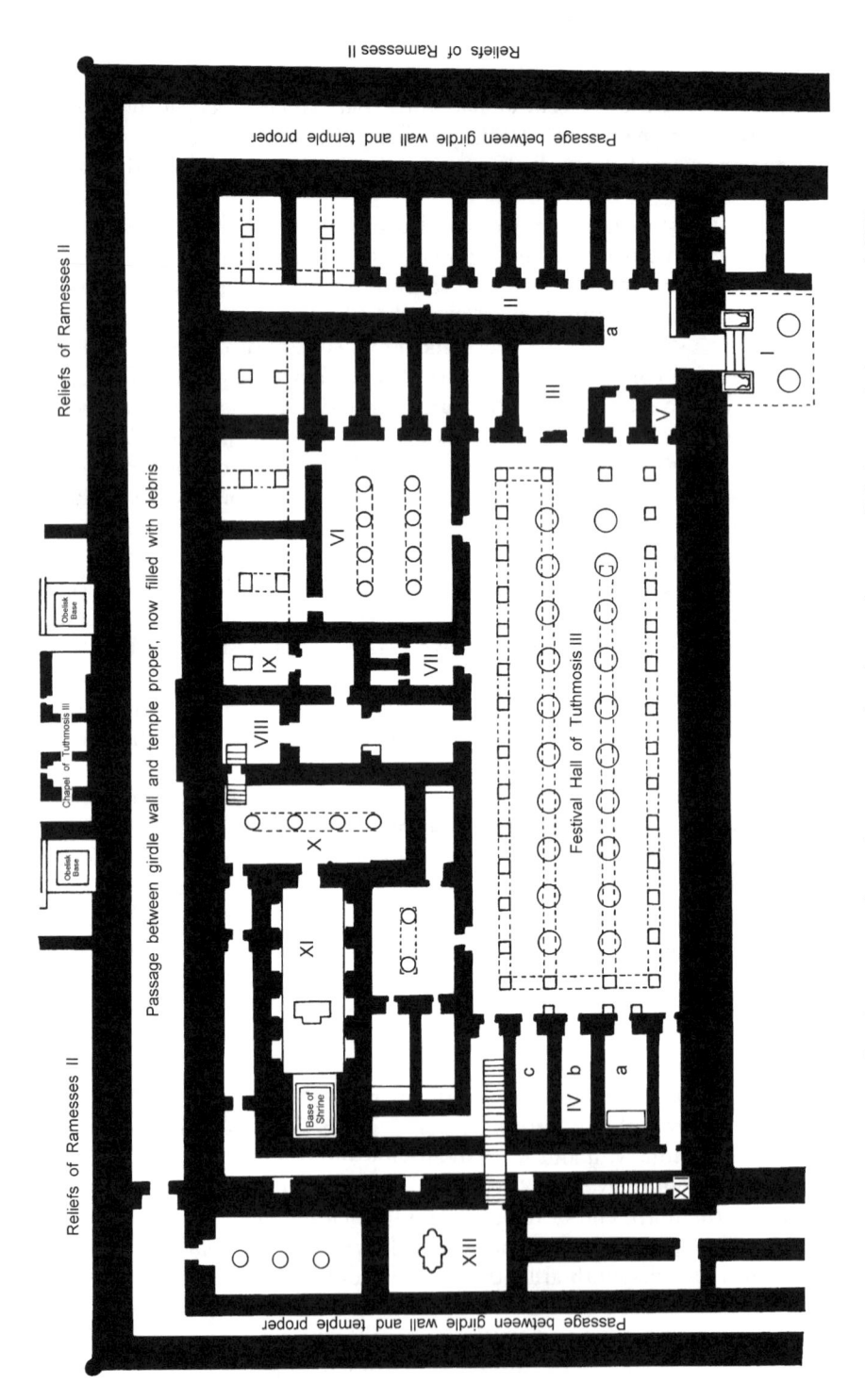

Figure 6.1 Plan of the Akh-Menu of Tuthmosis III (after Nelson, H., *Key plans showing locations of Theban temple decorations*: pl. VII).

pillars arranged in a rectangle to surround 20 columns (two lines of 10 each); these latter have unique capitals, often referred to as 'tent-peg' design. This appellation was used because it was thought that the columns replicated in stone the poles that would have supported Tuthmosis III's tent whilst he was on campaign. Another theory concerning this unusual feature is that the capitals reproduce the original wooden supports used in the archaic shrines of Upper and Lower Egypt, whose forms were still used at kings' coronations and jubilees (Spencer 1984: 236). This would accord with the fact that the column shafts of the hall were painted to resemble wood. The ceiling of this hall was painted deep blue with gold stars, and illumination was provided by clerestory windows formed by the central columns being higher than the two side aisles of pillars.

At the north end of the hall are three chapels (IV a,b,c). On account of their ruinous condition, it is hard to be completely certain concerning their function, but nothing indicates that these were bark chapels, although probably dedicated to Amun, Mut and Khonsu respectively. In fact, these chapels would have been too narrow to admit the sacred barks and, moreover, their entrances did not line up on the processional axes and left no room for manoeuvring the boats into position. What little is left of the walls of these chapels show scenes of royal statues being transported from Karnak to the temple of Mut and their return. Further scenes in the corridor behind these chapels show further processions with royal statues, and finally a scene of Tuthmosis III before funerary chapels at Buto, symbolising the tombs of his royal ancestors. There are other rooms, too, within Akh-Menu where royal predecessors are depicted and, in particular, the famous Chamber of Ancestors (V) at the southern end of the central hall. The reliefs we see in this room today are actually copies, since the originals were removed to the Musée du Louvre in Paris in 1843: they show Tuthmosis III offering to 61 of his royal ancestors. The dedicatory inscription within the southern chamber of Akh-Menu requires the king 'to inscribe the names of the fathers, to set down their offering portions, to fashion their images ... and to offer to them great and divine oblations'. The fact that the royal statues, depicted in the chapels (IV a,b,c) at the opposite end of the central hall, would pass before the Chamber of Ancestors on their processions must be of relevance.

Access to all parts of the complex could be gained from the central hall. First, opening off the south-east corner, there was a suite of rooms, including a columned hall, chapels and storage chambers, all dedicated to Sokar, a funerary deity (VI): the rites which would have been performed here were linked to death, regeneration and rebirth. The second doorway opening off the east side of the central hall led into a small vestibule and two chapels, seemingly dedicated to the cult of the king himself (VII), which should be considered as part of the funerary aspect of the temple. The rooms entered through the next doorway, which was on the axial way of both Ipet-Sut and Akh-Menu, led into the start of the solar section of the complex. Three small chambers, one behind the other through ever-narrowing doorways, were ranged along this central axis: the first chamber contained scenes of the king's coronation, the second had scenes of the Theban Ennead, and the third and final chamber was the sanctuary that, from the remaining inscriptions, was dedicated to Amun-Kamutef, the iphthyphallic form of Amun (VIII). From the second of these chambers, a door in its south wall led into another vestibule and sanctuary (IX), almost entirely reworked by Alexander who, it appears, adhered closely to the chamber's original decor. This second sanctuary was dedicated to the falcon god, Horus, representing the king himself. It seems strange for there to be two distinct sanctuaries side-by-side, but it has been persuasively argued that we have here not two sanctuaries but a double one (Barguet 1962: 285–6). This suggestion acquires credence from the curious fact that, in these chambers, the scenes on their eastern (rear) walls are not orientated to the centre of each wall, as one would normally expect, but are angled into the south-east and north-east corners respectively, thus, in effect, converging upon the wall that separates them – that wall becoming, so to speak, the central axis of one double sanctuary dedicated to both the king and Amun-Re merging as one; surely a unique architectural concept.

It is interesting to note that this chamber (IX) lies directly east of the small group of three chambers (VII) linked to Akh-Menu's funerary aspect, all dedicated to the cult of the deified king. Can one see in this arrangement a parallel with the great Theban mortuary temples on the West Bank where habitually such a suite of royal cult rooms was to be found adjoining the sanctuary of Amun?

But let us return to the axial sanctuary itself (VIII), which holds further surprises. The entrance to this sanctuary would have been through double doors: within the chamber, and approached by several steps, once stood an enormous alabaster socle, almost 1.5 m in height, which very nearly occupied the entire space (Varille 1950: 127–8). Upon this would have stood the processional statue of Amun-Kamutef, possibly within some lightweight portable shrine. Although the socle extended almost to the side walls, there was a small opening raised 0.85 m off the ground in the north wall. Today, with very little of the socle left, this opening has been equipped with some steps to facilitate access for the visitor to the suite beyond – the famous 'Botanical Garden' (X). But no such steps could possibly have existed originally, there being simply no space to contrive them. What, then, was the purpose of this opening? It would seem that the height of the socle with the god's shrine upon it completely masked this secret entrance which led through the Botanical Garden to the most sacred hidden sanctuary of Amun (XI) where the profoundest mysteries of the cult would have taken place – only the king himself, or the high priest, could have used this carefully hidden entrance by mounting the steps on to the alabaster socle and then stepping down through the opening (Lauffray 1969: 196). It should be recalled, as we consider this carefully concealed sanctuary, that the god Amun was always termed 'the Hidden One', an indication of his divine mystery. A feature to note before leaving this room is that the floor is largely composed of great sandstone architraves of a building of Hatshepsut, which is particularly interesting when one considers that it was at this point that Karnak's original enclosure wall ran and where, presumably, the unidentified eastern building of Hatshepsut once stood, both demolished by Tuthmosis III in order to construct Akh-Menu (Carlotti 2001: 23).

The 'Botanical Garden' (X) is justly famous for its beautiful naturalistic décor showing plants, birds and animals that Tuthmosis had seen or brought back from his Syrian campaigns, but these reliefs occupy only the base of the walls of this chamber, and of the Holy of Holies into which it leads, the upper parts of the walls which would perhaps have explained some of the mysteries are largely destroyed. Within the innermost sanctuary (XI) where the decorative scheme continued, four niches were to be found in both the east and west walls, while in a great recess cut into the north (rear) wall stood a polished quartzite socle on whose surface can still be seen the grooves in which would have stood a gilded naos to hide the most sacred image of the god. An imposing offering table of red granite in the form of a *hotep*-sign still stands before the altar. It is impossible to be sure what function the eight niches in the sanctuary served, but each one seemed to be a tiny shrine in its own right, crowned with an individual lintel inscribed with the royal protocol beneath a winged disk and each closed by double doors of wood; between each niche is a scene of the king before a divinity. It has been surmised that these niches might well have contained images of the Theban Ennead, who feature quite prominently in other parts of the temple.

Recently an intriguing anomaly has come to light in this innermost sanctuary: the axis of the great naos in its alcove is slightly askew from the rest of the room (as, it was found, are also some of the foundation blocks of its eastern wall), and the suggestion has been put forward by the excavators that the naos had been preserved from some previous construction on this site, as were the foundation blocks (Lauffray 1969: 201). A tempting thought occurs: could it have been the altar, still *in situ*, from a demolished Akh-Menu of Tuthmosis I or from Hatshepsut's *Ntry-mnw* perhaps?

At the north-east corner of the 'festival' hall is a staircase leading to an upper solar sanctuary; however, this staircase is not original but one contrived by later kings. The original stairway, which was much wider and less steep (XII), can still be seen in the north wall off the corridor that runs behind the three chapels already discussed (IV), and it ascends to a great platform formed against part of the north wall of the Akh-Menu complex. Upon this platform is the high solar sanctuary (XIII). All the decoration here is of Ramesside date, the only evidence of Tuthmosis III's work is a fine alabaster offering table composed of four *hotep*-symbols, usually known as a Heliopolitan-type solar altar, exactly similar to that which still exists in the sun-temple of Neuserre of Dynasty V at Abu Gurob. Behind this altar in the east wall, an opening

Plate 6.1 Staircase within Akh-Menu leading to the solar sanctuary.

had been introduced to permit the rays of the rising sun to penetrate the chamber and probably to fall upon the altar, though this is now thought to have been part of the later reworking of this chapel. From the top of the stairway, where it attained the platform, a ramp led off to the east from the landing outside the solar sanctuary up to the terrace or roof area of the temple. Along the wall bordering this ramp ran a long inscription, the whole enclosed within an extended cartouche:

> (Tuthmosis III) has made it as a memorial for his father Amun-Re, the act of making for him a beautiful monument, a marvel such as has never yet been seen, since he loves him more than all the gods; that he may be given life, stability, power like Re for ever.

Both the stairway and the ramp were of grand proportions indicating a processional way. Certainly the statue of Amun would have been brought in procession to the solar sanctuary, or even to the terrace to greet the rising sun. On special festivals, it is possible that the sacred bark might have been carried there also, but it is not clear whether this was feasible due to its size and the difficulty in manoeuvring it.

Having completed his Akh-Menu enclosure at the eastern end of Karnak, Tuthmosis III then constructed a great sandstone girdle wall which completely encircled both the Akh-Menu and the main Amun temple on three sides. It stretched from the north wing of the Fifth Pylon right round the eastern end of the temple until it joined the south wing of the Fourth Pylon, leaving an ambulatory corridor between the two walls.

This brief description of the general layout of Akh-Menu gives some idea of the great complexity and many unusual features of this special temple: small wonder, therefore, that arguments and theories concerning its true function abound. The decision to build Akh-Menu was taken by Tuthmosis in Year 23 of his reign: as monuments of this scale were usually undertaken to commemorate some great occasion such as a coronation or sed-festival, might it be the case that this project was to mark Tuthmosis' full accession to power in Year 22 after Hatshepsut's death? One fact is quite certain: the Akh-Menu's function was totally different from that of Ipet-Sut and, as such, it had its own distinct priesthood as we learn from the great inscription Tuthmosis had carved on the southern outer wall. In it he referred to a 'temple priesthood of my father Amun-Re in Akh-Menu in conjunction with the regular temple priesthood of the House of Amun in Ipet-Sut ...' (Gardiner 1952: 16). Whereas the normal cultic rites were performed in Karnak proper, Akh-Menu was clearly something apart, where very particular rites relating to Tuthmosis III himself were enacted. Later in Karnak's history, Akh-Menu's original purpose became overlaid, and very probably became the main sanctuary of the entire temple, though there is little doubt that the Middle Kingdom temple itself still continued to function in some form.

Certainly Akh-Menu's different sections each had a vital part to play. The heart of the temple lay in the secret sanctuary where Amun – truly the Hidden One – protected by the Ennead in their niches, looked out upon his creation, the perfect living world represented by the Botanical Garden. And we have seen the strange 'double' sanctuary on the axial way where the king and Amun-Kamutef, the procreative aspect of Amun, seem to merge into one. To the south-east was the funerary area, encompassing the Sokarian rooms, and chambers dedicated to the royal cult where the divinised king, as Horus, was regenerated and reborn after having passed through the rites of Sokar: his final empowerment took place through solar rites. Tuthmosis also included his royal ancestors in many of these sacred ceremonies, and he stated clearly that Akh-Menu was 'a monument for his fathers, the kings of Upper and Lower Egypt'. The entire complex he designated as 'a temple of millions of years' – truly a memorial to perpetuate their names and his own divine cult.

All these ceremonies, while having obvious connections with coronation and sed-festival rites, go far beyond them, for this was a temple not only of the divine cult, but of the divine king, whose god-given powers were perpetuated in this amazing monument's architectural symbolism. What deeply veiled rituals were enacted within the secluded sanctuary, we cannot begin to guess, but in the course of these unknown and mysterious ceremonies, the king communed directly with Amun, receiving the god's divine power, renewal and life.

It is often assumed that a 'temple of millions of years' was a designation applied only to a king's mortuary foundation. While a mortuary foundation certainly was such a temple, the term actually denoted a monument that was dedicated to the cult of the divine king. Akh-Menu is a prime example of just such a monument, as is the magnificent temple of Seti I at Abydos: neither of these was, of course, a mortuary temple. Other instances of 'temples of millions of years' are known at Karnak, as subsequent chapters will show.

The magnificence of Akh-Menu can sometimes dim one's perception of the great amount of other building work that Tuthmosis III undertook at Karnak. He transformed much of the central area of Ipet-Sut and of the southern processional way; he dug the Sacred Lake that still exists today, and built a massive wall enclosing the entire temple precinct.

Central Karnak

Exactly when, and in what order, Tuthmosis III made his alterations and additions to central Karnak is still debated. The reworking of this area was extensive and undoubtedly carried out in stages, but a likely progression is, as suggested by Peter Dorman (Dorman 1988: 56), that the architectural changes made by Tuthmosis show two different concepts for the processional approach to the sanctuary of Amun. The first of these involved the Fourth, Fifth and Sixth Pylons, originally giving access to a series of unroofed courts, with the façade of the Middle Kingdom temple at the far end, while the building of the Sixth Pylon simply divided the courtyard of Tuthmosis I into two shallow, open courts surrounded by pillared porticoes on three sides. Much later in his reign, Tuthmosis III converted the axis of the temple into a covered corridor through the existing three pylons and two new portals, with openings on either side into small roofed courts.

This great transformation took place over many years, from the erection of the Sixth Pylon early in his sole reign right through to the reworking of the Wadjet Hall, which must have been towards the end of his life since the work there was completed by his son and successor, Amenhotep II. So, let us look at this whole central area which is still entered through the Fourth Pylon.

The Wadjet Hall, which Tuthmosis I constructed between the Fourth and Fifth Pylons, is, as we see it today, largely the transformation wrought by Tuthmosis III. His first act was to enclose each of the obelisks of Hatshepsut within a masonry coating which in appearance was akin to the two towers of a small pylon: the gateway that once existed between them, thought to have been of granite or limestone, has since disappeared. These two towers were joined to the Fifth Pylon by two walls, each pierced by a doorway: the one to the north named 'the great doorway (called) "Menkheperre-is-great-of-offerings"' and to the south 'the great doorway (called) "Menkheperre-is-pure-of-offerings"'. This formed an area which acted as a type of vestibule in which were found several offering statues of the king: these, together with the named doorways, provided a most appropriate antechamber to the next court, to the rear of which stood the suite of offering rooms, the Palace of Maat.

Tuthmosis decided to re-roof the Wadjet Hall, the wooden ceiling of which had been removed by Hatshepsut to facilitate the erection of her obelisks. In fact, he declared that he found the hall so full of water after a violent storm that it had to be baled out (*URK* IV: 839). Since he decided to roof it with stone slabs, he found it necessary to augment the number of columns in order to support this great weight: it has even been suggested that the masonry he constructed round his stepmother's obelisks was more to support the ceiling than to hide her work, particularly as the top of the obelisks, sheathed in gold, still stood above the roof, flashing and glinting in the sunshine. In any event, enclosing her obelisks in mini-pylon towers with a central gateway and then roofing the hall certainly added to the 'corridor' effect at which he was aiming (Bjorkman 1971: 75).

Whereas five cedar-wood columns, aligned north to south in the Wadjet Hall, had been erected by Tuthmosis I, his grandson increased this to fourteen sandstone columns in two rows. An inscription of Tuthmosis III in the northern half of the hall describes the transformation in that section: 'Then my Majesty made four papyrus columns, two more than were already found in the north part; there are (now) six papyrus columns in total covered in fine gold'. He dealt similarly with the southern, and larger, part of the hall, erecting another eight columns. To support the great weight of the ceiling's stone slabs, Tuthmosis lined the hall with another masonry skin and in the niches created by its supporting piers, he placed some of the many statues of Tuthmosis I which were standing in the peristyle court through the Fifth Pylon.

Standing in the Wadjet Hall today, all these additions make it look crowded and out of proportion, but it should be remembered that it was in this hall that, as a young priestly acolyte, Tuthmosis III claimed that the statue of Amun, whilst in procession, had stopped before him and signalled him as the future king. In order to accommodate a festival procession of the god with his full retinue of priests and attendant officials, one must visualise the very much more spacious hall that existed in the time of Tuthmosis I and Tuthmosis II.

In the peristyle court of Tuthmosis I beyond the Fifth Pylon, Tuthmosis III continued his alterations by erecting further masonry walls which enveloped the two central columns of the court, thus forming two chambers to the left and right of the axial way. This central aisle, due to all the additional walls and chambers, had now become, as already described, a virtual corridor leading from the entrance at the Fourth Pylon right through to the bark sanctuary. The approach to this sacred area was embellished with much beautiful relief work, often gilded (Lacau 1956: 221–50). The doorway of the antechamber to the Sixth Pylon was plated with gold, the fixing points for which can still be seen in the stone: the jambs of this doorway also highlight something of unique importance. On these west-facing door jambs, the king is shown being led by Atum (on the north jamb) and by Montu (on the south) into the presence of Amun. Normally these scenes would have been centred on the main east–west axis, but in this case they are actually both orientated to the south (Chevrier 1955: 13–14). This is unprecedented, since it appears to indicate that the king's customary 'royal ascent' towards the sanctuary had been halted at this point and diverted instead towards the south. The way leads through a court to a chamber in which an immense sandstone dais, nearly a metre in height and approached by a stairway, can still be seen today. On its surface is the outline of a shrine bordered by square pillars forming a peripteral chapel, and the whole surrounded by royal Osiride statues.

What was this enigmatic chamber towards which the gods led Tuthmosis III? It has been suggested that this was, in effect, a 'coronation seat' (Barguet 1953: 148): within this chapel Tuthmosis approached Amun to be consecrated and enthroned at his coronation; after which, having communed directly with the god and been sanctified by him, the king could now return to the original way and was in a spiritual state to enter the Holy of Holies. Doubtless this very sacred chapel would have been used subsequently at the great royal festivals, such as the sed-festival and the anniversary of the coronation, where once again Amun would confer his divine blessing personally upon the king before the latter proceeded to the sanctuary.

The name of this chapel is known to us thanks to an inscription left in the tomb of a very powerful official named Menkheperresoneb who, amongst other things, was the High Priest of Amun. In his tomb, this great man spoke of erecting 'a secluded sanctuary' at Karnak 'made of solid granite as a monolith . . . inlaid with fine gold and pillars of sandstone inlaid with gold of the best of the deserts . . . called "Menkheperre-raises-the-crowns-of-Amun"' (*URK* IV: 927–33). Further inscriptions in the tomb refer more than once to his title of 'Overseer of craftsmen in "Menkheperre-raises-the-crowns-of-Amun"', and in another instance he lists his titles thus:

> The Chancellor of Lower Egypt, overseer of the priests of the South and the North, administrator of the two thrones of the god, overseer of important offices, overseer of the double treasuries of gold and silver, superintendent of works in 'Menkheperre-raises-the-crowns-of- Amun', set over the mysteries of the Two Ladies, High Priest of Amun, Menkheperresoneb. (Davies, N. 1933a: 11, 13, pls X, XIV)

In such a catalogue of great and powerful titles, the fact that he yet again picked out this chapel for specific mention must surely indicate its exceptional importance.

Across the peristyle court of Tuthmosis I beyond the Fifth Pylon, Tuthmosis III, early in his reign, erected the Sixth Pylon: its towers were of sandstone and its gateway was of granite covered in electrum. This magnificent portal marked a very important entrance which gave access to the area immediately in front of the bark sanctuary. Tuthmosis himself wrote: 'My Majesty erected for him a great gateway of gold (named) "Amun-Senior-in-Prestige"'. It should be noted that in a temple such as Karnak, each gateway was an independent feature, not considered part of the wall in which it stood. The inscriptions on these doorways were totally separate from those on its supporting walls, and each had its own personal name, usually incorporating the name and attributes of a god in the belief that these would be manifest within that part of the temple, thus benefiting its royal builder. Hence the doorway jambs of the Sixth Pylon show Tuthmosis before Amun 'adoring the god four times' and processing towards the sanctuary preceded by a divinity; while on the walls of the pylon itself, the traditional scene of the king victorious over defeated enemies (in this case specifically at Megiddo) can be seen.

The new peristyle court which was formed by the Sixth Pylon was subdivided by Tuthmosis when he built walls which joined each end of the pylon to the Palace of Maat, thus creating a central hall and two courts – a northern and a southern – each of which contained six papyrus columns whose bases and stems were entirely covered in gold leaf. In order to achieve this, Tuthmosis had obviously by this time dismantled the Chapelle Rouge, and had also reworked and enlarged the central area within the Palace of Maat to accommodate his own new bark-shrine of red granite, altering at the same time much of the offering rooms' decoration and substituting his own cartouche, or that of his father, for Hatshepsut's. The splendid granite doorways, covered in gold, of Hatshepsut's bark-shrine were reused by Tuthmosis in his reworking of this area (Lacau

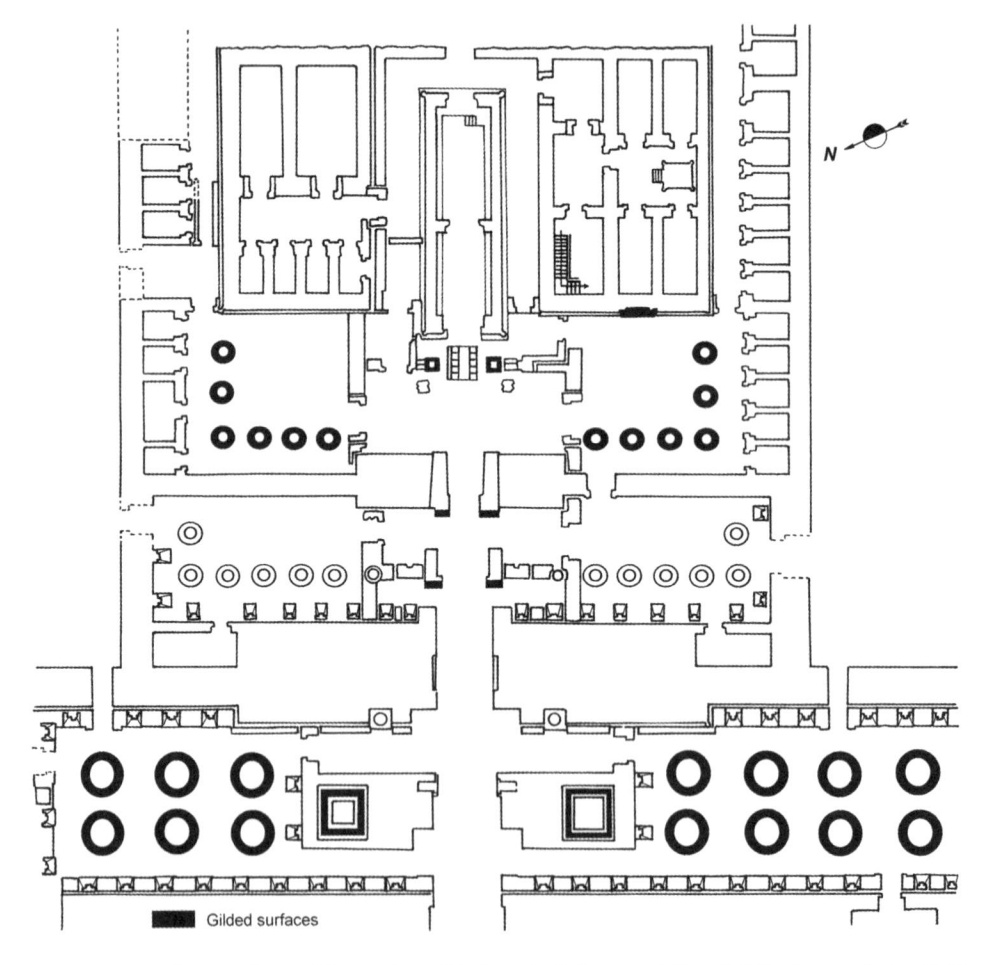

Figure 6.2 Plan showing the gold decoration of Tuthmosis III in central Karnak (after Lacau, P., in *ASAE* 53: 251).

1956: 237–40), which was a logical step since these portals were already carved in his name within the Chapelle Rouge. What had been the rear (eastern) doorway, named 'Menkheperre-is-great-in-the-power-of-Amun', was used within the Palace of Maat to communicate between its central area and its northern suite of rooms, and the Chapelle Rouge's western doorway, 'Menkheperre-is-pure-in-the-exultation-of-Amun', was now placed in the wall that gave access to the southern court. The central doorway within the Chapelle Rouge was bonded into its structure and therefore could not be reused, but Tuthmosis III took its name 'Menkheperre-is-permanently-praised-before-Amun' for the entrance door to the northern court, thus completing the use of these symbolic doorways (URK IV: 167; Nims 1969: 70, 72[vi]).

Just in advance of the bark-shrine, the king built a small girdle peristyle which protected the shrine's entrance. And it is here that the two magnificent so-called 'heraldic' pillars can still be seen today; originally they too would have been ornamented with gold. It has been suggested that these exceptional pillars had some special significance during the performance of the unification rite (*sm3-t3wy*) which was enacted during coronation and sed-festival ceremonies (Barguet 1962: 130). Between these pillars, the small peripteral area was adorned with yet more golden-covered columns. The whole effect must have been awe-inspiring indeed, and it is small wonder that Tuthmosis described it as being 'comparable to the horizon of heaven'. One cannot but recall in this regard the vision in the Christian tradition of the philosopher Emanuel Swedenborg (1688–1772): 'I have seen palaces in heaven whose magnificence was beyond description. Above they glittered as if made of pure gold and below as if made of precious stones' (Swedenborg 1909: 81[185]). It seems that the Egyptian vision, many centuries earlier, was almost identical, and one which they translated into a concrete form upon earth (Fig. 6.2).

In the midst of this rich and magnificent work of Tuthmosis III, it seems ironic that the focal point of all this splendour, the shrine of the sacred bark, should have been so totally destroyed. Only a few scattered blocks and fragments of the king's rose granite shrine remain: 'Lo, my Majesty erected for him (Amun) an august shrine (named) "The-Favourite-Place-of-Amun"....'. The name is identical to that of the Chapelle Rouge, and it is still debated whether this inscription of Tuthmosis referred to Hatshepsut's shrine, which he initially claimed as his own construction, or whether he transferred the name to the granite shrine which later replaced it.

Returning to the northern and southern courts in this area: an entrance in their north and south walls respectively gave access to the small chambers constructed initially by Amenhotep I in limestone, which had been demolished by Hatshepsut and which Tuthmosis III had replaced in sandstone. These chambers were dedicated to the memory of his ancestors, to Amenhotep I in particular, and of course to Tuthmosis himself. They were all more or less uniform in size barring one only, to the north, which was considerably larger and, according to the inscription on its walls, was an incense room (Lacau 1954: 192). One is tempted to speculate as to whether this room occupies the site of the one constructed by Hatshepsut which Tuthmosis perhaps destroyed in his reworking of the area. Depictions of incense trees from Punt, as well as piles of various incense pellets adorn the walls along with Tuthmosis' dedication:

> He made it as his monument for his father Amun, Lord of the Thrones of the Two Lands, in making for him a storeroom for incense ... in order to

prepare the precious essence so that each day shall be always in the perfume of the divine.

The southern court is distinguished by the remains of what must have been a quite spectacular feature on the outside west wall of Hatshepsut's offering chambers. This was a magnificent stela in the form of a false-door which once boasted a figure of Amun in blue (i.e. inlaid with either lapis lazuli or turquoise) while the hieroglyphs of the accompanying inscription were inlaid with gold and lapis (Barguet 1962: 127). An altar would almost undoubtedly have stood before this false-door and, in the course of the divine rites enacted there, the 'essence' of the offerings would have passed through the false-door to the chambers behind, wherein today can still be seen a relief of Amun enthroned and receiving these offerings.

On the southern outer wall of Hatshepsut's offering chambers is an inscription of Tuthmosis III known as the 'Texte de la Jeunesse', which purports to be autobiographical. Part of this great inscription shows a scene, whose content we have touched on before, of Tuthmosis seated within a pavilion: the dais upon which he is enthroned is decorated with two lions flanked by the *sm3-t3wy* symbol (the binding of the two heraldic plants of Upper and Lower Egypt) (Habachi 1985: 350ff.). In front of the pavilion runs the text of forty-nine columns: these give an account of how the young Tuthmosis was chosen to be king by Amun, how he was given his titulary by the gods themselves, and how, when he finally ascended the throne as sole king, he made many offerings and dedicated many monuments to the god in gratitude: finally, there is a

Plate 6.2 A relief of a lion flanking Tuthmosis III within a pavilion.

calendar of religious festivals. Further along the wall to the east is another and almost identical scene, but the king in question here is Senusret I, and it appears that this is a copy of an original scene, faithfully reproduced by Tuthmosis, which the king, or possibly his stepmother, had demolished. Sadly, the long inscription which had once accompanied it has been all but destroyed, leaving just the beginning of a text dated to Year 9 of Senusret which speaks of a 'sitting of the king in the Audience Hall; the courtiers and the Great Ones of the Palace were admitted in order to execute efficiently the desires of his Majesty ...' (Gabolde 1998: 40–3). And there it breaks off, having just whet our appetites for what would seem to have been a historical inscription: very probably the announcement by Senusret of his decision to build a temple for Amun-Re. Remarkably, a third version of this scene was inscribed by Tuthmosis on the southern outer wall of Akh-Menu, once again showing the king enthroned before his courtiers to whom he addresses a speech concerning the founding of Akh-Menu.

It will have been noted that Tuthmosis III showed a profound reverence for his royal ancestors: this is just one example of his efforts to conserve or reproduce important elements of his predecessors' work; the reconstructed chapels of Amenhotep I being another.

> My Majesty has made many monuments in my name ... while the name of my father abides on his own monuments, and the names of the kings of Upper and Lower Egypt abide on their monuments in the House of Amun-Re, Lord of Karnak, for ever and ever.

Just as significant is the emphasis he put on the cult of his ancestors in many parts of Karnak, and in particular in Akh-Menu: 'My Majesty has commanded the perpetuation of the names of my fathers, the refurbishing of their offerings, the fashioning of their images ... and divine offerings anew' (BAR II: para. 604).

Another very important inscription, or series of inscriptions, known as the Annals of Tuthmosis III, is found on some of the walls surrounding the bark sanctuary and other walls in the court preceding it. These tell of the king's many military campaigns and are full of fascinating historical detail: the text appears to be much more factual and less overblown and boastful than was normally the case when pharaohs gave accounts of their exploits. In fact, he stated quite plainly that 'I have not uttered exaggeration in order to boast of that which I did saying "I have done something" even though my Majesty had not done it ... I have not done anything against which contradiction might be uttered ...' (BAR II: para. 570). In many of his inscriptions, the king refers to his wish to make a durable record of the 'great deeds which he had accomplished' – in other words, in stone – as well as being written upon 'a leather roll in the temple of Amun' (*URK* IV: 662). At the start of this great collection of historical annals stands a magnificent relief of Tuthmosis dedicating a vast array of beautiful and costly artefacts to the greater glory of Amun and his temple: first and foremost amongst them two towering obelisks, probably those destined to be erected before the Seventh Pylon, followed by a breathtaking display of ornaments, offering tables, vessels, necklaces – all of exquisite design (Wreszinski 1923: pl. 33b). It is fascinating to learn from an inscription over a particular vase that it was 'of costly stone, which his Majesty made according to the design of his own heart'. The manufacture of some of these vessels is shown in the tomb of Menkheperresoneb, the High Priest of Amun, and here too it is stated that the vessels were of Tuthmosis' own design (Davies, N. 1933a: 11). Other instances are known which also tell a similar story: it seems this great warrior king was a man of many parts. A study of this wonderfully detailed relief brings home to the observer just how immense was the wealth that the New Kingdom pharaohs had at their disposal.

The Southern Approach

> Lo, my Majesty found the Southern Pylon of mud-brick, the Southern Gateway ... stone in the lesser constructions, the double door-leaves of cedar, the columns of wood. Then my Majesty made it of ... its gateway of granite, its great door-leaf of copper, the name of which was made 'Amun, Great-of-Diadems'... (Nims 1969: 70[viii])

Thus wrote Tuthmosis III concerning the Seventh Pylon which he claims to have erected to replace the ruinous gateway on the southern approach. There can be little doubt that the 'Southern Gateway' to which he referred was that of Amenhotep I, built of limestone and set in the early mud-brick enclosure wall, although current work has shown that gateway to have been situated somewhat further to the south.

Built of sandstone with a rose granite gateway, the Seventh Pylon was decorated on its south face with traditional scenes of the king massacring his enemies, and was adorned with four great flagstaffs of cedar, each tipped with gold. Finally, two colossi of Tuthmosis III and two granite obelisks stood at this imposing entrance: today it leads into the so-called Court of the Cachette, but originally access to this whole area must have been through the Southern Gateway of Amenhotep I.

The east wings of the Seventh and Eighth Pylons are connected to each other by a wall which is pierced by two doorways, one of which is an entrance of particular interest (Barguet 1962: 266 and n. 1; Pillet 1939: 247ff.). This is presented in relief as a pylon in miniature: small pylon towers with classic torus-moulding flank the doorway which was fronted by two flagstaffs and two royal statues of Senusret I. In fact, what is here represented is a scaled-down replica of one of the monumental entrances of Karnak: the Seventh Pylon itself has been suggested, although not every detail is correct since the two obelisks which stand before the Seventh Pylon are not shown. The embellishment of the temple's monumental gateways with gold, electrum and precious stones like lapis lazuli and turquoise is well attested: can such adornment be visualised for this replica in miniature? If the importance of the shrine was as great as it would seem, then such décor is certainly possible. To add to the somewhat unusual feature of a miniature replica pylon is the curious fact that this entrance to Tuthmosis' shrine appears to be reproduced elsewhere in a relief (or perhaps this relief also represents the Seventh Pylon) – in chambers of Tuthmosis III to the north-west of the court which enclosed the central bark sanctuary to be exact, thought to be his so-called 'House of Gold' (see below, p. 90).

As to the monument itself, the gateway gives access to the alabaster bark-shrine 'Menkheperre-is-enduring-of-monuments'; 'Enduring-of-monuments' was also the name of the alabaster shrine of Amenhotep I, which that of Tuthmosis probably replaced on this site. Tuthmosis' shrine was constructed in two stages: initially the central kiosk was surrounded by a peristyle of square pillars dating to the king's first sed-festival in Year 30. A second, and larger, ambulatory of pillars joined by intercolumnar walls formed a court round the monument, and bears the date of Tuthmosis' second jubilee, Year 33. In the thickness of the entrance gateway there is the first of five shallow steps of rose granite which ascended to a platform upon which the kiosk stood; two monolithic walls of alabaster are still *in situ*, and these once supported a ceiling of the same material. The remains of a socle upon which the bark would have rested can still be seen in the centre of the shrine; while at the rear of the shrine five other steps lead down to the eastern doorway. The axis of this bark-shrine was aligned with that of the Sacred Lake, also constructed by Tuthmosis III, and the eastern doorway of the shrine led out on to a tribune overlooking the Lake. On account of this, it is tempting to speculate whether the shrine might have been built especially for certain water-borne religious rites and festivals held upon the Lake. Certainly there was a ritual known as 'Rowing the Deity on the Lake' which would have entailed carrying the god's image itself down to the bank and placing it on a boat upon the water. A point to note is that the western entrance to the bark-shrine had a width of 2.20 m, while the opening to the rear measured only 1.66 m, thus making it impossible for the bark itself and its cortège to pass through to the east. But, of course, one could readily visualise the god's statue being lifted from its bark and carried out on to the tribune to oversee water-borne rites from there. In fact, an inscription of Tuthmosis upon the rear wall of Karnak stated that 'my Majesty commanded to have made a statue fashioned as a living likeness, conforming to the beauty of my Majesty for rowing in procession . . . the statue for the water procession on the lake . . .' (*URK* IV: 1257). It can well be imagined that the god would have been carried out to impart his divine blessing upon the proceedings.

As we have seen, the bark itself, of precious wood and gold, was developed for the solemn transfer of the image of Amun within a closed and veiled chapel upon its deck: and the shrine holding it was very simple, open at both ends upon its axis, its west door being wide enough to accommodate the priests who carried the sacred bark on their shoulders. The eastern door at the rear needed only to allow access for the portable statue to be carried in and out, usually from the temple sanctuary – but in this particular case, on to the tribune or down to the Sacred Lake. Maps of Karnak from the early twentieth century showed a stairway descending to the very edge of the Lake, though there is no sign at all of this feature today, if, indeed, it ever existed (Barguet 1962: 267 n. 2). It is not possible to know what rites took place to which this shrine was central, but, in any event, the rich materials employed in its construction and the grandeur of its entrance indicate that this was a very special monument.

A Sacred Lake was, of course, an essential element in temple life and ritual: it had many functions. Tuthmosis III states on Karnak's walls that it was he who dug the 'Southern Lake', the one with which the alabaster bark-shrine had an obvious connection. Quite what the Lake looked like in his day can only be conjectured, because the Nubian pharaoh Taharqa (Dynasty XXV) undertook some extensive reconstruction, giving it the form that still exists today.

But in addition to the Southern Lake, there are several references from different periods of Karnak's history, including the reign of Tuthmosis III, to a 'Northern Lake' (Nims 1955: 117). We know of various officials who held posts connected with this Northern Lake: for example, 'overseer of the artisans of the Northern Lake of Amun' and 'guardian of the Northern Lake of Amun' (Hall 1925: pl. 19). But where was this lake to be found? No archaeological evidence for its existence has yet come to light. Was it a natural pool or an artificial basin? It has even been suggested that the pool might have been 'seasonal'; in other words, that it came and went with the changes in the water-table occasioned by the annual inundation.

Obelisks

It is known that Tuthmosis erected at least three pairs of obelisks at Karnak, as well as planning the 'unique', or single, obelisk which now stands in the Piazza San Giovanni in Laterano, Rome. It seems remarkable that not one of them survives in its original location, and, despite the many references made to them by the king himself and by his nobles, it is not at all certain just where many of these great shafts of stone originally stood.

The general consensus is that Tuthmosis celebrated five sed-festivals and on each occasion obelisks were set up to commemorate the event: the first three pairs were erected at Karnak *circa* Years 30, 33 and 36; the fourth pair was at Heliopolis (it is one of these that now stands on the Thames Embankment in London); and for his fifth sed-festival, the king commissioned the single 'Lateran' obelisk, but it would appear that he died while it was still being decorated, and it was left to Tuthmosis IV to erect it at the spot intended for it by his grandfather.

A magnificent dedicatory scene inscribed in the Corridor of Annals within the Palace of Maat depicts Tuthmosis III dedicating, amongst other offerings, two gold-topped obelisks to Amun (Wreszinski 1923: pl.33b); another pair is shown in the tomb of Puyemre, a great official of the king (Davies, N. 1922: pl. 37). Two other powerful men also claimed involvement in the erection of obelisks: Yamu-nedjeh, Controller of Works and Royal Architect, and Menkheperreseneb, the High Priest of Amun; however, there is a total lack of details as to which obelisks these might be or to their location (Habachi 1984: 72–3).

A pair of obelisks certainly stood before the south face of the Seventh Pylon, and it is one of these which was transported to Istanbul in the fourth century AD. It is made of red granite and stands today to a height of nearly 20 m; however, part of the lower half is missing, so its true height is unknown but was probably in the region of 30 m or more. The opening of the text on one side of this Istanbul obelisk corresponds exactly with that on one of the obelisks (the right-hand one) featured in the offering scene in the Corridor of Annals, leading to the conclusion that this scene showed the obelisks that were erected before the Seventh Pylon. But an interesting point to note here is that the different numbers written in the inscriptions upon each obelisk in this offering scene are thought to indicate that they were actually two different pairs (Habachi 1984: 72): so that only one of them represents the pair erected before the Seventh Pylon, while the other (the left-hand one) must represent one of Tuthmosis' other pairs, probably the pair which had stood before the Fourth Pylon because the dedication makes reference to the 'double door' of the temple, i.e. the main entrance. Equally, the direction of the hieroglyphs in the inscriptions shown on the two obelisks in the scene both face the same way: if they had been a matching pair, the inscriptions would have been centred to face each other in the traditional way.

Tuthmosis III also erected obelisks at the temple's main entrance – the Fourth Pylon at that time – and their bases can still be seen partially embedded in the Third Pylon (erected later by Amenhotep III), and fragments of their broken shafts lie on the ground. It would appear, therefore, that the king erected this pair within the festival court of his father, Tuthmosis II, sandwiched between the obelisks of Tuthmosis I and Tuthmosis II, a remarkable feat when one considers the tight spaces involved. His obelisks were, in fact, a mere 2.1 m from those of Tuthmosis I and 2.4 m from those of Tuthmosis II (Gabolde 1987: 152 n. 23); but then Tuthmosis III often displayed great ingenuity in his skilful placing of monuments between those of earlier monarchs without having to demolish them. In fact, the king actually mentioned the care that he took 'not to damage' the constructions of his ancestors, and that he 'did not touch one stone in order to remove it' – statements which seem mostly to be true.

Where the great king's third pair of obelisks was sited is not known and no trace has ever been found of them, but more of this later.

We are better informed, however, concerning the Lateran obelisk, the tallest known example of all obelisks. When Tuthmosis III commissioned this great shaft, it was, apparently, a completely novel idea: the king himself wrote that it was 'the very first time of erecting a single obelisk in Thebes'. His dedicatory inscription stated that it was intended to stand 'in the upper court of the temple in the neighbourhood of Ipet-Sut', which describes exactly where it was eventually placed by the king's grandson, the future Tuthmosis IV. Sometime before Tuthmosis III's death in Year 53, the cut granite obelisk, measuring more than 33 m in height, was delivered to a stonemason's yard to the south of Karnak to be decorated and inscribed, where it remained until it was found and erected by Tuthmosis IV in memory of his illustrious grandfather (Nims 1971: 109). Today its sandstone socle with torus-moulding still stands within a later temple of Ramesses II, but originally there had been a simple colonnaded approach.

Why a single obelisk? Was this another special project of Tuthmosis III, who, as we have already seen, was a great innovator and even used his own designs? Or was it a religious concept where the god became personified by the obelisk? Certainly this accords with the motif, particularly employed on some scarabs, where a king is depicted adoring a single obelisk. In this respect, is it a coincidence that Tuthmosis III instituted a cult for his obelisks? In his list of feasts and offerings, Tuthmosis instructed that there should be 'divine offerings for the four obelisks' (BAR II: para. 563). If they did indeed personify the god, such an act would be a logical one.

This covers the current state of knowledge on Tuthmosis III's stone obelisks, but the story does not end there. Mention has already been made of the noble, Puyemre, whose titles included Chancellor of Lower Egypt, God's Father, Superintendent of Upper Egypt, Overseer of the temple of Amun at Karnak. Within his tomb is a scene of the great man receiving the overseers of work who are presenting a fabulous array of rich artefacts for the temple treasury headed, first and foremost, by two obelisks coloured gold and between which are inscribed the words 'two great obelisks of gold (or (?) electrum)'; furthermore, somewhat unusually, the directors and overseers of work standing before Puyemre acknowledge to him the difficulty they had experienced in manufacturing these particular obelisks (Davies, N. 1922: pl. 37). It has been suggested that the two obelisks in question are those which were cast from solid electrum and the inscriptions of which were inlaid with lapis lazuli; these had apparently stood in advance of the peripteral entry to the bark sanctuary. The inscription accompanying the presentation of these obelisks states: 'See the great and perfect monuments which the king Menkheperre has made for his father Amun at Karnak, of silver and gold (electrum) and of every kind of splendid and costly stone (lapis)' (Desroches-Noblecourt 1951: 48).

The existence of these amazing artefacts is known from an Assyrian text of Assurbanipal who, when he sacked Thebes in 656 BC, stated that: 'I removed from their place and carried away to the land of Assyria, the two great obelisks made of pure electrum of which the weight is of 2,500 talents and which stood at the door of the temple (i.e. sanctuary)' (Desroches-Noblecourt 1951: 58). The bark sanctuary is known to have been the place where they stood from the time of Tuthmosis III because they were almost always shown in front of that shrine in the various scenes depicting the departure of the sacred bark on procession. Made under the supervision of Puyemre, these obelisks have been calculated to have stood to a height of around 7 m each and to weigh in total about 80 tonnes (Desroches-Noblecourt 1951: 60). It is small wonder that the directors of work made reference to the difficulties they had encountered in the manufacture of these first-known examples cast from solid metal – the technology must have been very new. And certainly it would have been surprising if Assurbanipal had undertaken the extremely arduous and technically difficult task of carrying off two full-sized obelisks of stone and transporting them all the way back to Assyria; but what a different matter if they had been of solid gold or electrum – all 80 tonnes of it. The spoils of war indeed!

As already noted, since the obelisks shown in the offering scene in the Corridor of Annals are thought to represent two different pairs, could these famous obelisks depicted in Puyemre's tomb be the third pair – not of stone, but of electrum – of which no trace has ever been found? And there is another small clue to add weight to this theory. It has already been mentioned that Tuthmosis III instructed that offerings be made to his obelisks – but always he referred to his 'four great obelisks', never to six. The electrum obelisks were surely something quite apart.

In this context, it is interesting to note that in Puyemre's tomb are also shown two obelisks fashioned from incense or aromatic gum (Davies, N. 1922: pl. 32). While small obelisk-shaped 'cakes' of incense are well known, these particular examples must have been quite impressive, for it has been estimated that they stood at something over 2 m in height and were painted to resemble red granite. Were these destined perhaps as cult offerings to the solid electrum obelisks?

'White loaves' or 'cakes' for cult offerings were a common commodity and came in many shapes and sizes, but were most usually a conical shape (Davies, N. 1922: 85 n. 5). However, these 'white loaves' were on occasion formed of other substances than the habitual ones of bread, cake or incense. Amazingly, there are instances of conical 'loaves' of lapis, malachite, and even gold and silver dust for cult offerings. Such dazzling displays of wealth stagger the imagination, but the vast quantities of booty that Tuthmosis III, in particular, must have brought back to Egypt from his campaigns made the unbelievably lavish and sumptuous aggrandisement of Amun's temple a reality. The profusion of gold and precious stones used in its adornment perhaps explains the vivid description used by Puyemre: 'The temple is in festival, it is adored by all ... its terrace is aglow, its columns illuminated, its blue is brighter than ... (?) sacred pool'.

Other buildings

Against the eastern end of Karnak, Tuthmosis III erected an open chapel which, despite being on the main east–west axis of the temple, did not communicate with it at all, being separated from it by the enclosure wall of Akh-Menu and Ipet-Sut. This chapel, built on the occasion of his first sed-festival in Year 30, contained a large naos which incorporated a statue of Tuthmosis and Amun seated side-by-side, the entire naos and statue being carved from a single huge block of alabaster. The statue is very damaged and there is some disagreement as to the identity of the figure beside the king: a female goddess, rather than Amun, has been suggested. The king must have built this chapel at the same time as his great sandstone temple enclosure wall since its blocks are keyed into the wall, and also because, for the entire width of the chapel, the enclosure wall becomes vertical and not battered as it is everywhere else (Nims 1971: 109–10). The whole area of the chapel is fronted by a peripteral court that has a façade of six Osiride columns with intercolumnar walls and three rooms flanking the great naos. Later, under Nectanebo I, two further flanking chapels were added. Finally, Tuthmosis erected a small colonnade leading to the temple entrance or even, it is speculated, to the intended site of the single obelisk which he had commissioned, but whose erection he did not live to see.

Tuthmosis declared of this monument: 'My Majesty erected for him (Amun) a proper place of hearing ... and I erected the shrine therein from a single block of stone'. This 'temple of the Hearing Ear' was undoubtedly a place to which the ordinary people of Thebes had access in order to present their prayers, pleas and oracle-questions to the god and, as such, was a very special shrine which continued to develop in size and importance over the centuries, being greatly enhanced by Ramesses II and subsequent kings.

Blocks from yet another alabaster shrine of Tuthmosis were found in the fill of the Third Pylon. It appears to have been a way-station for the sacred bark, which had actually been built through the thickness of one of the walls of the festival court of his father, Tuthmosis II, thus giving, presumably, direct access to the court. As there is no defacement of Amun's name, it seems that it had been dismantled before the Amarna period, either by Tuthmosis IV when he reworked the festival court or, more likely perhaps, by Amenhotep III when he cleared the area to construct the Third Pylon. This beautiful little shrine, measuring around 3.75 m wide and 6.5 m long with double doors at either end, had a ceiling decorated with stars and a central band of text giving the king's name and claiming that this building was 'in pure alabaster of Hatnub, in a single stone on each side' – an accurate description.

In the midst of all these great building works, Tuthmosis III did not forget to add to the many gardens whose beauty scented and enhanced Karnak's splendour:

> My Majesty made for him (Amun) a garden for the first time, planted with every pleasant tree, in order to offer vegetables therefrom for divine offerings every day, which my Majesty founded anew as an increase of that which was formerly ... with beautiful maidens of the whole land. (BAR II: para. 567)

This picturesque reference to 'beautiful maidens' leaves one wondering what their function might have been. Did they perhaps belong to Amun's 'harem' (or, indeed, the king's), or were they an order of priestesses who tended the temple gardens? Possibly they were merely members of the temple personnel (of which there must have been large numbers), but clearly decorative members.

Another building of Tuthmosis III to which references have been known for some while was a 'House of Gold'. This title conjures up rich images, but it was not, as one might have thought, some type of treasury but, in fact, a place where newly created

THE NEW KINGDOM

artefacts were 'given life' and animated through special rites. Each of the Karnak temples (Amun, Mut, Khonsu) was reputed to have had one, but their whereabouts remain unknown. However, a recent study made upon a suite of rooms situated on the north side of the temple between the enclosure walls of Tuthmosis I and Tuthmosis III offers a possible solution to the siting of the House of Gold of Amun (Traunecker 1989: 89–111). This suite of rooms comprises a number of interesting features, including several richly decorated magazines built on two levels which open upon an inner corridor. To the west of these magazines lie two chambers, one of especial interest – in fact, an interpretation of its reliefs has led to the suggestion that in this suite of rooms we have the House of Gold constructed by Tuthmosis III (Fig. 6.3).

It is known that the function of a House of Gold was to endow statues with divine life

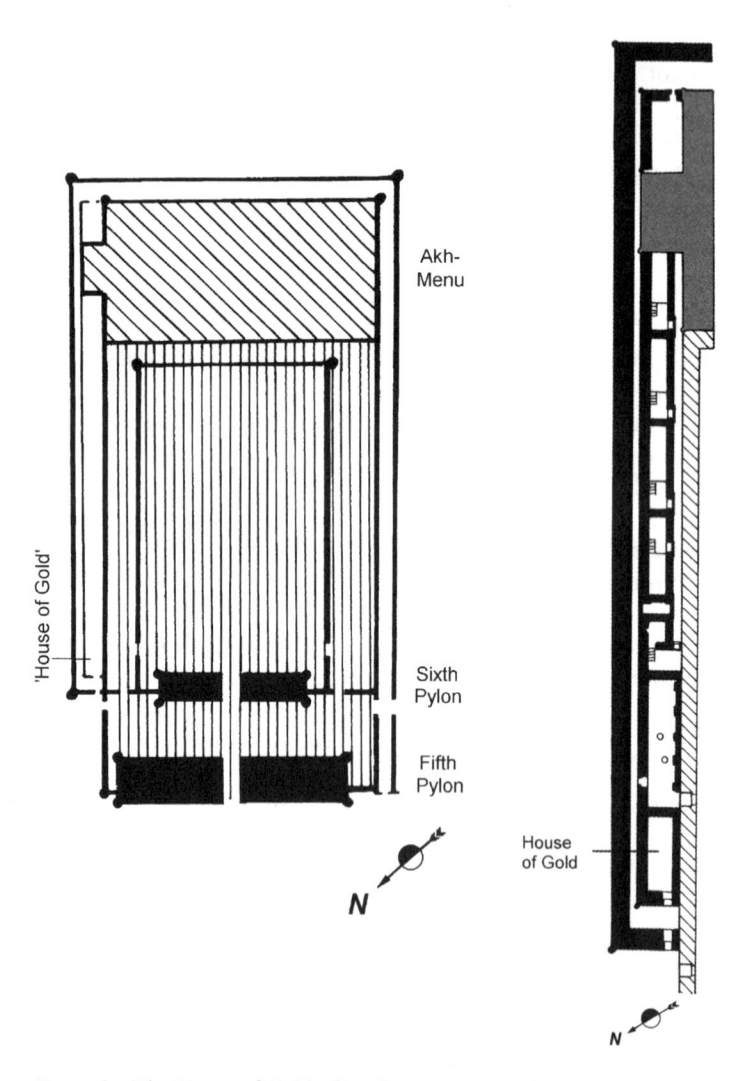

Figure 6.3 The House of Gold of Tuthmosis III. (a) Sketch plan showing its position. (b) Plan of the magazines (after Traunecker, C., in *CRIPEL* 11, 90–1, figs. 1 and 2).

through the performance of various ceremonies including, in particular, the Opening of the Mouth: the depiction of just such a rite is to be seen within this chamber. It is true that the reliefs are much damaged, but it can be seen that the east (or back) wall has scenes of Tuthmosis dedicating huge piles of offerings to Amun, representing the booty from the king's military campaigns. The south wall is occupied by a scene of navigation, comprising three tableaux each showing the sacred river-bark; the north wall has reliefs of the king erecting flagstaffs before a pylon which is fronted by obelisks and royal statues. Many of these scenes are rare indeed. While the offering scene on the east wall appears fairly standard, the words spoken by Amun are not – for he thanks the king specifically for the artefacts which have been manufactured from precious wood (cedar-of-Lebanon) and for those made from the finest gold of foreign lands. These artefacts are then shown on the south wall to be a new river-bark (Userhet) with all its rich accoutrements, certainly the most prestigious of all artefacts that the king could consecrate to the god for his personal use. Very tellingly in this scene, Tuthmosis is shown performing the rite of the Opening of the Mouth upon the ram's head on the ship's prow, with the assistance of the god Ptah – the Memphite creator god who 'created and fashioned the gods with his own hands' – and who traditionally presided over ceremonies in the House of Gold. It is worth remembering, too, that a depiction of the Opening of the Mouth rite was extremely rare on temple walls, being normally confined to funerary contexts.

Finally, the north wall contains a scene, unique of its type, depicting the king, attended by his two viziers and other court officials, erecting two great flagstaffs in front of a pylon (Traunecker 1989: 99–100, fig. 6). It has already been stated that this was thought to have represented either the Seventh Pylon or, more questionably, the miniature pylon before Tuthmosis III's alabaster bark-shrine which opened off the court between the Seventh and Eighth Pylons. In either case, it was difficult to understand why such a relief was to be found in this particular location. However, it takes on a special significance if the chamber with its attendant magazines was indeed the House of Gold where, not only new statues and artefacts, but indeed all temple regalia (such as, in this instance, flagstaffs), was to be imbued with life and power after having been manufactured in the temple workshops elsewhere. These workshops were likely to have been situated adjacent to the so-called Treasury (*pr-ḥd*) of Tuthmosis I, which was near the western entrance to this suite of rooms; here, coincidentally, an offering scene to Amenhotep I and Ahmes-Nefertari was to be found in the entrance passage (Loeben 1987b: 240). The siting of this relief has long been a puzzle, but it should be recalled that these two deified royal ancestors had been adopted by Theban artisans as their 'patron saints', and one can readily visualise the workmen carrying their new handicraft through the western entrance into the House of Gold, perhaps pausing to do homage by this most appropriate scene. It is difficult to see any other reason for such a relief to be found so unexpectedly in this area.

Other less substantial buildings of Tuthmosis III must undoubtedly have existed, though very often there only remains textual evidence for them. One such reference speaks of an enclosure for the sacred geese of Amun, but we are ignorant of its siting. A fowl-yard somewhere around the area of the Sacred Lake is known from as early a reign as that of Senusret I, and the remains of one from Dynasty XXIX can still be seen in that area. 'My Majesty created flocks of geese for him (Amun) in order to fill the fowl-yard ...' wrote Tuthmosis in his Annals. Was this yard also situated on the south bank of the Sacred Lake? A stela of Seti II of Dynasty XIX was excavated in that region, in which he claimed to have built the yard anew. Was the yard he rebuilt that of Tuthmosis III? It is quite possible.

From the time of Tuthmosis' death in Year 54 until the end of ancient Egyptian civilisation, Karnak changed comparatively little: it certainly expanded, but the basic layout had reached its ultimate form. Although the king's grandfather, Tuthmosis I, had formalised state temple design, it was under Tuthmosis III that it reached its apogee. Upon entering through the great pylon gateway, there lay in succession an entrance court, a hypostyle hall, a hall of offerings (containing the bark-shrine), an intermediate court and the sanctuary: a form that was not to alter. In relation to Karnak as it appears today, the cult temple, Ipet-Sut itself, stretched from the Fourth Pylon to the main sanctuary in the Middle Kingdom court. All the courts, pylons and columned halls that developed in front of Ipet-Sut only served to separate yet further the sacred from the profane.

Tuthmosis III had been a mighty king and warrior, and also a prolific and innovative builder who, in addition to what was new, had altered, adapted and enhanced to his own design what was already there, whilst demolishing very little. It is true to say that while Karnak undeniably grew bigger, it certainly never exceeded the perfect form and standard of exquisite decoration that it achieved under Tuthmosis, due not only to the unparalleled wealth lavished upon it, but more particularly to the inspiration of a vastly talented man.

7

AMENHOTEP II AND TUTHMOSIS IV

Amenhotep II

For the last two years of his reign, Tuthmosis III associated his son, Amenhotep II, on the throne with him. Amenhotep was the son of Tuthmosis' Great Royal Wife, Meryetre Hatshepsut, and the young man had early acquired a reputation as an athlete of great physical strength. His skill as an archer was clearly remarkable and he himself was obviously proud of his prowess with a bow, for many representations of him in this pursuit are known; the most famous being, perhaps, a scene on a block from Karnak where Amenhotep is shown in a speeding chariot shooting arrows through a great copper target. The remains of some of his longbows were found in his tomb, an indication of the pleasure he obtained from this sport which he obviously wished to continue in the next world. Archery was not his only pastime: he was renowned as an oarsman of prodigious strength and he was also a skilled horseman.

In the tomb of a military officer named Amenemhab, who had accompanied Tuthmosis III on his Asiatic campaigns, the death of the great king and the accession of Amenhotep II to sole rule was recorded thus:

> Lo, the king completed his lifetime of many years, splendid in valour, in might and in triumph, from Year 1 to Year 54, third month of the second season, the last day of the month under the Majesty of King Menkheperre, justified. He mounted to heaven, he joined the sun, the divine limbs mingling with him who begat him ... When the morning brightened, the sun arose and the heavens shone, King Aakheperure, Son of Re, Amenhotep, given life, was established upon the throne of his father; he assumed the royal titulary ...
> (BAR II: para. 808)

I think it would be fair to say, in modern parlance, that Tuthmosis III must have been a hard act to follow, and it would seem that this was the view amongst Egypt's subjugated territories for, upon the death of Tuthmosis, some of the Asiatic city-states rebelled and Amenhotep had to undertake several military campaigns to deal with the problem, which ended in Year 10 with the signing of a treaty with the Mitanni and the Hittites who, according to Amenhotep, sued for peace.

Not only was Amenhotep a strong man physically, but he appears to have been a somewhat cruel and ruthless one: textual evidence speaks of how he personally killed seven Asiatic princes and had them 'placed head downwards at the prow of his Majesty's ship'. Six of these unfortunates were then hung from the walls of Thebes and the seventh likewise at Napata. On another occasion, we hear how 'all the adult males of Retjenu, their children and their wives . . . were made into living prisoners. Two ditches were made around all of them and it was filled with fire'. At Karnak he listed the rebels which 'my Majesty slew . . . who are prostrate in their blood'. Not surprisingly, it seemed that such tactics quickly instilled fear into any potential rebels, for the rest of Amenhotep II's reign was peaceful.

Despite the peace and prosperity that Egypt enjoyed, Amenhotep was, on the whole, content not to undertake massive new building projects at Karnak, but merely to embellish what was already there and to complete his father's unfinished work. There were, nonetheless, several significant works of his, although the majority of these were dismantled by later kings. However, some of the re-employed blocks are today being studied, and evidence is amassing to show that Amenhotep probably undertook more building work at Karnak then he is credited with. Perhaps he was justified in his oft-repeated claim to be 'one abundant of monuments'.

The largest of the known monuments is sited on the eastern side of the court between the Ninth and Tenth Pylons. This sandstone building, which measures around 37 m in width and 20 m in depth, was constructed for the king's sed-festival, and has variously been described as a festival temple, shrine, kiosk or edifice, but Amenhotep himself named it 'the temple of Aakheperure (called) "'Amun-rejoices-when-he-comes-to-behold-the-beauty-of-Thebes"'. Today, the entire building stands on an elevated base and is approached by a gentle ramp leading up to a colonnade which is fronted by a portico of fourteen square pillars; from there, a red granite doorway gives access to a large pillared hall occupying the full depth of the monument, which is flanked to north and south by other rooms and chapels. Until very recently, archaeologists believed that Seti I of Dynasty XIX, having found this jubilee monument of his ancestor in decay and much damaged by Amarna zealots, had rebuilt it as a bark repository, using much of the original material. It seemed that, originally, Amenhotep's building had opened to the east as well as the west; however, the eastern entrance had been closed by Seti by the placing of a large false-door stela in the eastern wall before he dedicated the rebuilt monument to Amun as a bark-shrine (Fig. 7.1).

A strange feature of this monument, and completely atypical of ancient Egyptian architecture, is that none of its angles is at ninety degrees, and that the ground plan actually describes a parallelogram (Lauffray 1979: 143–4). Was it truly built like this by Amenhotep, or was it a deliberate reconstruction in this form by its renovator? Recent research has led to the conclusion that, no matter who was the instigator of this anomaly, it was no accident, but seemed to have been an attempt to orientate the building to various arrangements of sacred emplacements and processional routes; but more of this later.

After long research into this building and the whole general area, it has been discovered that the monument was originally quite different in both form and function, and that it was sited in a different location altogether. New evidence places Amenhotep's edifice in front of the Eighth Pylon in the form of a festival court (perhaps similar in layout to that of Tuthmosis II in front of the Fourth Pylon) (van Siclen 1990: 78). Since the last king of Dynasty XVIII, Horemheb, was the constructor of the Ninth and Tenth Pylons along the southern processional way, and since Amenhotep's reconstructed edifice abuts a wall of Horemheb which connects the eastern wings of the two pylons, it is apparent that Horemheb felt the need to remove and rebuild

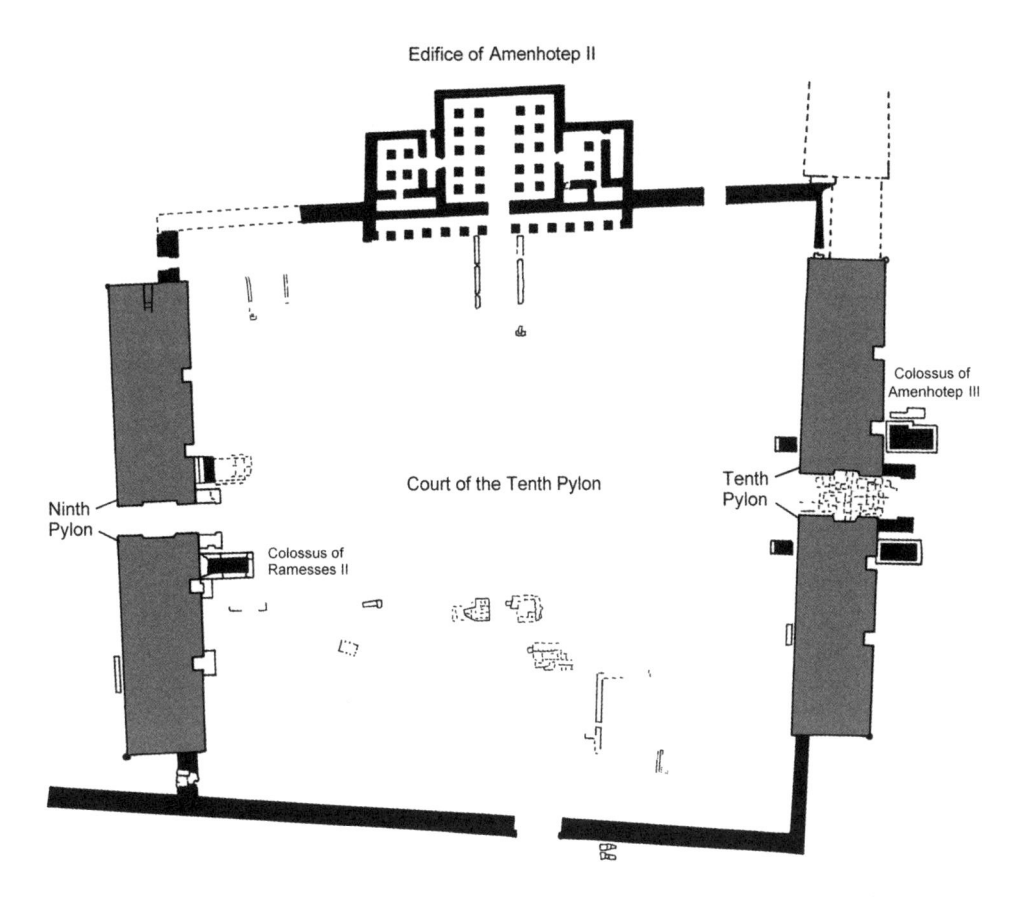

Figure 7.1 Plan of the position of the Edifice of Amenhotep II (after Lauffray, J., *Karnak d'Égypte*: 138).

the monument (which in its original position would have impeded his vision of a new extension of the southern approach), placing it in a new form where we see it today; later, Seti I completed and decorated it. The walls of Amenhotep's reconstructed monument are orientated to the Ninth and Tenth Pylons, but these pylons themselves are not aligned on one another. In this orientation, then, lies the probable cause of the strange angles that can be observed in Amenhotep's edifice as it now stands. The building must have stood in its original form and location until after the Amarna period, not only because of the defacement and subsequent restoration of all the figures of Amun, but also because of the *talatat*-blocks from Amarna-period monuments that have come to light in the foundations of its later reconstruction. Further evidence for the original placing and function of Amenhotep's edifice can be seen in the discovery of features from many interior and exterior doorways, the tops of small pylon blocks and the remains of flagpole embrasures (van Siclen 1990: 83), as well as elements pertaining to the king's mother, Queen Meryetre Hatshepsut (where a parallel can be seen in the festival court of his son, Tuthmosis IV, who also honoured *his* mother in this way). The siting of an entrance gateway to Amenhotep's monument in its original placement has recently been located in the court between the Eighth and Ninth Pylons.

Plate 7.1 The reconstructed Edifice of Amenhotep II.

The existence of another, smaller, monument of Amenhotep came to light when a huge 86-tonne block of alabaster was found in the fill of the Third Pylon, which proved to be part of the roof of a shrine. Subsequently, another block of 60 tonnes and several smaller blocks were recovered. Somewhat later, the two side walls of the shrine were also found; they were each of solid alabaster measuring 1 m thick, and had been recarved and reused by Ramesses II as stelae which he had placed before the pylon of a small temple within the Mut precinct. This alabaster construction was not a bark-shrine, but was more like an enormous naos in design with a portico surrounding it on three sides. Nor was it a free-standing structure, for it was originally set through one wall with the rear of the shrine abutting another wall. Exactly where such a structure could have stood is uncertain, but it had to be where two walls stood parallel in close proximity. Because of this feature, it has been suggested that the two walls in question were the south wall of Tuthmosis II's festival court and the north wall of the court of the Seventh Pylon (now called the Court of the Cachette) (van Siclen 1986: 38), although into which of these two courts the shrine was orientated is not clear; the probability lies with the court of the Seventh Pylon. The shrine's function is also unclear and there are not many clues to give any firm indication. Sed-festival references on the monument are few and fairly stereotyped, and two scenes on the façade labelled 'the appearance of the king' can have a variety of meanings: the accession, the coronation, or merely the monarch's participation in certain rites. It is possible that the shrine should be viewed as a 'Station of the King' where he would have stood to oversee festivals and processions. The uncertainty of its function is well encapsulated in the words of C. van

Siclen (who published the monument): 'It is quite possible that the true nature of the building would not have been evident to any but the gods' (van Siclen 1986: 12).

As to Amenhotep's other work at Karnak, the most notable was the completion of his father's work in the Wadjet Hall. It has not been ascertained whether it was Tuthmosis III who replaced the columns in the southern part of the hall, which Amenhotep II then inscribed in his own name and embellished with gold, or whether it was Amenhotep who was responsible for the entire job: probably the former. Amenhotep claimed that 'he made it as his monument for his father Amun-Re, making for him august papyriform columns for the southern Wadjet Hall wrought with gold in large quantity as a work of eternity', but he gives very little detail about these columns or their condition, unlike his father who gave a full description of the poor state of the wooden columns of Tuthmosis I, which he then replaced with sandstone ones. Since the reworking of the Wadjet Hall was one of the last projects undertaken by Tuthmosis III, it is quite likely that he never completed its decoration, and that in all probability the southern columns, while erected by Tuthmosis, were decorated by his son who claimed it all as his own work; it was certainly Amenhotep who inscribed the mini-pylons which his father had erected around Hatshepsut's obelisks within the hall.

The texts which Amenhotep had inscribed on the columns in the southern Wadjet Hall also give information on other work he had undertaken: 'I made for him a shrine of gold, its floor being of silver ... it is more beautiful than the multitude of stars ...'; 'I presented to him two bases of gold for shrines ... with statues and sphinxes of my Majesty in the two chapels to each side ...'. Neither of these seems to refer to a sandstone chapel, which the king erected in the southern part of the Wadjet Hall to commemorate his victories over the Asiatics. Some of its blocks survive showing the king leading serried ranks of prisoners before Amun, and listing the conquered lands.

Amenhotep also figures prominently on the Eighth Pylon where, in traditional pose, he is shown massacring prisoners before the god. This scene replaced an earlier one, and the texts that had accompanied it had certainly been of Hatshepsut: these had later been suppressed by Tuthmosis III. Surprisingly, Tuthmosis did not inscribe anything in their place – perhaps because he decided to erect a new pylon (the Seventh) instead – and it was left to Amenhotep to redecorate the pylon and provide it with flagstaffs.

One of the inscriptions Amenhotep placed on a Wadjet Hall column contains the phrase: 'I made for him a garden anew'. In the tomb of Sennefer, an important noble who lived during Amenhotep's reign and who included amongst his many titles 'the Overseer of the Gardens of Amun', is a representation of such a garden with its groves of trees, vine trellises, lotus pools, plants and flowers – access to which is shown to be through an imposing stone gateway. Whether this is the actual garden to which the king's inscription referred cannot be ascertained, but the jambs of a red granite gateway have been unearthed to the south of the Second Pylon entrance (van Siclen 1982: 15) – just the area where, in Dynasty XVIII, such a garden is likely to have been sited. The inscription on these jambs reads:

> He (the king) has made as his monument for his father Amun-Re ... a cool and holy place (named) 'Aakheperure-satisfies-Amun' by decorating it with a pool (named) 'Libation-of-Amun' in sandstone, the gateway of granite, the

door-leaves of copper. It is his Majesty who sanctifies this pool, adorned with reeds, and planted with sedges, lotuses, herbs, rushes and lotus-buds ... (van Siclen 1982: 16)

Also depicted in Sennefer's tomb is 'The granary of the Temple of Amun' which shows an entrance gate opening upon a balustraded stairway that led up to a raised altar; the whole is set within a large enclosure piled high with heaps of grain. There is no reference as to where this granary might have been situated: certainly it would have been outside the precinct of the temple proper, but logically it must surely have been adjacent to the Nile in order to receive the cargoes of grain that would have arrived by boat.

The temple of Karnak was, of course, primarily a religious foundation, but in order to function as such, it had a large administrative section to organise and provide all that was necessary for the countless ceremonies, services and rituals constantly taking place, as well as for the great state festivals which often lasted for days, even weeks, on end. We have already seen evidence of bakeries, kitchens, workshops and gardens from the Middle Kingdom onwards which were used for this very purpose. Horticulture was clearly vital for the production of a great variety of offerings in the form of fruit, flowers, vegetables, grain for loaves and beer, and grapes for wine. Since the gardens that adorned the precincts of Karnak were limited in size and were, to a large extent, decorative, it is obvious that the bulk of the produce came from outside the temple walls – very often from some distance, such as the supplies of grain already mentioned. Recently, during the drainage of a canal area to the north of the Montu precinct at Karnak, a sandstone lintel and the remains of some sixteen-sided columns were discovered, all bearing the name of Amenhotep II. The inscriptions speak of the founding of a 'divine vineyard' in the area to supply produce for Amun (Hegazy *et al.* 1993: 207). It is known that by the Ramesside Period the 'Estate of Amun' owned vast areas of land throughout Egypt, the income from which formed the basis of the wealth of the temple and in part supplied the offerings for its altars; and no doubt this wealth in land was already accruing in the mid-XVIIIth Dynasty. However, this is the first known mention of a vineyard being dedicated personally to the god by the king. The inscription further informs us that this land was to provide 'all kinds of vegetables', so it would seem to have been more than just a vineyard, but a garden and an orchard in addition. Considering its proximity, perhaps it should be viewed as an annexe of the Garden of Amun in the west front of Karnak.

As already mentioned, it would seem that Amenhotep's building programme was more extensive than previously thought. Research is still proceeding on the many architectural elements that have been found widely scattered giving tantalisingly ephemeral glimpses of what once had been. Commemorative scarabs tell of obelisks erected at Karnak by the king, although no remains have ever been found and their position is unknown. However, since Amenhotep seems to have built a new southern entrance to Karnak with his gateway and festival court, this would certainly have been the most obvious place to have raised them.

Amenhotep II also decorated and inscribed some blocks along the corridor leading to Tuthmosis III's Akh-Menu, and he added his name to his father's 'coronation chapel'. Did he, too, approach this chapel to be enthroned by Amun? Did subsequent kings do likewise? Some time later in its history, however, this chapel was adapted to accommodate the god's bark on its procession to Akh-Menu, and its whole function altered. Traces of other work of Amenhotep are known from the bark-shrine within the temple of Khonsu and from the temple of Opet: both temples obviously having earlier incarnations than their present form. Architectural fragments from other monuments and sundry inscribed blocks all attest to a variety of building schemes now lost. Perhaps the continuing research will provide some answers.

Tuthmosis IV

The fourth Tuthmosis came to the throne upon the death of his father, Amenhotep II. It is not certain whether he was the heir apparent, and there does not appear to have been any period of co-regency; however, Tuthmosis' accession to the Horus throne seems to have been a smooth one, so it is quite possible that any older sons had predeceased Amenhotep. That Tuthmosis was not the original heir apparent is perhaps inherent in the text of the famous Sphinx stela in which the kingship of the Two Lands is promised to him by the god Re-Horakhte in return for clearing away the sand from the god's image.

Tuthmosis' mother, Tiaa, was probably a secondary queen of Amenhotep II for she does not appear as Great Royal Wife on any of his monuments – a title that she seemed only to acquire during her son's reign when she rose to a very prominent position (Grajetzki 2005: 56), completely overshadowing Tuthmosis' own queens, and figuring with her son on his monuments and beside him in statue groups: in these instances she was always accorded the title of Great Royal Wife and King's Mother. A block from an unprovenanced temple of Tuthmosis IV shows part of a divine birth scene (Bryan 1991: 206, fig. 39), indicating perhaps that the king wished to emphasise his mother's pre-eminence as queen as well as his own royal and divine credentials. Possibly because of the startling fact that Hatshepsut had been able to follow her husband, Tuthmosis II, and occupy the Throne of the Two Lands, subsequent kings seemed to keep their Great Royal Wives very much in the background. While early Dynasty XVIII queens had enjoyed great prominence, the queens of Tuthmosis III, Amenhotep II and Tuthmosis IV rarely, if ever, featured on the walls of their husband's monuments or appeared with them in statuary. In all these cases, it was during the reigns of their sons that these queens came to be recognised and honoured as 'Great Royal Wife and mother of the king'.

While a date of Year 8 is the highest known for Tuthmosis IV, he probably reigned for considerably longer, during which time he undertook some military activity in Nubia and Syria, and a treaty with the Mitanni was sealed by Tuthmosis' marriage to a Mitannian princess.

When it comes to the king's work at Karnak, there is very little left to see today; nevertheless, a detailed study of various elements has shown that Tuthmosis IV did indeed undertake some major construction work, much of which was quite impressive; but, as with his father and with all subsequent kings, his work merely embellished and extended the area that lay outside that central and most sacred core of the temple, Ipet-Sut.

His major monument, however, did not enlarge the existing precinct – although it certainly embellished it – for he contrived to build a court with a double peristyle *within* the festival court of Tuthmosis II. In effect, Tuthmosis IV built one monument inside another: the two being complementary (Grimal and Larché 1993: ix). Over one thousand sandstone blocks from this peristyle court were found in the core of the Third Pylon, which has made it possible to restore in part what had once stood in front of the Fourth Pylon; and, indeed, the remains of a wall from the court can still be seen against the north-west corner of this pylon. It seems that Tuthmosis IV had no desire to demolish his predecessor's work (a rare wish in itself) but he adapted it, using its monumental gates and reworking the interior to accommodate his peristyle court of square pillars which measured around 70 m wide by 40 m deep. At least twenty-five pillars are known – undoubtedly only a fraction of the original number, for the construction was designated 'a court which is in front, of excellent hard stone, surrounded by pillars' (Letellier 1979: 55). These are almost exactly the words used by Ramesses II to describe the court that *he* built at the front of Luxor temple ('a court which is in front of its temple, surrounded by pillars') (Barguet 1962: 95). It seems, then, that we should envisage Tuthmosis' court as being somewhat in the style of the later one of Ramesses at Luxor, which is, of course, still extant.

A section of Tuthmosis' pillared court is currently undergoing reconstruction by the French and Egyptian archaeological teams within Karnak's Open Air Museum, thus giving today's visitor an impression of this structure's erstwhile grandeur.

The reliefs from Tuthmosis IV's court make it apparent that its function was almost precisely that of Tuthmosis II's before it: the dedication of offerings, the presentation of tribute, the ceremonies surrounding the departure and arrival of the sacred bark in procession, the purification of the king and priests before they entered the holiest areas of the temple, and certain semi-public rituals.

One relief on the court's south wall is of particular interest as it shows the king and his mother Queen Tiaa stretching the cord with the goddess Sefkhet-Abu at the foundation ceremony (Chevrier 1951: 568, fig. 1). Queens were not customarily involved in such ceremonies, and this scene has no known parallel until Ptolemaic times when a queen is depicted participating in brick-moulding activity for the temple at Tod (Bryan 1991: 100, n. 44). The uniqueness of this scene has led to speculation as to whether the peristyle court could possibly be the 'House of Tiaa in the Temple of Amun' referred to in the Wilbour Papyrus (Bryan 1991: 101). In other words, did she share in the dedication of this court with her son, since no other separate chapel or shrine has ever been found in her name? At the very least, her inclusion in this scene indicates her extraordinarily high status.

Within his peristyle court, Tuthmosis constructed a bark-shrine of alabaster named 'Tuthmosis-who-receives-the-crowns-of-Amun'. Its name would seem to indicate some kind of kingship ceremony (Barguet 1962: 317). The likelihood of its being a sed-festival is slight since none of its reliefs bears this possibility out, and in so comparatively short a reign, it is unlikely that the king ever celebrated such a festival. The more likely scenario is that it commemorated the king's coronation.

The shrine was approximately 7 m long, 5.15 m high and 4.65 m wide, and probably stood in the south-west corner of the court: today it has been re-erected in the Open Air Museum, where its fine relief work can be admired. Among the beautifully executed scenes in the shrine's interior is one depicting the sacred bark on its socle. A reference on the Lateran obelisk, erected by Tuthmosis IV, tells of a renewal of Amun's state-barge, Userhet, which carried the sacred bark on water-borne processions. Could this alabaster shrine have been commissioned especially to commemorate the new barge and its precious cargo? And what could have been a better or more appropriate festival for which this was undertaken than the king's coronation?

The decoration of Tuthmosis' shrine was, however, incomplete and his son and successor, Amenhotep III, added his own name and reliefs sometime after his father's demise; he likewise inscribed his name in the alabaster shrine of his grandfather, Amenhotep II, which also stood in this area. But further, the alabaster shrine of Tuthmosis IV is known to have stood up against that of Tuthmosis III, thus raising the amazing likelihood that all three alabaster shrines were sited concurrently within the same immediate environs. It is hard to imagine what their configuration could possibly have been, before Amenhotep III eventually swept them all away to construct the mighty Third Pylon.

Tuthmosis IV was to embellish this area yet further by his work on the Fourth Pylon. He did not claim to have built the original pylon or its gateway (these were the work of Tuthmosis I), but to have enlarged them. His dedication text reads: 'Then my Majesty acted, making a great doorway as his monument, extending and magnifying it greatly ... Its height was great, it reaching the sky. Its rays inundated the Two Lands ...'. It appears, therefore, that he reworked the central part of the pylon, raising its height and renewing its gateway (Bryan 1991: 170), and the fact that he mentioned that its 'rays inundated the Two Lands' probably meant that he decorated the entrance and the flagstaffs with gold.

However, this was not the full extent of Tuthmosis' work in the area, for a block from his peristyle court, mentioning the door of the Fourth Pylon, states: 'The great door (named) "Amun-is-powerful-of-prestige"... ebony, the porch (*sbḫt*) in gold and many precious stones' (Letellier 1979: 57–8). Literally a *sbḫt* was a screen-walled portico protecting an important entrance, and the doorway of the Fourth Pylon was, at that time, certainly the most important entrance at Karnak, giving access, as it did, to the inner precincts of Ipet-Sut: it was here that the king would have undergone ritual purification by the gods before entering the temple.

Although there are virtually no physical remains of this porch today, we are fortunate in having two representations of it that give a clear picture of its form (Yoyotte 1953: 28–30): one is on the above-mentioned block, and the other is from the tomb of the Second Prophet of Amun, Amenhotep Si-se (Davies, N. 1923: pl. XII). These both show a roof supported by two lotus columns, between which can be seen a doorway topped by a lintel and cornice; this probably depicts the actual door of the Fourth Pylon. The likelihood is that the lotus columns were of wood resting on stone bases, and one of these bases can still be seen in place. According to the inscriptions, the porch, its columns and its ceiling were gilded – in all probability coated in gold or electrum, as, of course, was the door of the Fourth Pylon itself. A sumptuous and awe-inspiring sight indeed. Yoyotte also proposes the possibility that the porch is represented in a wall painting within the tomb of Neferhotep (Yoyotte 1953: 32–3; Davies, N. 1933b: pl. XLI)(Fig. 7.2).

It is not known for certain whether Tuthmosis IV erected any obelisks of his own at Karnak: a red granite fragment of one from Karnak, now in the Cairo Museum, has been ascribed to him, but his cartouche does not appear on the fragment and there is no other record of its existence or where it stood. However, his erection of Tuthmosis III's single 'Lateran' obelisk is well known.

Figure 7.2 The porch of the Fourth Pylon (from the tomb of Amenhotep Si-se) (after Yoyotte, J., *CdE* 55 (1953): 28, fig. 7).

> Tuthmosis (IV) ... it was his Majesty who beautified the single, very great obelisk, being one which his father, the King of Upper and Lower Egypt, Menkheperre, had brought, after his Majesty found this obelisk, it having spent 35 years lying on its side in the hands of craftsmen on the south side of Karnak ...

Tuthmosis IV added his own lines of inscription either side of those of Tuthmosis III, and covered its pyramidion with electrum before setting it up where his grandfather had originally intended – that is, in front of the Eastern Temple. Incidentally, Tuthmosis IV's inscription also provides us with the interesting information that there were ateliers and workshops situated 'on the south side of Karnak'.

By the time Tuthmosis IV had raised the Lateran obelisk in honour of his grandfather, eleven of these great stone needles – most capped with gold – had been erected upon the main axial way of the temple of Amun. There were no less than six in front of the Fourth Pylon (two each of Tuthmosis I, II and III), two of Hatshepsut in the Wadjet Hall and two more of hers at the eastern end of the temple, and finally the single 'Lateran' obelisk. In addition, of course, there were obelisks on the southern processional way, such as those of Tuthmosis III before the Seventh Pylon, and the possible but unknown ones of Amenhotep II and of Tuthmosis IV himself.

Quite an impressive array of statuary of Tuthmosis IV adorned Karnak's precincts, and in this regard, another detail in the decoration of the tomb of Amenhotep Si-se, mentioned above, is worth noting. Featured on the walls of this tomb is a representation of a colossal statue of Tuthmosis named 'Amun-who-hears-prayers', which is very similar in design to an actual quartzite statue of the king found at Karnak. Could this statue have stood on the approach to the Eastern Temple – the 'temple of the Hearing Ear' – where the townspeople of Thebes, who had no access to the main temple, could come and present their prayers and petitions to the god? To endorse this possibility, we know that, somewhat later, a cult statue of the deified Ramesses II named 'Ramesses-who-hears-prayers' once stood in the area for this very purpose.

Another unusual statue in black granite of the king shows Tuthmosis IV represented as a falcon. This is of particular interest because a relief on one of the peristyle court blocks depicts a group of statues of the king being dedicated to Amun, one of which does indeed represent Tuthmosis as a falcon (Letellier 1979: 57; Bryan 1991: 179–180). Could this be the very same statue? It cannot be ruled out.

In his reign of ten years or possibly longer, it can be seen that Tuthmosis IV accomplished quite a substantial building programme at Karnak. It is ironic, perhaps, that it was his own son, Amenhotep III, who almost completely removed his father's monuments and consigned them to virtual oblivion until the present day. Now, once again, we can have some conception of the very fine work achieved by Tuthmosis, and it is, moreover, due in very great part to the early incarceration of these buildings within the Third Pylon that they have been so well preserved for us.

8

AMENHOTEP III AND THE PROCESSIONAL WAYS

Amenhotep III

When Amenhotep III succeeded his father on the throne in *c.*1386 BC, he inherited a kingdom that was immensely prosperous and powerful. After decades of military campaigning and foreign conquests undertaken by his predecessors, vast quantities of tribute in the form of gold as well as precious and exotic products were annually poured into Egypt's state coffers from every corner of her huge empire. Amenhotep himself, however, had no desire to conduct further foreign campaigns, preferring instead the diplomatic touch with his neighbours and the encouragement of trade. Nevertheless, early in his reign, he did undertake a few relatively unimportant military expeditions which he proceeded to claim as glorious conquests, referring to himself as a mighty warrior and boasting of many other great (though imaginary) victories.

In truth, the only type of campaign Amenhotep wished to pursue was that of self-glorification, which he did with enthusiasm. Theoretically, every Egyptian king was a god, standing at the interface between the human and divine worlds, a myth which Amenhotep never failed to promote – and there are aspects of his reign which seem to indicate that he almost believed his own publicity. In temples throughout Egypt and its empire, the cult of the deified king was established, sometimes a cult no less great than that of Amun himself. Inscriptions referred to Amenhotep as Amun's 'living image upon earth' or as 'an image a million times great' and as 'the dazzling sun disk of all lands' – all epithets he himself chose. Amenhotep's Great Royal Wife Tiye, although a commoner by birth, was, upon her marriage, dubbed by her husband as having become 'the wife of a mighty king' and she, too, was given a temple dedicated to her cult.

At home, Amenhotep indulged in worldly pleasures of unparalleled luxury: opulence was the order of the day. He encouraged and patronised every form of the arts, creating a sophisticated and cosmopolitan society. This interest in the arts, coupled with his innate, if extravagant, good taste, were to be reflected in the splendour of his building programme, with its grandiose architecture, design and decoration.

In order to glorify Amun and himself in the Theban area, Amenhotep's vision encompassed a huge ritual complex that would link the temples of Amun, Mut and Khonsu at Karnak with that of Amun at Luxor for the Festival of Opet, and which would also incorporate the West Bank mortuary temples for the Beautiful Feast of the Valley (Kemp 1989: 203, fig. 71). In fact, the celebration of these important festivals had become the decisive influence in the development of this great ritual site. As we saw earlier, Hatshepsut was the ruler who either instituted or greatly enhanced the Festival of Opet and, indeed, by so doing, she was to change the whole focus of Karnak's ritual ceremonies; though it would be true to say that it was Amenhotep III who brought Hatshepsut's vision to full fruition when he promoted the festival to a huge religious and state occasion.

Whatever temple or shrine existed at Luxor in the earlier reigns of Dynasty XVIII, he now demolished in order to build a glorious new temple: it is important to note, however, that this temple was not orientated on the Nile, but on Karnak itself, thus stating Luxor's dependent link. While in Hatshepsut's day the Festival of Opet had lasted approximately eleven days, it now began to expand, so that by the time of Ramesses III in Dynasty XX, the celebrations continued for twenty-seven days, and it had become the most important of all the religious festivals.

The basic idea of celebrating the reigning king's divine conception and birth had developed into an increasingly complex series of rituals and ceremonies culminating, from Amenhotep III's time, in a mystical union between king and god, from which the king emerged as a transfigured and divinised being – this was the cult of the royal *ka*, to which end the new temple at Luxor was particularly directed (Bell 1985: 281). Perhaps we should see a parallel here to the rituals held within Tuthmosis III's Akh-Menu.

During Amenhotep III's reign, the procession of the sacred bark from Karnak to Luxor was probably accomplished by river both ways. Amun was certainly now attended by the statues of Mut and Khonsu also. Amun's river-barge, Userhet ('Mighty-of-Prow'), carried the god's image contained within its veiled shrine upon the portable bark, and by the reign of Tutankhamun (and very probably earlier), Mut and Khonsu each had their own personal river-barge to carry their sacred barks likewise. The processions must have been wonderful to behold, and it is small wonder that huge crowds gathered to watch the spectacle and throw themselves wholeheartedly into the festivities.

But to return to Karnak itself and to Amenhotep's building scheme there, described as 'Amenhotep, Ruler of Thebes, distinguished of monuments in the Temple of Karnak, abundant with marvels'. Most marvellous of all was his magnificent Third Pylon, a structure that has provided Egyptologists with a huge amount of information and an array of beautiful monuments to study. When Amenhotep came to the throne, Karnak's main entrance was the Fourth Pylon, fronted by the peristyle hall of his father, Tuthmosis IV. Initially, Amenhotep did his filial duty by completing his father's unfinished monuments, such as the alabaster shrine, and by adding limestone gateways into the courtyard that stood before the peristyle hall; it is quite possible that he completed the hall as well. However, a little later, Amenhotep swept away the whole courtyard and hall complex along with two of the three pairs of obelisks which stood in advance of it, not to mention the many smaller monuments clustered around this very significant point at which the two temple axes crossed, in order to commence his grand scheme. Only some blocks of one of the limestone gates remain in that area today, their original cartouches reworked by Seti I and Ramesses III (Fig. 8.1a).

It might seem strange that Amenhotep felt compelled to demolish his father's festival court and so many other monuments of his predecessors when there was obviously plenty of open space further to the west; but, as already mentioned, the huge ritual significance of this area could not be ignored by a monarch so bent upon creating a work that would forever ensure the glory of his name. Now, with a new perspective and a new route for the great Festival of Opet, as well as a glorious new temple at Luxor in which to celebrate it, Amenhotep must indeed have felt confident of immortality.

At the time of its construction, the Third Pylon formed the new monumental entrance to the temple: upon docking at the quay, the temple would have been approached through a gateway, which is believed by some to have opened upon the colonnade of fourteen papyrus columns, each measuring 25 m in height, which led to a vestibule before the great pylon entrance. Today, this beautiful colonnade forms the central aisle of the later Hypostyle Hall, and until recently scholars were relatively certain that these great columns dated to Amenhotep III (Chevrier 1956: 36) because their foundations, consisting of two great mud-brick massifs running east–west in parallel, are totally independent from those of the Hypostyle Hall, and also because blocks from demolished buildings of his son, Akhenaten, were found under all the columns of the Hypostyle Hall, but not under the colonnade columns. Moreover, one cannot but be impressed by its similarity to that other glorious colonnade at Luxor temple. However, the identity of the builder of the Karnak colonnade has long been in dispute: the argument arose principally over the depiction of what is assumed to be the Third Pylon painted in the tomb of Neferhotep, an official in the reign of Ay about sixty years after Amenhotep III (Davies, N. 1933b: pl. XLI).

There is no absolute proof that the scene in Neferhotep's tomb actually represents Karnak, but many of the features portrayed can still be found *in situ*: the canal leading from the Nile ending at a quay with a landing stage for disembarkation is clearly shown, as is the temple garden and an avenue of trees leading to the Third Pylon, behind which lie in succession the obelisk of Tuthmosis I, the Fourth Pylon with its wooden porch, the Fifth Pylon and the sanctuary. Where, then, is the colonnade? There is no cut-and-dried answer to this, and it continues to be argued over, especially since there are no cartouches of Amenhotep III on any of the columns. However, since the colonnade is not the only feature that is lacking in Neferhotep's representation of this entrance, could the omission be put down to artistic licence? But more of this contentious question later (Fig. 8.1b).

The Third Pylon itself was built of sandstone with eight great flagstaffs of cedar in niches against the western face, each topped with a fluttering pennant, while either side of the central gateway a sphinx stood guard. The texts tell us that the mighty flagstaffs, which must have been almost 40 m high, were each fashioned from a single cedar-of-Lebanon trunk, the lower ends of which were sheathed in bronze and the tips plated with electrum. Such magnificence must have been awe-inspiring which was, no doubt, part of the intention. Our knowledge of its appearance is due to a relief of Tutankhamun's reign at Luxor temple; such knowledge would otherwise be lost to us because the rear wall of the later Hypostyle Hall of Seti I and Ramesses II was built hard up against the western façade of the pylon, and it is difficult today to distinguish what must once have been an astonishing and wondrous sight. One must rely on Amenhotep III's own words to bring its splendours to life:

> making a very large pylon for him before the face of Amun-Re of Karnak, adorned all over with gold. On its door, the shadow of the god is like a ram set with real lapis lazuli, worked with gold and many costly stones. Its floor is inlaid with silver, the gates opposite it stand firm. The stelae are of lapis lazuli, one on each side. Its towers reach up to the sky like the supports of heaven, its flagmasts, adorned with electrum, shine brighter than the sky. (BAR II: para. 889)

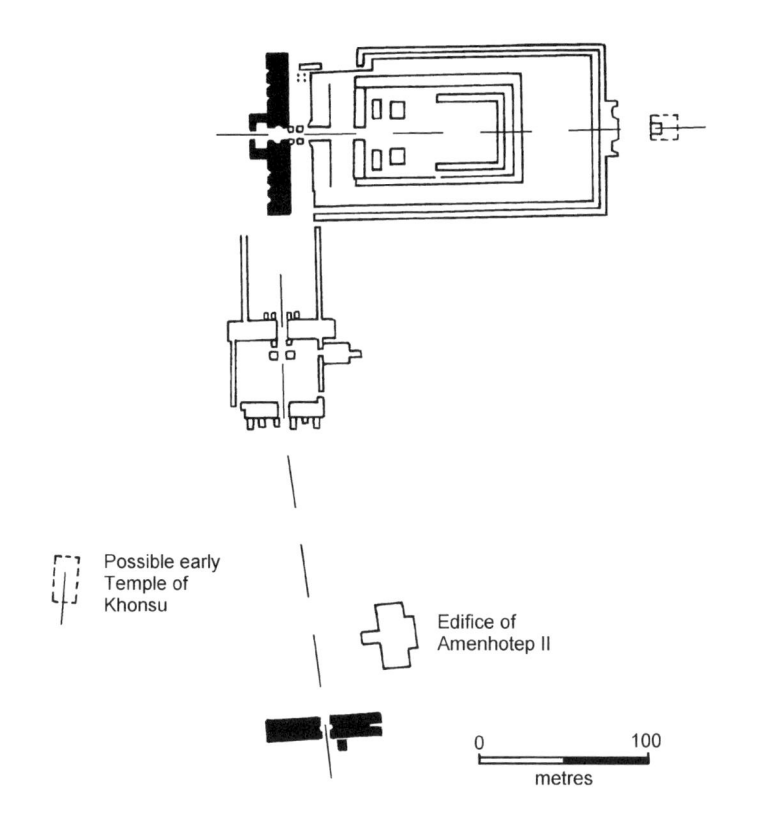

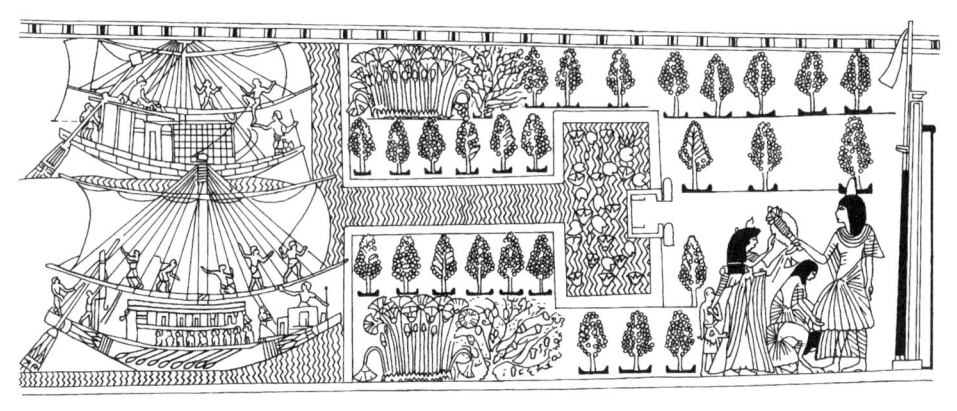

Figure 8.1 The constructions of Amenhotep III. (a) Sketch plan of the constructions (shown in black). (b) Canal and basin in front of the temple (from the tomb of Neferhotep TT49) (after Aufrère, S. *et al.*, *L'Égypte Restituée*: 98 and 127 respectively).

Such a description might seem somewhat exaggerated, but much of it can be verified. The adornment of such monuments with gold and electrum, and inlays of lapis lazuli and turquoise are well attested. But what do we make of a floor inlaid with silver? There is textual evidence that Amenhotep endowed other temples – Luxor and Soleb for instance – in a similar fashion (*URK* IV: 1654–5). It has been suggested that this silver floor of the temple entrance was where the sacred processional bark would have been stationed in order to proclaim oracles: certainly, later oracle texts speak of a 'silver floor' (Sauneron and Vérité 1969: 251 n. 1). The most conclusive evidence for its existence, however, is to be seen in the drilled holes which have been found in the passageway paving-blocks of the pylon: these would have been used to fasten the metal sheets to the floor. Although the name of the Third Pylon has not survived, the fact that it too – as with the Fourth, Fifth and Sixth Pylons – had the god's figure represented as a ram inset upon the door, would seem to indicate another name incorporating the homonym *šfyt* ('prestige') within it. Because none of the central doors of Karnak's mighty pylons survives, one must try to visualise great cedar doors, clad with bronze, inlaid with silver, gold or electrum and encrusted with semi-precious stones, which would have shut off the sacred precinct from the outside world. The heavy door-leaves swung upon massive bronze hinges set in granite sockets and were closed by bronze bolts. The richness of the pylon's decoration can scarcely be imagined when one looks at what now remains.

Sadly, no record remains to acquaint us with the finances required to undertake these huge projects. But from Amenhotep III's reign a list does survive of the precious metals used in the adjacent temple of Montu: 31,485 *deben* of electrum, 25,182 *deben* of gold, 4,620 *deben* of copper, 14,342 *deben* of bronze, 6,406 *deben* of lapis lazuli, 1,731 *deben* of carnelian and 1,075 *deben* of turquoise (*URK* IV: 1668). (Alan Gardiner gives one *deben* an approximate weight of 100 grammes (Gardiner 1973: 200).) Such staggering quantities become even more incredible when the comparative smallness of this temple is set against the size of Amenhotep's other works at Thebes: Karnak itself, Luxor temple, the vast funerary complex on the West Bank, in addition to all his other temples and palaces throughout Egypt and into Nubia.

The east face of the Third Pylon, which today stands to about half its original height, is much more visible than the west and was extensively decorated. The south wing contains a lengthy text, while the north wing bears a splendid scene of Amun's great river-bark, Userhet, being towed by the king's barge. Userhet was richly adorned from stem to stern: 'its hull is ornamented with silver and worked with gold for its entire length; the great shrine is of electrum that fills the land with brightness, its bows ... bear crowns whose serpents twine along its two sides'. It is shown carrying the god's processional bark within a naos, before which can be seen flags and obelisks – presumably of gilded wood – and Amenhotep himself appears twice standing before the naos and also behind it, accompanied by the smaller figure of a prince, thought to be the future Amenhotep IV (Akhenaten), although it has been argued that the figure represents Tutankhamun (Murnane 1993: 33), added when that king restored many of the Karnak monuments after the damage inflicted during the Amarna period. This richly decorated scene faces, very appropriately, the court whence the Opet procession would have departed on its southward journey to Luxor at that time.

But it was the interior, rather than the exterior, of the Third Pylon that was to astonish Egyptologists over the last century. From the foundations and core of the pylon were extracted a large number of monuments, some almost complete, some only fragmentary: well over one thousand blocks belonging to buildings dating from Dynasty XI onwards have been recovered, including blocks from constructions of Amenhotep III himself. It has been suggested that initially the king had erected a central gateway with vestibule, these being set into an enclosure wall, all of which he subsequently demolished to build his pylon.

Generally speaking, the foundations of the vast majority of Egypt's massive pylons, walls and columns were remarkably inadequate for the great structures that they support, but in this case the foundations of Karnak's Third Pylon, in which all these blocks were found, were extraordinarily deep (around 6 m). This is a tremendous depth which, according to earlier thinking, was due to the fact that it had once been the site of an earlier quay and basin (Chevrier 1971: 74). A new basin would then obviously have had to be excavated further to the west, and this was thought to have been sited where the Second Pylon was constructed later by Horemheb. These claims have recently been disputed, and work undertaken in areas around the Second and Third Pylons has revealed no evidence of earlier basins. Be that as it may, the original basin (if it ever existed) having been drained, or alternatively huge foundations pits having been dug, its immense depth was filled with the many dismantled monuments, thus forming the mighty foundations for the Third Pylon.

However, Henri Chevrier who, along with Maurice Pillet, was responsible for clearing the pylon, reported that despite there being more blocks to dispose of, the filling unaccountably stopped at the ancient soil level; the blocking stones within the rest of the foundations, he stated, were by and large all new and rough-cut (Chevrier 1971: 74). Most of these filling blocks had large cursive hieroglyphs painted in red on their sides which, according to Pillet, can be translated as 'for the great pylon ... of Karnak' (Pillet 1925: 9). Such red-painted marks were used to identify the blocks cut from quarries, thus ensuring that they arrived at the correct destination for the correct monument. Quarry-marks of this type are attested as far back as the Old Kingdom and continue into the Ptolemaic period at least.

We can only ponder the curious fact that the Third Pylon contained so many earlier monuments, apparently put into the foundations with great care and in a given order: many theories abound; none has been proven.

Further argument was occasioned by the dating of the last two pylons of the southern processional way, the Ninth and Tenth. These were initially both attributed to Horemheb and, indeed, they both are carved with his name, but the story is more complicated than that. It has long been wondered why these two pylons were not aligned on the same southern axis as the Seventh and Eighth. It is now thought that it was Amenhotep III who built the original Ninth Pylon, orientating it on his newly founded Temple of Mut, for it is certainly true that this pylon lines up exactly with the sphinx-lined way leading to the Mut enclosure, and it is the only pylon on the southern way that does, surely a significant fact (Barguet 1962: 252). Perhaps Amenhotep constructed this pylon in mud-brick. Or did he leave it unfinished? Whatever the reason might be, Horemheb was without doubt the constructor of the pylon we see today, which states his ownership quite clearly, and which contained within its core blocks of Akhenaten and Tutankhamun.

If Amenhotep did not inaugurate the building of the Ninth Pylon however, then we must envisage a huge open court between the Eighth Pylon of Hatshepsut and the Tenth Pylon which, for several reasons, it is possible to be certain was indeed the work of Amenhotep III (Murnane 1993: 33): the first being on account of the massive colossus of the king which stood at the temple entrance against the southern face of the Tenth Pylon to the east of its gateway. This mighty statue was erected under the direction of the king's great minister, architect and advisor, Amenhotep son of Hapu, who left an inscription on one of his own statues to commemorate the achievement (Barguet 1962: 246). It was obviously a mammoth undertaking for the colossus was fashioned from a single huge block of red quartzite quarried from Gebel Ahmar, near Cairo, which necessitated the construction of eight barges (presumably lashed together) in order to transport the monolith upstream to Thebes. This was accomplished with the aid of the army, who then had the task of conveying the block to Karnak itself and raising it to the upright position upon a vast socle of the same material in front of the east wing of the Tenth Pylon; but, according to Amenhotep son of Hapu, 'they wrought with joy, their hearts were glad, rejoicing and praising the good god (i.e. the king)'. Were there two of these giants? Certainly there is a matching socle on the west side of the pylon's gateway, and Amenhotep son of Hapu in his inscription sometimes used a plural ending in referring to his commission, and sometimes a singular. Opinion is divided on this, but some scholars maintain that the second base held a statue of Horemheb erected more than thirty years later. The fact that the single colossus of Amenhotep III bore the name 'Montu-of-Rulers' and that it had its own cult might indicate that it was a unique object and not one of a pair. Small wonder that it should have been revered when one considers that it stood about 18 m high (not including its socle), and probably well over 20 m when the crown, which was a separate element, was added; even the pylon would have been eclipsed by the scale of this statue. Today, sadly, only the feet of this once magnificent sculpture remain, but each of these measures an amazing 2.9 m in length.

This, then, is one certain reason for ascribing the Tenth Pylon to Amenhotep III; indeed, the pylon's foundations were formed of large newly cut blocks placed in deep trenches which would have been impossible to construct *after* the emplacement of the statue (Chevrier 1950: 435). Second, a recent close examination of the Tenth Pylon has shown that the first eight courses of the stonework of the two wings can be securely dated to Amenhotep III (Azim 1982b: 151) and, likewise, the red granite doorway had been commenced by him. Both these elements were subsequently completed and decorated by Horemheb.

It is not surprising that Amenhotep son of Hapu should have been sufficiently proud of this achievement to leave an inscription concerning it. As the king's architect and 'director of all works', he was responsible for many of his master's vast building schemes, and it is obvious that Amenhotep III held his minister in very high esteem, granting him not only the privilege of having several statues of himself placed along the two axes of Karnak temple, but also the unique honour of a personal funerary temple on the West Bank in the shadow of his sovereign's great mortuary foundation there.

Apart from these great works, Amenhotep III's lesser monuments are not well known. He seems to have constructed a new granary, some decorated blocks of which have survived (Kozloff and Bryan 1992: 102, 115 n. 88); in fact, amongst its reliefs is the only reference to Queen Tiye that is known from the entire Karnak complex (Eaton-Krauss 1993a: 52). Several granaries undoubtedly already existed: the granary constructed by Amenhotep II, for instance, was still in use; and it is inconceivable that

Tuthmosis III did not also construct extra granaries to store the grain necessary for producing the large amounts of sacramental bread that were required every day for the ever-increasing number of shrines and altars at Karnak, and for the great festivals that developed. Also, it should be remembered, grain was an exchangeable commodity in a world that had no monetary system, and stockpiles of grain added substantially to the wealth of Egypt and its king.

We have already seen that Amenhotep had erected at least one great colossus of himself, 'Montu-of-Rulers', which was undoubtedly a cult statue. But to a monarch so prone to self-laudation as Amenhotep III, it is reasonable to assume that other evidence of his cult is to be seen at Karnak, and two such depictions can be seen on the opposing faces of the south-east doorway embrasure leading into the Wadjet Hall between the Fourth and Fifth Pylons (Loeben 1987a: 214). These identical reliefs show a naos containing a life-size statue of Amenhotep standing on a sledge which, without doubt, represented a portable statue in (gilded) wood used both in festival processions and for the king's cult. A similar statue, but in stone, was found recently in the Luxor Temple cache.

Little else of Amenhotep III's work at Karnak remains to be seen, and it is ironic, perhaps, that the one item of his that sticks in the minds of countless people who visit the temple today is the monumental scarab of red granite which sits on a plinth beside the Sacred Lake. The irony lies in the fact that the scarab does not belong to Karnak at all, but was brought across the Nile from the king's mortuary temple, probably by the Nubian pharaoh Taharqa some seven hundred years later.

It seems unlikely that a king as flamboyant as Amenhotep III, and one who dedicated so much work to Amun, would not have erected obelisks at Karnak: although only one pair (from the Montu precinct to the north) are known. These obelisks were, incidentally, placed upon two red granite socles that once had held the obelisks of Tuthmosis II in his festival court. When Amenhotep dismantled that entire court, he removed the bases of Tuthmosis' obelisks wholesale to north Karnak in order to use them as socles for *his* obelisks at the Montu temple entrance (Gabolde 1987: 152–3).

The only other evidence concerning possible obelisks is to be found in an inscription on the east face of the Third Pylon: it is a list of the king's building work, which, alas, is now very fragmentary, but which ends with the word 'obelisks'. Similarly, there is mention of obelisks on the king's great stela on the West Bank. There can hardly be any doubt that Amenhotep would have erected a pair of obelisks in front of his great pylon entrance at Karnak, and it must be assumed that they were removed later when the Hypostyle Hall was constructed. This assumption is reinforced by the discovery at Aswan of an inscription of Humen, Overseer of Builders of Amun, on which he states: 'I controlled the work on six obelisks for his Majesty ...' (Habachi 1950: 15). These must have been destined for the temples of Thebes, and in particular for Karnak. Although the king who commissioned these six obelisks is not named by Humen, Amenhotep III is probably the only Dynasty XVIII king – other than Tuthmosis III – who could have undertaken such a great building programme and who had the resources to make it feasible. Since the names of the architects in charge of the cutting and erection of Tuthmosis III's obelisks are known, it makes it virtually certain that Humen's commission was carried out on behalf of Amenhotep.

There is no doubt that other constructions of Amenhotep did exist; many have totally vanished and are known through textual sources alone: for example it seems that he built a new palace called 'Nebmaatre-is-the-Brilliant-Shining-Sun-Disk' (O'Connor 2001: 158) which perhaps replaced the earlier palace of Tuthmosis I and Hatshepsut that must have been demolished as Karnak expanded westward. This would have been used primarily for administrative and ceremonial purposes, as was that of Hatshepsut, because Malkata, Amenhotep's famous palace on the West Bank, seems to have been favoured as his Residence and the place where he celebrated his sed-festivals in great style.

Another building of which no trace has been found and yet which Amenhotep himself described in great detail was a 'Maru', similar, one must imagine, to the one built by his son at Amarna. In the king's words, it was 'a place of recreation for my father (Amun) on his beautiful festival ...' and was surrounded by gardens enclosing its own sacred lake (or pool) (*URK* IV: 1651). As this description contained a reference to the Festival of Opet, was this 'Maru-Amun' to be found somewhere along the ceremonial route between Karnak and Luxor? It has been suggested that it might even have been Amenhotep's newly constructed Mut temple, which did indeed have its own lake (Manniche 1982: 271–3), but no firm evidence has yet been found to substantiate this. On the other hand, was this elusive building to be found on the West Bank where a great lake or harbour, the 'Birket Habu', adjoined Malkata palace? However, since there are, to date, only textual references for this mysterious 'Maru', these theories remain pure speculation.

Amenhotep III reigned about thirty-eight years, during which time Egypt enjoyed decades of peace and prosperity. Under his patronage, the arts reached their zenith of richness and sophistication, and his architectural vision transformed Karnak and Thebes into a huge religious complex of unparalleled grandeur. Small wonder, therefore, that posterity has dubbed him 'Amenhotep the Magnificent'.

The Processional Ways

With the reign of Amenhotep III, it is time to consider the layout of Karnak's ceremonial and processional avenues and approaches, since it was during that king's regnum that the concept to provide a vast network of linked sacred ways was truly initiated.

As mentioned previously, there is evidence for a processional route to the south, lined with some type of statuary, during the reign of Hatshepsut; also a few of the existing sphinxes have been tentatively attributed to Tuthmosis IV on stylistic grounds (Cabrol 1995a: 23–4), but it was Amenhotep III who first instituted the sphinx-lined avenues, so familiar to us today, and despite their having been usurped, reworked and repositioned many times by later kings, these paved alleyways, linking the various temples of Karnak with one another and with Luxor temple, were to remain very much as he visualised them.

Let us begin, appropriately enough, with the western approach to Karnak's main entrance. This would have been effected along a canal which led from the Nile to a basin and quay, as graphically illustrated in Neferhotep's tomb (Theban Tomb number 49 (TT 49)) (Davies, N. 1933b: pl. XLII). As we have seen, the original basin and quay for the Middle Kingdom and early New Kingdom temple are thought to have been moved progressively further west as the temple expanded under subsequent kings, but today the remains of even the latest (and largest) of these elements can scarcely be detected at the point where the modern visitor alights from the tourist coach, for the canal, basin and quay have all long since silted up and disappeared under modern buildings and roads. The only remaining feature is the tribune, or ceremonial platform, across which today's visitor walks to approach, via the sphinx-lined way, Karnak's entrance at the massive First Pylon.

Therefore, we must visualise a T-shaped basin over which projected this platform, which was approached on either side by a flight of steps leading up from the quay. It

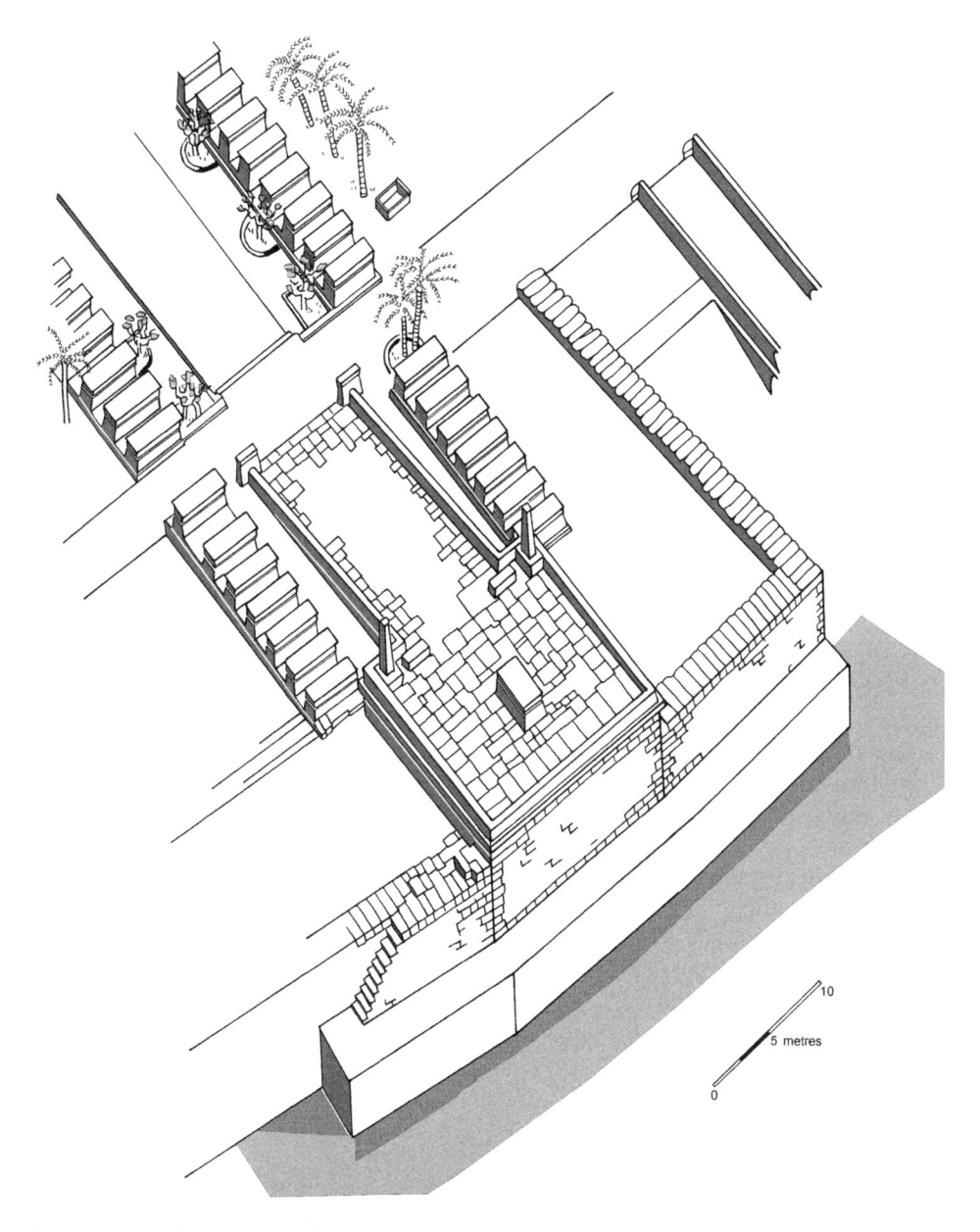

Figure 8.2 Artist's impression of Karnak's quay and tribune (after Lauffray, J., *Kemi* XXI: 82).

was here that the royal and divine boats would have docked, but the stairway up to the tribune, while suitable for people to ascend and descend, was far too narrow and steep to allow for the negotiation of the sacred bark from the deck of Userhet up to the tribune, where it was placed upon a centrally placed socle. It must therefore be assumed that one of the two ramps, which can still be seen to the south of the tribune, was where the sacred bark would have been brought ashore on the shoulders of its priestly bearers. One of these ramps is somewhat utilitarian and might well have been used for hauling Userhet ashore. In an area so adjacent to the sacred precinct, it is unlikely that such a ramp would have been used for the reception of grain or other commodities for the temple workshops: these would have been unloaded elsewhere. The other ramp is most elegantly constructed with low parapet walls that are engraved on one side with the titulary of Taharqa (Dynasty XXV) and on the other with a hymn, very possibly chanted by priests during the course of various rituals connected with the Nile and its inundation.

During these particular rites, it is probable that the sacred bark, or perhaps the god's processional statue within a light kiosk, would have been carried out on to the tribune, high above the water, to be placed upon the socle, with the trees and flowers of the temple gardens framing it behind: the impression must have been of the god coming forth from the sanctuary – the primaeval mound – to make contact with his creation at the all-important time of the inundation, upon which event the well-being of the entire land depended. It is noteworthy that the annual inundation heights were, in later dynasties, recorded upon the west face of the quay at this point.

The tribune, quay and ramps that have survived are quite late in date, and it is not possible to be certain what arrangement predated them, although part of a Ramesside avenue leading to a quay slightly to the south has been traced (Barguet 1962: 43). The tribune that we see today was thought to date to Dynasty XIX, due in part to the presence of the two small obelisks of Seti II. However, these almost certainly are not in their original positions since one of the inscribed faces of each base is hidden by the tribune's parapet wall. Following on the discovery of cornice blocks buried within the tribune which came from the great First Court of Sheshonk I (Lauffray 1979: 92), it must be admitted at the very least that the entire ensemble was massively reworked after Dynasty XXII, and possibly actually constructed at that time (Fig. 8.2).

The earlier Ramesside dromos, as stated above, is known to have deviated somewhat more to the south than the later one, presumably also to a quay. Very probably, these were destroyed by one of the devastating floods that occurred from time to time. Texts inform us that 'the quays of Thebes' were destroyed by just such a catastrophic event at the start of Dynasty XXI under Smendes, and that three thousand men had to be employed to quarry stone in order to rebuild them (BAR IV: para. 628–9).

Today, the visitor approaches the First Pylon by crossing the tribune, walking down a slight ramp and then along the paved avenue lined with ram-headed sphinxes (named very fittingly by the ancient Egyptians 'The Way of the Rams') to the temple entrance. The dromos (paved alley) has been attributed to Ramesses II, since the statuettes standing between the paws of the sphinxes bear his name, although there are possible traces of a more ancient name beneath (Nims 1955: 112). The sphinxes themselves appear to be the work of Amenhotep III; they are not, however, in their original location, having been placed at the western entrance to Karnak much later by Pinedjem I (one of the priest-kings of Dynasty XXI ruling at Thebes), whose name can be seen on each of the sphinxes today. This stretch of avenue is now about 20 m long, but it would have led originally to the Second Pylon – a length of approximately 52 m – at a time when that pylon was the temple's main entrance. At that period, the long avenue approaching the temple was bordered on the north side by the tripartite shrine of Seti II (Dynasty XIX) and to the south by the temple of Ramesses III (Dynasty XX). However, this long paved way was substantially shortened when Taharqa built his great kiosk before the Second Pylon, and was reduced even more by the construction of the great forecourt of Sheshonk I (Dynasty XXII) who then moved the sphinxes that had been enclosed by his building work to the north and south sides of the court, where they have remained to this day.

The excavation of the western dromos has brought to light the remains of a series of carefully constructed mud-brick troughs and connected water channels, proving that the avenue was bordered not only by sphinxes, but by trees and shrubs with their own 'self-watering' system (Lauffray 1979: 88). In addition, the entire avenue was screened within two parallel walls in order to shelter the god's procession to and from his sacred precinct.

The western approach remains an enigma, having been altered, reworked and extended many times, right through to the Ptolemaic period. Whether or not it was Amenhotep III who built the great colonnade in front of the Third Pylon, or whether it was he who lined the dromos with sphinxes, we can state with absolute certainty that he was the instigator of Karnak's network of sacred ways, and that his additions to the temple's main entrance would have been of unrivalled splendour.

The southern approach, with its several linked avenues, requires some consideration of its initial development. From an early date, the north–south axis of Karnak ran more or less parallel to the Nile and probably followed an ancient route from Luxor which passed in front of what was then Karnak's main entrance. How developed this route was at that time is not known, any more than is the earlier temple at Luxor. Two red granite architraves of Sebekhotep II (Dynasty XIII) were found at the entrance to Amenhotep III's great court at Luxor (Daressy 1926: 8), which might perhaps have come from an early temple on that spot; however, a quarry inscription of Ahmose at the very start of Dynasty XVIII states quite clearly that that king constructed a temple at Ipet-Resyt (Luxor) (*URK* IV: 25) – perhaps the temple that existed until Amenhotep's time. All that can be said with certainty is that a route between Karnak and Luxor existed, and that over the centuries, the north–south axis of Karnak was extended by four monumental gates, the Seventh, Eighth, Ninth and Tenth Pylons, marking the magnificent southern processional way to Luxor temple.

When Amenhotep III decided to build an entirely new temple at Luxor, and indeed a new temple for Mut outside Karnak's central precinct, the development of the sacred ways linking these temples was all part of his grand scheme. Whether he built a temple for Khonsu also is not known; there is no concrete evidence for it, only the possibility of an earlier avenue than the one that has survived. In fact, the Khonsu avenue is thought to be the oldest of all the sacred avenues of Karnak, but it was not linked with the processional route to Luxor; instead it led to a quay and basin that must have been connected by canal to the Nile (el-Molla *et al.* 1993: 246–8), although it has not been possible to trace its route due to the modern village in the area.

The approach to the Khonsu temple is lined with the figures of seated rams, the ram being an animal sacred to Amun: these are very distinctive, being somewhat larger

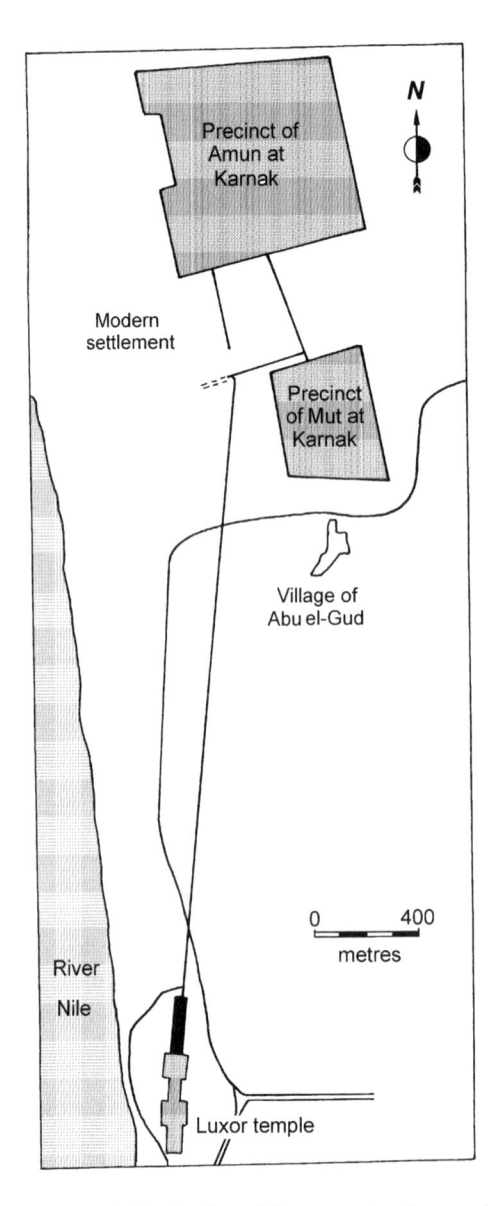

Figure 8.3 Sketch plan of the processional routes between the temples of Karnak and Luxor (after Hegazy, E., in *Journal of Ancient Chronology Forum* 3 (1989–90): 82).

than the criosphinxes (ram heads, lion bodies) and human-headed sphinxes that line the other avenues. Although they bear the name of Pinedjem I, they are known to be the work of Amenhotep III and may well have been brought by Pinedjem from the Mut precinct (Cabrol 1995b: 56), where a few identical ram-figures remain, or even have been transported from Amenhotep III's funerary temple on the West Bank, but research in this area is still continuing. This avenue, like the western dromos, was also planted with trees and bushes supplied with water from a purpose-built channel.

AMENHOTEP III AND THE PROCESSIONAL WAYS

The southern processional way exited the Karnak precinct through the gateway of the Tenth Pylon along a criosphinx-lined avenue towards the Mut temple enclosure: this dromos does not date to Amenhotep III but to Tutankhamun. It has been suggested that this avenue, too, was the work of Amenhotep III, but it is mere supposition since the avenue does indeed seem to have been initiated by the young king, even though the sphinxes themselves are not his. It has been shown that these have had rams' heads added to the bodies and a statuette of Tutankhamun then placed between their protective paws. The interesting point here is that the original heads of these criosphinxes had actually been human and that what remains of them have been clearly identified as being Akhenaten (with royal beard and *nemes* head-cover) and Nefertiti (with wig) (Eaton-Krauss 1993a: 54). They show the king and queen as being equal, and in this respect are unique. But from where did they come? In the light of the very latest research which has uncovered a processional way at east Karnak, the most likely answer is that Tutankhamun transferred them from Akhenaten's Aten temple there, replacing their heads with those of rams, and re-dedicating them to Amun. As if this hypothesis were not intriguing enough, another theory has proposed that the female sphinxes derived from an even earlier dromos from the time of Hatshepsut. Be that as it may, the positioning of all the sphinxes is quite random, showing clearly that they have been moved and reused.

Although the pedestals of the sphinxes bear the cartouches of Horemheb, they have quite obviously been added later over Tutankhamun's name and also over that of Ay, the latter king probably having completed the avenue after Tutankhamun's early death.

The final link in the chain that we have been discussing is the avenue that connects Karnak with Luxor, and many questions still remain concerning it. There is much work being undertaken to try to determine its age and the exact route that it followed: the avenue leaving Karnak for Luxor temple is known and the avenue leaving Luxor for Karnak is known, but where did they join up – as presumably they must once have done? At the moment, this is not known, although excavation is continuing with a view to exposing the entire length of the avenue. It is well known, however, that the avenue did not run in a straight line, but interconnected with the avenue of the Mut temple. It will be fascinating to discover its original route (Fig. 8.3).

An estimated 700 sphinxes lined the route between Karnak and Luxor temples (Hegazy 1989–90: 82–4), and its magnificence can scarcely be imagined. The sphinx-lined avenue which remains today in front of Luxor temple dates to Nectanebo I (Dynasty XXX); however, scenes in some New Kingdom tombs at Thebes imply that a processional way was already in existence during Dynasty XVIII, and certainly the Karnak end of the avenue is of a much earlier date. The Luxor end of Nectanebo's avenue commenced in the open court in front of Ramesses II's pylon. A slight ramp ascended to a doorway ('doors of true conifer wood') that gave access to the avenue; beside this door were found the remains of a red granite stela showing the king offering to the gods of Karnak: Amun, Mut, Khonsu and Montu. The avenue, which had a paved central walkway 5.7 m wide, was bordered by white-washed mud-brick walls, but stone blocks, some bearing the cartouche of Seti I and others of Ramesses II (Dynasty XIX), as well as some *talatat* of Akhenaten, have been found reinforcing two portals set within these walls (el-Saghir 1992: 183), which would clearly indicate that a dromos must have existed prior to that of Nectanebo. In addition, the brick walls at the commencement of the sacred way were also reinforced with stone blocks, these carved in the name of Seti II (el-Razik 1968: 157).

Another factor to be taken into account is that Nectanebo's avenue was of human-headed sphinxes (in his own likeness), while the Karnak end was ram-headed: if the sphinxes were destined to join up into one avenue, why (and where) did the type of sphinx change? In his building inscription, Nectanebo stated that at the end of the avenue he built a large pylon 'stretching to the sky in excellent everlasting work'. Was it at this pylon entrance that the sphinx avenue met the ram avenue (el-Razik 1968: 159)? This can only be speculated upon, for no evidence of the pylon has yet been found; moreover, it is not clear to which end of the avenue Nectanebo was referring.

The concept of this interlinked network of sacred ways began with Amenhotep III but was he the originator of them all? It is not possible to say at our present state of knowledge: however, they certainly underwent considerable restructuring by many later kings until the final addition by Nectanebo I. Let us conclude, therefore, with Nectanebo's dedication, carved on the base of one of his sphinxes, yet which could be said to sum up the entire complex and all the rulers who built or added to it: 'He (the king) built a beautiful road for his father Amun, bordered by walls, planted with trees and decorated with flowers . . . to celebrate the beautiful feast of procession to *'Ipt-Rsyt* (Luxor). No road more beautiful has ever existed before . . .' (el-Razik 1968: 157).

9

AMENHOTEP IV (AKHENATEN), TUTANKHAMUN AND AY

Amenhotep IV (Akhenaten)

The so-called Amarna period has sparked more controversy than any other period of Egyptian history, and has engendered countless theories and wild – even bizarre – speculation amongst both scholars and the public at large. Little of this will affect the account here, since the king in question, Amenhotep IV, left Thebes and Karnak behind him in about the fifth year of his reign in order to found a new capital city on virgin territory (Akhetaten/Tell el-Amarna) dedicated to his supreme deity, the Aten, the power imminent in the Sun Disk.

One of the major arguments of this period concerns the probability, or otherwise, of a co-regency between the young king and his father, Amenhotep III, and it is a subject that has given rise to much heated debate; but co-regency or not, it is true to say that Amenhotep IV did not appear on any of his father's monuments, unlike his brothers and sisters (Redford 1984: 57). This is unusual, to say the least, and it is hard to imagine the reason for this curious omission. Could it have been the strange appearance of the prince? Was there some congenital abnormality? The conjecture has been endless. However, his elder brother having predeceased him, it was the young Amenhotep who came to the throne under the name Neferkheperure Wa'enre Amenhotep. This last part he was to change shortly before he turned his back on Thebes, dropping 'Amenhotep', since it contained the hated element 'Amun' within it, and adopting the nomen Akhenaten, which incorporated the name of his deity.

Along with his name and the state religion, Akhenaten was also to change the entire art form, abandoning the traditions evolved over countless centuries. But let us begin with the start of his reign when he succeeded to the throne as Amenhotep IV and seemingly adhered, albeit very briefly, to the ancient traditions he had inherited. From this very early period, for example, must come the scarabs inscribed with 'Neferkheperure whom Amun-Re selected from millions' (Redford 1980: 22 and n. 161).

Almost immediately, as other rulers before him, the young king fulfilled his filial duty by completing two of his father's unfinished monuments at Karnak: he decorated the porch of the Third Pylon, adding a relief of himself smiting Egypt's enemies in the traditional style: he also worked on the Tenth Pylon. Every building of Amenhotep IV at Karnak has been so totally destroyed that it has taken decades of study to begin to see anything coherent in the smashed and widely scattered fragments of his various monuments. For this reason, some very large sandstone blocks, decorated in the traditional style showing Amenhotep IV offering to the falcon-headed sun-god,

Re-Horakhte, were thought to have come from a small temple or shrine dedicated to that god which had been erected at Karnak at the very start of the king's reign, although no mention of a *pr Rʿ-ḥr-3ḫty* (House of Re-Horakhte) was found on any of these blocks. Subsequent research has shown that the blocks probably originated, not from a temple but from an imposing gateway which the young king erected at the Tenth Pylon, also left unfinished by his father.

The suggestion that these blocks in traditional style had come from an early temple constructed by Amenhotep IV to the east, was based on the fact that this was an area already dedicated to the rising sun. However, one of these decorated blocks is still visible in the east wing of the Tenth Pylon bearing the inscription: 'the gate (called) "Neferkheperure Wa'enre is . . ."' (Redford 1984: 62 n. 8). Furthermore, an obelisk fragment in granite with an inscription and the name of Amenhotep IV on one face only was found in front of the south face of the Tenth Pylon (Aldred 1988: 88). The conclusion must be that such an obelisk(s) once stood before the aforementioned gateway.

Up to the present time, the Tenth Pylon has only been partially investigated, although it is known that its core contains much material relating to the early years of Amenhotep IV's reign, including an inscription of a Royal Address dated to Year 1. It will be fascinating indeed when this pylon's filling can be fully retrieved and studied.

The king had a new quarry opened at Gebel Silsileh in order to obtain the sandstone for his early gateway, and it was in this quarry that a stela was found which depicted Amenhotep IV worshipping Amun, obviously carved at the very outset of his reign (Redford 1984: 60). It is of particular interest for, although the king is shown worshipping Amun, the stela makes reference to 'the Great Benben of Re-Horakhte in Karnak'. 'The Great Benben of Re-Horakhte' was a squat obelisk which was the principal sun-symbol at Heliopolis. May not this be a very early indication of the change in doctrine that was coming?

These additions to his father's work apart, there is nothing traditional in Amenhotep IV's work, even during these early years at Thebes. Some time in Year 2 of his reign, the king announced that he was to celebrate a sed-festival – an extraordinary decision, since this ancient ritual of renewal and rejuvenation was customarily held around Year 30 of a king's reign (his father, for instance, held three such festivals in Years 30, 34 and 37), and although other rulers had, on occasion, held it at an earlier point in their reigns, nothing approaching a date as early as Year 2 had ever been known. Why did Amenhotep IV feel it necessary to celebrate this important festival at this stage? Was it to give life to his new theology with its concept of a single deity and its realistic art form? Did it rejuvenate the king in his role as sole intermediary with the Aten? In this context, it is surely of significance that where Re-Horakhte's figure crowned with the sun's disk had previously existed, it was now replaced by a representation of the Disk of the Aten to which a new epithet was attached: 'the great living Disk, which is in jubilee, who resides in (temple name) . . .'. It seems that this was a jubilee for both the king *and* the Aten. Whatever the reason, the sed-festival certainly seemed to act as the 'springboard' that launched the new religion; now a great building programme commenced.

Many years of research have been directed upon the tens of thousands of *talatat* found buried mainly within the core of the Second, Ninth and Tenth Pylons, but also in smaller quantities from various parts of Karnak and from other localities such as

Luxor and Medamud. These small sandstone blocks, with approximate dimensions of 52 cm × 26 cm × 22 cm, were devised and used by Amenhotep IV's architects for the speedy erection of buildings at Karnak, and later at Akhetaten. It should be remembered that despite their huge numbers, these *talatat* were in themselves small blocks of narrow width, and consequently great walls built solely of these would have been inherently unstable. The *talatat* should be considered therefore as facing blocks to both sides of mud-brick walls, thereby giving much greater stability.

Just how extensive Amenhotep IV's work at Karnak was has only recently been appreciated. The names of many newly constructed buildings at Karnak feature in the *talatat* inscriptions; however, several of these may simply have formed various parts of the four major structures which have been identified (Redford 1984: 63). The first of these was the *Gm-p3-'Itn* (translated as He-whom-the-Sun-Disk-has-Found): its existence had been known from early in the twentieth century, when it came to light during the modern digging works for Karnak's drainage canal. The temple was situated well to the east, outside Karnak's enclosure wall, and initially it was assumed that Amenhotep IV had wished to build his deity's temple away from the contaminated ground of Amun's residence, but this is probably not the case since some *talatat* actually infer a continuing cult of Amun at this early stage (Redford 1980: 22), probably side by side with the new cult of the Sun Disk (Aldred 1988: 263). Certainly a high priest of Amun, named May, is attested from a quarry inscription as late as Year 4 of Amenhotep IV's reign (Gabolde, M. 1998: 26). The more likely premise is that for a major temple like the *Gm-p3-'Itn* he needed the open space that existed to the east: his father, it should be remembered, had extended Karnak to the west by erecting the great Third Pylon, to the south by building the Tenth Pylon and the temple of Mut, and to the north the Montu complex. It seemed that his son had only one direction left which provided him with the space he required.

The *Gm-p3-'Itn* temple, therefore, was erected to the east of Karnak's enclosure wall, and despite being a construction of considerable dimensions (roughly 130 m × 216 m), its destruction was so complete that no foundations or piles of tumbled masonry were left to speak of its one-time existence. After decades of excavation and research, the temple has slowly yielded some of its secrets although, inevitably, many tantalising gaps and questions remain. The *Gm-p3-'Itn* stood within its own mud-brick enclosure and was orientated to the east, thus making it likely that there had once been a monumental approach from the west, but the destruction was such that this cannot be verified. However, an entry has been found midway in the western wall of the temple itself giving access through a colonnaded 'corridor' 11 m wide overall but with an entry width between the pillars of the corridor of only 4.5 m (Redford 1994: 488 and fig. 1). The intriguing aspect of this entrance is that the corridor has been found to originate somewhere within the present enclosure wall of Karnak (built much later by Nectanebo I), and seems to have run parallel to the north wall of the Dynasty XVIII temple (Redford 1994: 491). This has given rise to the suggestion that it led directly from the palace (sited to the north-west of Karnak) to the *Gm-p3-'Itn*, particularly since the majority of the scenes recovered from the corridor show repeated processions between palace and temple. It seems likely that Amenhotep IV took over the palace of his father 'Nebmaatre-is-the-Shining-Sun-Disk', renaming it in a somewhat similar style: '(Amenhotep)-rejoices-in-the-Horizon-of-the-Sun-Disk' (O'Connor 1995: 276–7). Some blocks depicting a large domain, very much in the

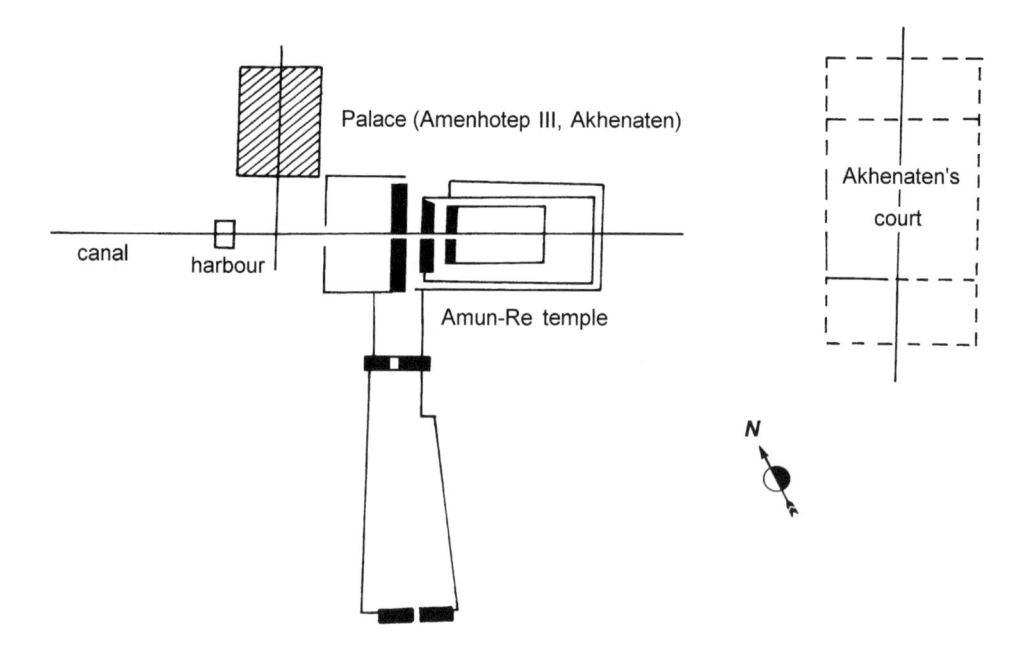

Figure 9.1 Possible siting of the palace of Amenhotep III and Akhenaten (after O'Connor, D., in *Ancient Egyptian Kingship*: 80, fig. 7.3).

Amarna style, showing luxurious accommodation surrounded by pavilioned gardens, have been found reused in various places around Karnak. Were these perhaps a depiction of the palace (Fig. 9.1)?

The entrance corridor of the *Gm-p3-'Itn* led into an open court surrounded by a peristyle of square pillars spaced 2 m apart; to the south of this court against each of the piers stood a colossus of Amenhotep IV, depicting him with the strange physical characteristics that have occasioned so much comment. The court's north side seems to have accommodated statues of different types, some of which were of the queen, Nefertiti (Redford 1994: 487). The walls of the court, all constructed of *talatat*, bore detailed scenes of the sed-festival – scenes which surprisingly retain much of the old iconography, including a few of the traditional gods and their emblems, perhaps because they were considered indispensable in the celebration of this ancient festival. Its name, the Court of the Great Ones, is perhaps significant in this context. Study of the surviving *talatat* has raised the possibility that the scenes on the north wall depicted rites related to Lower Egypt, and those on the south to Upper Egypt (Gohary 1992: 167–8; Redford 1984: 127), but this cannot be stated with complete certainty as yet. Since the sed-festival scenes that have been recovered all derive from the *Gm-p3-'Itn*, it is safe to assume that this temple was constructed especially for the celebration that took place in Year 2 to 3: and it is clear why Amenhotep's architects chose to use the small *talatat* blocks when faced with the task of erecting such a sizeable monument in so short a timescale.

Other monuments were to follow: notably a building named *Ḥwt-bnbn* (Mansion of the Benben) devoted to a solar cult, as its name might imply – the *bnbn* being the cult object in early Heliopolitan sun-temples. This structure was erected a little later in east Karnak, possibly within the confines of the *Gm-p3-'Itn* itself, but more probably adjacent to it: in any event, the *Ḥwt-bnbn* appears to have had a close association with the *Gm-p3-'Itn* since its full name was the *Ḥwt-bnbn-m-Gmt-p3-'Itn-m-pr-'Itn* (The Mansion of the Benben in *Gmt-p3-'Itn* in the house of the Aten). It should be noted immediately that whenever the full writing of the *Ḥwt-bnbn* was employed, the name of the *Gm-p3-'Itn* was written with the 't' feminine ending, i.e. *Gmt-p3-'Itn* (She-whom-the-Sun-Disk-has-Found) (Gohary 1979: 30). This is of particular interest when the decoration of the *Ḥwt-bnbn* is studied. When the many thousands of *talatat* deriving from all four monuments began to be analysed, it soon became apparent that Nefertiti was depicted much more frequently than her husband in the reliefs, more than twice as often in fact. The difference was too marked to be dismissed as being due to mere chance survival, and it was soon realised that a huge number of them derived from a building in which the queen featured as the sole officiant, making the offerings and performing the rituals – the king was nowhere to be seen: Nefertiti, and Nefertiti alone, was represented within this temple – the *Ḥwt-bnbn* (Redford 1984: 78). This was unprecedented since, in theory, the reigning monarch was the chief priest of all the gods and it was therefore the king alone who could be depicted performing the offering and other rites. This clear diversion from the accepted tradition makes the *Ḥwt-bnbn* all the more amazing, as it would seem to imply that here at Karnak there were complementary buildings (the *Gm-p3-'Itn* and the *Gmt-p3-'Itn*) representing the male and female aspects of the religion, other instances of which are known from this so-called Amarna period. Eric Hornung comments on the fact that Akhenaten refers to the Aten as the 'mother-father' god (Hornung 1983: 171).

The layout of this fascinating structure is unknown, but it certainly had a hall or colonnade of tall slender pillars, over 10 m in height, with courts fronted by elegant pylons whose entrances were topped with the 'broken' lintels, so typical of the Amarna architectural style. All the pillars were square: three sides bore identical reliefs, occupying the full length of the pillar, which depicted the queen, sometimes followed by a small daughter, shaking sistra in adoration of the god; the fourth side (presumably that which faced into the court) was divided into four registers, each showing the queen offering to the Aten (Fig. 9.2).

It has been suggested that a colonnade of these so-called 'Nefertiti pillars' had also stood somewhere in advance of Karnak's main entrance (the Third Pylon) (Loeben 1994: 41–3). The evidence for this lies in the fact that many of the *talatat* forming these pillars were found to have been deposited in roughly their original assembled state within the core of the Second Pylon, built later by Horemheb; it was thought that he had simply subsumed them where they stood into the pylon's masonry. However, some of the pillars appeared to have been deliberately up-ended and thus buried upside-down within the pylon (Smith and Redford 1976: 34); consequently, with no foundations to give any clue, this theory, as with so many others concerning the Amarna period, can only be considered speculation.

The existence of such a building (or buildings), in which Nefertiti alone was featured, poses many questions, particularly as several other instances of her prominent role at Karnak can be cited. One of the most noteworthy is the fact that she was on occasion represented in traditional male mode, such as wielding the mace or sword in scenes of smiting Egypt's enemies, while her throne is shown with prostrate captives around its base, and her carrying chair depicts her as a sphinx trampling foreign foes. It could

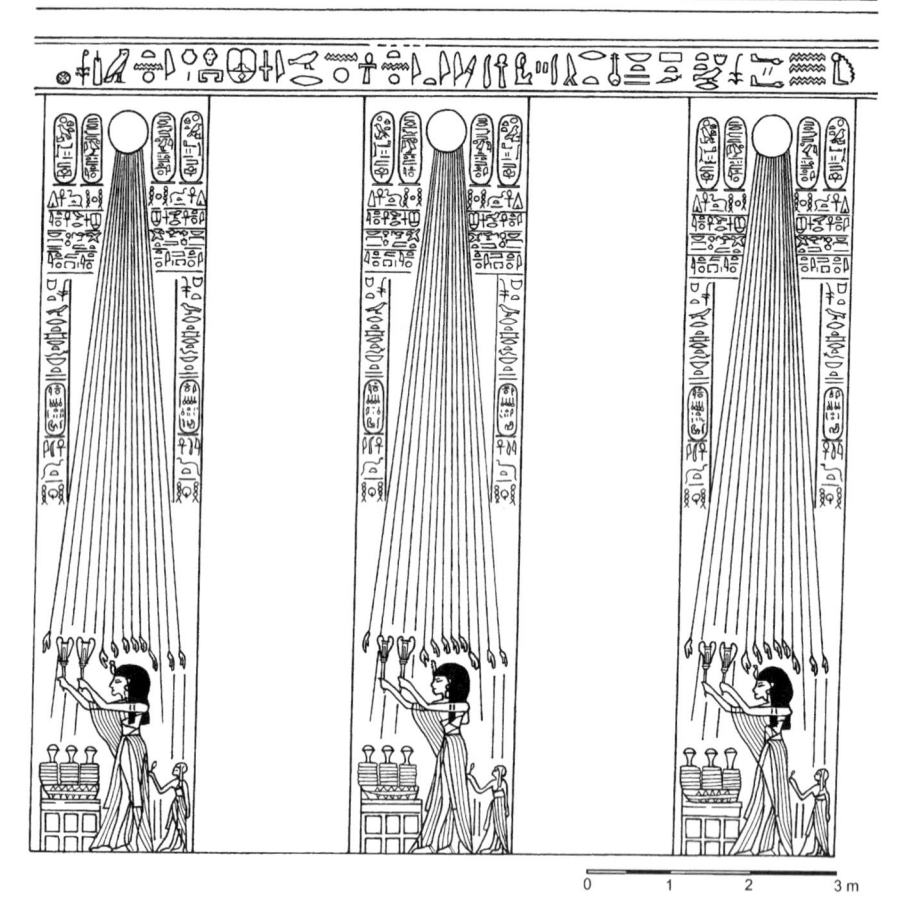

Figure 9.2 The 'Nefertiti pillars' in the *Ḥwt-bnbn* (after Redford, D., *Akhenaten, the Heretic King*: 77).

be argued that Hatshepsut, some centuries earlier, provided a precedent for some of these, but, unlike Hatshepsut, Nefertiti was not (according to the orthodox view) Queen Regnant and, again unlike her predecessor, her attire remained purely feminine. Nevertheless, further evidence of her prominence can be seen in the many reliefs that show her at Amenhotep's side receiving foreign tribute and homage, and assisting him in the distribution of rewards to loyal followers. But perhaps the most impressive evidence of her seeming equality with the king rests in the sphinx-lined avenue on the southern approach to Karnak, referred to in the previous chapter, where she and her husband were represented alternately in the form of human-headed sphinxes along that route (or possibly along a ceremonial approach to the *Gm-p3-'Itn* temple – see previous chapter): truly a unique testament to the queen's importance, and another example of the male/female emphasis already mentioned. However, the theory that Amenhotep IV and Nefertiti had reigned as co-rulers cannot be seriously entertained when it is observed how much the queen's role diminished after the move to Amarna in Year 5. The reason for this comparatively sudden and very marked decline in her prominence is hard to account for, and has given rise to yet more speculation. It would seem that the Theban triad of Amun, Mut and Khonsu, were transcribed into a new triad of Aten, king and queen, or god, male and female: a trinity that certainly seems to have been continued at Amarna.

The other two major monuments of Amenhotep IV at Karnak have been identified as *Tni-mnw-n-'Itn-r-nḥḥ* (Exalted-are-the-monuments-of-the-Aten-for-ever) and *Rwḏ-mnw-n-'Itn-r-nḥḥ* (Enduring-are-the-monuments-of-the-Aten-for-ever). These two structures had reliefs of offerings scenes, and in these it is Amenhotep who performed the rites. Other reliefs show the king and Nefertiti within a building that had double pylon towers at its entrance and a Window of Appearance, as well as many scenes of royal processions in chariots or palanquins, accompanied by soldiers, military officials, fan-bearers and courtiers of all kinds. Domestic scenes proliferate, with servants carrying wine jars and plates heaped with food, and also attending to such tasks as baking, brewing and grinding flour. The large number of scenes depicting the royal chariot and also the palanquin, is very noticeable (Lauffray 1979: 175–6) and appears linked to the appearance of the king in glory. This has led to a suggestion that perhaps these items were viewed as liturgical and processional objects – possibly a substitute for the sacred bark (Chappaz 1987: 114). Inscriptions accompanying such scenes make references to 'the great chariot of electrum like the Aton when he appears on the horizon'.

So what were these two sizeable edifices in which there was so much action, and where had they stood? Initially it was thought that one of them (the *Rwḏ-mnw*) must have been the palace, but probably they were cultic buildings, associated perhaps with the feasting that always accompanied the sed-festival celebrations. It is noticeable that no living quarters were indicated at all in either building: a feature that would certainly have been found within a palace complex.

As to their siting, there is virtually no evidence: the only clues lie, first, in the fact that the vast majority of their *talatat* were found in the Ninth Pylon and, second, that the names *Tni-mnw* and *Rwḏ-mnw* had formed part of the names of earlier buildings somewhere in this southern area of Karnak (Redford 1973: 85). It is noteworthy, also, that amongst the scenes from the *Tni-mnw talatat* are reliefs that show an area where birds were kept, presumably for offerings. It seems probable that this was the fowl-yard or aviary built by Tuthmosis III, and rebuilt and used by subsequent kings, that was close to the Sacred Lake.

However, when one looks at what space might have been available to accommodate these two substantial monuments, one is forced to conclude that the area to the east of Karnak was probably the only contender. A point worthy of consideration is that the *Gm-p3-'Itn*, as we know, was sited to the east of Karnak in the area lying north of the great temple's main east–west axis, with the southern wall of the *Gm-p3-'Itn* lying flush with that axis. Bearing in mind the ancient Egyptians' love of symmetry, it would seem reasonably logical to visualise the *Tni-mnw* and/or the *Rwḏ-mnw* as being sited on the southern side of that same axis, thus balancing the *Gm-p3-'Itn*.

In addition, the *Ḥwt-bnbn*, as mentioned above, was closely associated with the *Gm-p3-'Itn* and must also have been situated in this general area, and there is another indication as to the siting of this particular building. The *bnbn*-stone was a squat pyramidion-shaped object found in temples of the Heliopolitan solar cult, but in the case of the *Ḥwt-bnbn* at Karnak, the determinative attached to the writing of the name was always an obelisk, not the true *bnbn* symbol (Redford 1984: 74–5). Is it possible, therefore, to envisage that Nefertiti's temple was built adjacent to, or focused upon,

THE NEW KINGDOM

Plate 9.1 Shattered block showing a rare example of the cartouche of Akhenaten at Karnak.

the great single obelisk of Tuthmosis III (erected by Tuthmosis IV) in east Karnak (Vergnieux 1999: 156–8)? Unless further excavations should bring to light the remains of foundations for any of these buildings, it will remain uncertain.

Not until the very end of his residence in Thebes did Amenhotep IV change his name to Akhenaten: at the same time changing his Two Ladies name from 'Great-of-Kingship-in-Karnak' to 'Great-of-Kingship-in-Akhetaten' (Redford 1984: 149). This final rejection of every aspect relating to the god Amun, closely followed by the king's decision to leave Thebes and build a new city dedicated to the Aten, occurred in Year 5 of his reign. At his instruction, workmen commenced the task of chiselling out and plastering over every occurrence of the hated name Amenhotep and substituting Akhenaten in its place. When it is considered the number and size of the monuments of Amenhotep IV at Thebes, and of course elsewhere in Egypt, the enormity of the undertaking can be appreciated.

Tutankhamun and Ay

It is hard to imagine the scale of the impact that Akhenaten's religious 'revolution' had upon Egypt. Perhaps it impinged little upon the day-to-day existence of the general population, but upon the temples of Amun and their priesthoods, it is probably no exaggeration to say that the effect must have been cataclysmic. Certainly the scale of the destruction at Karnak, as elsewhere throughout the land, was vast, and much of it is still visible today; nonetheless, the damage was limited to an attempt to eradicate all visible signs of the name and image of Amun, as well as those of Egypt's other deities – with the exception of those gods whom Akhenaten himself had acknowledged, such as Re-Horakhte and Maat. Consequently, it was the reliefs, decorations and inscriptions that were the target of his destructive zeal rather than the buildings themselves. His determination to expunge the hated name of Amun from the record even extended to hacking out the first element of his own father's name, Amenhotep.

The many uncertainties concerning the death of Akhenaten and the brief reign of his ephemeral successor, Smenkhkare, may never be resolved, but it seems that Akhenaten's religion did not immediately die with him: it was to continue through Smenkhkare's reign and into that of Tutankhaton, only a boy at the time of his succession. The young king had, however, two powerful and wily advisers in the persons of Ay, his tutor, who had previously been a courtier and confidant of Akhenaten, and Horemheb, the Commander-in-Chief of the army. It was they who were instrumental in bringing the new king and his court back to Memphis, changing his name to Tutankhamun and, at the same time, reinstating the old religion and its gods, re-opening the temples and renewing the cults, especially that of Amun at Thebes. To these great programmes of regeneration and renewal, Tutankhamun put his name, but it was without doubt a plan of action instigated by his two powerful mentors.

The relationship between these influential men and their young charge was a complex one which engenders much debate even today. Who truly held the balance of power? Certainly it was not Tutankhamun himself, who was probably only about nine years of age when he became king. Various theories abound. Let us look at what Karnak might have to tell us on this score.

The most famous monument of Tutankhamun at Karnak is a large red granite stela, 2.5 m tall and incised with blue inlaid hieroglyphs, which stood against the Third Pylon – the temple entrance at that time – proclaiming the renewal of the Theban cult of Amun. For this reason it has been dubbed the Restoration Stela (Bennett 1939: 8–15), and its importance was such that a copy was erected in the temple of Montu at North Karnak: and although only some fragments of this second stela have survived, they are sufficient to prove that the two texts were identical. At the same time (and doubtless under the aegis of Ay and Horemheb), Tutankhaton was prevailed upon to change his name to Tutankhamun and to return to Thebes, thus strengthening the position of the king and the entire court.

The stela announced the young king's intention to suppress the evil which had engulfed the Two Lands and to make the temples 'flower anew'. If his words are to be taken literally, it must have been a huge undertaking – monuments were overgrown with weeds, shrines were deserted, halls and courts were used as public footpaths, and everywhere was a scene of desolation. But can this really be an accurate picture? Did Karnak actually stand empty during this entire period? Did so vast a temple fall into such a state of decay in what was a comparatively short space of time? Or was the Restoration Stela's description of the ruined temples somewhat exaggerated – perhaps a form of propaganda? With Akhenaten himself residing permanently at Akhetaten (Amarna), the boundaries of which he had vowed never to leave, can the entire priesthood of Amun truly have abandoned their god and their beliefs immediately and totally? Could it be that, during those intervening years, a few devout priests had quietly continued their daily rituals in some kind of private 'caretaker' capacity; or, alternatively, had they been persecuted and driven out by Akhenaten's iconoclasts?

We cannot know the answer to any of these questions: we have only the statements contained on the stela itself. They describe clearly the ruinous state of the temples which obviously had, first and foremost, to be restored; then the clergy must be reinstated and the cults revived; statues, altars, divine barks, incense burners, sacred vessels and implements for the necessary rituals of temple ceremony – all must be recreated, bigger and better than ever as Tutankhamun's own words tell us (Bennett 1939: 9):

> His Majesty meditated in his heart as to what was beneficial ... he fashioned an august statue of his father Amun upon thirteen carrying-poles; the holy image being of fine gold, lapis-lazuli, turquoise and every rare costly stone. Formerly, the majesty of this god had been upon (only) eleven carrying-poles.

The king then goes on to say that he built new monuments and new sanctuaries, endowing them with property; he re-established the cults and supplied them with rich offerings; he re-instated the priesthood and filled the temple storehouses with 'silver, gold, lapis lazuli, turquoise, rare and precious stones, linen, white cloth, oil, unguents, incense, myrrh ...'. Finally, the king commissioned new sacred barks to be fashioned from cedar-wood and worked with gold and precious metals, so that they should 'illumine the river'.

Tutankhamun, perhaps more than any other ruler, made a point of associating himself very visibly with Amun. In the circumstances in which he found himself, this was probably expedient. The policy can be seen clearly in the great number of statues which still exist of the young king assuming the form of Amun, as his very name – 'the Living Image of Amun' – implies. Although Amenhotep III seems to have been the first king to have adopted the use of the rebus (Johnson 2001: 88), it is noticeable with what frequency and upon what great variety of artefacts Tutankhamun employed the device.

Monuments of a lesser scale were not ignored. There survives a virtually complete restoration text of Tutankhamun engraved on a gateway from the time of Amenhotep III: 'The King of Upper and Lower Egypt, Lord of the Two Lands, Nebkheperure. He renewed the monument for his father Amun-Re, making for him a large storehouse anew for it had fallen into great ruin' (Schaden 1987a: 10). Furthermore, a sandstone stela, now in a storage magazine, depicts Tutankhamun standing before Amun, Mut and Senusret I. Once again, the ruling king desires to ally himself to Karnak's great founder – particularly appropriate perhaps at such a time of renewal.

To create order (*m3't*) out of chaos was the prime duty of every Egyptian ruler, and with his huge programme of restoration, it would be true to say that Tutankhamun did indeed fulfil this vital function.

However, so ambitious an undertaking, with all its attendant problems of organisation, finance and administration, can hardly have been the vision of a nine-year-old boy. Once again we are left wondering which of the king's two mentors was responsible: Ay or Horemheb. It was certainly Horemheb who usurped the Restoration Stela when he himself acquired the kingship, replacing Tutankhamun's cartouche with his own; possibly he felt it was no more than his due to lay claim to the honour of being the one who had restored the old religion, since he certainly was one of the 'strong men' of Tutankhamun's reign and in all probability had been the one who had made the decisions and got the work done. On the other hand, in the lunette at the top of the stela, it appears to be Ay who stands behind Tutankhamun, as he does on several other monuments of the young king. Was it Ay, therefore, who held the true power in Tutankhamun's reign, possibly in the capacity of regent, while Horemheb, an admittedly powerful official, was limited to implementing the decrees and commands of Tutankhamun/Ay? Moreover, Horemheb, in his capacity of head of the army, would have been engaged in securing Egypt's empire and borders, and restoring her power abroad following the disastrous Amarna era. Indeed, if it were *not* Ay who held the power, it is difficult to see how this elderly and somewhat colourless figure managed to succeed to the throne upon Tutankhamun's death. The other possibility to be considered is that Ay and Horemheb might have come to some kind of agreement between them, which at a time of such uncertainty, might well have been a wise expedient. But nonetheless, it should be remembered that, during this time, Horemheb began to construct for himself an admittedly lavish private tomb at Saqqara, but one in which there was little hint of any royal ambition, other than, perhaps, a scene where conquered foreigners are brought before him rather than the king. Ay, it seems, was the acknowledged and undisputed sovereign.

Apart from the Restoration Stela, there are only a few traces of the building programme undertaken in the temple of Amun during the reigns of Tutankhamun and Ay. Wherever such remains exist, they have all been ruthlessly usurped by Horemheb, as have the young king's restoration works. Yet Tutankhamun's work at Karnak was more extensive than is commonly realised and, while no building of his or of Ay remains standing, evidence testifying to their work continues to come to light. Tutankhamun's processional way between the Tenth Pylon and the Mut complex has already been touched upon, and several statues of the king still grace Karnak's precinct, most notably the red quartzite dyad of Amun and Amunet, in which the god's features are clearly those of the young ruler himself. In addition to these, an alabaster sphinx of Tutankhamun, once one of a pair, stands today against the southern upright of the entrance to Taharqa's kiosk, which precedes the Second Pylon; in the same area are two sandstone socles or altar bases. It is possible that these elements are the remnants of the Dynasty XVIII quay and perhaps a prototype of the later quay which even now has similar elements visible. Originally the two sphinxes would have stood at the foot of a gentle ramp that led to the quay, while the socles would have held two small obelisks – as their later counterparts do today.

In addition, there is some evidence, albeit meagre, of a possible gateway or substantial wall erected by Tutankhamun; its existence has been surmised from the discovery (in the area south of Karnak's main entrance) of a large and heavy block bearing his cartouches which, from its very dimensions, does not appear to belong to any of the known buildings of the young king. To add to the block's interest, it can be seen that Tutankhamun's cartouches have been usurped by both Horemheb and Ramesses II, indicating that this edifice remained in place for some considerable time. Finally, remnants are known of a limestone construction – perhaps a small shrine – bearing Tutankhamun's name in raised relief; these fragments appear to be reused *talatat*, so its date is probably very early in his reign.

The most interesting remains, however, are a series of architectural elements – blocks, lintels, architraves and the like – from a sandstone building of Tutankhamun and Ay, which have been discovered in various locations around Karnak, though the majority were found within the cores of the Second and Ninth Pylons (both of which were erected by Horemheb). Some of the elements were of a considerable size, and included parts of a pillared hall: it is clear that this was a monument of imposing dimensions. It is not certain, however, whether these elements derive from one or two buildings, but if it were only one, there certainly must have been two separate stages in its construction. One feature of the blocks which implies that they might have derived from separate buildings is that the names of two monuments are discernible: *Ḥwt Nb-ḫprw-Rʿ mri 'Imn grg W3st*, 'The Mansion of Nebkheperure, beloved of Amun, re-establishing Thebes', whose blocks were interred principally in the Ninth Pylon; and *Ḥwt Nb-ḫprw-Rʿ m W3st*, 'The Mansion of Nebkheperure in Thebes', the blocks from which were mostly found in the Second Pylon.

The first-mentioned monument, as its name implies, must have been constructed by Tutankhamun as part of his task to rebuild and enhance Karnak. In this particular building (or stage of building) Ay is associated with the king solely as a high official (possibly regent or vizier (Eaton-Krauss 1988: 3)), and named with his habitual appellation of Divine Father. What *was* the meaning of this enigmatic title? It was not a particularly rare one, and was held on occasion by high-ranking members of court, though for what purpose we are unsure. However, Ay obviously set great store by it, and it is thought that the title perhaps indicated a close personal connection to the royal family, either by blood or through marriage. Could this be the reason that Ay was able to succeed to the kingship? Whatever the answer, after the death of Tutankhamun, Ay kept his title of Divine Father, enclosing it within his own cartouche. This can be seen quite clearly on blocks from the second monument, 'The Mansion of Nebkheperure in Thebes'. Here Ay is depicted as king, his name given everywhere as the King of Upper and Lower Egypt, Son of Re, followed by his cartouches (Eaton-Krauss 1988: 4); yet within this second structure Tutankhamun also featured prominently. The decoration, though greatly damaged, is interesting: apart from standard religious themes, there are scenes of hunting and chariotry, and many military scenes showing troops with weapons, boats manned by soldiers, Nubian and Asiatic prisoners, and scenes of tribute. All these are shown in great detail, which raises the possibility that they portray genuine campaigns of Tutankhamun's reign. If that is indeed the case, then they must have been conducted by Horemheb, even if the young king had been in attendance. Obviously, re-establishing Egypt's power abroad was one of the priorities in the task of restoring the country to normality.

However, there are further reliefs that are unusual: these are, surprisingly, of a funerary nature. Throughout this second building, Ay states that he 'made it as his monument for his son, the Good God, Lord of the Two Lands, Nebkheperure', and he claims also that it was built for Tutankhamun as a 'Temple of Millions of Years'. The funerary inference in this is quite clear – but even more explicit is a relief that shows a funerary tent before which stands a procession of priests with standards; what remains of the inscription refers to 'who makes true-of-voice, [Nebkheperu]re . . .'. In the upper register, a line of mourners is depicted in attitudes of grief, behind whom can be seen several men dragging a small bark (Schaden 1988: 175). There seems little doubt that these are scenes of Tutankhamun's funeral.

What can be made of these puzzling and fragmentary scenes and inscriptions? Are we dealing with two separate structures, one built by Tutankhamun and a later one by Ay, or was this a single monument commenced by Tutankhamun and completed after his death by Ay, who dedicated it as a memorial to 'his son'? The evidence, such as it is, is not conclusive either way. However, it is something of a landmark construction, being the first known structure at Karnak to contain a funerary element; later in Karnak's history we shall see another.

There is no evidence for the siting of this monument, but a possible location has been suggested against the outside of the east wall of the Court of the Cachette, facing the Sacred Lake (Sa'ad 1975: 108). This theory was proposed on account of two symmetrical reliefs carved on this wall depicting Tutankhamun before the Theban triad, which was thought to have formed the rear wall of the monument. However, this location is disputed, and until there has been a detailed excavation of the site, the theory cannot be verified or otherwise. The centre of these two flanking scenes has fallen down, but its blocks lie on the ground and can be seen to show reliefs dedicated to Renenutet, goddess of the harvest, before whom stands Hapi, the Nile god, offering bread, fruit and flowers. One of Tutankhamun's titles is known to have been 'beloved of Renenutet', and certainly the goddess had a cult at Karnak. However, the scenes inscribed here, which show signs of having been encrusted with precious metals, seem to signify a most important area of the temple where offerings from the magazines, that were situated close to the Sacred Lake, were consecrated before entering the sacred area proper. Consequently, if this was an area specifically appointed for the dedication of

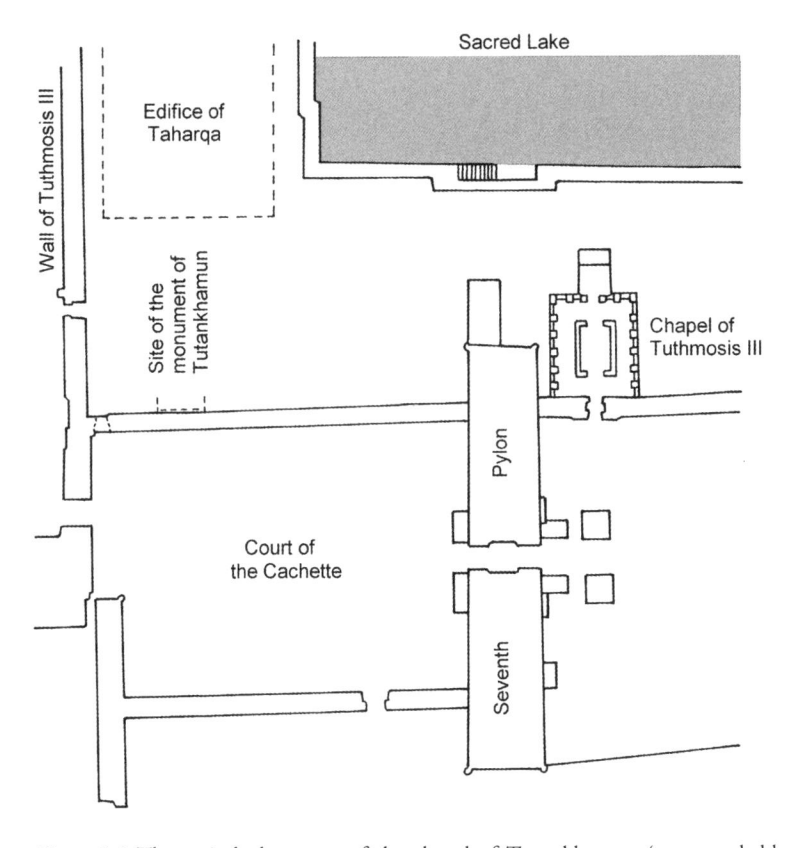

Figure 9.3 Theoretical placement of the chapel of Tutankhamun (more probably an area for the consecration of offerings) (after Sa'ad, R., in *Cahiers de Karnak* V: 107).

divine offerings, then it cannot have been the site of the Mansion-of-Nebkheperure-in-Thebes, which was more probably to be found somewhere on the main approach to the temple entrance (Fig. 9.3).

The remains of another stela of Tutankhamun (Schaden 1987b: 279), currently stored in one of the magazines at Karnak, has been linked to the offering chapel, mentioned above, although its precise location is not known (Le Saout and Ma'arouf 1987: 288). This was originally a large sandstone slab of considerable thickness, obviously free-standing since it was decorated on both faces as well as down its two sides. The king's cartouches are worshipped by *rekhyt*-birds, indicating that this stela might have stood where it could be seen by the few privileged personnel who had access to the courts of the southern processional way, though not to the heart of Ipet-Sut. On one side of the stela, the king is depicted offering a figure of the goddess Maat, the ultimate offering symbol, to Amun and Mut, while other scenes show multiple offerings of fruit, flowers and bouquets. In addition, as with the rear wall of the putative offering chapel itself, the stela was originally encrusted with gold and faience plaques.

After Tutankhamun's death, Ay appears to have continued the restoration programme at Karnak; his cartouches can still be seen on various structures, although invariably usurped or defaced by Horemheb.

Ay was a capable man, who has never really been given his full due. His career was completely overshadowed by the Amarna period with its many contentious issues, and later by the discovery of Tutankhamun's tomb with its fabulous treasures, which captured the world's imagination. Yet Ay must have been a most astute politician having spent the earlier years of his career as Akhenaten's tutor and adviser, and yet subsequently managing to retain the influence to steer Egypt back to orthodoxy. Eventually he was to rise to the highest office of all – that of pharaoh. But it was not a position he was to hold for long: by now he was an elderly man and his reign lasted only four years. Upon his death, the way was at last clear for the strong and ambitious commander of the army, Horemheb, to pick up the reins of supreme power.

10

HOREMHEB

The transfer of royal power to Horemheb seems to have taken place smoothly and with no sign of opposition. Possibly he had already made a pact with the powerful priesthood of Amun. It is significant perhaps that in his coronation decree, Horemheb stated that he appointed priests 'from the pick of the army'. As the former Commander-in-Chief, had he already placed his supporters in these influential positions during the short reign of Ay in order to facilitate his own elevation to the throne?

The coronation ceremony was of immense importance to Horemheb through which he sought to emphasise his legitimacy to the throne: an importance that he showed time and again in the coronation edict which he had inscribed on the back of a great black granite pair statue at Karnak (now in the Museo Egizeo, Turin, no. 1379) of himself and his queen Mutnodjmet. A second version of this edict was found in the Temple of Ptah at Memphis and a third in the Montu Temple at North Karnak: in fact, this latter inscription contains the significant phrase: 'It is commanded in heaven and heard in the temple of Ipet-Sut' (Davies, B. 1995: 70 l. 9).

The earlier part of Horemheb's life had been very much centred upon Memphis, the administrative capital, in the necropolis of which he had constructed a splendid tomb for himself and his family. His birthplace, too, was in the northern part of Egypt, probably in the town of Henen-Nesut, near the entrance to the Fayum, to which area he retained strong ties. Yet it was in the great temple of Amun-Re at Karnak in Thebes that he chose to hold his coronation, linking the ceremony there with the Festival of Opet at Luxor temple, thus tying himself irrevocably to the state religion of Amun-Re (Gardiner 1953: 22).

Horemheb was not of royal blood (although his queen was probably related to the Amarna royal family)(Grajetzki 2005: 65) and so he felt it necessary to employ a considerable amount of propaganda in establishing his credentials as a rightful heir to the Throne of the Two Lands. He described his career as a path that the gods had mapped out for him from birth, leading him inevitably towards kingship – he was their choice, and their favour was stressed by him again and again. By choosing Karnak as the site of his coronation, he was publicly allying himself with Amun-Re: 'Then did Horus proceed amid rejoicing ... to Ipet-Sut in order to induct him (Horemheb) into the presence of Amun for the handing over to him his office of king.'

It is a measure of the success of Horemheb's propaganda that he was later to be considered as the first legitimate king to rule after Amenhotep III (Gardiner 1953: 21): Akhenaten, Smenkhkare, Tutankhamun and Ay were all ignored since they were deemed to be tainted by their connection with Atenism.

We have seen in the previous chapter that Horemheb usurped almost all the restoration work carried out by both Tutankhamun and Ay, as well as their buildings at Karnak. However, he himself also undertook some restoration work, and in particular he restored many of the monuments of Tuthmosis III; in fact, on the wall between the Sixth Pylon and the bark sanctuary, he made a point of recording this particular work. Tuthmosis III was a king he clearly revered: perhaps his admiration was that of one soldier for another; certainly he would have admired the powerful and effective kingship exercised by Tuthmosis. Moreover, there is no doubt that Horemheb would have wished to associate himself firmly with the great kings of Dynasty XVIII.

In studying the blocks of the Mansion-of-Nebkheperure-in-Thebes, it is apparent that initially Horemheb had considered associating himself on that monument with Tutankhamun as his 'son' by replacing Ay's cartouches with his own and by abrading Ay's face, then polishing and recutting the stone in his own likeness. However, it seems that at some point he altered his mind and demolished the building (Eaton-Krauss 1988: 11). Despite wishing to appear as the legitimate successor by associating himself with Tutankhamun, it might be that Horemheb felt it was not expedient to display so visible a link with the Amarna period, and for this reason dismantled the monument. Or perhaps it was more mundane than that: since the Mansion-of-Nebkheperure-in-Thebes was located somewhere on the main approach to Karnak, Horemheb might well have demolished it in order to make way for the construction of the Second Pylon.

Horemheb was perhaps justified in taking, as one of the elements of his royal titulary, the Two Ladies name of 'Great of Marvels in Ipet-Sut', for great marvels he did indeed produce by constructing no less than three new pylons at Karnak: a great new main entrance to the temple (the Second Pylon), and two more pylons (the Ninth and Tenth) to extend the southern approach. It was an enormous undertaking. These massive entrances were, of course, highly symbolic in their form: the two great pylon towers represented the eastern and western horizons of Egypt between which the sun – in the form of a winged solar disc carved upon the lintel over the central gateway – was depicted as rising in a permanent act of creation (Fig. 10.1).

Until very recently, the Second Pylon had been in a parlous state of repair, which was due in part, so it was thought, to its having been built upon the site of the basin and quay that had served the Dynasty XVIII temple (as illustrated in Neferhotep's tomb (Davies, N. 1933b: pl. XLII)). This basin (if indeed it existed) was drained and filled mostly with fresh desert sand which did not provide sufficient stability for the mighty edifice that Horemheb erected, and as early as the Ptolemaic period, repair work to the towers had become necessary. By the time French excavators arrived at Karnak a century or more ago, the pylon was in danger of total collapse. Today, it has been dismantled and reconstructed, and we are able to appreciate some of its former glory.

The Second Pylon was even greater than Amenhotep III's Third Pylon, measuring about 98 m across, 14 m deep, and with a gateway over 30 m high – a truly imposing entrance. It was constructed of sandstone and had eight towering flagstaffs, each about 40 m in height, fitted into niches in the pylon's western face. Each flagstaff was fashioned from a single trunk of cedar-of-Lebanon, its lower end encased in bronze and its tip plated with electrum, from which fluttered long pennants. Against the northern massif the flagstaffs rested on bases of limestone and alabaster, and against the southern on bases of red and grey granite. The great doors of the pylon are now missing, but would have been constructed of precious wood from Asia, swung on huge

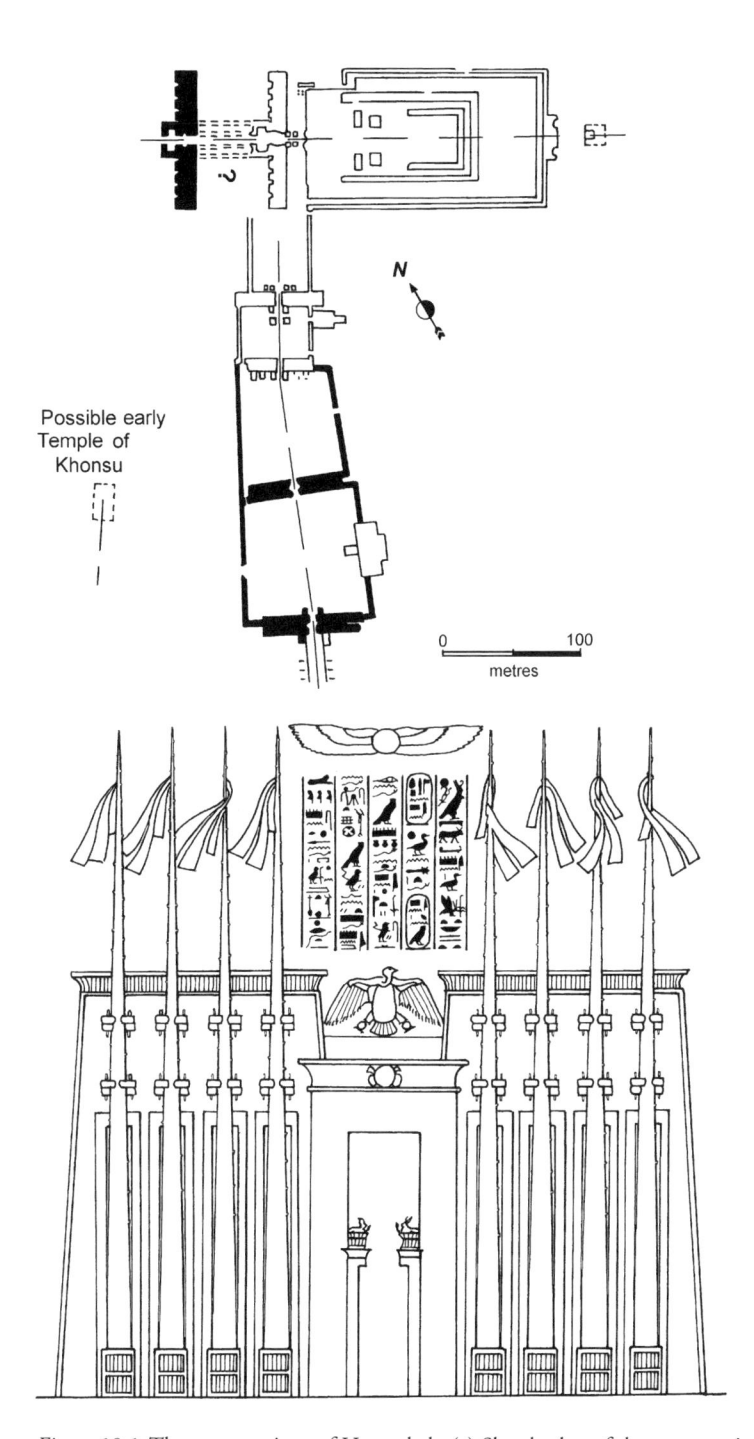

Figure 10.1 The constructions of Horemheb. (a) Sketch plan of the constructions (shown in black), (after Aufrère, S., *L'Égypte Restituée*: 98). (b) Façade of the Second Pylon as depicted on the walls of the temple of Khonsu (after Aldred, C. *et al.*, *Les Pharaons: l'Empire des Conquérants*: 306).

bronze hinges and closed with bronze bolts; the door-leaves would have been plated with copper and inlaid with gold or electrum. This whole magnificent façade bore the name of 'Illuminating Thebes', which is truly how it must have appeared to any of the awe-struck inhabitants of that city who gazed upon it, but who could never gain access to the divine power-house within, the pylons of which formed an impenetrable barrier to the sacred precincts.

It is small wonder that the Second Pylon's splendour inspired later kings to inscribe its likeness elsewhere: upon the walls of the nearby Temple of Khonsu, upon the side of a doorway adjacent to the Eighth Pylon, and in the great colonnade of Luxor Temple. It is thanks to these detailed representations that we learn of the special association that the great flagstaffs had with individual goddesses. The eight soaring wooden shafts were each dedicated to a goddess: 'The King of Upper and Lower Egypt ... has made it as his monument for his father Amun-Re: the flagpole Renutet ...'. Each pole bore an identical dedication text ending with the words 'the flagpole ...' followed by the name of a particular female deity (OI *Khonsu* I 1979: pl. 52). Those of Renutet, Hathor, Nekhbet, Mut and Amunet can still be read; sadly the last three inscriptions are damaged and the names of those goddesses are lost. It is reasonable to assume from this fascinating insight that these dedications were to be found inscribed upon all the flagstaffs that had once stood before Karnak's mighty pylon entrances.

To this majestic new entrance, Horemheb added a vestibule, the outside of which he decorated with traditional scenes of Egypt's enemies being slain by the king, while inside were scenes of the ruler being purified by Horus and Thoth before being led into the temple by Montu and Atum. One of the prime functions of a vestibule was to screen such rituals from profane eyes.

The decoration of the east face of the pylon was greatly damaged or, more often, completely recut when the Hypostyle Hall was constructed, but reliefs showing the procession of the sacred bark of Amun and the great state barge Userhet are still visible – scenes which Amenhotep III also had had inscribed on the east face of the Third Pylon.

The core of the Second Pylon, and also that of the Ninth, was found to contain thousands of *talatat* from the temples of Amenhotep IV (Akhenaten) and sections of the so-called 'Nefertiti pillars', as well as blocks from the Tutankhamun/Ay monuments. While it is undoubtedly clear that Horemheb began the demolition of the Aten temples at Karnak, the reaction against the Amarna period does not appear to have been so immediate or so violent as was first assumed: Horemheb seems to have pulled them down in an ordered way, as and when he required filling stone for his own building exploits. In this respect, his behaviour was no different from that of many kings before him, as we have seen.

Today, the doorway of the Second Pylon leads into the great Hypostyle Hall, but in Horemheb's day, it is contended, the Second Pylon was linked to the Third only by Amenhotep III's colonnade, screened on either side by stone walls (Chevrier 1956: 36). However, it is not universally accepted that the central colonnade *was* the work of Amenhotep III, and the evidence from the tomb of Neferhotep, who lived during the reign of Ay, is cited as proof. Was it Horemheb, therefore, who conceived the entire project (Seele 1940: 92)? Were the foundations of the Hypostyle Hall established by him? According to Henri Chevrier, who excavated much of the area, it was Horemheb's vision which did indeed undertake the commencement of the columned hall, though not its completion, since he (Chevrier) asserted that the foundations of the Second Pylon and the Hypostyle Hall were in fact joined into one system (Chevrier 1956: 37); more recent research, however, states that the foundations beneath the columns were actually much later – of Graeco-Roman date perhaps since they are of fired brick, presumably used in early restoration work, or even in more modern times (Brand 2000: 218).

While all this is still debated, it nevertheless does seem somewhat unlikely that Horemheb would have built the parallel stone walls either side of the colonnade if his plan had indeed been to construct a vast columned hall. Therefore, some authorities believe that Horemheb did no more than build the colonnade with its screening walls, and that it was Ramesses I who conceived and began construction of the true Hypostyle Hall; others maintain that the whole project was the work of Seti I. All this will be discussed in the next chapter, but it seems that these are questions which are likely to remain under discussion for some time yet.

As to the other two pylons ascribed to Horemheb, it is probable that he completed the Tenth Pylon before he began work on the Ninth, since the Tenth Pylon was left unfinished by its originator, Amenhotep III, who had only achieved the first eight courses (Azim 1982b: 151). Horemheb's completed pylon was constructed of sandstone, with four flagstaffs before the southern face; in the centre the red granite gateway, about 20 m in height, was inscribed with scenes of the king before the gods. As we have seen, a colossal figure of Amenhotep III stood on the east side of this entrance; whether its counterpart was also a colossus of that king cannot be verified since it is missing, but its socle was re-cut and re-inscribed to Horemheb. More tellingly, perhaps, its base was full of *talatat*.

With the completion of the Tenth Pylon, the point where two sacred ways (to Mut and to Luxor temples) merged into a single entrance, the southern processional way now could be said almost to equal the main east–west axis in its grandeur, especially as Horemheb had by this time dismantled the pillared hall of Amenhotep II in front of the Eighth Pylon and rebuilt it, in a very different form, on the east side of the court created by his construction of the Tenth Pylon. While the southern way was indeed impressive, its skewed appearance seemed out of keeping with the Egyptian love of symmetry; but this anomaly was a consequence of the fact that the Ninth Pylon had been built to line up with the axis of the Temple of Mut and the sacred way that led to it. Since this temple and its sacred way were the work of Amenhotep III, it has been assumed that the original Ninth Pylon was built by him also (Barguet 1962: 252). But the sandstone structure that stands there today was found once again to be filled with huge numbers of *talatat* of Amenhotep IV and also blocks of Tutankhamun and Ay, proving therefore that it must have been built *after* those rulers. It therefore appears that Amenhotep III had erected the original in mud-brick, a construction that Horemheb replaced with one of stone. Although the reliefs decorating the pylon were usurped by Ramesses II, IV and VI, there is no doubt that Horemheb was its builder. The west façade shows him seated on a throne decorated with the *sm3-t3wy* motif and with the names of the Nine Bows – Egypt's traditional enemies – written in rings below.

The Ninth Pylon had some unusual features which give an insight into the special significance of these structures. Although the towering flagstaffs have long since disappeared, recent excavation has revealed that the base of one of them had a bronze

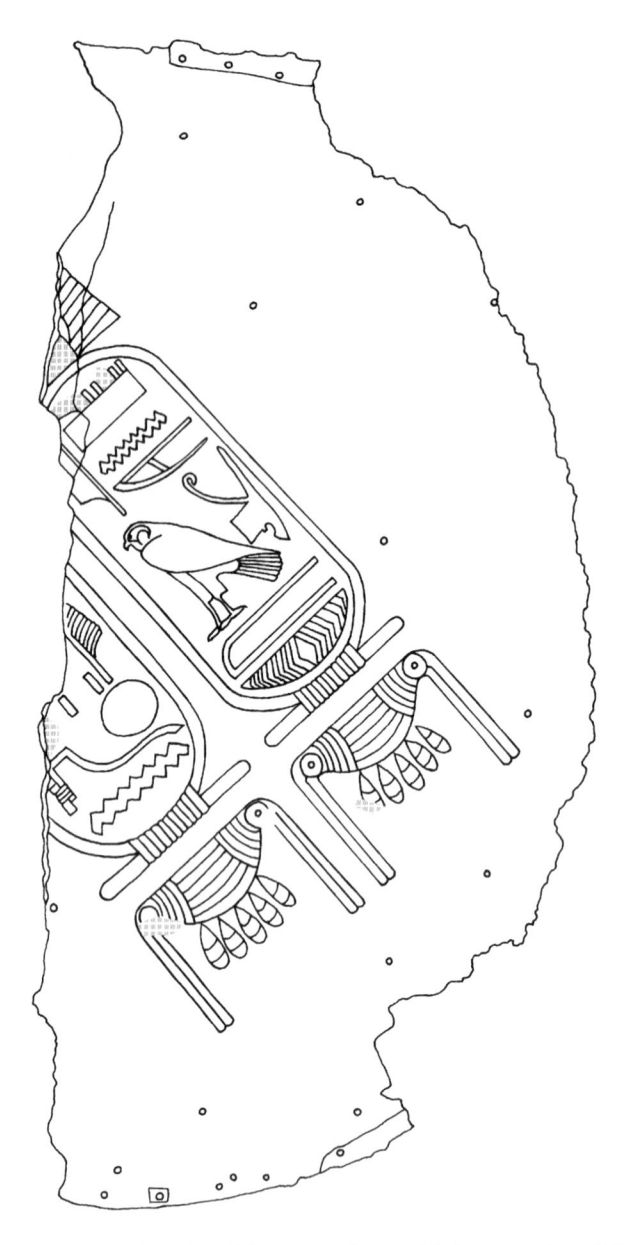

Figure 10.2 Drawing of the bronze plaque with the cartouches of Horemheb found beneath a flagstaff of the Ninth Pylon. (a) Drawing of the plaque as found. (b) Drawing of the plaque as it would have looked when complete (after Azim, M. *et al.*, *Cahiers de Karnak VII*: 86 and 88 respectively).

Figure 10.2 (continued).

plaque riveted to it inscribed with two large cartouches of Horemheb (Azim and Traunecker 1982: 88). From this plaque it has been possible to estimate an approximate diameter at the base of 1.5 m for each flagstaff. These plaques would have been completely hidden, and it is fascinating to reflect that the presence of the king's names, engraved with great care upon an object destined to be for ever invisible to men's eyes, indicates once again the measure of the religious significance of flagstaffs. It is worth remembering also the relief in Tuthmosis III's House of Gold where the king is seen erecting a flagstaff in a dedication ceremony before the highest officials of the land. Whatever their significance, it is certain that flagstaffs were more than mere decorative features, as is surely underlined by the fact that each one, as we have seen with the Second Pylon, was dedicated to a specific goddess (Fig. 10.2).

Perhaps the plaques should be equated with the customary foundation deposits found below pylons and other sacred buildings, perpetuating the holiness of the monument. But, here again, the Ninth Pylon was to produce surprises for the excavators. Certainly foundation deposits were found, but they had been placed not *under* the pylon in the usual manner, but *within* it (Azim 1982a: 93). The variety of objects in these deposits was wide: amongst them were inscribed bricks, objects in gold and faience, faience cartouches of Horemheb, model tools and implements.

Another unusual detail, possibly unique to the Ninth Pylon, can be observed at the foot of the narrow eastern face of the west massif where a doorway opens on to a staircase that gives internal access, as was customary, to the pylon's summit: there is no decoration here, but a niche above the stairway shows where a small flagstaff was fixed (Barguet 1962: 257) – an intriguing feature, given the obvious ritual importance of these objects.

Finally, against the north face of the western massif are the remains of two monolithic alabaster walls from a bark repository of Dynasty XVIII date (Barguet 1962: 256). No inscription remains, but it is tempting to see it as one of the six way-stations built along the southern processional route by Hatshepsut.

With the construction of these two southern pylons (the Ninth and Tenth), a large open court was thereby created between them, closed on either side with sandstone walls – the one to the east incorporating the façade of the rebuilt edifice of Amenhotep II. As little but the lower courses of these walls remain, it is impossible to know what the total decorative scheme might have been. There are remains of reliefs of Horemheb's showing a journey to Punt to bring back precious materials, as well as scenes of the sacred barks processing to and from Luxor temple for the Festival of Opet, but whether these latter scenes date to Horemheb or to Ramesses II, whose name can be seen, is not clear.

This court became the place, therefore, where the sacred barks of the Theban triad assembled before departing to Luxor, Horemheb having constructed a gateway in the western wall so that the bark of Khonsu might have direct access from his temple in order to join the cortège. In addition, it acted as another area between the sacred and the profane to which certain privileged officials and personnel had admittance; a place where oracles were proclaimed and where royal announcements could be displayed for public knowledge – including Horemheb's Decree (see below) and Ramesses II's marriage stela. Here, too, were placed statues of certain high officials, such as Amenhotep son of Hapu, who could act as intermediaries between petitioners and the gods.

Having constructed three such prestigious entrances complete with towering flagstaffs before them, it seems unlikely that Horemheb did not erect that other essential to pylon adornment – namely, obelisks. Certainly some fragments bearing his name have been unearthed around Karnak, but they seem to have come from relatively small obelisks and their inscriptions were fairly mundane. Perhaps Horemheb felt that Karnak was by now sufficiently equipped with such elements and preferred to devote his building energies to other projects.

Horemheb's building programme at Karnak was undoubtedly on a grand scale, but lesser works must also have existed. The scant remains of a small but interesting chapel dated to his reign certainly fall into this category. This was located between the magazines that stored food-offerings, situated south-west of the Sacred Lake, and the outer east wall of the court between the Eighth and Ninth Pylons. It lies alongside an inclined path that led down from the magazines towards a doorway which Horemheb had introduced into the wall of the court, giving access to the temple. This little chapel was perhaps the place where offerings were consecrated before they entered the hallowed precincts. We have already discussed the likelihood of an adjacent area being just such a place in Tutankhamun's time.

Horemheb's small construction was dedicated to Thoth and Amun: it would seem that Thoth's role was that of an 'administrator' who accounted for the daily offerings in the House of Amun (Goyon and Traunecker 1982: 362). The chapel of sandstone was reconstructed later by Osorkon III, and apparently stood within a small mud-brick enclosure with a stone gateway.

When Horemheb took, as another element of his royal titulary, the Horus name 'Mighty Bull with wise decisions', he probably spoke no more than the truth. He had inherited a country still suffering the after-effects of the Amarna period both at home and abroad. During his time as Commander-in-Chief of the Army and possibly as regent or deputy for the young Tutankhamun, he had certainly begun the task of restoring Egypt to some of its former glory, but it was only when he acquired the supreme power of kingship that he was able fully to implement much-needed reforms on almost every level: 'Now his Majesty took counsel with his heart concerning the protection of the entire land ... repelling wrong-doing and destroying falsehood ...' (Davies, B. 1995: 78, l. 9–10).

Thus it was that in the new court between the Ninth and Tenth Pylons, Horemheb caused a sandstone stela to be erected upon which was carved a decree announcing the re-establishment of law and order throughout the kingdom, effectively drawing a line under the Amarna period (Davies, B. 1995: 77–83). The decree dealt with much of the inefficiency, injustice and corruption that were a legacy of those years, and it was probably issued early in Horemheb's reign in order to stamp his authority on the kingship and the country from the very start; he was thus declaring the end of chaos and the beginning of the rule of Maat.

The decree gives us today a great deal of information on the judicial and administrative organisation, both national and regional, of the Two Lands; and, unlike other royal decrees, Horemheb's does not apply merely to a few special categories of people, but to every section of the population at large. Consequently, it is very likely that copies of this decree were put up in every major town and city throughout Egypt – one is certainly known from Abydos.

A wholesale reorganisation of the army was to follow, which Horemheb divided into two distinct units – an army of the South and an army of the North, each with its separate commander. As a military man himself, Horemheb would have known, more than most, how best to control this powerful force in the land: 'divide and rule' was surely his maxim here.

Horemheb's reign was firm and effective, during which Egypt prospered and grew strong again. The length of time he actually occupied the throne was in the region of thirty years, about half the time claimed by some inscriptions which gave dates of up to Regnal Year 59. It was soon realised, however, that in these cases Horemheb was counting his years, not from his own succession, but from the date of Amenhotep III's death – in other words, he was counting the intervening years of Akhenaten, Smenkhkare, Tutankhamun and Ay's reigns as his own.

Despite everything he had accomplished in returning Egypt to much of its former greatness, Horemheb lacked the one essential needed to ensure the future – he had no heir to form a stable dynasty that would maintain and continue what he had achieved. With the passing years, therefore, he turned more and more to a man whose assistance he had come increasingly to rely upon for the execution of many of his royal duties – the vizier, Pramesse. Like Horemheb himself, this man had a military background, having risen steadily through the ranks to become a general in the army, as well as a royal envoy engaged in diplomatic work at home and abroad. Later, as vizier, Pramesse was to become the ageing king's right-hand man, and eventually was given the title 'Deputy of his Majesty in the South and the North' – a title Horemheb himself had once held.

Two statues of this great official, who was destined for even higher things, stood against the north face of the Tenth Pylon: 'given by favour of the king' Pramesse asserts on them with pride, as well he might, for very few private individuals indeed were granted the privilege of a statue within Karnak's hallowed precincts.

Finally Horemheb proclaimed Pramesse as Crown Prince and his successor: 'Hereditary Prince in the Entire Land'. By this time, Pramesse was himself no longer in the first flush of youth, but he had both a son and a grandson – the start of that strong new dynasty which Horemheb so desired for Egypt's future well-being.

11

RAMESSES I AND SETI I

Upon the death of Horemheb, the void which that king had so feared was quickly filled by his appointed successor. The new ruler was a commoner by birth and had no royal connections whatsoever, either through blood or through marriage: his father being a troop commander in the army, and his wife being the daughter of a military man. With this background, then, but with a brilliant career behind him, Pramesse ascended the throne as Ramesses I. He was, of course, fully aware of his lack of any hereditary right to rule and he immediately set about establishing his legitimacy. Unlike Horemheb before him, he made no allusion on his public monuments to his pre-royal career. On a stela from Sinai, for example, he declared that the throne was destined for him from birth and that he was 'the son of Amun, born of Mut, to rule all that the sun encircles' (Davies, B. 1997: 196, l. 2).

Ramesses I, and his son and grandson likewise in their turn, strove to draw parallels through their titularies with the great kings of Dynasty XVIII. Ramesses chose his titulary deliberately to echo that of Ahmose, the founder of that illustrious dynasty, a role he himself hoped to emulate (Kitchen 1982: 18–19). However, while the Dynasty XVIII kings had been Theban princes, Ramesses and his forebears were northerners, and this too was reflected in his titulary with the Two Ladies name: 'Appearing as king like Atum'.

There is some evidence of a coronation at Thebes: this is based on the remains of a stela found reused at Medinet Habu on the West Bank (Brand 2000: 378). Its fragmentary inscription refers to Ramesses I as 'the bodily son of Re' and describes him as one 'who loves the gods of Thebes, who appears in the house of his father [Amun-Re] … who established him as ruler … his appointment as king upon the throne'. As can be seen from this, Ramesses certainly paid due homage to Amun as the all-powerful 'state' god who had ordained his kingship, but although Thebes was to remain the centre of religious power and Karnak continued to expand, political and secular power, however, slowly and inexorably began to move northwards.

The extent of Ramesses' work at Karnak is still debated: how much, if at all, was he involved in the scheme to build the great Hypostyle Hall? As we have already seen, the central avenue of columns has been variously attributed to Amenhotep III, Horemheb, Ramesses I and finally to Seti I. While arguments on the subject are still forthcoming, the latest research by an American team believes it can show that the entire hall was the work of Seti, and Seti alone (Brand 2000: 201). The Second Pylon was undoubtedly constructed by Horemheb, although Ramesses I added his name and some reliefs to its western face and to the vestibule at its entrance; but on the pylon's eastern face, the evidence is more equivocal. Certainly it can be observed that Horemheb's decorative scheme was erased and recarved in order to line up with the roof levels and architraves of the Hypostyle Hall when it was constructed at a later date; almost all that recarving can be securely dated to Seti I's reign, except for a few scenes high up beneath the roof line, which are in Ramesses I's name. It was assumed, therefore, that Ramesses had commenced the building of the Hypostyle Hall but had only had time to execute these few reliefs before his death, after a reign of only one to two years' duration.

It is necessary at this point to consider how the Hypostyle Hall was constructed in order to understand some of the arguments over the identity of its builder. As already stated, for a long time it was believed that Ramesses I had commenced the project by building the side walls, possibly the central colonnade (if, indeed, it was not already in place) and the multiple rows of columns, which were composed of a series of stone drums one upon another. As the blocks were put in place, the whole area was slowly filled with earthen ramps until the entire court was full of these embankments up to the roof level. When the construction work was finally achieved, the carving and painting of scenes could begin, starting at the very top and progressing steadily downwards, removing the earth bit by bit as each level of work was completed. This method would seem to explain why the only reliefs of Ramesses I are to be found at the topmost courses of the Hall's western wall (the rear of the Second Pylon), at which point it was assumed that he died, leaving the rest of the relief work to be carried out by his son (and grandson).

The current research work in the Hypostyle Hall disputes this theory and, after meticulous examination of the area, can state that, while the roof, the walls and the columns were erected with the use of embankments, the earth was at this juncture slowly removed as the stone was dressed and polished from top to bottom in preparation for the draughtsmen, artists and sculptors to outline, then carve and paint the scenes, these being done by means of wooden scaffolding (Brand 2000: 216–17). Ramesses I, they conclude, would never have had time to complete all this work in so short a reign, particularly since new scenes in his name have been located around the jambs of the western gateway into the Hall. Stylistically, all these supposed reliefs of Ramesses can actually be dated to his son, Seti, who dedicated them to his father's memory (Brand 2000: 201).

It is possible, however, that it was Ramesses I (or perhaps Horemheb) who had constructed the side walls that linked the Second and Third Pylons, thus creating a large open court. This would seem logical because immediately upon entering that court through the Second Pylon, to the left and right in the angles of the gateway and against the pylon's eastern face, Ramesses I introduced two balancing niches or shrines, each originally closed with double doors of wood. Each niche once contained a great stela, perhaps the stela of gold of which texts speak, and an alabaster floor bearing representations of Asiatic and Nubian prisoners between the symbolic Nine Bows (Legrain 1929: 149–50). Possibly these niches were 'Stations of the King' where Ramesses, or perhaps his statue, would have stood, or sat enthroned, on various ceremonial occasions with the enemies of Egypt depicted prostrate beneath his feet. It is probable that in the northern niche he would have been wearing the Red Crown, and in the southern the White Crown, as the ceremonies dictated. What should be particularly noticed is that if the central colonnade, or indeed the entire Hypostyle Hall, had already been constructed, the niches would have been completely blocked from view by the first two great columns which were placed almost directly in front of them (Brand 2000: 200). It is inconceivable that the king would consent neither to see nor be seen during any of the religious ceremonies enacted in this court. Consequently, it seems virtually certain that, during Ramesses' reign, the area served as an open forecourt to the main temple.

Ramesses I reigned about one-and-a-half years: he barely had time to start his tomb (just one antechamber, which had to be hastily pressed into service as a burial chamber), let alone a mortuary temple. Was he aware of his impending death? He certainly associated his son Seti very closely with him almost from the beginning of his reign. Seti campaigned abroad in his father's name, reviving a healthy respect for Egypt amongst the vassal states; he also undertook many duties at home alongside his father, helping to re-establish order and stability to the nation (Brand 2000: 379).

It is an interesting fact that Ramesside kings did not appoint co-regents in the accepted sense, but instead associated their designated successor with them without granting full kingship, unlike, for example, the co-regents of the Middle Kingdom. Sometimes that association conferred huge power and influence on the younger man, but nonetheless did not make him a ruler until such time as the current king died. Both Ramesses I and Seti I, as Crown Princes in their turn, held high-profile religious, civil and military offices, but remained the heir-apparent only (Brand 2000: 333–5). This system held true for Ramesses II also (despite his protestations to the contrary) and for later kings of the dynasty.

Despite this, the early Ramesside kings were, it seems, a close-knit family, and every new ruler made a great show of honouring his parents (Brand 2000: 373), as each in his turn strove to strengthen the new dynasty. Seti, when Crown Prince, referred to his father as 'discharging his kingship like Re' while he, Seti, 'was with him like a star at his side'. A statue from Medamud dedicated to Ramesses I by his son contained a similar refrain: Ramesses was 'in the likeness of Re' and Seti was 'the star of the land' (Kitchen 1982: 19). After the death of Ramesses, Seti, as dutiful and loving son, finished his father's tomb, built him a mortuary chapel within his, Seti's, own funerary endowment at Gurneh on the West Bank, and also constructed a small cenotaph, or memorial chapel, at Abydos on his father's behalf. In addition, he had various scenes carved in Ramesses' name within the Hypostyle Hall at Karnak, scenes which have led to much controversy, as we have seen. Later, Seti was to honour his mother, Sitre, by providing her with a tomb in a hitherto little-used valley on the West Bank at Thebes. Previously, it had been the usual custom for a queen to be interred within her husband's tomb: Sitre was the first queen to be buried in an inscribed and decorated tomb of her own in that specially designated area, which subsequently became known as the Valley of the Queens. The titles Seti gave his mother, while not uncommon, are typical of this close-knit family and speak much of his devotion: 'King's Wife, God's Wife, Great Queen-Mother, Lady of the Two Lands, Mistress of South and North, Possessor of grace, Sweet of love . . .', not uncommon epithets, perhaps, but they have a resonance which is hard to deny.

The new king, like his father before him, formed his titulary with care. Seti modelled his name, as he hoped to model his kingship, upon two much-admired predecessors – Tuthmosis III, a great soldier, and Amenhotep III, a great builder (Kitchen 1987: 131–2). In both roles, it can be fairly said that Seti I achieved his own measure of greatness, roles which served to strengthen his claim to legitimate kingship.

The early years of his reign were much occupied with campaigning as he strove to put down a number of serious rebellions, to restore Egypt's fortunes and status abroad, and to ensure that annual tribute from her vassal regions, and booty from her army's expeditions, would once again flow unimpeded into Egypt's coffers. In addition, he worked the turquoise mines in Sinai, the gold mines in Nubia and in the eastern desert, where he provided wells and settlements for the workers. He certainly would have needed the wealth that was brought back from successful military campaigning, as well as ensuring that he had access to a constant supply of precious stones and metals, for the great building programme he was planning.

It is interesting that at this early stage of his reign, before his construction work in the temple of Amun had begun, that Seti recorded a description of his first military campaign on a sandstone stela which he chose to erect in the Temple of Ptah at Karnak (Brand 2000: 221). The choice of such a venue speaks of a special regard for Ptah of Memphis: the Ramesside family, it should be recalled, were of northern origin. Later, under Ramesses II, there is another unusual instance of this particular regard.

While Seti was indeed to prove a great builder, in the mould of Amenhotep III, the earliest years of his reign were occupied with completing the restoration programme of the many monuments damaged in the Amarna period which were still in need of attention. Throughout Karnak, Seti's name is to be seen with the simple inscription: 'A renewal of monuments which the King of Upper and Lower Egypt, Menmaatre, Son of Re, Seti, made in the house of his father, Amun-Re'. This formula appears on such 'high-profile' sites as the Fourth Pylon, the Wadjet Hall, Hatshepsut's obelisks, Tuthmosis III's bark-shrine, the Sixth, Seventh and Eighth Pylons, the Eastern Temple, the Kamutef chapel, and various prominent and important stelae. It is of particular interest (and some curiosity) that Seti should have restored the defaced inscriptions on the obelisks of Hatshepsut, even though her name was subsequently to be omitted from his famous king-list at Abydos.

Amongst the list of his restorations must also be placed the Edifice of Amenhotep II, but in this particular case Seti's work was considerably more extensive. As stated above, Horemheb had dismantled, moved and rebuilt this structure in a different form, though it appears he had not had time to undertake any redecoration. It is probable that he died before he could begin the re-carving of this monument: this was almost entirely undertaken by Seti I. Some of the pillars from the original building had been reused in the new edifice, and where divine images remained on them, Seti reworked them: but quite a few pillars had not been reused, and sections of these had been built into the newly constructed walls with their decorated faces turned inwards to leave their blank faces exposed (Brand 2000: 81). These were then carved by Seti, sometimes in his own name and sometimes in the name, though not the style, of Amenhotep II.

It was in Year 2 of his reign that Seti commenced one of the most astounding architectural undertakings of the ancient world: the construction of the great Hypostyle Hall at Karnak. This particular area of the temple has called forth just about every superlative in the book, from the very earliest travellers right through to the countless tour parties that flock to Karnak today. Every tourist stops, stares, exclaims and photographs the structure that Seti I himself described as his 'work of eternity'. It would surely gratify him, and indeed any Egyptian monarch, in the unceasing quest for eternal life, to know that over three thousand years later people still gazed in awe and wonder at his achievement.

As the second king of a new and non-royal dynasty, still anxious to strengthen its claim to the throne, it was in Seti's own interests to build and dedicate magnificent monuments to the gods, and to undertake successful foreign conquests in their name. Seti's military campaigning had gone well, and for this reason also 'it pleased his heart to make a memorial for his father Amun, seeing that he (Amun) had given him (Seti) courage and victory'. Now the king was left to ponder long and hard on how to enhance Karnak in fitting style. His own words, carved on one of the Hypostyle Hall's architraves, perfectly sums up his deliberations: 'Now as for the Good God (Seti) whose heart is set on making monuments, he lies awake, unable to sleep, while seeking to perform beneficial deeds . . .' (Brand 1999: 23). Obviously his sleepless nights paid off, for soon the mighty work began on the structure that most appropriately bore the name 'Seti-is-beneficial-in-the-House-of-Amun'. 'And', continued Seti, 'it was his Majesty who gave the instructions, who guided the work on his monument'. This last comment surely endorses the view that the Hypostyle Hall was entirely Seti's work. Egyptian kings might well have been prone to bombastic claims and to usurping other rulers' monuments, but it is hard to believe that Seti would have carved so personal and heartfelt a statement on the usurped building of a predecessor.

Having made the decision to construct and dedicate a magnificent monument to the glory of Amun, Seti directed his architects to the huge open court that lay between the Second and Third Pylons, and in this space was created the edifice that will continue to immortalise the name of Seti I for generations to come (Fig. 11.1).

Nearly every description (and there are many indeed) of the Hypostyle Hall makes use of the term 'a forest of columns', and it is easy to see why, when one contemplates the 134 columns packed into an area measuring 103 m wide and 52 m deep. The central aisle, which is on the main east–west axis of the temple, was composed of 12 gigantic open-papyrus columns, each reaching, with its abacus, a height of 22.4 m, and supporting a ceiling of stone slabs decorated with stars. To the north and south sides of this central colonnade stood 122 papyrus-bud columns, each nearly 15 m high, arranged in twelve rows of nine columns and two rows of seven. The difference in roof levels occasioned by the disparity in heights between the two types of column allowed for a system of clerestory windows to be inserted along the top of the central colonnade, thus permitting a dim, filtered light to penetrate the sacred space below. The roof would have been accessible from both the Second and Third Pylons, and recent work on the hall has found the remains of a rounded parapet enclosing the raised area above the colonnade, leading to the conclusion that astronomical observations of the night sky probably took place there (Lauffray 1979: 112).

Seti's decoration of the Hypostyle Hall was of an exceptionally high standard: his work encompassed the entire northern half of the hall and many of the wall scenes on the southern side, all in the finest raised relief; he also carved the exterior north wall in sunk relief. These exterior scenes, which extend around the east and west corners of the outer wall, show Seti's triumphant campaigns in Syria and Palestine (to the east of the gateway) and similarly against the Libyans and Hittites (to the west), each scene ending with the presentation of booty to the Theban Triad. There is much of significant historical interest to be learned from the reliefs, and much still to be argued over with regards to the chronology of these campaigns, the climax of which was, perhaps, Seti's triumphant capture of Kadesh (or, in fact, recapture, since in this he was emulating the achievement of his much-admired predecessor, Tuthmosis III). The magnificently

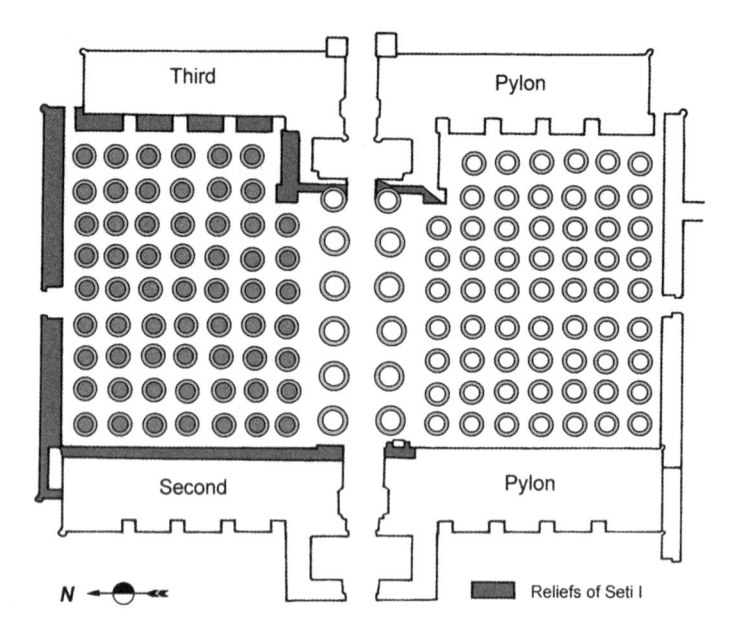

Figure 11.1 Plan of the Great Hypostyle Hall showing the extent of the decoration of Seti I (after Brand, P., *The Monuments of Seti I*: Plan I).

carved reliefs of warfare and conquest, full of life and vigour, trumpet Seti's victories by putting paeans of praise for the king into the mouth of Amun himself:

> I cause the foreign lands . . . to come to you with their tribute, laden with silver, gold, lapis lazuli and every noble gem . . . I cause them to see your Majesty as Lord of Radiance, you shine in their faces like my very image. I cause them to see your Majesty arrayed in full panoply when you take up the weapons of war upon the chariot . . . mighty in power, unstoppable in heaven and earth.
> (Kitchen 1993: 22)

At the other end of the scale from this grandiose rhetoric, the exuberant reliefs and texts also contain small and unusual scenes worth noting, including one of tree-felling in Lebanon, whose cedars formed a great source of precious wood so essential for the temples of Egypt: 'The chiefs of Lebanon, they cut timbers for the great river-barge Userhet and likewise for the great flagstaves of Amun.'

Inside the hall a remarkable variety of themes was employed: many are standard scenes of Seti offering to the gods and performing the daily cult, but there are also reliefs showing the hall's foundation ceremony, the baptism and coronation of the king and his royal progress, and lively scenes of hunting, fowling and of the chase, as well as many varied representations of the royal and sacred barks. All the scenes were executed in the highest quality raised relief, so typical of Seti I's reign, and they were then picked out and painted in glowing colours. In one inscription, Seti claimed of the central colonnade that 'its august open-papyrus columns are of electrum' (Rondot 1997: 24). It has to be said, however, that close inspection of these columns has shown no evidence at all of plating with precious metal, but plenty of gilding was almost certainly employed within the hall.

One of the interesting points concerning the Hypostyle Hall, and one which Seti himself stressed time and again, is that it was conceived as a temple in itself (Brand 2000: 386): 'The temple (called) Seti-is-beneficial-in-the-House-of-Amun', and which the king described many times as being 'a great and sacred temple in excellent sandstone'. The expression 'Seti-is-beneficial' was mirrored in several other of Seti's monuments throughout Egypt: his mortuary temple at Gurneh, the Ptah temple at Memphis, the Osirieion at Abydos, probably the temple of Re at Heliopolis, and perhaps a Seth foundation in the Delta (Brand 1999: 132). The use of *3ḫ* ('beneficial' in this context, rather than 'glorious' or 'shining') is of particular significance, since the building of such monuments was considered as being beneficial to the gods and consequently to Egypt and the king (Brand 1999: 33).

The term *ḥwt-nṯr* (temple), frequently used by Seti to describe the Hypostyle Hall, implied that it was in some senses an autonomous foundation, and the fact that it had its own specific cult aspect of Amun, named Amun-Atum-Re-in-Thebes, underlines the view that it should be considered as a temple in its own right (Rondot 1997: 135; Spencer 1984: 50). To have such a foundation within the Karnak precinct was not unprecedented: Tuthmosis III's Akh-Menu was another, which, as we have seen, had its own separate priesthood. A further indication of the Hall's autonomy is that it had its own treasury, and there are texts within the hall that describe the presentation of precious metals destined particularly for 'the temple (called) Seti-is-beneficial-in-the-House-of-Amun'. In addition, we know of two officials of this period whose titles, listed in their tombs, included, in the one case 'Scribe of the treasury in "the temple (called) Seti-is-beneficial-in-the-House-of-Amun"', and in the other 'Steward of the treasury in "the temple (called) Seti-is-beneficial-in-the-House-of-Amun"'. And furthermore, the Hall had its own endowments of land, making it a wealthy foundation in its own right. If the Hall's Treasury was akin to the *pr-ḥḏ* of Tuthmosis I, then doubtless the produce from this land would have been directed to it.

However, it seems that Seti's great hall was to serve several other functions. Apart from its designation as a temple, it was also intended to be a cult place for the *ka* of Seti I: thus it is often referred to in the inscriptions as a 'temple of millions of years', and several of the Hypostyle Hall's architraves record this particular function (Rondot 1997: 144). It should be noted once again that such a building within the Karnak complex was not unique: once more we can cite the Akh-Menu, and the small temple of Tutankhamun, discussed in Chapter 9, also bore this name: later kings were to follow suit.

Several descriptions recorded within the hall make use of the term *wb3* (Spencer 1984: 9), usually translated as an 'entry area' or 'forecourt'. They speak of Seti 'making splendid its (Karnak's) *wb3* with a perfect and great monument', and also of Seti building his 'temple (called) Seti-is-beneficial-in-the-House-of-Amun in the axis of Ipet-Sut, a *wb3* made august with open-papyrus columns'; and a third time as 'the great monument in the *wb3* of his temple'. The word *wb3* is of interest and can be translated in a variety of ways, which has led to many interpretations as to Seti's meaning when he used it in apposition to the term *ḥwt-nṯr* (temple). A great deal of research has taken place recently on the inscriptions within the Hypostyle Hall which show that the purpose of the inscribed texts was to give the necessary information required for the religious functioning of the hall. These studies suggest that the intended meaning of *wb3* was a cultic, rather than an architectural, one, and that in these terms it meant an 'accessible' area in contrast to *št3*, an 'inaccessible' area. This theory gains credence from the fact that images of *rekhyt*-birds (symbolising the people of Egypt) worshipping the king's cartouches are to be seen round the base of the hall's columns; also texts bearing the legends 'a place of acclamation for the people' (Kitchen 1996: 362) and 'all men are astounded at seeing it (the Hall)' (Rondot 1997: 10) are inscribed on its architraves. The inference here must surely be that, on some particular occasions, certain privileged members of the public were granted access. Since Seti also mentions the reception within the Hall of foreign tribute, should it be considered as a festival court in the same vein as those of Tuthmosis II and Tuthmosis IV?

Another, and very important, function of the hall was that it acted as a vast *ḥnw* (resting place) (Rondot 1997: 143–4). This is the only known use of the term with reference to so huge an edifice: it usually denoted a small structure where a statue or bark could receive cult offerings. But, along with allied terms, such as *st-ḥ'w* (the place of appearances) and *st-ḥtp* (the place of resting)(Rondot 1997: 141–2, 144), it indicates that the Hypostyle Hall was viewed in some respects as a bark repository, and this is borne out by the numerous reliefs of the sacred barks to be seen on the walls. As is so often the case in ancient Egyptian texts, there are different levels of interpretation and meaning. The terms *st-ḥ'w* and *st-ḥtp*, while obviously having reference in the Hypostyle Hall context to the god and his sacred bark, also have other connotations. *St-ḥ'w*, for example, was the term used to denote the place of the king's coronation, the ceremonies of which are depicted on the walls of the Hall. In addition, the two expressions *st-ḥ'w* and *st-ḥtp* were used with reference to the rising and setting of the sun. It is easy to see the close connection between all these uses and the subtle interchange of function between god, king and sacred ritual contained within them.

The hall remained the route taken by the processions for the Festival of Opet and the Beautiful Feast of the Valley and others, as it had during Horemheb's reign, even though at that time the area was an open forecourt. Thus, it seems, the sacred barks assembled there, because the texts tell us that the hall was 'the place of appearance (*st-ḥ'w*) of Amun, the King of the Gods, Mut and Khonsu following him ...'. In one or two inscriptions, the central colonnade, with its open papyrus columns, is referred to as a separate entity, being distinguished as 'a temple that is surrounded by closed papyrus columns'. This was possibly to emphasise the particular importance of the east–west axis of the hall, since this was where the sacred barks rested.

When one stands in the Hypostyle Hall today with its profusion of columns, it is hard to imagine how these great festival processions managed to assemble there, particularly as the barks grew ever more lavish in size and adornment:

> The Good God (Seti) who performs benefactions for his father the King of the Gods, and who enlarges his river-barge in conformity with his status in heaven, being wrought with the best gold of the deserts, made to glitter with every kind of precious stone – the face of Amun in gold, the wig in lapis lazuli, the insignia of Re upon his brow, his statue [...] supporting the sky and his sacred image within it – it illumined the deep waters with its beauty. (Kitchen 1993: 179)

The width of the column bases, and their proximity to one another, must have made any movement, not to mention manoeuvring, of the barks and their retinues virtually impossible except in the main east–west axis and, to some extent, the secondary north–south axis. However, it appears that some attention was paid to these difficulties: for, upon passing through the Second Pylon, it can be observed that the first three pairs of columns show signs of repairs of Graeco-Roman date up to a height of around 7 m. It seems that the columns were cut away to allow construction of 'a kiosk of light material' (Barguet 1962: 77), which was later to be removed. As well as having the effect of slightly widening the entrance by the cutting away of the columns to accommodate this kiosk, the structure itself would have veiled the sacred barks from profane eyes: such a construction is shown in three reliefs within the Hypostyle Hall.

It is difficult while standing amidst the tumbled remains of Karnak today to visualise the glory and grandeur of the temple in its hey-day. But perhaps in the awe-inspiring remains of the Hypostyle Hall, it is still possible to get a sense of the divine power that it once generated, for, as Seti himself described it, 'its perfections attain the very heights of heaven'. When the great gates and side doors were closed, the only light that could penetrate into the hall was through the stone grilles of the clerestory windows, many metres above, filtering downwards in thin shafts of dappled sunlight, catching on the gilding and brilliantly painted scenes, suffusing the darkness with hints of jewel-like colours so that the sacred area glowed and glinted softly within its dim, incense-laden interior. Who could not have been filled with a sense of awe and reverence in such a place?

In addition to the majestic Hypostyle Hall and his extensive restoration programme, there is evidence of other work undertaken by Seti at Karnak – such as blocks from certain of his buildings found incorporated into the Khonsu temple pylon, and remains of stelae and some statuary scattered at various locations around the precinct. Amongst these, two very fine pieces in alabaster, a statue and a stela, stand out. They were stylistically very similar and clearly came from the same workshop. The stela is firmly dated to Year 1 and its inscription states that it was erected 'opposite the Mansion of the Prince at the Place of Appearances of the Majesty of Re' – which Paul Barguet asserts was the main sanctuary of Re at Karnak, situated at the top of a stairway to the north of the Akh-Menu complex (Barguet 1962: 276–7). There is clear evidence on the stela's lunette of inlays of semi-precious stones and faience on a background of sheet-gold, while the text below was in blue pigment (Brand 2000: 219–220). Such decoration against the lustrous white alabaster would have illumined the dimmest of sanctuaries.

Similarly, the alabaster statue of the king (Brand 2000: 222–3) was also ornamented with inlays on the *nemes*-headdress, eyes and eyebrows, collar and kilt, while the inscriptions on the base were again in blue pigment. It is possible that so magnificent a piece of work was a cult statue of Seti, or perhaps the main effigy of the king at Karnak. It certainly was intended to emphasise the divinity of his kingship, the inscription calling him 'the bodily son of Re' and 'mighty heir of Amun-Re'. Standing about 2.38 m in height, the statue might not be classed as a colossus, but what it lacked in size, it certainly made up for in richness. If this was indeed the cult statue, the likelihood is that it originally stood somewhere within the Hypostyle Hall itself. However, its dedicatory inscription bears no cult name and is quite simple: 'He has wrought for his father the making of a statue in pure alabaster to establish his name in the house of his father Amun'.

In contrast to Seti's grand undertakings at Karnak, there is a small artefact known which, despite only being in a very fragmentary state, nonetheless is of great interest. The three remaining pieces of this intriguing object are in three separate collections, and only one of them has a probable Theban provenance; but that they all came from the same object – a temple model executed in dark grey granite (Berg 1990: 94) – is certain. Another such model, also of Seti I's reign, is well known: it represents the entrance to the temple of Re at Heliopolis and has been published in detail by Alexander Badawy (Badawy 1973).

The temple model under discussion here, however, featured the names and titles of Amun, as well as mentioning Thebes in general and Karnak in particular (Berg 1990: 101). From what little remains, it is not possible to say whether this might have represented an actual construction at Karnak – in the same way that the other known example represented the temple at Heliopolis – or whether it was intended to be a votive offering representing no particular edifice. Unlike the Heliopolitan model, the sockets that still exist on the base of the Karnak model are so fragmentary as to be impossible to restore, but the approximate dimensions of the base can be estimated at 81 cm wide, 104 cm deep, with a height of 26 cm. The scenes around the four sides show Seti kneeling and offering to (presumably) Amun. Badawy believes that these models were used in the temple foundation rite entitled 'Presenting the House to its Lord' where the king was shown dedicating a *sh*-shrine before the god. Badawy states further that what is being presented is a model merely of the entrance façade, not the whole temple (Badawy 1973: 8). Such a foundation scene with a *sh*-shrine is shown twice on the walls of the Hypostyle Hall. However, the *sh*-shrine is known from a variety of contexts, and Badawy's conclusions are not universally accepted. Apart from these two examples, none other is known. So were these models unique to Seti's reign, and what was their function? At the moment, there are no certain answers to these questions (Fig. 11.2).

Having considered Seti's work at Karnak, it is perhaps worth adding a small postscript to the record which, while being largely supposition, is nonetheless an interesting possibility. Two stelae (Brand 1997: 101), both dated to Year 9 of the king, can be seen carved into the cliff-face not far from the Aswan granite quarries. One states: 'His Majesty ordered to be made for himself large statues of black granite . . . the crowns thereof from quartzite of the Red Mountain', and the other: 'His Majesty ordered and charged numerous workmen to make very great obelisks, and great and wonderful statues . . . he made great barges for transporting them.'

By Year 9, many of Seti's building projects must have been nearing completion, and it is logical to assume that at this point he would have been wishing to adorn them with statuary and obelisks. However, there is a marked lack of such monuments in Seti's name: none of his known statues is a colossus, despite the commissioning of 'great statues' of which both Aswan stelae speak. Similarly, the paucity of obelisks in the king's name is surprising: one is known from Heliopolis, and another, smaller one, can still be seen only partly extracted in the quarry. To these two must now be added the recent recovery of an obelisk from the sea-bed at Alexandria. How does one account for this lack of such essential temple adornment from a king noted for the magnificence of his building programme?

The highest known date for Seti's reign is Year 11: assuming, therefore, that he died during that year, it is very probable that the statues and obelisks referred to in the Year 9

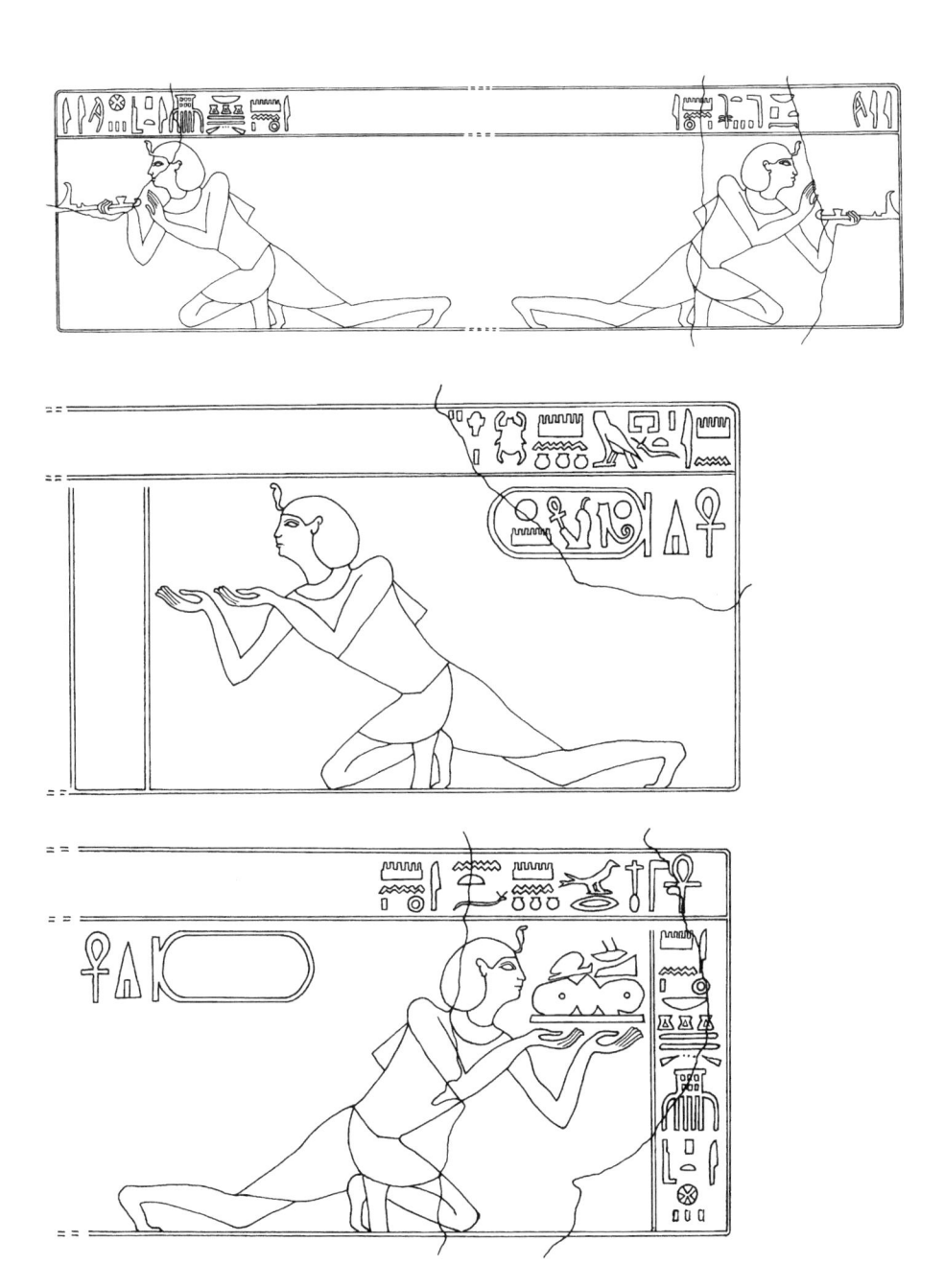

Figure 11.2 Temple model showing the names of Amun and Ipet-Sut. (a) Reconstruction of the front; (b) Reconstruction of the left side; (c) Reconstruction of the right side (after Berg, D., in *SAK* 17: 97 and 99).

stelae were left unfinished and consequently his son, Ramesses II, would have inherited a legacy of uninscribed but virtually completed temple furniture. It has been noted that the obelisks of Ramesses II which fronted Luxor temple bear the very early form of his name (only in use up to Year 2 of his reign) (Brand 1997: 108). In addition, his Luxor colossi bear the cult name 'Ruler-of-the-Two-Lands', which is precisely the title used by Seti on his Aswan stelae when referring to the black granite statues. The Luxor colossi are carved from black grano-diorite and have, incidentally, crowns of red quartzite, exactly as stated on Seti's stelae (Brand 1997: 112). It must be a real possibility that these stone monuments inscribed for Ramesses II were actually those commissioned by his father, and it seems somewhat ironic, therefore, that it was Ramesses, as Crown Prince, who had been put in charge of this expedition. By extrapolating on this train of thought, it can surely not be impossible to imagine that some of this statuary, and indeed obelisks as well, might have been intended by Seti to grace Karnak's precincts had he lived long enough to complete the project.

Seti I proved himself to be a prolific builder with a magnificent and widespread construction programme. The fine raised relief work, for which he is justly famous, customarily portrays him bowing, kneeling, sometimes even prostrate, before the deity – an unusual feature, since hitherto in Egyptian reliefs, the king had always been shown standing upright. As a commoner, from a new ruling family of less than two years, Seti was anxious to show his gratitude and devotion to the gods who had raised him to such honours.

Not unsurprisingly, Seti's work was to prove an inspiration to later kings, just as Dynasty XVIII had been an inspiration to Seti; even his reliefs and texts were to provide a model for many later Ramesside kings who used, virtually wholesale, passages from Seti's texts.

By the time of Seti I's death, the dynastic succession was secure and the institution of Egyptian kingship had been restored to something akin to its height under the rulers that Seti so admired – Tuthmosis III and Amenhotep III. Although to some extent his military and architectural achievements were overshadowed by those of his son Ramesses II, renowned for his aggressive self-promotion, Seti I's reign nonetheless ranks among the greatest. When, today, one surveys the beauty of the monuments raised by him to the glory of his god, with their exquisite scenes worked in delicate raised relief, one can be forgiven for wishing that this remarkable monarch, both warrior and builder, might have lived longer and so had more time to bequeath to his people and to posterity more of this artistic legacy.

12

RAMESSES II TO THE END OF DYNASTY XIX

Ramesses II

Ramesses II, it would be fair to say, is, in the majority of people's minds, the epitome of the all-powerful Egyptian pharaoh. There is small wonder in this, for his self-publicity knew no bounds, and his name and image, even today, are carried in seemingly endless profusion on temple walls, obelisks and colossi throughout Egypt while statues, columns and artefacts bearing his familiar cartouches adorn the world's museums. He was, indeed, the greatest builder of monuments in Egypt's history, and those that he did not build, he frequently usurped, stamping his name and persona upon them. To add to his fame, he has been equated, rightly or wrongly, with the pharaoh of the Exodus and, as a consequence, has 'starred' in many of Hollywood's biblical epics, and has featured in all manner of literature from poetry to popular novels. Such high-profile exposure, which has ensured that his name is still being spoken millennia after his death, could only have pleased Ramesses in that it granted him the eternal life that was the ultimate desire of every ancient Egyptian.

Upon the death of Seti I, the country was prosperous and peaceful, and the transfer of power to the Crown Prince, Ramesses, was smooth and secure. Although in his dedicatory inscription at Abydos, Ramesses claims that his father appointed him as king (i.e. co-regent) during his (Seti's) lifetime, Seti himself makes no such statement (Brand 2000: 330); Ramesses was most certainly *prince*-regent but not *co*-regent. It was to be the start of an amazing sixty-seven year reign, which perhaps goes some way towards explaining the plethora of monuments he left behind. During this time he was to celebrate fourteen sed-festivals and father over one hundred children – Ramesses, without doubt, was determined that his name should 'exist for millions of years'.

Seti, it seems, did not die at Thebes, but somewhere in the north of the country. Here it was, therefore, that his son made arrangements for the great king's mummification – traditionally seventy days – and, although Ramesses' formal accession had been announced immediately, the full coronation could not take place until Seti I had been interred in his magnificent tomb on the West Bank at Thebes with all the required funerary rituals, overseen by his son and heir. Having completed these necessary duties, the new king was able, as full pharaoh, to take part in the annual Festival of Opet at Thebes, all twenty-three days of it, during which time he could celebrate his coronation, as had Horemheb and Hatshepsut, and doubtless other rulers, before him. This great event was commemorated more than once upon the walls of Amun's temple at Karnak.

As mentioned in the previous chapter, the early Ramessides were a close-knit family. We have seen how Seti honoured his father, Ramesses I; now it was Ramesses II who said of *his* father that 'his (Ramesses') heart was tender towards him who begat him, and his breast yearned for him who brought him up' (BAR III: para. 260). Such warmly expressed sentiments speak of true attachment. In customary style, but with expressions of warm affection, Ramesses fulfilled his filial duty by completing his father's unfinished monuments: 'Compassion is a blessing; it is good that a son should be concerned to care about his father. I am determined to confer benefits on Menmaatre (Seti I) ...' (Kitchen 1982: 46). There can be little doubt that, due to the meticulous care of Seti's craftsmen in producing the exquisite, but time-consuming, raised relief-work which that king favoured, there was still much decoration to be completed after his death. This Ramesses was happy to undertake, leaving his own cartouche stamped on his father's buildings, although it was not long before the new king tired of the slow process of raised relief, which he soon abandoned in favour of the much faster sunk relief – a change of style very apparent within the Hypostyle Hall at Karnak, and one which showed a marked decline in the standard of workmanship. Ramesses seemed content in many instances to usurp his father's work by the simple expedient of replacing Seti's cartouche with his own; but, strangely, in other instances, he actually cut away his father's raised reliefs to replace them with identical scenes in sunk relief (Brand 2000: 202): perhaps his intention was to produce a uniformity of style that would persuade all who saw it of his 'ownership'. Furthermore, it is noticeable that Ramesses' usurpations are particularly marked in the areas his father had decorated that were adjacent to the central colonnade. It should be remembered, of course, that this was the area where people would have congregated for the great festival processions and other very particular ceremonies. There can be little doubt that subsequent generations, even up to the present day, have often been deceived by this ruse – and it is Ramesses II who has taken most of the credit for the Hypostyle Hall.

Did Ramesses attempt to usurp the entire hall and claim it as his own? It is interesting to see an inscription that he had added over Seti's decoration of the northern half of the hall's west wall: in it, Amun addresses Ramesses thus:

> I have given thee the office as King of Upper and Lower Egypt ... inasmuch as thou hast made a great monument for me in front of my temple which had been left an undecorated court from the reigns of the kings of Lower Egypt. I never put it in their hearts to undertake to embellish my monument; only to thee my son ... have I authorized it. (Redford 1986: 265)

From this, it would seem that Ramesses acknowledged the actual construction to have been undertaken by another, but that he, and he alone, had been responsible for its decoration, through direct instructions from the god himself.

However, before we condemn Ramesses for usurping his father's great work in order to glorify himself (although that was surely part of his intention), it should be remembered that a temple could not function on a king's behalf, or in the vital maintenance of universal order ($m3't$), unless the temple in question was in the name of that particular king (Rondot 1997: 151); and in a careful evaluation of Ramesses' various additions, alterations and suppressions of certain of Seti's inscriptions, it has become clear that the functions of the Hypostyle Hall differed in Ramesses' reign from those of his father. Also, there are many scenes indicating that Ramesses continued the cult of Seti's *ka* within the hall: we see various scenes of the deceased Seti being purified and receiving offerings from his son (Habachi 1969: 17), and of Ramesses in the role of funerary priest (*iwn-mwt.f*) speaking an offering formula in front of a naos containing a statue of his father, as well as depictions of Seti's statue on a royal bark before which Ramesses burns incense or pours a libation.

Although by the time of his death Seti had completed the decoration of more than half the Hypostyle Hall, the central colonnade of twelve great open-papyrus columns had been left with undecorated shafts; there is some evidence for thinking that Seti's draughtsmen had begun to trace scenes in black outline on the giant columns (Brand 2000: 216), but now it was left to Ramesses to accomplish their decoration as he wished. Work on these scenes and on the remainder of the Hypostyle Hall's reliefs was commenced early in his reign and, as might be expected, the name of the edifice was changed to 'Ramesses-is-beneficial-in-the-house-of-Amun'.

As with his father, the bases of these columns were adorned with images of the *rekhyt*-bird, denoting the ordinary people of Egypt, and a unique formula stating that the hall was 'the place where men honour the great name of his Majesty' was carved on the architraves above. The wording seems to indicate that not only were certain privileged members of the public granted access during the festival processions (which was certainly the case under Seti I), but that under Ramesses it also gave access for people to participate in specific rites of adoration associated with the cult of the *living* king – Ramesses II. Along with this aspect, it can be noted that later in his reign, Ramesses altered some of the reliefs pertaining to the cult of Seti's *ka* within the Hypostyle Hall to show instead the cult offerings being directed to *himself* (Kitchen 1999: 396). And in relation to this, he appears to have introduced at least two great cult statues of himself within the hall named 'Prince-of-princes-in-every-land' and 'Seed-of-Kamutef', the latter of which had connections with the Amun-Kamutef festival depicted on the hall's west side (inscribed by Seti, but again usurped by his son). Ramesses went further still: his father had inscribed a sequence of twenty-three scenes from the Ritual of Amenhotep I – the deified Dynasty XVIII king greatly revered as the founder of the New Kingdom temple. These scenes Ramesses usurped to show himself as being not only the officiant of the rites, but the *recipient* also (Nelson 1949: 202).

In addition to usurping much of his father's work in the Hypostyle Hall, Ramesses also suppressed the one certain monument attributable to his grandfather: the northern of the two great niches or shrines constructed by Ramesses I in the east face of the Second Pylon. Here, Ramesses II removed the original stela and/or statue and replaced it with an alabaster dyad, 5.5 m in height, of Amun and himself.

Despite the extent of Ramesses' work in the Hall, it is nonetheless worth remembering that, within this one structure, there were established the cults of no less than three royal *ka*s, Ramesses I, Seti I and Ramesses II – in this respect at least, the Hypostyle Hall could be regarded as a dynastic monument of the early Ramessides (Rondot 1997: 153).

In Year 5 of his reign, Ramesses II determined to recapture the city of Kadesh which his father had relinquished in a treaty with the Hittites. This famous battle was to form the major event of Ramesses' claim to military glory, despite the fact that it was by no means the Egyptian victory he asserted. Nevertheless, on the southern exterior wall of the Hypostyle Hall, in imitation of Seti's great battle scenes on the northern wall, Ramesses depicted his own great triumph at Kadesh. Not content with this, he also had it carved twice at the Ramesseum on the West Bank, three times at Luxor temple, and also at the temples of Abu Simbel and Abydos. This was propaganda of the most blatant kind. At Karnak, however, there was more to come: along the entire length of the western exterior walls of the southern processional way, stretching from the Hypostyle Hall to the Tenth Pylon, were a variety of military themes, including a battle with the Syrians, the storming of the fortress of Askalon ('the wretched town which his Majesty carried off because it was wicked ...'), and the text of the treaty with the Hittites of Year 21. However, the authorship of the scenes and texts relating to a Canaanite campaign has recently been disputed, and has been attributed instead to Ramesses' son, Merenptah. Further along this same wall was yet another depiction of the battle of Kadesh accompanied by a commentary, which has been dubbed the 'Bulletin'; and beyond this is a great text referred to as the 'Poem' which is in fact part poem, part prose, recounting the tale of Ramesses' heroic deeds (Davies, B. 1997: 55–96).

Heroic, on a personal basis, they certainly seem to have been, but the final outcome, nevertheless, was not the splendid victory that Ramesses claimed – rather, it might be described as a stalemate, which led eventually to an alliance or treaty with the Hittites many years later. This important historical event, which ensured peace between the two powers, was recorded on a stela carved into the same wall, mentioned above; the wording purported to be a copy of the treaty that had been engraved on a great silver tablet which the Hittite king, Hattusil III, sent to Ramesses (Kitchen 1982: 85).

The cementing of good relations between Egypt and Hatti did not end there. In Year 34 – the year of his second jubilee (sed-festival) – Ramesses II married a daughter of the Hittite king, an event also commemorated by a great stela at Karnak (Kitchen 1982: 85); a second stela, carved on an alabaster slab and giving an abbreviated version, was dedicated to the mother-goddess Mut and erected within her complex at Karnak, as well as copies at numerous other temples throughout Egypt. This was, after all, a hugely important public announcement of an international alliance, of which the king would obviously wish his people to be cognisant.

The Marriage Stela was erected against the south face of the Ninth Pylon, while balancing it on the other wing of the same pylon was another stela, but on a different theme; these two seem to have been set up in conjunction with one another, since copies of both were erected together elsewhere (most notably at Abu Simbel). On the second stela, the god Ptah makes mention of the peace treaty and of the marriage to the Hittite princess as part of a list of blessings he had bestowed upon the king; while on the Marriage Stela itself Ptah states: 'She was lovely in the estimation of his Majesty and he loved her more than anything together – a success and a victory which his father Ptah-Tatenen had decreed for him ...'. Another parallel in the two texts is the reference in both to momentous weather conditions. Ptah described it thus: 'I (Ptah) shook for you in order that I might foretell for you great and excellent wonders. The sky quivered ... the mountains, the waters, and the walls which are upon earth shook ...' (Goelet 1993: 35–6). It is widely believed today that the texts describe an earthquake, but that Ramesses, who as king was ultimately responsible for the well-being of Egypt, attempted to pass off such an event as a manifestation of the god's power on his behalf in order to cow the king's enemies and impress them with the might of Egypt's gods and of their son Ramesses.

This surprising emphasis in the House of Amun upon Ptah, the great god normally associated with Memphis, is an indication perhaps of the affiliation the early Ramessides had with the northern part of Egypt, from whence their family derived, and where the administrative capital, Memphis, was located. With the area so strategically important for military expeditions into Syria and Palestine and for the defence of Egypt's borders, both Seti I and Ramesses II spent much of their time in the north of the country, and Ramesses, of course, was to build himself a magnificent and, by all accounts, opulent new capital, Per-Ramesses, in the Delta.

But to return to Karnak: despite the fact that his name is to be seen everywhere, Ramesses left few actual monuments here – the bulk of his vast building programme was to be reserved for other parts of Egypt. But he did build a small temple of huge significance at the eastern end of Karnak, one which it seems was specifically designed to meet the spiritual needs, aspirations and prayers of the common people who appeared

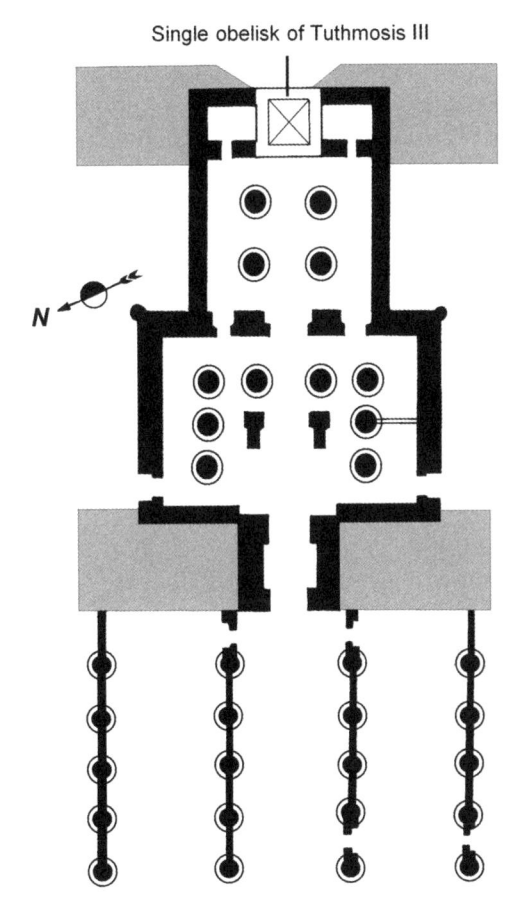

Figure 12.1 Plan of the Eastern Temple of Ramesses II with the additions of Taharqa and the Ptolemies. The single obelisk is at the western end (after Aldred, C. *et al.*, *Les Pharaons: l'Empire des Conquérants*: 306).

to have unrestricted access to this area. Generally referred to today as the Eastern Temple, it was in fact 'The Temple of Ramesses-beloved-of-Amun-who-hears-prayers'.

This monument was constructed between Years 40 and 50 by the high-priest of Amun, Bakenkhons, who described his work thus:

> I made for him (the king) the temple of 'Ramesses-Meriamon-who-hears-prayers' at the Upper Gateway of the Temple of Amun. I erected therein obelisks of granite, their points nearing the sky, the enclosure (*ḏ3ḏ3*) before it of stone, opposite Thebes, with a watered park and a garden planted with trees. I made two great doors of electrum, their tops joining heaven, and I hewed two great flagpoles in the august court before his temple. (Nims 1971: 108)

Today the monumental gateway that gives access to the Eastern Temple is that of Nectanebo I of Dynasty XXX, but the gateway's very presence at this spot, where the shattered remains of two red granite obelisks, and two sphinxes, dated to Ramesses II have been found, would indicate an original gateway and enclosure wall of his had once stood there, as Bakenkhons claimed, before being replaced by those of the later king.

Within the enclosure, the sandstone inner doorway into Ramesses' temple had the unusual distinction of being given two names: one in its capacity as entrance to the Eastern Temple – 'the great door (called) Usermaatre-and-Amun-are-those-who-hear-prayers', and the second name as the entrance to the temple of Amun – 'the Upper Gateway of the Domain of Amun'; both names are to be seen inscribed on the jambs of the doorway (Barguet 1962: 226). This entrance led through to a peristyle court of eight 16-sided columns; the columns themselves, plastered over and reworked by Ramesses, actually date to Tuthmosis III and were probably taken from the earlier king's colonnaded approach to *his* eastern temple. Set in the middle of this peristyle court were two colossal Osiride pillars of Ramesses II engraved with his royal titles. An interesting graffito depicting the sacred bark of Re-Horakhte can be seen on the base of the southern colossus (Barguet 1962: 228 n. 2, pl. XXIXc); since this eastern end of the temple was dedicated to Amun-Re-Horakhte as the rising sun, it was an apt choice of subject.

At the back of this court was a large niche, possibly in the form of a false-door; later in the Ptolemaic period, this was knocked through to form a central doorway, but in Ramesses' time the niche would have housed the cult statue of Ramesses-who-hears-prayers, or possibly a dyad of Ramesses-and-Amun-who-hear-prayers. To either side of this central feature was a doorway each showing Ramesses entering, the door to the left being named for Mut and that to the right for Khonsu. These doorways now lead into an inner hallway, which was a Ptolemaic adaptation of what, in Ramesses' time, was an open area without side-walls but with a short colonnaded approach (again reusing columns of Tuthmosis III) to the base of the great single obelisk of Tuthmosis III (Barguet 1950: 269f.). The obelisk probably became the sacred focal point of an open solar sanctuary, but it is uncertain whether this was the case in Ramesses' day. Opinion is divided: some believe that the obelisk became the sanctuary area only in Ptolemaic times, but others believe that Tuthmosis III had intended his obelisk to be erected as the central focus of veneration, though perhaps not within a specific sanctuary: he did not, of course, live to see the obelisk erected – that task was undertaken by his grandson, Tuthmosis IV. Ramesses II, however, found the single towering shaft still standing in his day and may well have retained it as a focus for the solar cult of his own Eastern Temple (Barguet 1962: 241).

The decoration of the Eastern Temple contains a strikingly large number of references to Ramesses' sed-festivals, leading to the inevitable conclusion that this was indeed a jubilee temple constructed for one of the king's many celebrations of the event (Barguet 1962: 300). One block names Ramesses as 'Lord of Jubilees in the House of Amun', which seems a singularly appropriate epithet for a ruler who celebrated no less than fourteen such festivals.

While Ramesses constructed no other complete monuments at Karnak, he decorated many of the hitherto blank walls, some of which have already been mentioned (i.e. the outer western walls of the southern processional way). Another great expanse that he decorated was the entire girdle wall constructed by Tuthmosis III around Ipet-Sut, which stretched from the wing of the Fourth Pylon in the south, stretching round the Akh-Menu complex, to the wing of the Fifth Pylon to the north. Tuthmosis had merely inscribed the top of this wall with a single band of text: beneath this, Ramesses was to carve two registers of scenes along the whole length of the north, east and south walls. Being the person he was, he claimed to have built 'the temple anew' and spoke of 'a wall reaching up to the sky'. In reality, apart from the decoration, the most that Ramesses might have done would have been some repair work (Kitchen 1999: 397). But there is a profusion of interesting scenes and, in particular, there is a depiction of Ramesses erecting two obelisks dedicated to Re-Horakhte. These were probably the very obelisks the king had erected at the entrance to the Eastern Temple, that whole area being, of course, dedicated to Amun-Re-Horakhte. Other scenes include a whole series of coronation ceremonies: the king leaving the palace, being carried by the Souls of Pe and Nekhen, being purified by the gods, the royal progress towards the sanctuary where he is crowned by two deities who hold ribbed palm-branches signifying millions of years, and finally the newly crowned king offering to Amun and all the gods of Egypt.

Was Ramesses II crowned at Karnak? Two schist statues of very similar design, found in the Karnak cache, make it a distinct possibility. The king is represented semi-prostrate, pushing forward in the one case a small shrine, and in the other a rebus of his name (Ramesses-beloved-of-Amun), a ploy of which he was particularly fond (Habachi 1969: 38). The surface of each base on which the king kneels is inscribed with branches of the sacred *išd*-tree (persea), on the leaves of which are written his throne-name. These statues may well have been commissioned for Ramesses' coronation since, at that ceremony, the king's titulary was officially proclaimed and inscribed by the gods on the leaves of the persea-tree; and further, the name seen on these statues was the early version of Ramesses' name, only in use up to Year 2, whereafter it changed.

One of the most famous, and certainly the most beautiful, statues of the king is that which now resides in the Museo Egizio, Turin (no. 1380), but which was discovered at Karnak. Executed in black granite, highly polished and of superb quality, this statue of Ramesses II depicts him as a young ruler, seated in majesty upon a throne, crowned with the so-called Blue Crown and holding the crook in his right hand. Was this masterpiece of sculpture commissioned for Ramesses' coronation? Or was it, as some scholars have posited, a statue of his father, Seti I (Eaton-Krauss 1993b: 16) – even, perhaps, one of the 'great statues in black granite' which Seti never completed, discussed in the last chapter, and which Ramesses took over on his accession?

While all kings were considered to be divine, having received power from the gods through the very act of being crowned, Ramesses II, more even than Amenhotep III, 'made of himself a manifestation of the sun-god on earth' (Kitchen 1982: 178). His temple building was unsurpassed in quantity (if not in quality), and he erected more statues of himself than any other king. A huge number of cult statues of Ramesses are known from Karnak: many of these show him beside one of the great deities and bear such names as 'Ptah-of-Ramesses', 'Amun-of-Ramesses', 'Re-of-Ramesses', 'Atum-of-Ramesses'. It can be clearly seen upon such of those dyads as have survived that the king was actually represented as the dominant figure of the two – better carved and finished, and often slightly larger: in such dyads, there is no doubt that Ramesses was claiming divine status. Similarly, one of the king's cult colossi, named 'Re-of-Rulers', is shown on a private stela with the stela-owner kneeling before the statue and worshipping it, clearly illustrating its divinity.

Many of the dyads mentioned above can be seen depicted on the girdle wall of Tuthmosis III (Barguet 1962: 212–13), already discussed, along with scenes of Ramesses offering before row upon row of Egypt's deities. This aligning of himself with the pantheon of gods was repeated in an unusual format on the interior western wall of the Court of the Cachette. Here the city of Thebes, personified as a goddess, praises Amun and asks him to grant the king continued victories. This is followed by many identical couplets in which Egypt's goddesses, one by one in geographic procession, endorse the sentiment. This particular sequence of scenes, known as the Litany of Victorious Thebes (cf. OI *Khonsu* II 1981: pl. 179), was not, in fact, original to Ramesses II. It appears to be a copy of a Litany of his father's, alas largely destroyed, on the walls of the Hypostyle Hall. Later kings were to take up the theme and include similar versions on their own monuments also.

The message of the divinity of Ramesses II was proclaimed in many ways, but of prime importance, of course, was his claim to divine birth. Scenes of this momentous event, represented in the traditional form used at Deir el-Bahri and Luxor temples for the births of Hatshepsut and Amenhotep III respectively, are to be found at the Ramesseum within the small temple dedicated to Ramesses' mother, Queen Tuya (Gaballa 1967: 303–4): two episodes from this sequence of scenes were repeated on the walls of the Hypostyle Hall. Here, as might be expected, Amun is claimed as the king's father. But a further, and more unusual, version of events can be found carved upon the great stela, set up in conjunction with the Marriage Stela against the south face of the Ninth Pylon. In this instance, it is Ptah who is the progenitor of the king: 'I am your father who begot you ... I assumed my form as the Ram, Lord of Mendes, and I implanted you in your august mother', and then Ptah acknowledges Ramesses as his son in front of the company of gods. Again, it is unusual to see Ptah being given such prominence in the temple of Amun (Goelet 1993: 32), but there is no doubt that Ramesses' affiliation with the north was growing ever stronger which manifested itself even in the Domain of Amun. Nonetheless, Thebes still remained, and would continue to do so, the religious capital of Egypt.

Posterity has long referred to this monarch as 'Ramesses the Great', and few would dispute his right to the title – his achievements on many fronts were great indeed. But his father, Seti I, was a hard act to follow: who knows what Seti would have achieved had he been granted as many years of life as his son. But when one surveys the accomplishments of these two great kings within the temple of Karnak, Ramesses might have claimed the greater glory, but to Seti goes the crown.

Merenptah to the end of Dynasty XIX

Because of the exceptional length of Ramesses II's reign, twelve of his sons predeceased him and it was the thirteenth son, Merenptah, born to the second of Ramesses' Great Royal Wives, Isetnofret, who in the fullness of time succeeded his father upon the throne. Several princes, including the high-profile Khaemwaset (who, in modern times, has been called 'the first Egyptologist' on account of his habit of restoring older, damaged monuments), were nominated in turn as heir-apparent, but each was to die before acceding to the highest office. Merenptah himself was by no means a young man when Ramesses finally 'flew to his horizon', but he had for some years been very much in control of Egypt's affairs on his father's behalf as the old king's health and strength faded.

Up to Year 39 of Ramesses' reign, Merenptah simply bore the title 'royal son', after which he began to acquire more grandiose titles including 'Commander-in-chief of the Army'; but it was not until Year 55 or later that 'Crown Prince' was added to these – obviously by this point all his older brothers having died. As with the earlier Ramessides, Merenptah was never appointed official co-regent, but in the latter years of his father's reign, he certainly deputised for the ageing monarch in nearly all matters.

There are many representations of Merenptah as Crown Prince, and at Karnak two are known: one can be seen on the outer southern wall of the Hypostyle Hall below his father's reliefs of the Battle of Kadesh. Here a procession of royal princes is shown leading Hittite captives before the Theban Triad. Since Merenptah is the thirteenth and last figure in this procession, it can be assumed that his titles as heir-apparent were added much later than the original carving, particularly as Ramesses had fought the Battle of Kadesh in Year 5 of his reign and Merenptah was not appointed Crown Prince before Year 55. There is even the possibility that it was Merenptah himself who added not only his new title, but even his actual figure, behind his twelve brothers. Also from Karnak, but found in the Court of the Cachette, came a limestone solar-disk originally belonging to a criosphinx which, on its supporting pillar, names Merenptah as Crown Prince no less than three times.

Relatively elderly as he was upon his accession, Merenptah nevertheless reigned for approximately ten years, during which time he was actively engaged in large-scale military campaigning, supported by his own son and heir, Seti-Merenptah, thus enabling Egypt to hold on to the empire in Palestine and to deal effectively with a Nubian rebellion. But without doubt, the most important event of his reign was the repulsing and crushing in Year 5 of a serious invasion by a coalition of the Libyans and the so-called Sea Peoples. Merenptah's resounding victory was justly represented in glorious terms upon the walls of Karnak: Egypt had been gravely threatened and it had been a fierce conflict indeed.

The walls upon which he chose to commemorate this great event were on the east side of the court that lay between the Seventh Pylon and the southern wall of the Hypostyle Hall (in other words, the Court of the Cachette), this being the first court on the processional route leading to Luxor temple, and the place where the sacred barks would have assembled for any procession by land (as opposed to travelling by river) to

Luxor. The wall in question actually dates to Tuthmosis III, but must have remained undecorated, for upon its length, Merenptah caused to be inscribed a full description of his campaign, known as the Great Inscription, followed to its right by the Victory Stela, a hymn of triumph underlining the king's role as Egypt's saviour, which was basically an abbreviated form of the Great Inscription, but in poetic style. In this, Merenptah seems to have emulated his father's 'Bulletin' and 'Poem' of the Battle of Kadesh, also inscribed upon the walls of Karnak, as we have seen.

Today the Great Inscription has lost about one-third of its content, due to the collapse of many blocks, but the full text originally comprised some 79 vertical columns telling of Merenptah's campaign against the Libyans and Sea Peoples from the planning, preparation and implementation through to its ultimate victory, including the king's triumphant return with booty and prisoners (Davies, B. 1997: 151–72). There is a heavy emphasis throughout the text on the god Ptah, which indicates that the Karnak inscription was almost certainly a copy of a Memphite version, which very probably stood within the Ptah temple there (Sourouzian 1989: 144). The tradition of inscribing great events at both Memphis and Thebes had become established since Dynasty XVIII, nevertheless the fact that Merenptah had inscribed it so prominently in Ipet-Sut would indicate a sense of loyalty to the great god of Thebes.

To the right of the Great Inscription is carved the Victory Stela which, like its neighbour, has also lost its upper part. The text was composed of 39 horizontal lines and is a copy of the very famous 'Israel Stela' found at Merenptah's funerary temple on the West Bank, but with a few differences in style and writing (Davies, B. 1997: 173–88). For instance, where the name of Ptah occurs on the Israel Stela, it has been replaced on the Victory Stela by that of Amun, and Karnak itself is specifically named. Here again, then, is evidence of Merenptah's sense of obligation and devotion to Amun.

To the extreme right on this wall, alongside the great texts, are a series of reliefs in registers depicting the king before the gods and, in particular, the age-old scene representing the king massacring his enemies before Amun (Sourouzian 1989: 146–7). The customary format of this traditional scene was to show balancing reliefs of the ruler in the White Crown executing his southern enemies on the one hand, and on the other, wearing the Red Crown, dispatching his northern enemies. However, in this particular case, Merenptah is shown only wearing the Red Crown, perhaps because the enemies, and indeed the battle, were all in the north; there is no balancing relief for the south. This is strange in itself, but in addition it is certainly most unusual that such a scene should appear neither on a pylon nor on an outside wall for all to see. There is, however, a possible answer to that.

Merenptah's main building programme was very much concentrated at Memphis, but that programme apart, he was not a great builder of monuments, and his major work at Thebes was on the West Bank, namely his funerary temple and his tomb; at Karnak he is represented, as we have seen, more by his historical inscriptions than anything else. His father and grandfather had built extensively at Karnak and all the pylons from the Second to the Tenth were by now fully decorated. Nevertheless, Merenptah wished to leave his mark upon the great temple as all other kings before him had done. Consequently, his impressive decoration of texts, stela and reliefs along the southern processional way was surely intended to be Merenptah's version of the famous dedicatory statement: 'he made it as his monument for his father Amun'.

This 'monument' was placed, not within the sacred heart of Ipet-Sut, but upon a wall that would have been seen by all those who participated in festival processions (Sourouzian 1989: 148–9), not least by the god himself, veiled within his sacred bark.

Despite the lack of building, Merenptah's name is fairly well attested at Karnak: he added his cartouches to many of his predecessors' monuments, or sometimes he usurped them by replacing earlier cartouches with his own. One case in point is a fine relief of a criosphinx protecting a royal personage between its paws, which can be seen on the same wall as the king's Great Inscription; here the original king's name – probably that of his father – has been chiselled out and Merenptah's carved in its place. Since this attractive relief precedes Merenptah's own full-scale decoration of this wall, he no doubt felt this was an appropriate and justifiable usurpation.

Merenptah also dedicated statuary and probably some sphinxes at Karnak; one statue in particular should be noted for it is indicative of the special devotion the king had for the god Ptah, obvious even within the temple of Amun. Carved in red granite, it depicts the king kneeling and holding before him a seated statue of Ptah: a rare representation, since kings were customarily seated alongside deities in such dyads (Sourouzian 1989: 154).

Egypt enjoyed relative prosperity during Merenptah's reign, and although he retained Per-Ramesses as the capital city, he had the time and the resources to focus most of his building activities at Memphis, seemingly his spiritual home. He certainly felt an affinity with Ptah: his name, of course, translates as 'Beloved-of-Ptah'. Memphis, therefore, was where the king chose to construct his famed palace, the magnificence of which was an indication to all who saw it (especially foreigners) of the king's power. Such work as Merenptah did carry out at Karnak was obviously sufficient for him to feel that he had paid due homage to Amun-Re and fulfilled his traditional sacred obligations in Egypt's religious heart.

What followed upon the death of Merenptah is uncertain and, despite much research, there are still unanswered questions. There is no doubt that Merenptah's named heir was his son Seti-Merenptah, who bore the titles 'Heir of the Two Lands, Generalissimo and Senior Prince' and who had been prominent throughout his father's reign; yet somehow a hitherto unknown contender named Amenmesse stepped forward at this point to bury the deceased king with all the necessary attendant rites and claim the throne. What had happened to Seti-Merenptah? The general conclusion is that the heir-apparent had been absent at the vital time of his father's death, possibly away on campaign or on a diplomatic mission, and Amenmesse had seized the moment to his advantage. But who was Amenmesse? His parentage is not known; possibly he was yet another son of Ramesses II, or even of Merenptah, by a minor wife, because without any royal blood at all, it is hard to see how he could have successfully snatched the throne – he must at the very least have had some very influential backers. Another theory suggests that Amenmesse married some unknown daughter of Ramesses II and made *that* his justification for assuming royal power. However, recent work in his tomb (KV 10) in the Valley of the Kings indicates that despite reliefs of two royal women on the walls (Takhat, previously thought to have been his mother, and Beketwerel, thought to have been his queen), these reliefs were actually applied on top of those of Amenmesse (Ertman 1993: 41–3), thus totally obliterating his work – a highly unlikely scenario if these ladies were indeed his mother and wife respectively. There is nothing else known from the historical record to date that links Amenmesse with either of these women, but work is continuing.

Amenmesse's tomb in the Valley of the Kings is his only known monument; however, he made sure that his name was liberally scattered around Karnak and other sites in Egypt, renewing and/or usurping his predecessors' works. But his reign was short and when he died in Year 4, the erstwhile Crown Prince, Seti-Merenptah, buried his rival with the required ceremonies and then, ascending the throne as Userkheperure Meryamun Seti II, he ruthlessly suppressed Amenmesse's name throughout Karnak and elsewhere, wherever he could find it. In the circumstances, this does not seem surprising.

Seti II's own name appears on monuments the length and breadth of Egypt and his work is perhaps more extensive than many give him credit for. Upon gaining the throne, Seti took as his titulary a series of names that were modelled upon those of his grandfather Ramesses II. He himself had been trained as a soldier and had been Commander-in-Chief of the army under his father, campaigning widely during Merenptah's reign. In keeping with that status, his newly adopted titles had a militaristic ring to them and, although at first he seemed undecided between two different series, names such as 'Strong-of-arm, subduing-the-Nine-Bows' and 'Great-of-dread-in-all-lands' set the general tone.

These names are proclaimed in true regal fashion on a double-sided sandstone stela announcing Seti's work within the temple which was set up on the north side of the sphinx-lined avenue approach to the front gateway of Karnak. The hieroglyphs, both front and back as well as down the thickness of the sides, are deeply cut and they and the entire stela would doubtless have been encrusted with brilliant inlays – a clear reference to Seti's divine kingship stated powerfully at the very entrance to the god's domain.

Progressively, the kings of Dynasty XVIII had advanced the temple entrance ever further westwards until Horemheb's reign when, after the construction of the Second Pylon, this push to the west stopped. Today, at the very place of alighting before the House of Amun, two red sandstone obelisks of Seti II stand in the north-eastern and south-eastern corners respectively of the tribune. These were not very tall by obelisk standards, measuring about 3.8 m, and each had a seated lion or sphinx beside it: only the northern one of these figures remains and its ruinous state allows no inscription to confirm whether they, too, were Seti's work. In any case, it seems unlikely that this configuration was the original one.

But the new king's largest monument in the area in front of the temple's main entrance was a triple bark-shrine (Chevrier and Drioton 1940) constructed on the north side of the approach avenue and at right angles to it, so that it bordered on the processional avenue and was a convenient and appropriate place for the sacred barks to pause. It is of especial interest in that this monument was the first entirely free-standing tripartite shrine at Karnak where the barks of the Theban triad were all accommodated side-by-side. Many single bark-shrines and way-stations had been built in and around the sacred precinct, and contiguous shrines to house the three barks are known within other complexes, such as Akh-Menu, but Seti's tripartite shrine, standing alone as it did, was at that time unique.

The building is of sandstone standing upon a quartzite base, and quartzite was also used for the doorways of the three chapels. The façade has a pronounced batter and is surmounted by a cornice and a frieze of Seti's cartouches interrupted by a winged solar disk over the central doorway. The whole is a simple construction of classic proportions, with a width of about 21 m, a depth of 16.5 m, and with surprisingly thick walls, in the eastern one of which was accommodated a staircase to the roof. The shrine comprised three parallel chapels, each entered separately through its own doorway in the façade. That of Amun in the centre is, as might be expected, the largest of the three, with the slightly smaller chapel of Mut entered to the west (left, when facing the monument) and that of Khonsu to the east (right).

However, there is more to this small monument than at first meets the eye. It is always referred to as a bark-shrine, and so indeed it is, but it also had other very important functions as indicated by Seti's own words. He stated that it was a temple of millions of years, 'its beautiful name is "the Mansion of Seti-Merenptah in the temple of Amun"', and added that he had built it for his father Amun in front of Ipet-Sut as a place to adore, worship and pray to the gods. While the term 'temple of millions of years' is often associated with funerary monuments, we have already seen that it can also refer to commemorative buildings or cenotaphs, of which there is more than one example at Karnak; and the statement that it was to be used for the adoration, prayer and praise of the gods is unusual and of significance.

First, in its capacity as a bark-shrine, it would have been used as a resting place for the barks of the Theban Triad during the great Festival of Opet and the Beautiful Feast of the Valley, as well as for various other processions and ceremonies. Here the priests, who bore the ornate barks upon their shoulders, could lower their sacred burden on to the socles in each appointed shrine, where certain rituals would then have been performed. While they remained within the shrine, the barks would, in the words of Georges Legrain, the shrine's excavator (Legrain 1929: 78), have imparted their 'divine benediction' upon it and upon its builder, Seti II, which was of supreme importance to the king, since this shrine also functioned as a cult chapel for his *ka*.

Although the reliefs and texts within the tripartite shrine are badly damaged, they have much to tell. Within the central chapel of Amun, three niches can be seen in the rear wall, and at the back of each niche is carved, not depictions of the god as might be expected, but a representation of the king standing upon a sledge, denoting, in effect, a royal statue. On the side walls of each niche can be seen the figure of a *iwnmutef*-priest offering to the statue, along with texts referring to the king's *ka*: such priests, as well as having funerary connections, also served as *ka*-priests. Thus, in addition to being a bark-station, this shrine of Seti's was obviously designed to perpetuate his cult.

But there are further revelations contained within the shrine's decoration. Apart from serving as a royal cult chapel, there are other funerary overtones. It can be noted that in each of the shrine's three chapels, the reliefs of the king depict him being followed by a young prince, named in the accompanying texts as 'the king's eldest son, Seti-Merenptah', and described always by the epithet 'true-of-voice', indicating that this young man had died. In addition, the texts state that the monument was dedicated to the prince by the royal favour of his father, and in one instance it declares that it was for the *ka* of Prince Seti-Merenptah – a funerary gift that could, by tradition, be granted only by the reigning monarch.

Here, therefore, we see a monument, small in size, but great in significance for the king, because not only was it a bark-shrine where the associated rituals which were enacted 'profited' Seti himself as the builder, but it also served as a cult chapel for the royal *ka*, both during his life and after his death. And in addition, it served as a funerary endowment granted to his one-time heir, but now deceased eldest son, Seti-Merenptah (Blyth 1999: 41–2).

Outside the shrine two colossi of Seti II once stood guarding the entrance, the bases of which can still be seen in position. The statues themselves today reside in the Museo Egizio, Turin, and the Musée du Louvre, Paris, respectively.

Seti's work within the central Ipet-Sut enclosure is mostly found around the sanctuary area and in Akh-Menu. Much of this work became necessary due to the increase in size of the sacred bark itself and in the number of priests required to carry it. Consequently, doorways around the sanctuary and within Akh-Menu, as well as associated aisles and passages traversed by the bark procession, needed considerable modification, a task which Seti undertook leaving numerous renewal texts in his name. Whilst widening the entrance of Akh-Menu, Seti also took the opportunity to usurp the two colossi of Tuthmosis III that stood there, and Seti's name in blue pigment can still be seen upon the northern (left-hand) one.

There is no shortage, however, of statuary of his own to be found at Karnak. Apart from the two huge statues that stood before his tripartite shrine, three sandstone statues of Seti were found within the Hypostyle Hall, although whether this was their original location is somewhat doubtful. Another fine statue of Seti found at Karnak now stands in The British Museum (EA 26). This striking sculpture has been referred to by J. Vandier as the most beautiful royal statue within that museum's large collection (Vandier 1958: 400), but again its original location at Karnak is unknown. All these statues were undoubtedly the work of Seti but, as we have just seen, he was not averse to usurping yet more, and a most interesting theory has recently been published (Sourouzian 1995: 528–9). The two colossi of Ramesses II that today stand in front of the Second Pylon are actually thought to have been usurped by that king from Tuthmosis III or possibly Hatshepsut: he moved them from their original position to what was, in Ramesses' time, the entrance to Karnak, where he re-cut and reinscribed them. But the colossi were not placed facing each other as they do today, but stood parallel on either side of the gateway. It was Seti II, the theory states, who re-employed them yet again, turning them to face one another when the construction of his tripartite shrine altered the processional route and reconfigured the whole entrance area. This would explain why his titulary is to be seen only upon the west-facing side of the bases.

Seti certainly strove to ensure that his name would be remembered at Karnak. Large inlaid faience plaques of his cartouches, surmounted by double plumes and sun-disk, were once set into the thickness of the gateway of the Ninth Pylon. These sizeable plaques, about 134 mm high, were brilliantly coloured in blue and gold in a white background, and the notches found in the pylon gateway, into which the cartouches were inserted, are very deep (Pillet 1922: 252). Similar notches of identical dimensions are known from the gateways of both the Fourth and Eighth Pylons: however, since no faience plaques have been recovered from these, there is no proof as to their ownership. Nevertheless, this particular form of decoration was one much employed by Seti II, and faience plaques of his cartouches are known deriving from the Ramesseum, Luxor temple and Mitrahineh, as well as others of unknown provenance. The backs of all the plaques found bear the imprint of some material upon which they had been placed to dry after manufacture, and they are scored with the outline of a Seth animal and another symbol, which perhaps served both as a means of identification and to aid the bonding of the mortar when being set into place. All the plaques without exception bear these same symbols.

Several stelae of Seti II are known from Karnak, one referring in particular to his work of constructing 'a fowl-yard anew'. This stela was discovered to the south of the Sacred Lake, very close to the Karnak storehouse; although the storehouse was rebuilt in Dynasty XXIX, Seti's fowl-yard was probably associated with an earlier version of this building. Tuthmosis III had mentioned the existence of a fowl-yard in his Annals (*URK* IV: 745) and a Karnak official bearing the title 'overseer of fowl-houses' is known from his reign. Later, the edifice entitled *Tni-mnw* of Amenhotep IV also had an associated fowl-yard (Redford 1973: 84–5). Whether these two attested examples were one and the same or separate entities is not known, but it is possible that by Seti's reign these buildings were somewhat dilapidated, necessitating a new fowl-yard to be constructed. It must have been sizeable, for Seti claims that it was 'filled with geese, cranes, *dndn*-birds, *wrd*-birds, ducks, doves, *mnw*-birds and *s'š3*-fowl in order to provide the divine offerings for his father Amun' (Berg 1987: 49).

It must be admitted that, for a ruler who occupied the throne for only six years, Seti II's building legacy at Karnak was not insubstantial. He himself emphasised his achievements in no uncertain fashion:

> The perfect living god, great of monuments in the house of his father Amun, who has made his divine images, who has beautified his domain and adorned his temple with excellent monuments of eternity, the King of Upper and Lower Egypt, the image of Amun, Lord of the Two Lands, Userkheperure-Meryamun, victorious king, who has accomplished magnificent actions, prodigious of monuments, rich in marvels, whose every intent is immediately achieved like those of his father, the King of the Gods. He has illumined Thebes with great monuments; no other king has done what he has done, the Son of Re of his body, his beloved, the possessor of crowns, Seti-Merenptah. (Barguet 1962: 118)

This exaggerated claim to 'prodigious' monuments, inscribed on a wall adjacent to the Sixth Pylon, might, in today's parlance, be considered somewhat 'over the top', nonetheless Seti's constructions are worthy of a great deal more attention than they are customarily afforded.

Following the death of Seti II, the royal succession becomes clouded in uncertainty. With the Crown Prince, Seti-Merenptah, having predeceased his father, it is generally thought that a young man named Siptah, perhaps another son by a second queen, ascended the throne. At one time this new ruler was thought to have been two separate persons, since he was initially called Ramesses-Siptah and later changed his name to Merenptah-Siptah. During his reign of approximately six years, it was very probably Seti II's Great Royal Wife Tauseret, the young king's putative stepmother, who acted as regent, aided by a shadowy foreign official known as Chancellor Bay. This enigmatic figure was very much the power behind the throne and, indeed, was even accorded a small tomb in the Valley of the Kings. Siptah's short reign was seemingly uneventful, and upon his death Tauseret assumed full Pharaonic powers, having a sole reign of about two years' duration. It is not surprising, therefore, that neither she nor Siptah appear to have left so much as their name upon the walls of Karnak.

This whole murky period of history to the end of Dynasty XIX was most appropriately dubbed the 'Time of Troubles' by subsequent dynasties, and only Seti II was ever acknowledged as having been a legitimate wearer of the Double Crown.

13

RAMESSES III AND DYNASTY XX

Exactly how Dynasty XIX came to an end is unclear, but its description as the 'Time of Troubles' obviously summed up how this obscure period was viewed by its successors. The founder and first king of the new dynasty, the Twentieth, was named Setnakhte, but who he was and where he came from is not known, nor whether he had any genuine claim to the throne.

There is very little background to Setnakhte on which to draw: a stela of his from Elephantine gives a version of events, as does the historical section of the Great Harris Papyrus, although this latter was compiled somewhat later, during the reign of Ramesses IV (Peden 1994a: 213). These documents relate that the gods wished to restore peace to Egypt after a period when 'the land was in confusion'. To this end, 'they established their son, who came forth from their bodies to be Ruler, upon their Great Seat', namely Setnakhte. The new king promptly quelled some Asiatic rebellions, renewed temple cults, and generally brought stability back to Egypt 'which had languished'.

According to the Great Harris Papyrus, one of the first acts of Setnakhte's short reign was to appoint his son, Ramesses, to be Crown Prince, thus ensuring, he hoped, a smooth succession. He only reigned some two to three years and, not unsurprisingly, seems to have done little building work in that time. Other than his cartouches on the Mut temple pylon, Setnakhte's name is not attested at Karnak. It was to be a different matter, however, with his son.

Crown Prince Ramesses came to the throne as Usermaatre Meriamun, Ramesses Heka-Iunu (Ruler in Heliopolis). He greatly admired Ramesses II who, although probably not a direct ancestor, was certainly a celebrated royal predecessor whom the new king took as his role-model, adopting a similar titulary, building style and even, he would have us believe, some military campaigns, in an attempt to emulate the earlier ruler's glorious career: he even went so far as to name his sons after those of his hero. Ramesses II's self-propaganda, it seems, had already made its mark.

Setnakhte's wish for a trouble-free transfer of power was achieved as Ramesses III acknowledged: 'I accepted my father's office joyfully and the land was content, rejoicing in peace' (Peden 1994a: 215). But the peace was to be short-lived: in Year 5 of his reign, Ramesses undertook his first large-scale military campaign against the Libyans; two years later, the Sea Peoples, who had recovered from the crushing defeat inflicted by Merenptah, were invading Egypt again, necessitating decisive and powerful action by Ramesses; in Year 11, the king was engaged in a second Libyan war. This was supposedly followed by campaigns against Hittites, Syrians and Nubians, but since reliefs and inscriptions relating to these events seem merely to be virtual carbon copies of those of Ramesses II, obviously a large question mark hangs over their veracity.

All these military triumphs Ramesses chose to emblazon in vivid style upon the walls of his huge mortuary temple at Medinet Habu on the West Bank at Thebes. His work at Karnak was less dramatic and more concerned with honouring the gods.

His major construction at Karnak was a bark-shrine of substantial proportions. Like Seti II before him, he placed it in the open area in front of the temple entrance, the Second Pylon, and at right-angles to it – but on the opposing side to that of Seti and closer to the pylon. Although its function was that of a bark-shrine, Ramesses in effect built a complete small temple with all the components of such a structure: pylon entrance, forecourt, vestibule and hypostyle hall – only the usual single sanctuary at the rear was replaced by three chapels to receive the barks of the Theban triad.

One of the remarkable aspects of this edifice was that it was built entirely of new materials, an extremely unusual occurrence for this period (Chevrier 1933: 21). The majority of constructions contained many reused elements: at Karnak, for example, Ramesses III built the Temple of Khonsu almost completely out of re-employed materials, and other buildings of his likewise. That his bark-shrine was so unusual in this respect is an interesting point on which to ponder: it is hard to imagine that it was mere coincidence. This small temple of Ramesses was clearly viewed by him as something exceptional dedicated to the god of Thebes – 'the temple of Ramesses Heka-Iunu in the domain of Amun', which was qualified as a 'mysterious horizon' constructed 'in a great and holy place upon sacred ground'.

The shrine was built of sandstone throughout, only the main gateway being of granite. In true temple style it had its own pylon entrance bearing traditional scenes of the king smiting Egypt's enemies, and was fronted by two colossi of the king, each about 6 m in height; the pylon only differed from Karnak's other such entrances in its lack of any flagstaffs. The pylon gateway gave access to a forecourt colonnaded on both its east and west sides by eight square pillars, each fronted by an Osiride statue of the king; the eight to the right wear the Red Crown of Lower Egypt and the eight to the left the White Crown of Upper Egypt. The western side of the court was decorated with scenes of the Festival of Min (or his Karnak counterpart, Amun-Kamutef); in these scenes the king is followed by two of his sons, Princes Ramesses and Amonhirkhopshef. The east side depicts episodes from the Festival of Amun and its attendant bark procession.

Behind the forecourt stands a four-columned vestibule leading through to a small hypostyle hall with the three bark chapels beyond. This entire inner area was built upon an elevated terrace well over a metre above the forecourt level; its parapet was crowned with a cavetto cornice and a frieze of uraei, and four more Osiride statues stood upon the parapet, two either side of the central approach ramp. The portico is decorated with scenes of the king before various deities, and from here a doorway gives access to the hypostyle hall. The jambs either side of this doorway show Ramesses entering: his figure was once covered in some precious metal, though only the holes left by the securing pins remain to be seen.

The small hypostyle hall, 21.25 m wide and only 9 m deep, has two lateral rows of four columns each supporting the roof: again the scenes are mostly standard ones of the king offering to the gods. However, one register contains, somewhat unusually, a relief of Queen Ahmes-Nefertari before Amun (OI *Reliefs* 1936: pl. 51B) – but more of her a little later. Opening off the rear of the hall are three bark chapels: that of Amun in the centre being the largest and also the highest, thus making possible the insertion of clerestory windows to admit some light. The chapel of Mut stands to the east of Amun's and that of Khonsu to the west. All three shrines have side rooms opening off them, perhaps a type of sacristy where priests could be purified and ritual implements stored. The chapel of Amun has two such annexes, one on each side towards the back of the shrine, while Mut and Khonsu have one apiece. That of Mut also gives access to a staircase leading to the roof terraces, and to a tiny roof-top chapel. Upon the roof, channels for the dispersal of rainwater led to six gargoyles, three each on the east and west sides respectively.

The three shrines, as might be expected, have reliefs of the sacred barks, but in addition, the Amun shrine has a version of the Litany of Victorious Thebes (OI *Reliefs* 1936: pls 56A and 59B), already known from monuments of both Seti I and Ramesses II.

The exterior of Ramesses' temple has some interesting reliefs: on the west wall, scenes of various battles against Syrians and Libyans are fairly stereotyped, unlike those at Medinet Habu. But also on this wall is a very full representation of the water-borne procession of the Festival of Opet with the royal barge, the sacred barks of the Theban triad and assorted sailing boats, accompanied by singers and dancers, some with musical instruments and some waving palm-branches. It certainly gives a flavour of the excitement and joy of the celebrations. On the eastern exterior wall are depictions of a Royal Progress: here we see the king leaving the palace accompanied by standards; then he is shown in a palanquin borne on the shoulders of the Souls of Pe and Nekhen with their jackal and hawk faces. There are also three royal decrees concerning the presentation to Amun of various cult objects (OI *Reliefs* 1936: pl. 108). These decrees are of particular interest for they tell us a great deal about temple furnishings in a period that witnessed the last flowering of Egypt's great age of empire.

The decrees were dated to Years 6, 7 and 16 respectively: they were, however, all carved at the same time, although quite distinct the one from the other. The first decree endowed two gold and silver offering-stands, complete with twenty gold vessels, on which were to be placed offerings of bread, beer, incense and fruit, the quantities of each being precisely specified. Since Ramesses' temple/bark-shrine had not been constructed by Year 6, this decree is obviously a copy of one already in existence and these rich offerings were clearly intended for the main Karnak temple.

The second decree of Year 7, only one year later, is quite different: 'His Majesty decrees to endow divine offerings which are to be offered to his father Amun-Re, King of the Gods, upon the arm of the statue of the King of Upper and Lower Egypt, Ramesses III . . .' (Nelson 1936: 236). An explanation of this somewhat strange wording can be seen in a relief on the other side of Ramesses' temple which shows the king offering in front of the Theban triad; beside the offering-table is a stand upon which rests a small statuette of the king himself kneeling with one arm raised in a ritual gesture and the other arm and shoulder bearing a container piled high with various loaves of bread. Similar reliefs to this one can be observed around Karnak, inscribed by other monarchs, the purpose being, presumably, to act as a permanent substitute for the king in the daily offering ritual.

The third decree, dated to Year 16, gives information concerning an endowment of which Ramesses appears to have been particularly proud, for he had it inscribed on the walls of his temple/bark-shrine no less than five times (Nelson 1936: 237 n. 18). The decree opens with the words: 'His Majesty has decreed to establish divine offerings for his father Amun-Re, King of the Gods, newly upon his great and august offering-table called Great-of-Food ...'. But this seems to have been no ordinary offering table because Ramesses claims that 'thousands of *deben*' of precious metal were used in its manufacture. 'I made for thee (Amun) a great offering table of silver in hammered work, mounted with electrum, the inlaid figures of *ktm*-gold, with statues of the king of gold in hammered work'. A representation of this artefact accompanies the text, and the inlaid gold figures, which are fecundity figures, and the hammered gold statues of the king can all be clearly seen. The name of the table, Great-of-Food, is also visible. It is small wonder that Ramesses was proud of this marvellous object.

These three decrees shed a glimmer of light upon the incredible richness of decoration, furnishings and equipment that adorned the temple of Karnak which, in its heyday, must surely have defied description. The stupendous wealth that was lavished upon Amun and his domain gives some small indication of the honour and reverence in which the mighty god of Thebes was held.

There is another document which paints a similar picture, but it cannot be so accurately dated: it is known to be Ramesside and, since it mentions the temple at Medinet Habu, it cannot predate Ramesses III. The inscription giving the information was carved on the base of a statue of an official who was 'overseer of works in the House of Amun-Re, King of the Gods'. This man's responsibilities covered:

> all monuments of his (Amun's) house and in his house of gold, its ceiling and its walls being of gold and its pavement of pure silver ... I rendered service to the statues that are upon the Great Seat, these likewise of good gold, the fans, both round and of single plume, and the sacred eyes being of gold. (Gardiner 1948: 20–1)

This description almost certainly referred to the main sanctuary, while a further text relates to other areas:

> I was overseer of works for thy Ogdoad of sun-worshipping baboons which is in thy forecourt, I was overseer of works for thy columns of gold which had hitherto been painted blue, I was overseer of works for thy Ram, the great champion of Thebes, established in thy forecourt for ever.

Alan Gardiner comments that this is the only known reference to a colossal statue of the Ram, an animal sacred to Amun (Gardiner 1948: 21 and n. 10). It is by the recovery of these precious snippets of information, admittedly in some cases rather overblown, that we today can begin to visualise not only the richness of the temple decoration but, more unusually, the layout and disposition of some of its furniture which has long since disappeared.

There is evidence to show that Ramesses erected a small kiosk, or chapel of purification, in front of Karnak, probably where the sphinx-lined approach avenue stopped a little short of the Second Pylon. Here, on the north–south axis of the entrance to his bark-shrine/temple, stood this kiosk, now destroyed, but from which a large alabaster basin, sunk into the pavement, has been recovered (Grandet 1993: 248). The basin would have been used in the king's ritual purification before he entered the bark-shrine or Amun's main temple; various other implements of gold and silver were also used in this rite, and these are described in some detail in the Great Harris Papyrus. The papyrus also informs us that Ramesses erected two great gilded columns in front of the Second Pylon's entrance vestibule, supporting a light wooden roof that was similarly gilded and inlaid with precious stones. The columns were said to have rested upon silver bases (Grandet 1993: 249): this use of silver in such a context would indeed be unusual, but silver was obviously a metal that Ramesses liked to employ, as we have just seen. In any event, that there was a liberal use of all types of precious material there can be no doubt.

Ramesses' temple-cum-bark-shrine was his principal construction at Karnak in honour of Amun-Re: he also built a temple in honour of Khonsu within the Karnak precinct, and one dedicated to Mut within her own precinct. It can be assumed that all three were richly decorated as well as richly endowed.

The actual construction date of these temples within the Karnak complex is not known, but it is generally thought that Ramesses' first and greatest project, his mortuary temple on the West Bank, was completed around Year 12 and, consequently, that his major work at Karnak probably commenced towards the end of, or after, that period (Grandet 1993: 247); he had, after all, been very much occupied with years of warfare.

Sometime in Year 5, Ramesses III inscribed on the base of the Third Pylon's east face a decree announcing his intention to undertake an inspection of major temples (Peden 1994a: 187). It was ten years before this was implemented, the delay perhaps being due to his preoccupation with the wars. These would undoubtedly have been a drain on the state coffers, but once victory had been achieved and peace established, the king could turn his attention to temple finances, including reorganising the cults, carrying out any necessary repairs, and generally putting their affairs in order. To this end, in Year 15, an official named Penpato who bore the title Chief Archivist of the Treasury (Grandet 1993: 220) was given the commission to inspect the gods' temples, 'their treasuries, granaries and divine offerings, to make their temples flourish anew' (Peden 1994a: 189). A text regarding this undertaking can be seen at Tod and at Elephantine; at Karnak it was inscribed along the base of the west wall of the court between the Ninth and Tenth Pylons. Some of the results of Penpato's inspections were included in the Great Harris Papyrus: by Year 22, for example, Ramesses had altered all the endowments to Karnak – a huge and expensive undertaking in itself, since they were all considerably increased.

The Great Harris Papyrus (Papyrus Harris I, now in The British Museum) is the largest and most comprehensive document ever found in Egypt: about 42 m in length, comprising 117 columns of text on 76 'pages' of papyrus. It was actually compiled during the reign of Ramesses IV, but relates very largely to that of Ramesses III. The papyrus purports to be a complete list of all the temple endowments made by Ramesses III and their reconfirmation by Ramesses IV, with the purpose of validating the succession of the latter.

Amongst the myriad facts, figures and statistics that the papyrus gives, it is revealed that Karnak acted as the repository for all Egypt's temple archives. Earlier, Tuthmosis III's Annals had alluded to this fact, and now Ramesses III indicates something very similar:

> I made for thee (Amun) great tablets of silver ... bearing the decrees and inventories of the houses and temples which I made in Egypt in order to administer them in thy name ... I made for thee other tablets of copper ... with the house-regulations of the temples ... (BAR IV: para. 202).

This information is given under the section of the papyrus pertaining to the Great Amun Temple at Karnak. Many centuries later, the Roman historian Tacitus had occasion to refer to the historical archives housed at Karnak.

Ramesses III's other construction work at Karnak was not on the grand scale of many of his predecessors, but neither was it negligible. Amongst his works, he provided the main sanctuary with a fine naos in which to house the sacred image of Amun, this naos being carved from a single block of red granite and closed with a door of gold (Grandet 1993: 252). Red granite was also used for two small obelisks which were unearthed in the court between the Ninth and Tenth Pylons, although whether they were originally sited within this court is not known.

The meagre remains of a mud-brick enclosure wall attributable to Ramesses III can still be seen to the north of the Third and Fourth Pylons, and a stone gateway set in this wall bore the name 'Ramesses Heka-Iunu is he who sees the beauty of Amun' (Barguet 1962: 35–6, 83–4)). At the northern end of the court between these two pylons, another stone doorway, aligned on the former, and some mud-brick walls also bear Ramesses' name, but the function of the building to which they belonged is undetermined (Grandet 1993: 241).

Like several of his predecessors, Ramesses wished to add his name to Tuthmosis III's Akh-Menu complex; in particular, within the elevated solar sanctuary on the north side. Inscribed scenes show the king, followed by the Souls of Pe and Nekhen, worshipping the rising sun, as well as depictions of pharaoh before the Theban triad and other deities. All the scenes on the north and south walls are directed towards the east where the rays of the rising sun were allowed to penetrate the sanctuary through an opening or 'window', possibly an innovation of this date. The decoration is certainly Ramesside in style, with Ramesses III's names very apparent. However, they do appear to be carved over earlier cartouches, some of which might well be those of Amenmesse of the previous dynasty.

Another important set of scenes which Ramesses III added to an earlier monument was a series of reliefs upon the north face of the Eighth Pylon illustrating his coronation.

Ramesses III's other work in Amun's temple consisted of little more than adding his name, sometimes with accompanying texts, on his predecessors' monuments. Many of the texts are found running beneath earlier kings' scenes in long inscriptions, often referred to as 'bandeau texts'. Frequently they consist merely of standard repetitions of the royal titulary, but on occasion they give information of some interest. It was a ploy which came into vogue at Karnak during the Ramesside period. The longest of these ran round the entire girdle wall that enclosed the Middle Kingdom temple and the Akh-Menu complex on its three sides. This wall, constructed by Tuthmosis III, had been comprehensively decorated by Ramesses II; now Ramesses III added his own text with his names and titles along the base of the whole enclosure (PM II 1972: 127). These bandeaux were, of course, an easy way for a ruler to ensure that his name would remain visible for eternity within the temple with a minimum of time, trouble and expense. However, in the case of Ramesses III, these additions often took the form of brilliantly coloured and inlaid faience tiles showing his name within the 'palace-façade' motif, and these ornamented the base of many walls, pylons and gateways within the central temple and along the processional ways (Grandet 1993: 247): their brilliance must have been visually stunning.

There is a small but interesting adaptation attached by Ramesses III to one part of Seti I's battle reliefs on the northern outside wall of the Great Hypostyle Hall that is worth noting. The scene in question is one depicting Seti leading Hittite prisoners before the Theban triad who are shown within a naos. Ramesses III added six of his own cartouches beneath the naos, which he provided with small wooden uprights supporting a roof whose beams, fitted into notches in the wall above, are still visible (Grandet 1993: 251). The relief of this naos was, therefore, transformed into a cult image, obviously gilded and inlaid, in front of which those people who had no access to the Hypostyle Hall could make offerings and manifest their devotion to the Theban triad.

Finally, a few, largely unremarkable and damaged stelae of Ramesses' reign can be found at various locations around Karnak; however, a very large double-stela still stands in the Court of the Cachette. Dated to Year 20, the left-hand stela records a conversation between the king and the gods, and the right-hand section concerns the praise accorded to Ramesses by the gods for his work in renewing their temples, supplying divine offerings, and organising their cults and priesthoods (Peden 1994a: 117–31).

To return for a moment to the scene, mentioned above, of Queen Ahmes-Nefertari inscribed within the hypostyle hall of Ramesses' temple/bark-shrine: in addition to this unusual representation, another depiction of the deified queen, also inscribed by Ramesses III, is to be seen in the court of offerings between the Fifth and Sixth Pylons on the approach to Karnak's central shrine. Here it is a case of a block of alabaster inserted into a sandstone wall on which is depicted Ramesses, preceded by a small figure of Ahmes-Nefertari, offering an image of the goddess Maat to Amun. The precious scene shows the queen in fine raised relief that imitates Dynasty XVIII style, while the figure of Amun was, in its original state, covered in gold (Barguet 1962: 113 n. 6); the king himself, however, was carved in sunk relief. This intriguing tableau must be compared with the similar one to be found at the entrance to Tuthmosis III's House of Gold. At that location, as we have seen, it was originally a question of the king offering to the deified Amenhotep I and Ahmes-Nefertari. Later, in Ramesside times, when Ahmes-Nefertari became more prominent than Amenhotep, the blocks containing Amenhotep's figure were removed and replaced by alabaster blocks carved in the likeness of Amun. Here again, the deities are in raised relief and the king in sunk relief (Barguet 1962: 210). It seems probable that there was some cultic significance in this.

The cult of Ahmes-Nefertari became widespread in Ramesside times, while that of Amenhotep declined. H.H. Nelson comments upon the fact that during the Ramesside period the deified Amenhotep I was 'conspicuous only by his absence' (Nelson 1949: 345). Further scenes of the queen can be found in a variety of locations around Karnak, one of especial interest being in the Great Hypostyle Hall of Seti I where the queen is shown as having her own sacred bark. Recent work has uncovered a possible temple dedicated to Amenhotep I and Ahmes-Nefertari at North Karnak, and this might well have been where her sacred bark resided (Loeben 1987b: 238).

From all this it can be seen that while, under Ramesses III, the temple of Amun did not acquire a host of new monuments, as might have been expected from so great a king, it nonetheless was adorned with an immensely rich provision of temple furniture, decoration and cult objects.

Ramesses III reigned some thirty-two years and has often been dubbed 'the last of the great pharaohs'. His achievements were certainly notable, and did indeed to some extent emulate those of his much-admired role-model, Ramesses II. He had fought and won several major conflicts, repelling serious foreign invasions, as well as undertaking great building and reform programmes. However, throughout his reign, minor incursions of Libyans continued sporadically until by the time of his death they had infiltrated as far south as Thebes itself, probably through the western deserts and oases. In addition, there was unrest at home, including the famous 'strikes' by the Valley of the Kings' workforce at Deir el-Medina, and finally, and most dramatically, there was an assassination attempt upon the king's life. Whether Ramesses survived this is not absolutely clear, but his death did occur close to the event; nonetheless, his eldest surviving son, the Crown Prince, Ramesses (IV) succeeded him without any apparent challenge to his kingship. After the death of Ramesses III, there was a marked decline in temple building, not only at Karnak, but throughout Egypt generally; but it would be fair to say, of course, that by now the greatness of Egypt itself was in decline.

Ramesses IV was the fifth son of Ramesses III (Kitchen 1972: 186), but his four older brothers had predeceased him. By Year 22 of his father's reign, the young Ramesses had been appointed heir-apparent and was depicted as such in the reliefs of the Festival of Min in the forecourt of Ramesses III's temple/bark-shrine at Karnak. Following him in these reliefs, as already mentioned, is his younger brother, Amonhirkhopshef, later to become Ramesses VI, while Ramesses IV's *own* son was to rule as Ramesses V between the reigns of his father and his uncle.

While still Crown Prince, Ramesses IV appears to have undertaken some military campaigning on his father's behalf, which raised his profile throughout Egypt as Ramesses III's intended heir. Even more telling in this regard is a scene to be found in the tomb of Amenemope on the West Bank at Thebes where the tomb-owner is shown being invested as the new High Priest of Mut by Crown Prince Ramesses, while the reigning king, Ramesses III, looks on (Gaballa and Kitchen 1981: 176–7). This is quite without precedent, and indicates very clearly how determined Ramesses III was that all should know that his son Ramesses, his chosen successor, was destined to be the next monarch (Peden 1994b: 9–10). Ramesses IV, upon gaining the throne, put his own personal emphasis on his right to rule: 'I am a legitimate ruler, I did not usurp, I am in the place of the one who begot me ...'. In a dedication text within the Akh-Menu complex, he asserted in the time-honoured way that he had been chosen to rule by Amun-Re himself (Peden 1994b: 37).

Ramesses IV's reign lasted no more than six to seven years, and although he erected no buildings at Karnak, he certainly ensured that his name would be forever remembered there: he was 'the one who sanctifies the temple of Amun, King of the Gods, with monuments of eternal workmanship'. This somewhat overstates the case, it must be said, but his cartouches are certainly present throughout the temple precinct. A great proportion of the columns within the Hypostyle Hall of Seti I (a building with which many later kings wished to be associated) bear the names and titles of Ramesses IV, and bandeau texts of his are spread along the base of many of Karnak's walls, particularly those that line the southern processional way.

The largest monument that Ramesses IV left at Karnak was his so-called Festal Stela, which was carved on the eastern wall of the Court of the Cachette. This stela describes the king's visits to the temples of Re at Heliopolis, of Ptah at Memphis, and of Amun at Thebes which, being undertaken in his first regnal year, were very probably on the occasion of his coronation, when the new ruler traditionally visited the principal temples of Egypt's major deities. The text speaks of the miraculous recording of the king's name upon the leaves of the sacred *išd*-tree: at Re's temple the inscription was made in the god's 'secret colour as if of gold ... those who were beside him (the king) saw it and gave a shout to the height of heaven ... this had not happened to them (the king's ancestors) as it had for his Majesty' (Peden 1994a: 159). Likewise in Ptah's temple, the cartouches were said to be inscribed in the god's own writing. Unfortunately, the part of the stela relating to Amun's contribution to these miracles is damaged and only the description of the subsequent rejoicing and feasting remains to be read, but it was very probably in much the same vein. The text ends with several lists of divine offerings designated, one imagines, for the celebrations that took place at Karnak to commemorate this great event.

Ramesses IV's name is seen elsewhere in Karnak: on the obelisks of Tuthmosis I and on various walls from the Fourth Pylon through to Akh-Menu; he also undertook extensive decoration within the temple of Khonsu. He certainly ensured that his name would not be forgotten. His early prayers to Osiris (Peden 1994a: 151) to be granted as many years of life as his illustrious namesake, Ramesses II, were not heeded however, and in Year 7 he was laid to rest in his tomb by his son and successor, Ramesses V.

Subsequent kings of Dynasty XX, through to Ramesses XI, while erecting few monuments of their own, did not adopt a policy of usurping the work of earlier kings, although it is true that they had a tendency to *add* their own names alongside those of their forebears. However, the later rulers of this dynasty were certainly adept at usurping each other's cartouches on walls, statues and stelae, leaving a veritable jigsaw puzzle of reworked Ramesside titularies.

The name of Ramesses V occurs but rarely in Karnak: he reigned only four years, to be succeeded by his uncle, Ramesses VI, who himself usurped a great number of statues and reliefs; in particular, he seemed to wish to be associated with the southern processional way where the bandeau texts of his elder brother, Ramesses IV, were heavily usurped, as well as those that occupied prominent positions in other areas of Karnak. This concentration upon the usurpation of Ramesses IV's cartouches has led to suggestions that Ramesses VI deliberately persecuted his brother's memory, but it seems much more likely that economic considerations were the underlying factor in all this (Kitchen 1972: 192): a further indication being that the mammoth, but unfinished, funerary temple of Ramesses IV was usurped first by Ramesses V and then again by Ramesses VI (Peden 1994b: 81). These Ramesside kings might have been short of funds but there seemed to be no lack of grandiose schemes: the funerary monument commenced by Ramesses IV, and usurped by his son and his brother, would have been larger, had it been completed, than the Ramesseum (Peden 1994b: 49).

In the early part of his eight-year reign, Ramesses VI was apparently preoccupied with the problem of Libyan marauders who were mounting ever more serious raids as far south as Thebes, to such an extent that the burial of Ramesses V appears to have

Plate 13.1 Cartouche of Ramesses IV usurped by Ramesses VI (from the Wadjet Hall).

been postponed until Year 2 of his successor, by which time Ramesses VI had, it seems, finally managed to crush the invaders. The impression he leaves is of an aggressive and war-like pharaoh, in the mould of Ramesses II upon whose titulary he had modelled his own: 'strong-armed, defeating myriads' being a typical example. To celebrate his victory over the Libyans, he had a triumphal scene carved on Karnak's entrance (the Second Pylon), the last such relief until the reign of Sheshonk I of Dynasty XXII, some two centuries later (Amer 1985: 67 and n. 13); he also commemorated the event by erecting a dramatic statue of himself holding down a subjugated Libyan prisoner by his hair.

Although the kings were now residing permanently in the north, Thebes still remained Egypt's religious capital which the pharaoh and his court would visit on the occasion of all the great festivals: one text speaks of a state occasion when Ramesses VI came south to celebrate the Beautiful Feast of the Valley and to install his daughter Isis in the important post of God's Wife of Amun at Karnak, an event attended by the highest officials of the land (Amer 1985: 68).

Ramesses VI was succeeded by his son, Ramesses VII who, although he reigned for seven years, left nothing but a few usurpations at Karnak. *His* successor, Ramesses VIII, was the last son of Ramesses III: he reigned for one year only and is not attested at Karnak.

During this time, the High Priest of Amun, Ramessesnakht, who held office from the reign of Ramesses IV through to the early years of Ramesses IX, was growing increasingly rich and influential, and it is not over-fanciful to see in him the first of the priestly officials who were eventually going to assume almost regal status in the south and, in so doing, to divide the country (Peden 1994b: 80). Two statues of this powerful man are known from Karnak, as well as wall reliefs of him before the gods – an occurrence unheard of before this time – but a sign of the coming change in status and power.

With Ramesses IX, work at Karnak was once again being undertaken. This was largely carried out under the auspices of a new High Priest of Amun, Amenhotep, son of the aforementioned Ramessesnakht. He continued in the same vein as his father, claiming much of the glory for his work and constantly raising his personal profile by leaving highly visible records around the temple of his achievements there. While these activities were ostensibly undertaken for Amun by Ramesses IX, Amenhotep made very sure that his own part in the proceedings would be acknowledged for eternity.

The work of Ramesses IX and his High Priest was centred along Karnak's north–south axis, i.e. along the southern processional route, through a great gateway leading into the court between the Third and Fourth Pylons, and then out towards North Karnak and the temple of Montu, where further work was undertaken. This programme commenced, so Amenhotep informs us, with the construction of a portico, with a richly decorated double-leaved door, in front of the south face of the Eighth Pylon. Passing through this portico and pylon, a statue of Amenhotep, portrayed as a seated scribe, was placed against the south face of the Seventh Pylon; upon the statue base was inscribed a record of his work around Karnak telling of the 'excellent and many monuments which he made in the House of Amun-Re, King of the Gods, in the great name of Ramesses IX'. This whole area is a veritable monument to Amenhotep himself, for in addition he inscribed texts on the inside east wall of the court concerning further works of his, while on the outside wall is carved a large scene showing him being rewarded by the king for these great works. The remarkable feature here is that Amenhotep's figure standing before Ramesses is depicted as being equal in stature and importance to that of the king (Smith, W.S. 1965: 374, fig. 367). A further text, in which Amenhotep speaks of his restoration work upon the dwelling of the High-Priests that had been erected in the time of Senusret I, can be seen in the south-east corner of the same court, while an autobiographical text was inscribed on the outer rear wall of Tuthmosis III's alabaster bark-shrine just outside the court. In addition, a side door in the east wall, constructed by Tuthmosis III but left undecorated, bears reliefs of Amenhotep, one of which shows the seated figure of Amun receiving homage – not from the king, as would be expected, but from Amenhotep himself (Lefebvre 1929: 184ff.).

Leaving this court through the Seventh Pylon, the monumental gateway of Ramesses IX rises majestically at the northern end of this last court. It is one of the Temple of Amun's great entrances giving access from the southern processional way into the heart of the main temple where the two axes meet, and named by the king 'the great door (called) Neferkare-Setepenre-is-the-one-who-adorns-monuments-in-the-temple-of-Amun'. Two large, but very damaged sandstone sphinxes guard the gateway. It has been suggested that these replaced older ones, since an adjacent relief shows a young king Merenptah kneeling between the paws of a sphinx.

The gateway in its original state must have been imposing: today its cornice and winged sun-disk are missing, but when complete its height would have been about 7.5 m, while the width of the whole façade decorated by Ramesses IX extended to 21 m (Amer 1999: 3). A detailed examination of the reliefs has revealed that this was a festival gateway, through which all the processions to and from Luxor came and went. Registers of scenes show Ramesses IX before the Theban triad, many mirroring those within the Great Hypostyle Hall of Seti I. In particular, the sacred barks of Mut and Khonsu are depicted joining that of Amun within the Hypostyle Hall for great festive occasions and for processing out through the temple's main entrance for all river-borne festivals and processions (Amer 1999: 32).

In the court between the Third and Fourth Pylons stands a large, but damaged, stela of Ramesses IX inscribed with a hymn of praise to Amun; this is somewhat similar to the double-stela of Ramesses III in the Court of the Cachette, mentioned above, and it is probable that the missing part would have recorded Amun's reply. While this is an interesting, but fairly standard document, another document, this time on papyrus, is more unusual and gives a rare glimpse into the more day-to-day affairs of ordinary men in a pharaoh's employ. The papyrus was destined for Karnak's temple archives and takes the form of a letter addressed to the High Priest Ramessesnakht. This very fact dates the letter to early in the reign of Ramesses IX, because a little later Ramessesnakht was succeeded in his office by his son Amenhotep. The text concerns the need to obtain galena (a form of eye-paint) 'with all haste' for the king. We learn that the first expedition to obtain this eye-paint had been a disaster because the quality of the product sent to Ramesses IX had been sub-standard and the royal physicians had pronounced it 'worthless . . . and not fit for the use of Pharaoh' (Peden 1994a: 109). It was sent back forthwith with orders to acquire 'particularly good eye-paint'. We do not know the end of this little saga, but the perusal of this archive document, concerning such a mundane and practical matter, imparts a wonderful sense of the daily round that occupied the time of many levels of the temple personnel.

Ramesses IX enjoyed a reign of 18 to 19 years, but conditions at home were deteriorating: Libyan raiding parties were yet again threatening Thebes, while famines, food shortages and the pillaging of royal tombs were becoming a social scourge. Ramesses IX was succeeded by yet another Ramesses (X), possibly his son, but a king who left almost no record of his name at Karnak. The final king of Dynasty XX, Ramesses XI, was to rule for 29 years during which time the institution of monarchy, greatly weakened and undermined, was to undergo a fundamental change.

The early years of Ramesses XI were marked by crises at home; there was rampant lawlessness and social unrest on a large scale throughout Egypt. At this time, the King's Son (or Viceroy) of Kush, a powerful official named Panehsy, using the Nubian militia under his control, restored order in the Theban area and, with the king resident in the north of the country, assumed unchallenged power in the south. This remained the position for many years until, in about Year 19 of Ramesses XI, Panehsy vanished from the scene. Whether there had been a power struggle is not clear, but in his place a military officer named Herihor appeared as the new High Priest of Amun who, in addition, bore the titles of Generalissimo, King's Son of Kush and even Vizier. With so many high offices now vested in one person, Herihor's power was unassailable: he became *de facto* ruler of an area that stretched from Nubia in the south to El-Hibeh in middle Egypt. He quickly arranged to have his right to rule endorsed by an oracle of Khonsu and confirmed by Amun at Karnak. A declaration to this effect can be seen upon a stela in the Temple of Khonsu: although very badly damaged, it is noticeable that the text is peppered with the phrase: 'and the god agreed exceedingly, exceedingly' (Peden 1994a: 183). There was to be no doubt on this matter. Assuming more and more kingly attributes, Herihor pronounced this time as the start of an era of 'renaissance' (Egyp. *wḥm mswt*: the repeating of births) and began to date his 'reign' from Year 1 of this era, corresponding to Year 19 of Ramesses XI.

From this time Egypt was, to all intents and purposes, divided in two with a king as nominal ruler living in the north of the country, while the south was under the jurisdiction of a military pontiff, the High Priest of Amun and Generalissimo. This combined title, unknown before now, was one that Herihor's successors were to retain, along with its inherent powers: a state of affairs that was to last for three hundred years (Kitchen 1973: 250).

While Ramesses XI continued as king, residing in the north, Herihor took upon himself the decoration of the Khonsu temple, left incomplete by Ramesses III and IV. Initially he inscribed its hypostyle hall in the name of Ramesses XI, naming himself as High Priest, but later he decorated the entire forecourt in his sole name, adopting a royal titulary and enclosing a prenomen and nomen within cartouches. Amongst these titles he stressed his affiliation to the Theban area and its god: 'Strong Bull, Son of Amun' and 'Performing benefactions in Karnak for his father Amun'. Further, he appropriated the traditional royal announcement that he was 'appearing upon the throne of the living Horus . . . chosen of Amun himself', and had a sequence of scenes depicting his 'coronation' carved upon the temple walls; he even showed himself celebrating that most important of royal rites, a sed-festival. All aspects of divine ritual, normally reserved solely for the monarch, were now shown with Herihor as the celebrant, including one of the most essential royal functions – offering Maat to the god for the maintenance of universal order. There could be no doubting his kingly pretensions.

In the temple of Amun itself, Herihor's cartouches appear on the columns and walls of the Great Hypostyle Hall, that most prestigious of Ramesside monuments with which every king wished to be associated. It is thought that at this time there was a special link between the Temple of Khonsu and the Great Hypostyle Hall of the Temple of Amun (Roth 1983: 46–8). The Second Pylon, which was the entrance to the Hall, was depicted in great detail by Herihor on the wall of the Khonsu temple courtyard (OI *Khonsu* I 1979: pl. 52), and this pylon is also to be seen represented in the tomb of Herihor's immediate predecessor, Panehsy. Similarly, Herihor's 'royal' name appears in the Hall and in the Khonsu temple, but nowhere else at Karnak: however, it is interesting to note that all administrative documents are in his name of High Priest, King's Son of Kush, or Vizier, but never king (Kitchen 1973: 251).

Herihor's 'reign' lasted only seven years and he died before Ramesses XI. He was succeeded in the south as High Priest and Generalissimo by his son Piankh, who never used any kingly titles; in fact, generally speaking, he used only the simple title of General. This can be seen in an inscription of Piankh on the outer north face of the Edifice of Amenhotep II concerning an oracle confirming the appointment of a lesser official in the post of Scribe of the Storehouse of the Estate of Amun (Nims 1948: 157ff.). While Herihor, and then Piankh, controlled the southern half of the country, another possible son of Herihor, named Smendes (Egyp. Nesubanebdjed) (Wente 1967: 174), controlled the north with as much power as Herihor in the south, even while Ramesses XI was alive and resident there. However, with the death of Ramesses in Year 29 (or Year 11 of the Renaissance), it was to be a very different matter.

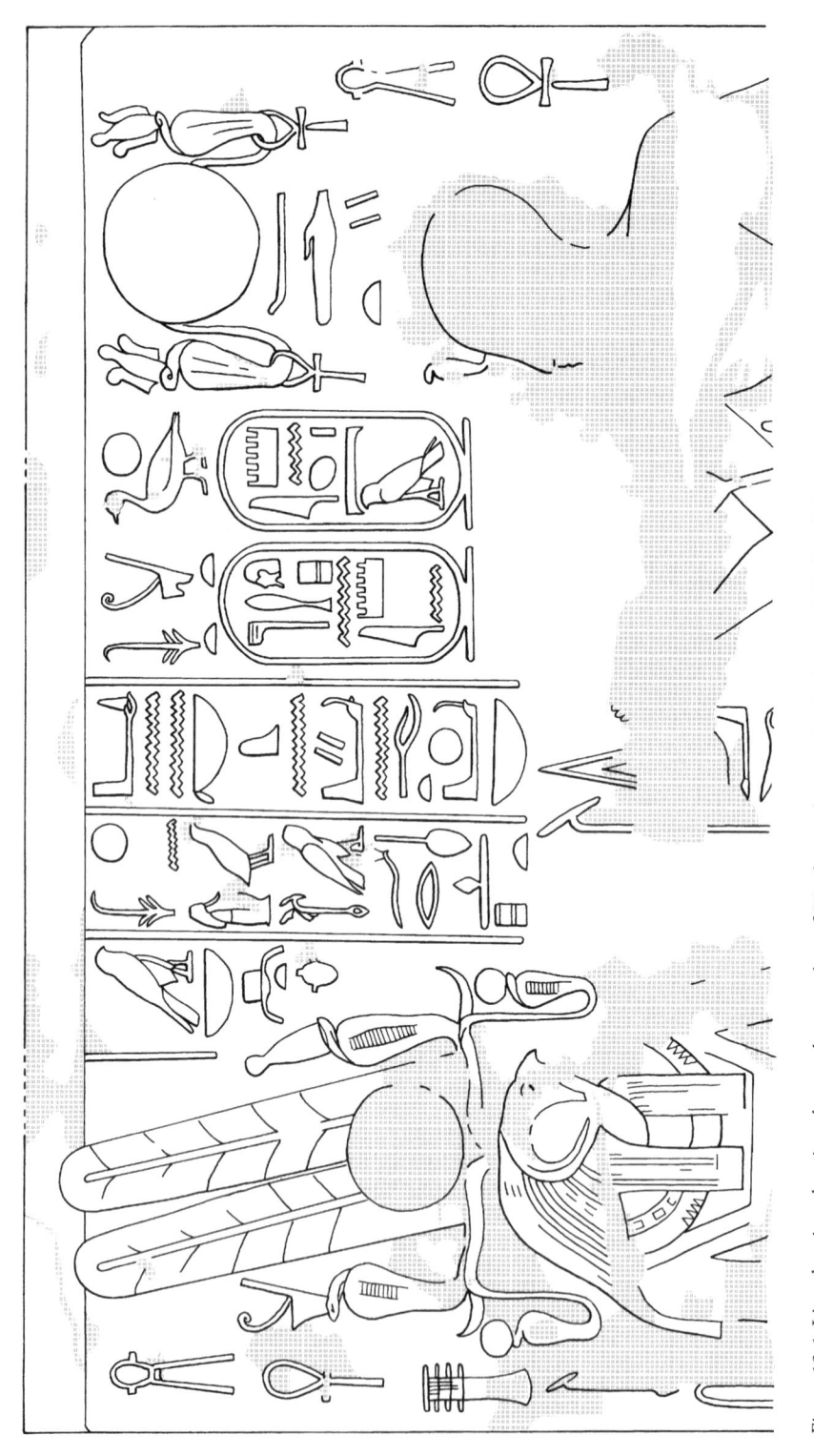

Figure 13.1 Line drawing showing the royal cartouches of Herihor to be seen in the hypostyle halls of the temples of Amun and Khonsu (after *The Temple of Khonsu*, vol. I: pl. 7).

Part 3

THE LATE PERIOD

14

DYNASTY XXI, DYNASTIES XXII–XXIV (LIBYAN PERIOD) AND DYNASTY XXV (NUBIAN PERIOD)

Dynasty XXI and Dynasties XXII–XXIV (Libyan period)

Upon the death of Ramesses XI, Smendes, whose wife is thought to have been a daughter of Ramesses, moved swiftly to consolidate his power by pronouncing himself king of the entire country, perhaps using his wife's royal connections as his justification. Although his actual power-base was limited to the north, he was generally accepted throughout Egypt as the new ruler and founder of Dynasty XXI. Meanwhile, the military High Priests of Amun continued to hold sway over the south, and when Piankh died, he was succeeded by his son Pinedjem (I), who himself seems to have married a daughter of Smendes (Kitchen 1973: 259): the inference from this being that the whole arrangement was an amicable one and mutually agreeable to both parties.

While Piankh, despite his undoubted power, was happy to use the simple title of General, Pinedjem was very much more ambitious and, like his grandfather Herihor, had royal aspirations. It was of significance, surely, that he named his son Menkheperre and his daughter Maatkare (Kitchen 1973: 258, 260), the respective prenomens of those great monarchs of Dynasty XVIII, Tuthmosis III and Hatshepsut. Initially he retained his titles of High Priest and Generalissimo, but he took the opportunity to install in front of the Second Pylon an Osiride colossus named for himself but usurped from an earlier Ramesside ruler. Further, he usurped the entire avenue of sphinxes that led from the quay to Karnak's main entrance, inscribing each one with his name, as well as supplying sphinxes to line the approach to the Temple of Khonsu. These latter may well have been removed from another sphinx-lined avenue dated to Amenhotep III which led to the Mut precinct, or may even have been brought over from Amenhotep's mortuary temple on the West Bank, no mean undertaking in itself. This information is gleaned from a rather vague text of Pinedjem's queen inscribed upon the base of a Sekhmet statue from the temple of Mut (Cabrol 1995b: 56). However, it was not until about Year 15 of Smendes that Pinedjem openly took a full royal titulary and pronounced himself King of Upper and Lower Egypt upon the Khonsu temple's pylon and gateway. A year later he appointed his son Menkheperre to the position of High Priest of Amun, while he himself was referred to as King Pinedjem on monuments and administrative documents alike. Menkheperre's name is attested at Karnak in two instances: in an action similar to that of Ramesses III, Menkheperre announced an inspection of all Theban temples; also a stela in his name, found in the Eastern Temple at Karnak, records the building of 'a very great wall' to the north of the temple where the houses of the general populace were beginning to encroach upon the sacred precinct

(Barguet 1962: 36–7). Two sons of Menkheperre were to succeed him in the post of High Priest, but neither he nor they ever affected kingly titles.

The remainder of Dynasty XXI's rulers and High Priests of Amun were to leave no traces at Karnak. Meanwhile, during the reign of Psusennes II, the last ruler of the dynasty, a man of Libyan extraction, whose family had settled in Egypt six generations earlier, rose to prominence to become both Commander-in-Chief of the Army and close adviser to the king. This military strong-man, named Sheshonk, was undoubtedly the most powerful individual in Egypt, so that, upon the death of Psusennes, with no obvious successor, it was Sheshonk who assumed the crown and was the first king of the so-called Libyan Dynasty (Dynasty XXII).

Sheshonk took prompt action to establish his authority. In order to ensure that the Theban pontiffs were under his control and did not operate a separate power-base in the south, he appointed members of his own family to all the key posts throughout Egypt: his son Iuput became High Priest of Amun and Generalissimo as well as Governor of Upper Egypt. Sheshonk had, in effect, reunified Egypt under one ruler: 'the one whom Re caused to appear as king to unite the Two Lands' (Kitchen 1973: 288–9). And with Sheshonk there was to be a return to a true monumental building programme once again.

Having achieved peace and stability at home, much of the remainder of Sheshonk's 21-year reign was taken up with campaigning, principally in Palestine, but also in Nubia, in order to regain some of Egypt's erstwhile foreign domination. His military triumphs, both north and south, ensured that tribute was once more flowing into the state coffers. His successful campaigns completed, the renewed wealth could now be employed in ambitious building works at home.

Amun being the god to whom Sheshonk was particularly devoted ensured that Karnak was the temple to which the king's activities in this field were principally directed. To honour the god of Thebes, Sheshonk inaugurated the building of a great forecourt in front of the Second Pylon at Karnak, a court that measured 81 m in depth and 101 m in width (enclosing an area of about 9,000 m^2, named 'The Mansion of Hedjkheperre Setepenre (Sheshonk) in Thebes'. A special quarry to provide the stone for this huge construction was opened in the sandstone quarries of Gebel Silsileh (Caminos 1952: 50), where a large stela was left commemorating the event. The king's son Iuput, the High Priest, seems to have been largely instrumental in the conception of the great court and his name features almost as prominently on the stela as that of his father. Moreover, as this project was undertaken towards the very end of Sheshonk's reign, it seems probable that Iuput was indeed the force behind it. The architect, Horemsaf, who carved the stela, tells us that he 'executed the opening of the quarry anew as the beginning of the work which the First Prophet of Amun-Re, Generalissimo and Army Leader Iuput ... son of the king ... did for his lord and for Amun-Re'.

Horemsaf further informs us:

> It was his Majesty who gave directions to build a very great pylon ... to illumine Thebes by erecting its doors of millions of cubits, to make a festival hall for the House of his father Amun-Re, King of the Gods, and to surround it with statues and a colonnade.

With the quarrying well underway, Horemsaf travelled north to the king's residence in order to report on the progress: 'All that thou hast said is being accomplished' (Caminos 1952: 51).

Sheshonk's 'festival court' enclosed completely the triple bark-shrine of Seti II on the north side and the front half of Ramesses III's temple/bark-shrine on the south. Along the court's north and south walls the colonnades, formed of closed papyrus columns, referred to in Horemsaf's stela, were constructed but never decorated: in all probability Sheshonk died before his vision was completed. However, some of the cornice blocks from the colonnade, decorated with Sheshonk's cartouches, have been found reused in the foundations of the tribune above the quay (Lauffray 1979: 92).

It is highly likely that the king had also planned a great pylon entrance, but this too was never achieved, and the court was perhaps hurriedly closed at the front by a mud-brick wall with a central gate. The section of the sphinx-lined avenue that had become enclosed within the new court was dismantled and the sphinxes placed against the northern and southern colonnades, where they can still be seen today.

From an early stage of the modern excavation work at Karnak, it was suggested by some that the First Pylon which stands at the entrance to Karnak today was also built by Sheshonk, but Henri Chevrier, and subsequent scholars, have pointed out the very different, and much later, building techniques involved in its construction, thus discounting the theory (Caminos 1952: 61).

Apart from the main western entrance, doorways also gave access to the forecourt on both the northern and southern sides. The northern one is small and unremarkable, but the southern gateway in the south-east corner is a magnificent entrance, known as the Bubastite Gate, which is inscribed and decorated in Sheshonk's name, and with a dedication text on the architrave. On the outside wall, a great triumphal scene was carved commemorating the king's campaigns against Israel and Judah. Sheshonk is depicted smiting his enemies before Amun who proffers the *khepesh*-sword of victory to the king; behind the figure of the god can be seen listed row upon row of captured towns and cities, their names enclosed in crenellated rings; while below the god stands the female personification of 'Victorious Thebes', likewise holding yet more names of vanquished cities: in all, 165 towns and cities are listed as having been conquered. This famous scene has prompted the suggestion that the façade of the Bubastite Gate represented the 'great pylon' referred to by Horemsaf in his stela.

The decoration of the gateway was never completed, but on the pilasters there are registers of scenes showing Sheshonk before the gods, always followed by his son Iuput; there are also a few scenes added by later kings of the dynasty.

Sheshonk's name is attested elsewhere at Karnak, especially in the hall adjacent to Tuthmosis III's Annals close to the central bark sanctuary. Unfortunately, the texts on the walls are very damaged, but they refer to the king's campaigns in Nubia and also to the tribute dedicated to Amun from victories in Palestine. In addition, Sheshonk erected a victory stela in the same hall, of which only fragments are now legible. Originally it was over a metre in height, carved in red quartzite, and once again the king's son Iuput features prominently with Sheshonk before Amun and Khonsu.

An interesting feature, now rather difficult to read due to weathering and also somewhat obscured under the modern road, was a series of Nile levels recorded on the western quay front. Amounting to 45 inscriptions in all, they covered a period beginning with Sheshonk I, through Dynasties XXII to XXV, and ending in the reign of Psamtik I, first king of Dynasty XXVI. A notable example from the reign of Osorkon III (Dynasty XXIII) records a particularly high level in Year 3: a corresponding text at Luxor temple tells us that 'the water rose covering the earth to its limits, it overran the two banks ... All the temples of Thebes were like marshes' (von Beckerath 1966: 44–5; BAR IV: para. 743). There is even a reference to fish being seen in the temple!

Building on the scale undertaken by Sheshonk had not taken place in the temple of Amun for several centuries; it took this powerful man to restore Egypt to some of its former glory, but it was to be a further two centuries before Karnak was to witness anything comparable.

During this span of time, a succession of kings and High Priests of Amun came and went, few leaving any mark upon the development of Karnak, the sum total of their work amounting to no more than a scattering of cartouches, a few statues, or an inscribed scene or text. The one exception was, however, the narrative of a Prince Osorkon, son of Takeloth II, who lived at the end of Dynasty XXII. Not only was this man the acknowledged Crown Prince, but his father also appointed him High Priest of Amun, Generalissimo and Army Leader, Governor of the South. Prince Osorkon was apparently welcomed in Thebes where he restored order after quelling a local rebellion, after which he issued five decrees to benefit Karnak with renewed offerings. For the next few years, he made regular visits to Thebes bringing shiploads of provisions and offerings for the great Theban festivals; but some years later another more serious rebellion broke out amounting to a prolonged and full-scale civil war. Years of bitter conflict ensued, which even this warrior-prince could not control, and peace could only be obtained through conciliation. Prince Osorkon left the annals of all these exploits and more in 77 long columns of autobiographical text upon the Bubastite Portal (Caminos 1958).

While the kings and High Priests left little witness to their reigns in the temple of Amun at Thebes, another form of monument began to emerge within the general precinct of Karnak, which was dedicated to Osiris, although the figure of Amun was always dominant in the decoration. Amun at this time had become associated with Osiris as the dying night sun, reborn the next day as Re, and an area to the north-east of the New Kingdom enclosure wall of Amun's temple became dedicated to this aspect of the cult (Robins 1997: 214). The monuments in question were small individual chapels, the first being erected during Dynasty XXII, but the majority during the so-called Nubian dynasty (Dynasty XXV). Six chapels were built in a row over a period in this northern area, which were later to become isolated by the construction of an enclosure wall around the Montu precinct incorporating these six small structures; individual access to them was, however, provided by the construction of a separate gateway for each one through the enclosure wall.

Closely associated with these chapels were the high-ranking priestesses who held the office of God's Wife of Amun at Karnak. Although this office had been known as early as Dynasty XVIII, it was only during the later dynasties that it became one of supreme importance, the incumbent's power and wealth exceeding that of the High Priest, whose influence dwindled to a mere sacerdotal role. The holder of the office of God's Wife, to which was added the title of Divine Adoratrix, was at this date always a king's unmarried daughter or sister, thus ensuring the loyalty of the Theban hierarchy: and on occasion it was she who could legally appoint her own successor in order to ensure that power passed smoothly and remained within the ruling family. On the walls of these Karnak chapels, the God's Wife of Amun soon adopted regal iconography, using two cartouches, wearing the royal uraeus on her brow, even celebrating sed-festivals, and indeed her power was little short of that of a monarch. The impressive funerary monuments on the West Bank of these powerful women contain ritual scenes previously solely the preserve of kings (Fazzini 1988: 24, pl. XL.1).

The first of the Karnak chapels was erected in Dynasty XXII during the reign of Osorkon II; it comprised two rooms with a small forecourt. The original name of the chapel was Osiris Wep-Ished, but today it is customarily referred to as 'Temple J': recent work has shown that it was dedicated to Isis, while its precinct was referred to as 'the Great Mound of the God', i.e. Osiris' burial place. In later dynasties, at certain festivals, the statue of Amun would process around this sector. Although very ruinous, some interesting reliefs remain, including one depicting seven Hathors in procession (PM II 1972: 203(J)). The 'Seven Hathors' traditionally pronounced the destiny of a new-born child (comparable perhaps to the fairy godmothers in 'The Sleeping Beauty' of our own tradition), and in this scene, they are associated with a young or re-born god – perhaps Amun-Re, born anew each day. The entire chapel was rich in Osirian and solar iconography.

Osorkon II was responsible for a second chapel, this time in association with his son Takeloth II and the God's Wife of Amun Karomama, whose beautiful and famous statuette resides today in the Musée du Louvre in Paris.

In the following dynasty, Osorkon III, in association with his daughter Shepenwepet (I), the God's Wife of Amun, and his son Takeloth (III), High Priest of Amun, erected another chapel, this time dedicated to Osiris Heka-Djet (Ruler of Eternity), which is still quite well preserved. Today this chapel stands hard up against Karnak's great enclosure wall, which was built considerably later by Nectanebo I (Dynasty XXX), but originally it stood outside the temple's earlier enclosure and had a small mud-brick girdle wall of its own with a stone entrance where the names and figures of Osorkon III, Takeloth III and Shepenwepet (I) can still be seen. The two innermost rooms are of this period, the forecourt and first chamber being added later, in the Nubian period. Although dedicated to Osiris, he and other gods are not represented as frequently as Amun; as with the gods, so with the humans, and it is Shepenwepet, Osorkon's daughter and Takeloth's sister, who is depicted more often than either king. Her role as celebrant of the offering ceremonial (Fazzini 1988: 20) and propitiator of the gods is emphatically stressed.

Some of the relief-work is highly unusual, often unique, such as a depiction of Shepenwepet wearing two Double Crowns (Legrain 1900b: 131; Fazzini 1988: 20): a scene showing a human, other than the sovereign, with such a headdress would be startling enough – this representation is quite extraordinary. She also bears the full cartouches of royalty: The Lady of the Two Lands, United with the Heart of Amun, Lady of Epiphanies, Shepenwepet I, Merytmut IV, God's Wife of Amun, Adoratrix of the God (Kitchen 1973: 356). Another unique relief, commemorating the elevation of Osorkon III's son Takeloth to the position of co-regent with his father, depicts the two kings back-to-back kneeling beneath two *išd*-trees: Amun writes the names of Osorkon upon the leaves of one tree, while Atum writes those of Takeloth upon the other (Legrain 1900b: 131–2). While the motif of the king's name written on the *išd*-tree is a part of royal iconography frequently seen on

THE LATE PERIOD

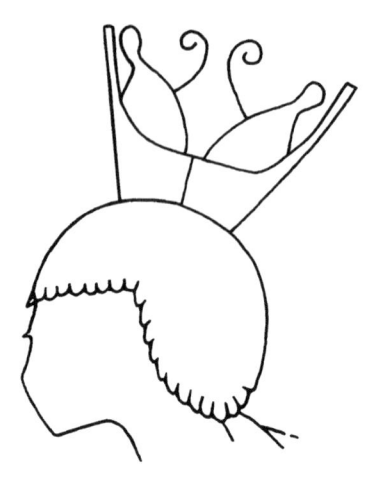

Figure 14.1 Drawing of Shepenwepet I wearing two double crowns, from the Chapel of Osiris Heka-Djet (after Legrain, G., in *RecTrav* 22: 131).

temple walls, this is the first and last occurrence of such a dual scene (Fazzini 1988: 21).

On what would have been the façade of the original building is an eye-catching false-door which is carved as a series of seven doors one within the other, giving a remarkable three-dimensional effect; it has been suggested as a 'perspectival rendering of a temple' (Fazzini 1988: 21). It was very probably used as an offering place, and at the very back of the false-door is a shallow niche, now blank, but perhaps originally containing a statue or some other focal point for the offering cult.

Throughout Dynasties XXII and XXIII, Nubia was slowly gaining in power and independence. Sheshonk I had been the last Egyptian ruler effectively to control that land and its products: a hundred years later, Nubia was to become a kingdom in its own right. The Nubian élite, after centuries of domination by their northern neighbours, had undoubtedly absorbed many aspects of Egypt's culture and religious beliefs; now under powerful monarchs of their own, an expansion northwards began.

Kashta, a young and active Nubian king, pushed into the south of Upper Egypt and assumed the title of King of Upper and Lower Egypt, although his sphere of influence probably extended no further north than Aswan, where he left a stela. Kashta's son, Piankhy (or Piye, to give him his true Napatan name), continued his father's ambitious drive, making advances still further into Upper Egypt until his power stretched well into the Theban area where he also claimed kingship, even while Takeloth III still reigned in the Delta. To underpin this claim, Piye installed his sister, Amenirdis (I), as God's Wife of Amun elect at Karnak, where the current God's Wife, Shepenwepet (I), daughter of Osorkon III and sister of Takeloth, was obliged to 'adopt' Amenirdis as her official successor (Fazzini 1988: 4).

Later in his reign, Piye campaigned as far north as Memphis, eventually subduing the whole of Egypt, but nonetheless decided subsequently to return to his native Nubia without consolidating his conquests, although he left his sister Amenirdis holding power at Karnak. This remained the *status quo* until his death when his brother and successor, Shabaka, ascended the throne. The new king, however, was not content with

Plate 14.1 False door on the façade of the chapel of Osiris Heka-Djet.

this situation: powerful families in the north were asserting their independent authority over an ever-widening area. Shabaka wasted no time therefore, in marching north to reconquer the whole country.

Dynasty XXV (Nubian period)

Once firmly established as ruler of both Egypt and Nubia, Shabaka was in a position to inaugurate a new round of building activity, much of it concentrated in the Theban area. He himself freely acknowledged Amun's role in his triumph, and his work at Karnak, though none of it monumental in scale, reflected his gratitude.

The new king's first undertaking within the Temple of Amun was the restoration of the 'golden' porch that Tuthmosis IV had constructed before the Fourth Pylon. Now, many centuries later, Shabaka found it in disrepair and set about renewing it. His dedication speaks of:

> making for it (the pylon door) a plating of fine gold ... that his Majesty had brought back, thanks to the victories that had been granted to him by his father Amun, as well as a great porch covered in fine gold, its two columns being clad with electrum, the two bases supporting them with pure silver.

It is somewhat intriguing that in this renewal text, when referring to the two columns, Shabaka uses hieroglyphs representing one lotus column and one papyrus column (Leclant 1951: 107, 112 and fig. 5). Did he perhaps replace the two open-papyrus columns of Tuthmosis IV's original porch with one each of lotus and papyrus, somewhat in the style of Tuthmosis III's 'heraldic' pillars?

Other restoration texts of the king were inscribed in this area and it is noticeable that Shabaka appears to have been careful not to usurp any of the existing scenes or texts of Tuthmosis IV, nor to claim any merit for the porch itself. Quite the reverse – where damage had occurred over the years, Shabaka, in his renewal work, faithfully reproduced Tuthmosis IV's cartouches (Barguet 1962: 90). Seemingly, he strove to restore the porch to its original condition, showing considerable respect for the memory of his Dynasty XVIII predecessor.

Shabaka must have had control of a good supply of gold, whether from his victories or from the mines in his native Nubia, is not known – perhaps from both. Endowed with this, the king felt it appropriate to build both a Treasury and a House of Gold at Karnak. As we saw with the Treasury, or *pr-ḥd*, of Tuthmosis I, it was a building designed to hold much of the produce of the land, destined for use in offering rituals, and which was surrounded by bakeries, breweries and a variety of workshops. Shabaka's treasury, however, seems to have been more closely associated with the temple proper and it is possible that many of the precious artefacts used in the offering rituals were housed, maybe even manufactured, here. From this building and its workshops, any new statues would have been carried to the House of Gold, where the Opening-of-the-Mouth ceremony was then performed in order to imbue them with divine life.

Sadly, the remnants of these two buildings of Shabaka are negligible indeed. The House of Gold stood immediately north of the Third Pylon where remains of four rows of sandstone columns and an area of paving can be seen. A dedication text inscribed on some of the recovered column-drums declares that the king had built for Amun 'a

House of Gold ... in order to create there the statues of the gods of the south and of the north, and to open their mouths ...' (Barguet 1962: 17 n. 6). The Treasury of Shabaka was situated between the north wall of the Akh-Menu complex and the great enclosure wall of Nectanebo I (built later). The *pr-ḥd* itself was a mud-brick construction, now completely destroyed, but it had a colonnaded entrance of twelve sandstone columns either side of a north–south axis. The remains that are left show that each column had four lines of text in blue pigment down its length, among them a dedication formula referring to a *pr-ḥd* 'full of beautiful things for divine offerings' (Barguet 1962: 38 n. 7).

Two chapels dedicated to Osiris were constructed during Shabaka's reign. The chapel of Osiris Neb-Ankh (Lord of Life) had a small pylon-like entrance, a forecourt and two interconnected chambers. Although today it is very ruinous, the cartouches of Shabaka and the God's Wife of Amun, Amenirdis (I), flank the main entrance. On either side of the door of one of the inner chambers is a niche formed by four small naoi carved one inside the other – a similar three-dimensional technique, though smaller and less dramatic, to the great false-door, already mentioned, in the earlier chapel of Osiris Heka-Djet. A beautiful alabaster statue of Amenirdis (now in the Cairo Museum) was found in the chapel of Osiris Neb-Ankh, which is probably where it originally stood, for the chapel name is inscribed on the statue-base (Leclant 1965: 96).

The second chapel, which bore the name Osiris-Onnophris-in-the-heart-of-the-persea-tree (*ḥry ib p3 išd*), was mostly constructed of mud-brick with an inner chapel of limestone, approached through a series of small courts; it also boasted a small stone approach-colonnade. A lintel from the chapel's outer doorway bears three cartouches: to the left Shepenwepet (I), in the centre Osiris-Onnophris, and to the right Amenirdis (I) (Leclant 1965: 43–4). The jambs of the doorway of the chapel façade show the two God's Wives, one to each side, embracing Amun in an uncharacteristically intimate fashion, with one arm hanging around the god's neck and the other across his chest (Fazzini 1988: 20). This is a reversal of the customary scene in which the god embraces his 'wife'.

As well as a new gateway added to the Ptah temple and some work in the Montu precinct, other buildings of Shabaka obviously existed at Karnak because various blocks bearing his name have been found reused in several locations, in particular built into the entrance to the Edifice of Taharqa (Parker *et al.* 1979: 6) near the Sacred Lake. Whether these latter blocks, of which there are quite a number, came from a building Shabaka had previously erected at that very spot, or whether Taharqa had dismantled some construction of his uncle's elsewhere, cannot be determined.

Shabaka's reign lasted some fourteen years, during which time he had coped skilfully with the impending threat from the Assyrians to the north. Upon his death he was succeeded by his nephew, Shabitku, son of Piye. From the outset of the new king's reign, Assyrian power was in the ascendant, and Shabitku dispatched his younger brother, Taharqa, with an army to counter this menace. Eventually the Assyrians withdrew rather than take on the Egyptian army at that time: Shabitku's remaining decade of rule was peaceful.

The work that the king undertook at Karnak did not amount to much. A small free-standing chapel dedicated to Amun was erected south of the Sacred Lake, but there is nothing to be seen of this now because, in the nineteenth century, Karl Lepsius removed it (and its close neighbour, dated to Osorkon III) in its entirety to Berlin

(Leclant 1965: 59–60). More visible is the addition that Shabitku and the God's Wife of Amun, Amenirdis (I), made to the chapel of Osiris Heka-Djet: this was in the form of a broad chamber that extended across the entire front of the original building of Dynasty XXIII. The façade of the new chamber bears a full-size tableau of Shabitku before Amun, who hands the king a *khepesh*-sword, *w3s*-sceptre and sed-festival signs; while on the jambs of the entrance doorway Amenirdis can be seen to one side and Shepenwepet (I) the other. Whether the elderly Shepenwepet was still alive at this point is uncertain – her cartouches are very few in number compared to those of Amenirdis (Leclant 1965: 50), and it is certainly known that sometime during Shabitku's reign, Amenirdis 'adopted' Shepenwepet (II), her niece and Shabitku's sister, as her successor. However, the cartouches of Shepenwepet II are different from those of her earlier namesake, so it can be ascertained that it is indeed Shepenwepet I who features in the chapel. It was Amenirdis, however, who recorded the dedication text at the chapel entrance: 'The great doorway of the God's Wife, the Divine Adoratrix, Amenirdis, whom the people adore, in the house of her father Osiris, Ruler of Eternity': neither the king nor Shepenwepet are mentioned. Inside the chamber a relief of Amenirdis can be seen presenting the temple to Amun, not to Osiris, despite the dedicatory inscription.

Taharqa

Shabitku died at Memphis and it was there that his younger brother Taharqa was crowned: in Taharqa's own words he 'received the crown in Memphis, after the Falcon flew to heaven' – the Falcon being, of course, the deceased king. Taharqa's reign was to last twenty-six years during which time he achieved a truly monumental building programme: with him we hear an echo of bygone glories (Fig. 14.2a).

As a devout worshipper of Amun, Taharqa rejoiced in glorifying the god's temple at Karnak with spectacular constructions. Even when disaster struck, as it did in Year 6 of his reign in the form of a catastrophic flood which overwhelmed the land, he still managed to marvel at the god's goodness in bestowing 'four wonders' upon Egypt, despite the huge amount of damage that had ensued. Taharqa recorded this unprecedented event upon a series of stelae and scarabs, amongst them a granite stela in the Temple of Kawa in Nubia (Macadam 1949: 27). Upon it the king claimed that he had been praying for floods in order to prevent famine, but when they came, they 'penetrated the hills of Upper Egypt, overtopped the mounds of Lower Egypt, and the land became a primordial ocean . . . there was no distinguishing the land'. Nonetheless, Taharqa counted his blessings quite literally (the 'four wonders') and announced that the flood had 'caused the cultivation to be good', had 'slain the rats and snakes', had 'kept away the devouring of locusts' and had given Egypt 'an incalculable harvest'. This must surely rate, in today's terms, as positive thinking in the highest degree.

Taharqa had the height of this record flood inscribed upon the west face of the quay at Karnak's entrance. Doubtless repairs were necessary to the temple after such an event, and an important official of the time, the Fourth Prophet of Amun at Karnak, Montuemhat, recorded that he had repaired all the temple walls 'of fine white sandstone to keep off the flood . . . when it came' (BAR IV: para. 914). Four other Nile levels were inscribed by Taharqa on the quayside during his reign, more than any other king. But, as we shall see, water was an element that seemed to hold a particular significance for this king.

Evidence of this, for example, is to be found at the southern end of the quay where two paved ramps descend down to the water's edge (Lauffray 1979: 94). The wider of the two is undecorated and probably served some utilitarian purpose, but the other is quite elegantly constructed and was clearly a processional ramp used in rites associated with the inundation which brought a renewal of life to the land. Low parapet walls border this ramp, their internal faces inscribed on the one side with Taharqa's titulary and on the other with a hymn which was probably chanted as the priests descended to the water in order to fill precious vessels with the renewed and purified waters during the Festival of the New Year, which was celebrated at the start of the annual inundation (Traunecker *et al.* 1981: 90). It is very likely that the king erected some sort of adjacent chapel for use in the course of these and allied ceremonies – quite possibly where the chapel of Hakor stands today, beneath which the remains of earlier walls have been found. It is certain that the ramp would have been but one element in a ritual complex linked to the Nile festivities.

These interesting works of Taharqa outside the temple entrance are now left behind as today's visitor enters Amun's precinct through the massive First Pylon. Immediately the eye is caught by the sight of a single towering column, a photograph of which graces almost every guide book to Karnak. Having duly admired it, however, the visitor is swept on into the wonder of the Hypostyle Hall without a backward glance. This is sad, for Taharqa's construction to which this column belonged was a wonder of its own: to our knowledge it is unique, although its true function eludes us and remains something of a mystery.

This one elegant column is the sole survivor of ten such columns belonging to a building erected in front of the Second Pylon. Frequently designated 'the kiosk of Taharqa', it is, in fact, no such thing since, traditionally, a kiosk would have been roofed, while the width of this columned structure was so great (16.25 m) as to make roofing it, even in timber, an impossibility. It stood close to, but quite independent of, the Second Pylon; thus in no way could it be said to have resembled a vestibule, having quite separate entry and exit doors of its own, and it was not linked to any other building (Lauffray 1979: 102–3) (Figs. 14.2b, 14.3).

The structure, paved in red granite, comprised two rows of five open-papyrus columns, built of small limestone blocks, and soaring to a height of 18.87 m, almost equalling that of the gigantic central columns of Seti I's Hypostyle Hall (Arnold 1999: 51). The intercolumnar screen walls, still visible today, were added later in Ptolemaic times. The two main entrances at the west and east ends were identical in design, and there were also entrances on the north and south sides between the second and third columns. A paved way, bordered with low stone parapet walls, extended from Karnak's entrance gate to the structure's west front where the remains of two granite colossi have been found; these statues doubtless stood one to each side, while some short distance west of them two pedestal bases probably once supported small obelisks.

This was clearly a special monument, but what was its function? Being open to the sky both at the top and the sides, it cannot have functioned as a bark-station, notwithstanding the alabaster base that is to be found on the east–west axis within it. Originally this base was assumed to be a socle for the sacred bark, but the sheer size and height of the polished block preclude that as a theory; it was almost undoubtedly an altar, which, it should be added, has been shown to predate Taharqa's construction. An unroofed structure, as this monument was, would indicate solar rites of some

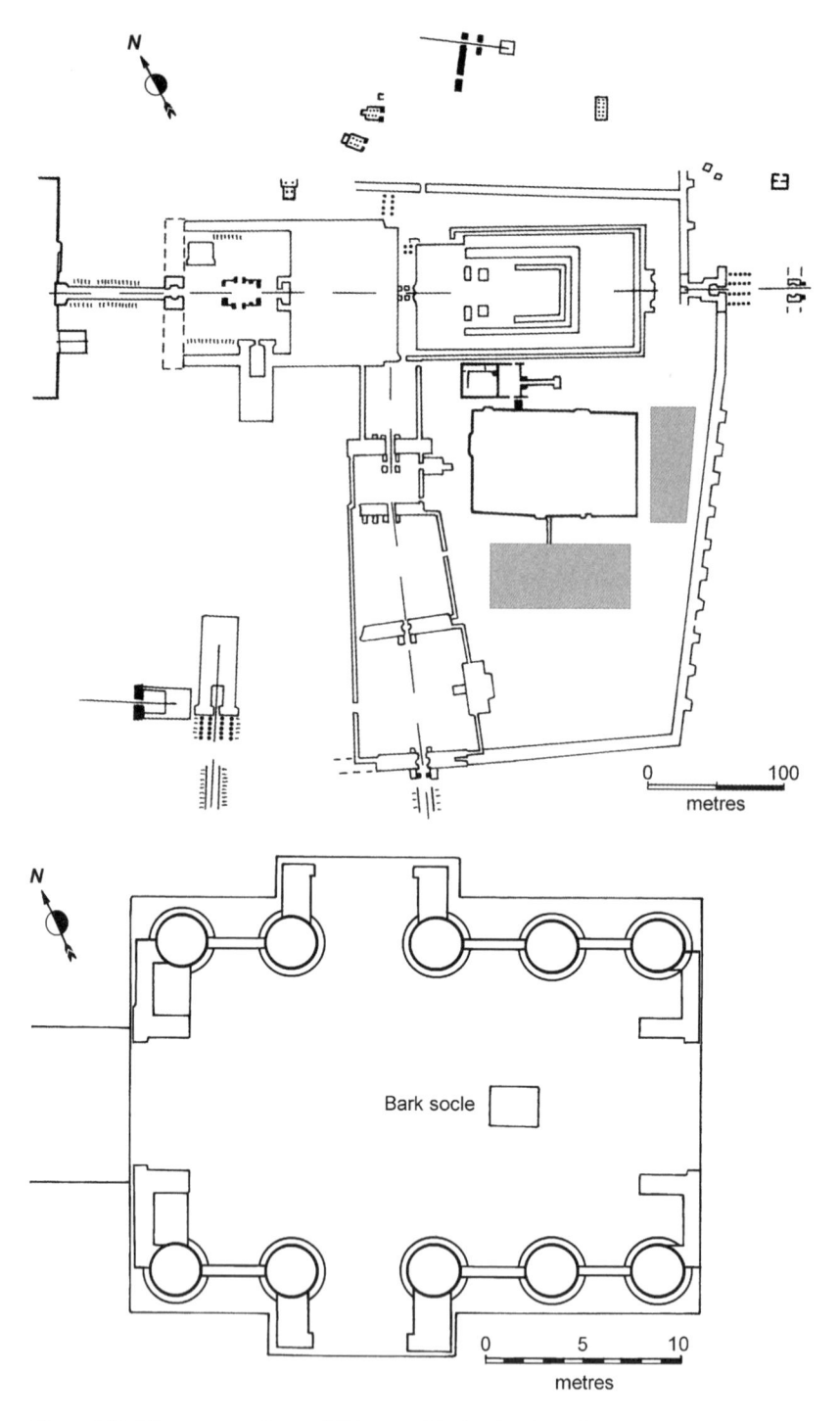

Figure 14.2 The constructions of Taharqa. (a) Sketch plan of the constructions (shown in black) (after Aufrère, S. *et al.*, *L'Égypte Restituée*: 106). (b) Plan of the 'kiosk' of Taharqa in the First Court of the Temple of Amun (after Arnold, D., *Temples of the Last Pharaohs*: 53).

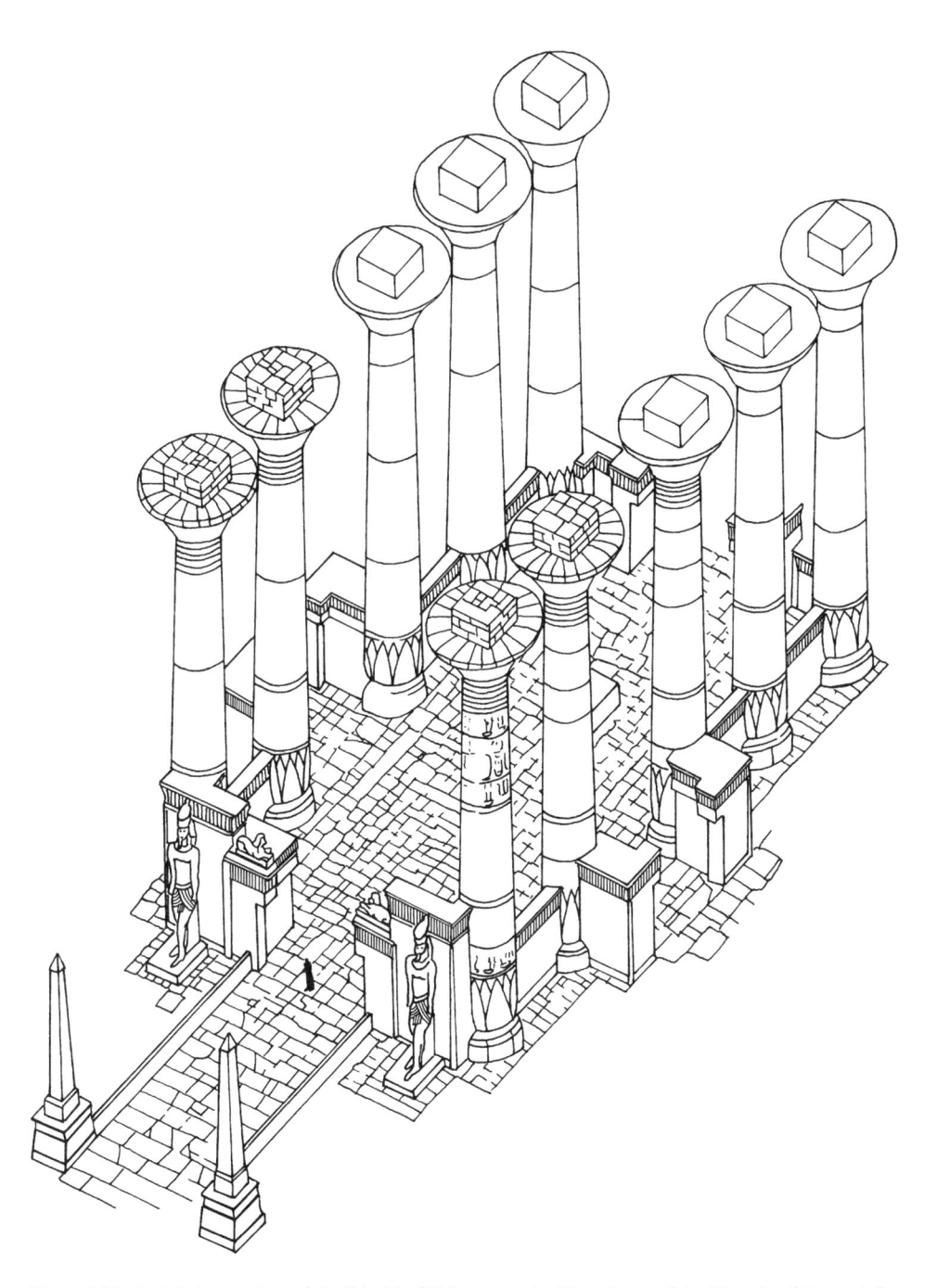

Figure 14.3 Artist's impression of the 'kiosk' of Taharqa in the First Court of the Temple of Amun (after Lauffray, J., *Karnak d'Égypte*: 102).

kind. A late text from the temple at Esna describes the ceremony of 'Union with the Sun', which was enacted on certain festival days in front of the temple, during the course of which divine offerings were introduced from the sides of the court – which would certainly explain the side entrances of Taharqa's monument, a somewhat strange feature. Previously this early morning rite, which re-invigorated the god's image with cosmic life, was conducted on the roof, or in the high solar temple of Akh-Menu, but in later periods was customarily held before the temple entrance (Lauffray 1979: 107).

There are further unusual features that have occasioned speculation. It has been suggested that the imposing columns of Taharqa's structure might once have been crowned with figures or emblems of the gods: a few such columns from buildings of other dynasties *are* known, although of smaller dimensions. One example stands today in the grounds of the Cairo Museum: of red granite, and measuring 4 m in height, it is surmounted by a kneeling figure of Merenptah protected by the outstretched wings of a falcon. To add weight to this as a possibility is the fact that Taharqa's monument has been found to be standing on the site of an earlier structure (Lauffray 1979: 107). A large number of holes were uncovered beneath the paving slabs: although of small diameter, they certainly were not left by scaffolding poles, but could well have held a series of wooden masts topped with divine emblems, as can be seen on many representations of the river barge Userhet where they adorn the front and back of the cabin that houses the divine image (an example of which can be seen in relief upon the east wall of the Second Pylon). Such wooden masts date back to those erected at the front entrance of the earliest predynastic temples. Were Taharqa's mighty columns versions of these translated into stone (Fig. 14.4)?

Although the intention of this book is to cover only the temple of Amun within the Karnak complex, it is necessary in the case of Taharqa to view his various entrance colonnades as an entity, since his purpose seems to have been to erect one at the main entrance to each temple: those of Amun, Montu, Khonsu, Mut and the Eastern Temple of Amun-Re-Horakhte each received one. The great structure at the west front of Amun's temple that we have just been discussing is often referred to as one of these colonnades but, as already indicated, it is unique in both form and function, and differs from the rest. The colonnade that once stood before the Mut sanctuary has all but disappeared, but the three remaining are, however, very similar in design to one another, each comprising four rows of five open-papyrus columns, all in the region of 9.5 m. in height, the columns of each row being linked by intercolumnar walls, mainly decorated with coronation and offering scenes (Fazzini 1988: pl. IX.2). These colonnaded 'porches' of Taharqa were distinctively paved with red or black granite slabs for the central nave and with limestone or alabaster for the two side aisles. In addition, the porches were architecturally joined to the temple façade, and were also roofed, although that which stood in front of the Montu temple had to incorporate the obelisks of Amenhotep III within its structure, which obviously caused roofing problems. In addition, the Montu colonnade yielded substantial foundation deposits bearing Taharqa's name.

Alongside this colonnaded approach to the Montu temple, there existed a small structure which can certainly be dubbed a 'kiosk'. It had its own small pylon and a gate with a 'broken' lintel, and the kiosk itself stood upon an elevated platform approached by a ramp and stairway: these gave access to a long room lined on three sides by columns. There is no clue as to its purpose, but the columns were of wood giving the

Figure 14.4 Example of wooden masts bearing emblems erected before a temple entrance (after Lauffray, J., in *Kemi* XX: 162).

structure a somewhat temporary feel, and it is possible to see it as a type of throne room in which the king sat in state to hear petitions and to administer justice (Arnold 1999: 54).

Within the colonnade that Taharqa had added to the Eastern Temple, two statue groups of four baboons adoring the rising sun have been found in the central aisle. Regarding these, it is worthwhile to note that Papyrus Bologna 1094 (Caminos 1954: 28–30), one of a 'miscellany' of Ramesside documents, contains a reference to 'eight baboons who are in the forecourt', followed closely by a reference to 'the great door of Baki'. The name Baki might well be an abbreviation of the name of the architect of Ramesses II's Eastern Temple, Bakenkhons. Another reference on a Late Period situla in The British Museum (BM 38212) also mentions eight baboons 'at the Upper Gateway', an appellation often given to this eastern entrance to Karnak. None of this can, of course, be taken as conclusive proof that it is the baboons still present in Taharqa's eastern colonnade which are being referred to, but it is, nonetheless, an interesting possibility.

At this point, it is perhaps appropriate to mention a structure referred to by the ancient Egyptians as a *d3d3* (Spencer 1984: 130–3), but whose nature and function is uncertain, and often debated. There are several textual references which derive from Karnak relating to these mysterious buildings, and the general inference is that they were erected in front of temples and buildings of special importance. One of the more specific references was that of Bakenkhons, who recorded that he had constructed 'a *d3d3* of stone' in front of the Eastern Temple's main gateway, exactly where Taharqa built his eastern colonnade upon the foundations of some earlier structure – perhaps Bakenkhons' *ḏ3ḏ3*. This possibility gains credence from the discovery within Taharqa's colonnade of a stela in the name of Menkheperre, son of Pinedjem I (Dynasty XXI), upon which he makes mention of constructing a wall that stretched 'from the *ḏ3ḏ3* of Amun to the Treasury north of Amun's domain' (this last being, presumably, the *pr-ḥḏ* of Tuthmosis I, since that of Shabaka did not exist in the time of Pinedjem I). Another stela of the same prince refers to Amun, when in procession, stopping at a *ḏ3ḏ3*; exactly which entrance this might have been the reference does not specify, but the context implies that of the main temple. Could this *ḏ3ḏ3* perhaps have been the earlier structure that had originally stood where the great colonnade of Taharqa now stands in front of the Second Pylon? And should one consider all the various colonnaded porches erected by Taharqa in front of Karnak's temples as being *ḏ3ḏ3*s (Barguet 1962: 302)? Another *ḏ3ḏ3* is known to have stood before the Temple of Opet: this structure might well have been a kiosk (thought to date to Taharqa), the remains of which were found in front of that temple's later pylon (Leclant 1965: 82).

Although the spectacular colonnade in front of the Second Pylon is the monument at Karnak most commonly associated with Taharqa, he did, in fact, build another fascinating and unique monument, usually known by the name of 'The Edifice of the Lake'. Situated between the north-west angle of the Sacred Lake and the southern enclosure wall of Amun's temple, this building is very ruinous and consequently most visitors pass by without a glance, scarcely realising that it is there at all: the reason for this being that the monument is partly subterranean. The superstructure remains only as a pile of tumbled stone, thus attracting little attention, but the rooms below ground are quite well preserved.

This is a puzzling and enigmatic monument that has no parallels, although it should be said that many reused blocks from a building of Shabaka, decorated in powerful Nubian style, have been found incorporated within the edifice; so much so, in fact, that it has been postulated that Taharqa's monument might have replaced an earlier one of his uncle upon this spot (Parker *et al.* 1979: 6).

Taharqa's edifice was dedicated to Re-Horakhte, which would explain the open solar court above ground, while the subterranean rooms symbolised the sun's nocturnal passage through the underworld. One must assume that the rituals enacted both below and above ground were complementary to one another, but sadly nothing of the upper courts remains to give any clues to this part of the ceremonies. However, it is apparent from Taharqa's participation in all the rites that they are closely connected with those of cosmic (or universal) kingship (Fig. 14.5).

While much of the superstructure can only be guessed at, systematic excavation has recovered some architectural features. It was evidently built upon a high terrace of sandstone blocks; this sizeable platform measured 29 m east to west and 25 m north to south and was approached on its eastern side by a ramp. The central area of the building was too large to have been roofed, so this was undoubtedly an open court which was fronted by a columned portico, the existence of this latter feature being indicated by the discovery of architraves decorated on both sides, as well as column-drums and abaci (Parker *et al.* 1979: 5). Decorated blocks from the internal walls of the court have been found, and there are extensive reliefs still existing on the exterior walls of the monument, particularly on the north side. These latter show, amongst them, the series of scenes usually considered as preliminary rites to the coronation, i.e. the king leaves the palace, is purified by the gods, is conducted into the presence of the Theban triad, makes offerings, recites formulae, and receives divine life and power. However, in this case, the scenes appear to relate more to the preparatory stages of whatever rites were to be enacted by the king within the Edifice.

Access to the monument was, as already mentioned, via a ramp which was found within a mud-brick court at the building's eastern end. This court had three doorways: one in the north wall, a corresponding one in the south wall leading, via a stairway 1.5 m wide, to the Sacred Lake, and a third in the east wall which gave access to a 'nilometer', though this term is actually a misnomer, for it is no such thing. The doorway in the court's eastern wall leads into a vestibule, decorated with reliefs, whence a covered passage slopes downward for about 30 m to the water level, doubtless viewed for ritual purposes as the primaeval waters of Nun. Clearly there was a ritual connection between Taharqa's edifice and the waters of both the Sacred Lake and the 'nilometer' (Parker *et al.* 1979: 81), all three being accessible from the mud-brick forecourt. This link is indicative once again of the importance to Taharqa of the cult of water: it is hardly surprising, therefore, that it was he who was responsible for the definitive aspect of the Sacred Lake as we see it today.

Within the Edifice itself, a doorway in the back wall of the solar court leads through to a sloping passage with a central staircase which descends in a south-to-north direction to the subterranean sector of the monument. At the bottom of the staircase are two antechambers which give access to the first of three rooms in succession, each one leading directly into the next, on a west-to-east axis. These chambers are both roofed and paved with sandstone slabs, and the walls are decorated with scenes and inscriptions relating to the setting of the sun, its descent into the underworld and its journey through the night. One chamber contains scenes from the Rites of the Mound of Djeme, whose funerary cults and rituals are difficult to interpret. Since the Mound of Djeme was situated on the West Bank at Thebes, the subsequent scenes record the Rites of the Divine Re-entrance in which the king welcomes the god's return from the domain of the dead.

The last of the three rooms is badly damaged, but the scenes depict the mystical union of Amun with Re prior to his rebirth as the morning sun (Khepri). In this respect, it should be recalled that the colossal red granite scarab of Amenhotep III, originally sited in his funerary temple on the West Bank, was actually transported to its present location beside the Sacred Lake by Taharqa, without doubt as part of the ritual concerning the rebirth of the sun as enacted within the Edifice. The text engraved on the scarab declares that it was 'Khepri who arose from the earth': a powerful symbol of the entire *raison d'être* of the Edifice.

The walls of the staircase that leads down to the underground complex are inscribed with scenes from the Litany of the Sun: on one side Amun descends past scenes depicting Osirian forms of Re, while on the other side, he ascends past solar forms of Re to emerge reborn. In other words, the god had descended into the underworld (the subterranean chambers) through which he had passed before being born again as Re and appearing out of the darkness of night into the light of day within the solar court where he is received with rapture (Parker *et al.* 1979: 83).

Within this unique monument, it can be noted that the very prominent Theban religious figure of the Divine Adoratrix plays only a minor role. She is depicted assisting

Plate 14.2 The entrance to the so-called 'Nilometer' attached to Taharqa's Edifice of the Lake.

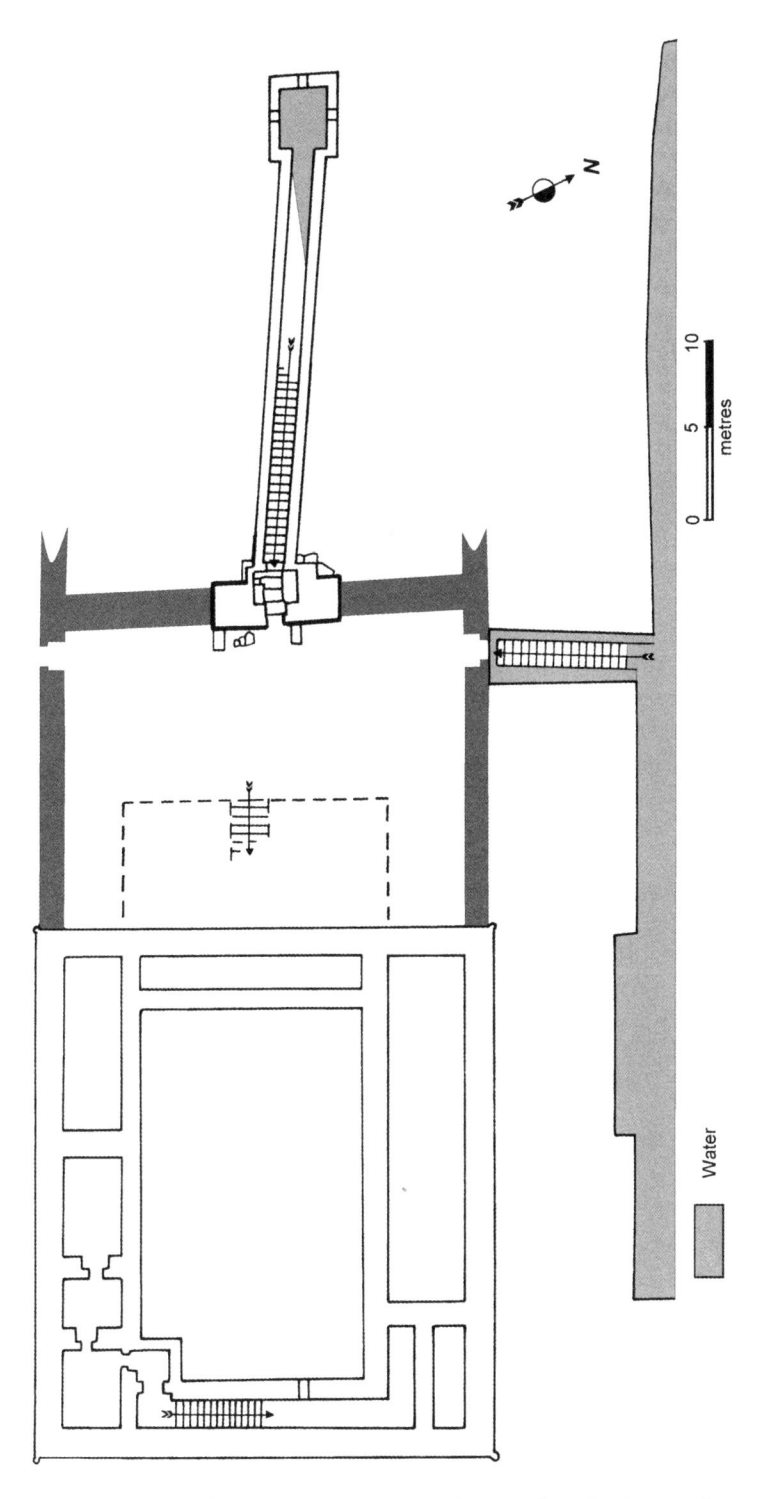

Figure 14.5 Plan of the subterranean rooms of the Edifice of Taharqa (after Parker, R. *et al.*, *The Edifice of Taharqa*: pl. IA).

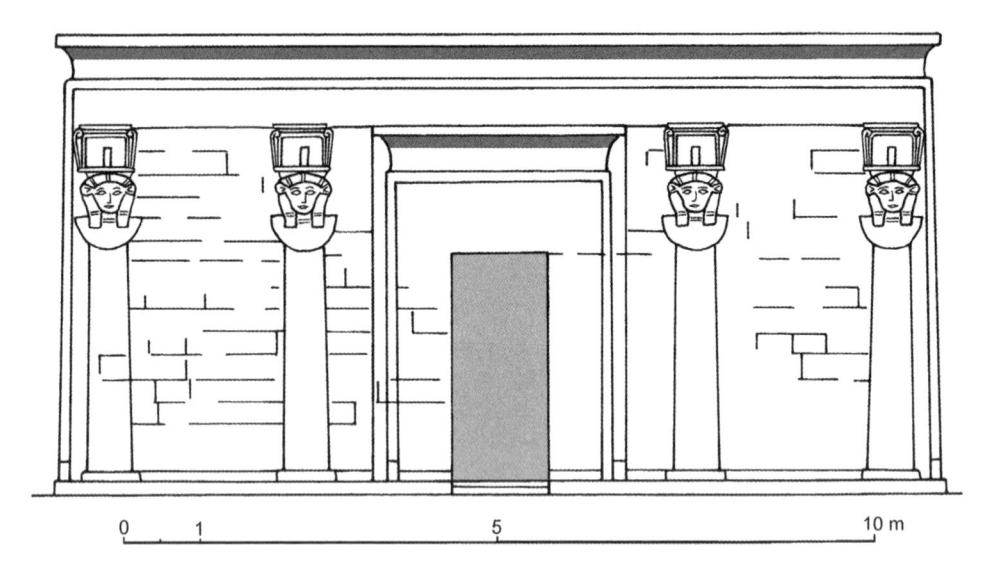

Figure 14.6 Hathor façade to the Chapel of the Divine Adoratrices (after Arnold, D., *Temples of the Last Pharaohs*: 55).

in some of the rituals but is never mentioned by name, whereas Taharqa himself is named time and again as officiant at, and celebrant of, these rites.

In the tradition of his immediate predecessors, however, there was no shortage of Osirian chapels dedicated by Taharqa in which his sister, the God's Wife of Amun, Shepenwepet II, and his daughter, Amenirdis II (Shepenwepet's adopted successor), feature prominently. In all, three such chapels were constructed: one known as the Edifice of the Divine Adoratrices stood somewhere within what was later to become the Montu enclosure. This chapel's exact position is uncertain for it was razed to the ground; however, sufficient elements of it have been recovered from the foundations of a nearby Ptolemaic building to enable a reconstruction on paper. Built of sandstone, it had a façade measuring about 10 m across fronted by a portico of four Hathor columns. Either side of the entrance doorway are reliefs of Shepenwepet and Amenirdis each being led, as it were, into the chapel by a 'blue' Amun (probably the god's figure was inlaid with lapis lazuli, or painted to look so). The interior comprised a large hall with two decorated chambers of equal size sited at one end, while in the centre of the hall stood an open-ended kiosk or naos (Robichon *et al.* 1954: fig. 117). There is no evidence of the king featuring in this chapel at all – the reliefs are entirely of the God's Wife and her successor, and it has been suggested that the Hathor façade was intended to emphasise the purely feminine aspect of this chapel (Arnold 1999: 54).

A second chapel is also rather unusual. This one, dedicated to Osiris Neb-Ankh, was situated north of Karnak's Third Pylon along the way leading to the Ptah temple. Built mainly of mud-brick, it had, however, a stone chapel, the lintel of which carried a central cartouche inscribed for Osiris Neb-Ankh with Taharqa shown offering to the left and Shepenwepet II and Amenirdis II offering to the right. What makes this chapel so unusual is its size, which is remarkable for its tiny proportions: a first chamber measuring 2.26 m high, 2.11 m wide and 1.98 m deep gives access through a door no higher than 1.24 m into a minute second room 1.32 m in length by 0.57 m in width. Legrain, who excavated the chapel, wrote: 'It is, I believe, the smallest religious monument in Egypt, and lost within the immensity of Karnak' (Legrain 1902: 209). One cannot help but wonder what rites could possibly have taken place in so miniscule a construction.

The third chapel stands to the west of the Montu enclosure and was dedicated to Osiris Pededankh (the-one-who-continually-gives-life), or sometimes called more simply Osiris, Lord of Eternity. Taharqa's construction was built upon the remains of an earlier Dynasty XVIII chapel, perhaps dating from Tuthmosis III's reign. The walls of the Nubian king's building were of mud-brick, but doorways, door-sills and columns were of sandstone; the entrance jambs bear reliefs of Taharqa to one side and Shepenwepet II the other. Two fine black granite statues of Taharqa were found here, but whether they originated from this chapel or from the Montu temple has not been determined. A very beautiful votive case was also unearthed here; composed of bronze sheets inlaid with gold and silver work showing the God's Wife before the Theban Triad, it bears the legend 'Shepenwepet, daughter of Piye' (Leclant 1965: 104).

Taharqa's building activity at Karnak ranged over the entire sacred complex. In addition to the work detailed above, he renewed the gates of the Second and Tenth Pylons, and left additional scenes and texts at various locations within the Amun temple; he also added two gates on the approach to the Ptah temple, developed further the original temple of Opet, as well as undertaking considerable works at the Montu and Mut temples, including the renewal of their Sacred Lakes.

The first half of Taharqa's twenty-six-year reign had been peaceful but, in the second half, Egypt became embroiled in a protracted and ultimately disastrous struggle against the might of Assyria. In Year 17, the Assyrian army under King Esarhaddon attacked Egypt but was defeated by Taharqa; notwithstanding this setback, in Year 20 Esarhaddon tried again and this time he triumphed. However, despite the Assyrian king's victory, when the army withdrew from Egypt, Taharqa was able to re-establish himself. Hearing of this, Esarhaddon marched yet again on Egypt, but died *en route*, and it was his successor Assurbanipal who this time defeated the Egyptian army, penetrating as far as Thebes, thus forcing Taharqa to flee to the safety of Napata. In an attempt to prevent a recurrence of the Nubian king's pretensions to Egypt, on this occasion when the Assyrians withdrew, Assurbanipal left a vassal prince, Necho of Sais, ruling in the north. Undeterred by this, Taharqa was able once more to extend his own rule northwards, reigning again from Thebes and Nubia.

Quite advanced in years by this time, Taharqa chose to associate his nephew Tanutamun with him upon the throne, and from this brief co-regency (if such it can be named) comes the only building at Thebes that bears Tanutamun's name. This was a chapel erected at Karnak, south of the Tenth Pylon and to the east of the sphinx avenue that linked Amun's temple to that of Mut. Dedicated to Osiris-Ptah Neb-Ankh by Taharqa and Tanutamun jointly, the chapel comprised two stone chambers preceded by a mud-brick forecourt with four columns (Leclant 1965: 111–13), (Fig. 14.7).

After Taharqa's death, Tanutamun claimed kingship over all Egypt, advancing north to Memphis and the Delta, killing Necho of Sais in battle. When news of this audacity reached Assurbanipal in Assyria, he lost no time in dispatching his armies once again to Egypt where they quickly crushed all opposition and marched south to Thebes, while

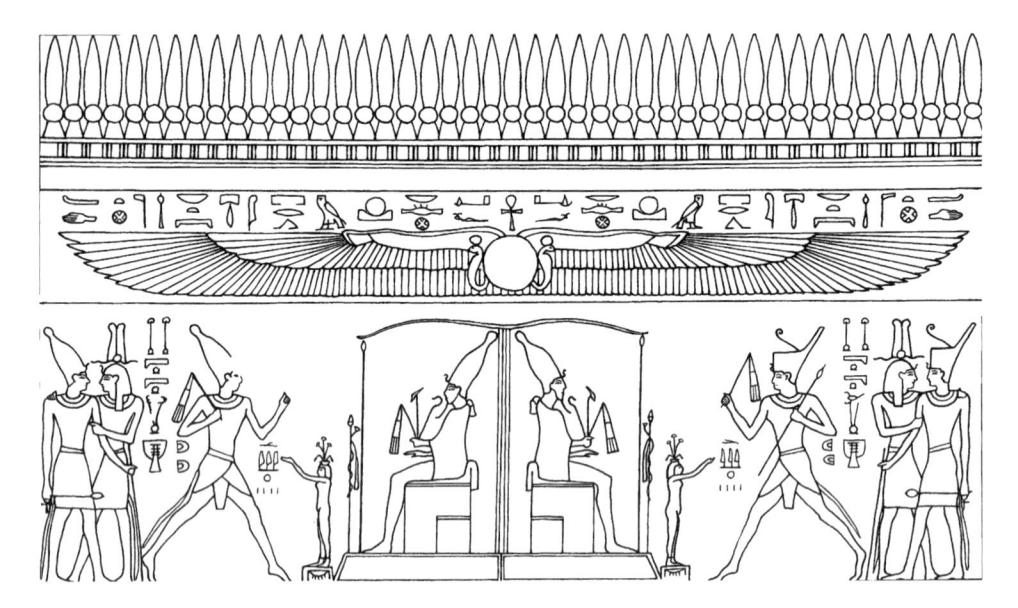

Figure 14.7 Lintel from the chapel of Osiris-Ptah Neb-Ankh showing Taharqa and Tanutamun (after Fazzini, R., *Egypt, Dynasty XXII–XXV*: pl. XXI.3).

Tanutamun sought refuge in Napata as Taharqa had previously done. But this time, the Assyrians ruthlessly sacked and looted Thebes, stripping the temples and carrying off untold booty. Karnak, founded as it had been in the Middle Kingdom and enriched by every king over the course of more than fourteen centuries, must have yielded incalculable treasure: for example, the solid electrum obelisks of Tuthmosis III. Such wealth, plundered by the Assyrians, can scarcely be imagined; neither can the sense of horror and outrage suffered by the Egyptians at the desecration of their most sacred places.

Despite this, and despite the absence of Tanutamun in Nubia and the appointment of another vassal prince, Psamtik (I), in the north, the Thebans, acknowledging no allegiance to a northern ruler, continued to date events to Tanutamun's reign, though in truth the area was ruled by the God's Wife of Amun, Shepenwepet II, in conjunction with the Fourth Prophet of Amun, Montuemhat, Mayor of Thebes and Governor of the South. This powerful individual, who had risen to prominence in Taharqa's reign, left an inscription in the Temple of Mut which, as we have already seen, recorded his work repairing the ravages of the exceptional Nile flood in Year 6 of Taharqa: he also spoke of the necessity to purify Karnak's temples 'after there had been an invasion of unclean foreigners in the south' – perhaps referring to the Assyrian onslaught. A new sacred bark was commissioned, as well as new divine statues, often processional ones, since Montuemhat frequently describes them as having 'two staves'. His power undoubtedly increased considerably after Taharqa's death and Tanutamun's defeat, although he must have been a witness to the devastating sack of Thebes. Nevertheless, he, along with Shepenwepet, remained in a position of power well into the reign of Psamtik I of Dynasty XXVI, as we shall see.

15

DYNASTIES XXVI–XXX

The Saite Dynasty (Dynasty XXVI)

Before the Assyrians finally withdrew from Egypt, they had established another vassal prince in the north, Psamtik, son of the slain Necho of Sais, who effectively ruled an area that included Sais, Memphis and Athribis. As Assyrian power in the whole region began to wane, Psamtik's power by contrast increased within Egypt itself, and he quickly extended his rule to include the whole Delta. Finally, with strong allies holding Middle Egypt on his behalf, Psamtik was able to look southwards: by Year 9 of his taking power, he had become undisputed ruler of the entire land.

This goal was achieved not by civil war or military force, but by a stratagem that was already a tried and tested one. Throughout history, nations have made peace, agreed treaties, formed unions through the time-honoured expedient of the giving in marriage of the daughter of one royal house to the king or prince of another. In the case of Psamtik, it was what might be termed a variation on a theme. He decreed that his daughter Nitocris should be presented to Amun and become the adopted successor of the God's Wife of Amun, Shepenwepet II, and her immediate heir, Amenirdis II, both scions of the Kushite royal dynasty. Psamtik declared: 'I have given to him (Amun) my daughter to be God's Wife ... surely he will be gratified with her worship'. The king was extremely diplomatic in his handling of this affair stating unequivocally: 'I will not do what in fact should not be done and expel an heir from his seat ...'. He therefore kept the current incumbents, as well as the Fourth Prophet of Amun, the great official Montuemhat, in their posts for their natural lives, but meanwhile began to appoint his own followers to positions of power in the south. Nitocris herself was to choose a personal staff loyal to her father.

Psamtik seemingly won the approval of his Theban subjects by a dazzling display of royal pageantry. We are most fortunate in having a detailed description of the momentous event of Nitocris' 'adoption' recorded on a red granite stela found in Karnak's forecourt close to the tripartite shrine of Seti II (Caminos 1964: 71–101). It is unfortunate that the top part of the stela is missing, but the narrative pertaining to the king's decision and his daughter's journey south remains to a large extent intact. 'Regnal year 9, first month of the inundation, day 28, departure from the king's private apartments of his eldest daughter, clad in fine linen and adorned with new turquoise ...'. The princess probably set sail from Sais (but possibly Memphis) accompanied by a great flotilla, richly equipped and laden with splendid provisions.

Regnal year 9, second month of the inundation, day 14 (a little over two weeks later) they arrived at the city of the gods, Thebes. As she advanced, she found Thebes with throngs of men and crowds of women, standing and rejoicing to meet her.

The narrative goes on to say that Shepenwepet and Amenirdis also rejoiced to meet her and welcomed her into the sacred confines of Ipet-Sut, as did the god himself, Amun-Re. The great stela concludes with a list of the many endowments granted to Nitocris by her father and others in the form of land, grain, beer, bread, fowl and the like. 'I have endowed her better than those who were before her' declared Psamtik (Caminos 1964: 74), who clearly wished his daughter to be the wealthiest of all God's Wives and, since she would in time inherit all the property of her two predecessors in the post, she undoubtedly would have been.

What seems to be a pictorial rendering of this great event is recorded upon some blocks which derive from the temple of Mut (Kitchen 1973: 236–9). The reliefs thereon have been much discussed, but are generally thought to depict the arrival of Nitocris at Thebes, showing her laden ships docking at Karnak's quay. One of the vessels is designated 'the barge of the Harem of Amun', and other boats are also named as belonging to the god. Nitocris, who was to be inaugurated into Amun's harem, and eventually to become its chief, would doubtless have been greeted by, or accompanied by such vessels. A female figure, dressed in flowing robes and with arms upraised, is shown standing upon the quay: it has been suggested that this is no less a personage than the God's Wife, Shepenwepet herself, coming to meet her adoptive daughter. Fragmentary though the scenes are, a minimum of thirteen boats can be discerned, with perhaps as many as twenty or more having once been depicted.

With Nitocris installed as successor to the Kushite God's Wives, Psamtik's hold over the south was well and truly established, but Sais was his capital and it was in the north that he and his heirs built extensively, erecting many imposing temples, shrines and chapels. Psamtik's reign ushered in a period of some 140 years during which Egypt remained free of foreign domination, and the country once again attained some stability, while trade and artistic endeavour enjoyed a renaissance. Yet for the dynasty's entire duration no new temples were constructed in the south of the country by any of the Saite kings, and virtually no work was undertaken at Karnak, other than some Osirian chapels in the names of Nitocris and her immediate successor, Ankhnesneferibre, the daughter of Psamtik II, the third king of the dynasty.

Nitocris herself remained in high office for well over sixty years and a variety of buildings at Karnak can be attributed to her, extending over the reigns of several kings. Two of these were erected in conjunction with her father. A chapel dedicated to Osiris Neb-ankh-di-heb-sed (lord of life, who gives sed-festivals), was one of the line of six that were later to be enclosed within the Montu precinct: it is one of the better preserved Osirian chapels. The paved approach, up a marked incline to the gateway in the Montu enclosure wall, was constructed somewhat later when that wall was built, but the paving overlies an earlier approach which perhaps was the original one. It led to a vestibule with four papyrus columns preceding the pylon-like façade of the sandstone chapel which housed three rooms, one at the front and two cult rooms behind (Leclant 1965: 94, fig. 27a). The discovery in the area of a thick circle or ring of black granite, which appears to have supported a small flagpole (Robichon and Christophe 1951:

35), indicates the possibility that flagstaffs might once have adorned the chapel façade or the gateway to it. The chapel's reliefs feature Psamtik and Nitocris, whose figure is frequently followed by that of her steward, Pasaba.

Another, more problematic, building of Nitocris is to be found west of the Montu precinct, much ruined and partially buried under a modern village. It seems to have been a sizeable construction, to such an extent that it has been referred to as a temple rather than a chapel; but such remnants of the monument as are available to study are difficult to interpret. It does not seem to be another Osirian complex. Although Psamtik's name and figure are to be seen, it is above all Nitocris who is featured. The most obvious architectural element still seen today is a double range of columns, linked by intercolumnar walls, leading through two doors to a monumental gateway set in an enclosure wall: this gate would undoubtedly have given entrance to the principal areas of the building (Robichon and Christophe 1951: 98). The intercolumnar walls were topped with a cornice and were decorated with a series of ritual scenes showing Nitocris being purified, presented to the gods, and crowned as God's Wife by Amun himself. One scene actually depicts Nitocris herself enthroned and receiving offerings. Part of the cornice consisted of a frieze of twelve cartouches repeating the name of Nitocris under three alternating headings: God's Wife of Amun, Divine Adoratrix and King's Daughter (Robichon and Christophe 1951: 107). Osiris does not seem to feature in this building at all.

Nitocris' name is attested quite widely elsewhere at Karnak, although often on blocks whose exact provenance is not known; it is clear, however, that other constructions in her name once existed.

After a reign of over fifty years, Psamtik was succeeded by his son Necho (II) whose additions to Karnak, despite fifteen years of rule, were minimal. Some fragments of a black granite stela in his name were found in front of the Second Pylon; more interesting, however, are the jumbled remains of a strange brick construction in the north-east sector of Karnak, adjacent to the court that precedes the Eastern Temple. The building, whose bricks were stamped with Necho's cartouches (Leclère 1996: 11), was composed of several vaulted chambers of varying size which contained many tiny Osiride figurines within small brick cavities built one upon another. It has been suggested that this represented the tomb of Osiris which, considering the strong Osirian link with this whole area of Karnak at that time, seems quite possible. Excavation is still continuing, and remains of similar constructions of an earlier date have recently come to light; some, it seems, as far back as the New Kingdom (Leclère 1996: 12).

The name of Necho's son, Psamtik II, who succeeded him, is attested at Karnak on several small monuments: a granite gate in front of Hatshepsut's small temple of Amun-Kamutef on the processional way to the Mut temple, and a lintel from an Osirian chapel built in conjunction with Nitocris and his daughter, Ankhnesneferibre, who in the first year of his reign was adopted by Nitocris as her future successor. By far the most noticeable mark that Psamtik II left on Karnak, however, was the systematic destruction or usurpation of all cartouches of the Kushite kings (Yoyotte 1951: 238–9). This targeting of the previous dynasty appeared to derive from a campaign that Psamtik undertook against Nubia in the third year of his reign (Kitchen 1973: 406 and n. 962–3), details of which he had carved upon a red granite stela set up in front of the Second Pylon. No Kushite building at Karnak was spared his attention, and one cannot but wonder what had occasioned such particular venom.

Psamtik II was succeeded in turn by *his* son Apries (Wahibre), of whom there is no record at all at Karnak. His reign was marked by struggles both at home and abroad, and it was a high-ranking military officer named Ahmose (Amasis) who eventually claimed the throne after the death of Apries in battle. Ahmose (II) then married the dead king's sister, perhaps in an attempt to legitimise his right to the throne.

Throughout this turbulent time, the Saite dynasty continued its hold over the Theban area through the offices of Ankhnesneferibre, daughter of Psamtik II, God's Wife elect until the death of Nitocris in Year 4 of Apries. Like her long-lived predecessor, Ankhnesneferibre was to hold her elevated post, as well as that of High Priest of Amun (Kitchen 1973: 480) (a very unusual office for a woman), for a period of about sixty years until the final collapse of the dynasty and the start of the First Persian Period.

Ahmose II built two Osirian chapels, one in association with Nitocris, the other with Ankhnesneferibre, both situated close together north of the great Hypostyle Hall, along the route to the Ptah temple (PM II 1972: 193). The chapel of Ankhnesneferibre was enlarged during the reign of Ahmose's son, Psamtik III, who also constructed another chapel with her not far from the columned building of Nitocris, described above, and likewise largely buried under local houses. All these chapels are very ruinous.

A monument of Ankhnesneferibre of some interest was a jubilee porch (Robichon *et al.* 1954: 128ff.), very probably erected on the approach to the Hathor-fronted temple of the earlier God's Wives, Shepenwepet II and Amenirdis II. This bears the first sure evidence of a God's Wife being granted a sed-festival, normally a rite conducted only by a reigning monarch.

Psamtik III's reign was brief: in his second year, the Persian army, led by King Cambyses, invaded Egypt. Sais, Memphis, Heliopolis, all fell to the Persians who then marched south to complete their conquest of the entire country: 121 years of Persian domination had begun.

Dynasties XXVII–XXIX

Throughout this long period of foreign domination (termed Dynasty XXVII), the Persian occupiers apparently remained indifferent to Egyptian religious observance in its most celebrated state temple at Thebes: scarcely a vestige of their presence can be found at Karnak apart from a column drum bearing the inscription: 'the one who accomplishes the rites, the King of Upper and Lower Egypt, Darius (I)' (Traunecker 1980: 210), and a fragment of beautifully worked bronze also in his name. It must be assumed from this that the normal cults and rituals quietly continued there unopposed. But with the death of the Persian king, Darius II, in 405 BC, the local ruler of Sais, Amyrtaeus (Amonortais), took the opportunity to rebel successfully against Egypt's overlords and to declare himself king, establishing a new dynasty, the XXVIIIth, of which he was the sole ruler. Virtually nothing is known of his reign, not even an existing cartouche, but he had shaken off the Persian yoke and once again there was to be a period of native Egyptian rule.

The following dynasty (the XXIXth) was to see the first expansion (albeit modest) of Karnak since the days of Taharqa, more than 250 years earlier: this was inaugurated by Nepherites (Nefaurud) I, ruling from his capital at Mendes. After the long period of Persian domination, followed by the struggles of Amyrtaeus to found a native dynasty, the kings of Dynasty XXIX were anxious to establish a dynamic renewal of the theology of Amun at the religious capital, Thebes. This they felt would underpin their power and reinforce their dynasty.

Consequently, during his six-year reign, Nepherites was to commence a way-station for the bark of Amun in front of the Bubastite Court: unique in its design, work on the shrine was to be continued during the one-year reign of his successor, Psamut (Pshenmut), but was largely constructed and completed by the dynasty's last ruler, Hakor (Achoris) (Arnold 1999: 100). In addition to this important monument, Nepherites appears to be the ruler responsible for a small temple named 'Khonsu-who-rules-in-Thebes' constructed beyond the south-east angle of Karnak's girdle wall. It was in this building that Champollion found the celebrated Stela of Bakhtan. Now almost totally destroyed, the temple was excavated in the nineteenth century by Karl Lepsius when it was still in a reasonable state of preservation, standing within its own enclosure.

Apart from his work on the above-mentioned way-station, Psamut in his brief reign also seems to have built, or possibly renewed, a storehouse for divine offerings ('the great pure storehouse of Amun-Re, Lord of the Thrones of the Two Lands, Foremost of Ipet-Sut') close to the Sacred Lake: a vital necessity in the reinvigoration of the temple's many cults. Due to the fact that Psamut's reign lasted only one year, the suggestion that Nepherites was the initial constructor of this storehouse is often put forward, but Psamut's name is by far the most prominent in this building and it is generally ascribed to him (Berg 1987: 52), although Hakor undoubtedly completed some of the decoration (Fig. 15.1).

The storehouse, constructed on a platform 4.5 m high, was a sizeable one with a facade width of 55.5 m and a depth of 45.5 m. Although built of mud-brick, it had sandstone doorways throughout, as well as stone columns and several stone chapels. The edifice was in two parts: the rear section, which was entirely roofed, was composed of three parallel units, each entered through its own doorway that led into a corridor with magazines opening off to left and right. At the end of each corridor was a small chapel containing scenes of offering to Amun or the Theban triad and a naos that stood against the rear wall (Traunecker 1987a: 150). The front section of the building comprised an open court, access to which was through doors in the north, east and west walls; a portico of eight stone columns lined the façade of the entrance to the rear section of the storehouse, while in the court's north-east angle was an area that probably served as an abattoir. The northern wall of the court was also pierced by a covered ramp leading to the Sacred Lake whereby the geese, sacred to Amun, and various other water-fowl could descend and ascend safely to and from the water. From outside the court's west door, a pathway descended at a gentle incline to the gate that gave access to the court between the Eighth and Ninth Pylons, past the small chapel, referred to above, that was dedicated to Amun and to Thoth in his capacity as the 'administrator' who audited the daily divine offerings (Fig. 15.2).

Inscriptions within Psamut's building speak of it as the place where these daily offerings were prepared and consecrated and, indeed, an altar and some purification basins have been found there (Traunecker 1987a: 149). All this indicates that the edifice was, perhaps, more than a mere storehouse – it has even been referred to as a temple. However, this type of 'treasury', 'magazine' or 'storage' block goes back to Dynasty XII at least, where the scribes would sit in the central corridors checking goods in and out of the storage chambers. As the revenue of the Amun temple was part of the god's estate, it is not surprising that chapels were introduced at the end of the corridors, thus

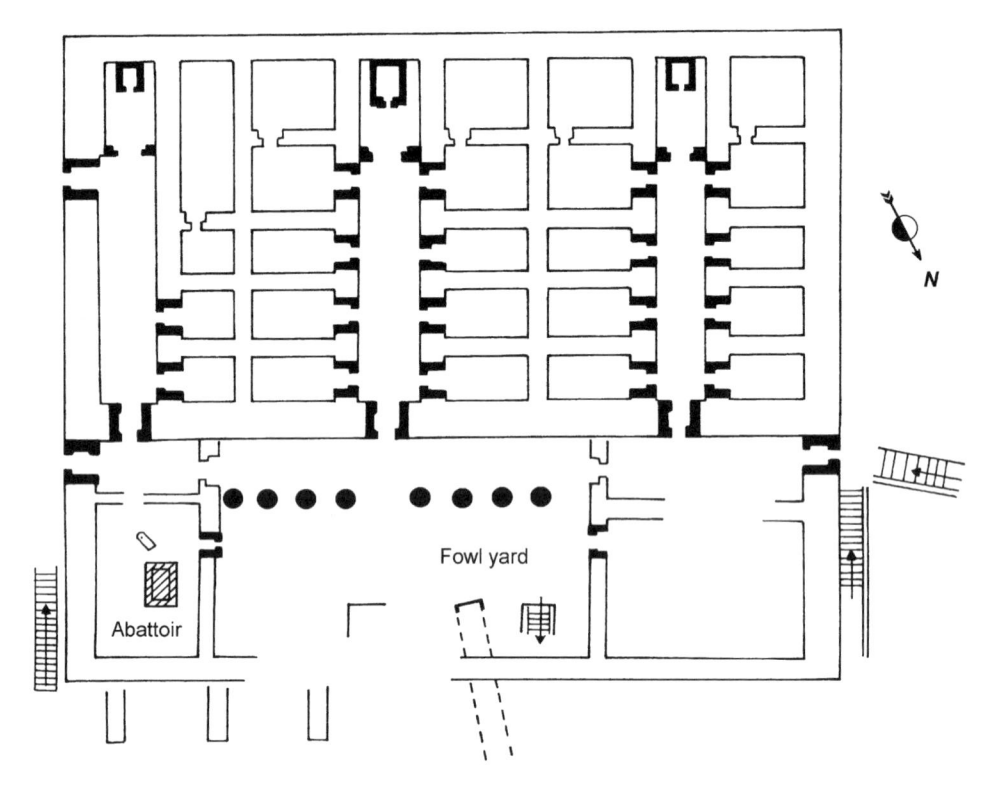

Figure 15.1 Plan of the storehouse of Psamut (after Traunecker, C., in *RdE* 38: 161).

implying the supervisory presence of Amun. In any event, it is certain that important religious rites connected with the consecration of offerings took place there.

The best known monument dating to this dynasty, however, is the so-called Chapel of Achoris (Hakor), situated outside Karnak's front entrance to the south-west. Despite the name given to it, the chapel was the work of three kings in turn: begun by Nepherites, continued by Psamut and completed by Hakor (Traunecker *et al.* 1981: 18). It was, in fact, a way-station for the sacred bark of Amun, the last such resting-place for the bark before being loaded on board the great barge Userhet for its journey to Luxor temple or across to the West Bank. Due to the extreme length of Userhet at this period of Egyptian history and the flotilla of accompanying boats and barges necessary to tow and manoeuvre it, it is highly probable that the quay extended at least as far as the level of this way-station, and probably beyond. Today, any evidence of this has long since vanished under modern concrete (Fig. 15.3).

The design of the chapel was unique due to the fact that at this point the processional route turned ninety degrees, having approached from the dromos lying to the north and then turned to the west towards the Nile where Userhet was moored. The bark-repository, or way-station, was constructed over this right-angle turn, so that the bark could enter, prow first, through the north door, then be placed upon the socle in the sanctuary while the porters realigned themselves to carry the bark out sideways through the west door towards the quay, thus facilitating its embarkation. The chapel could

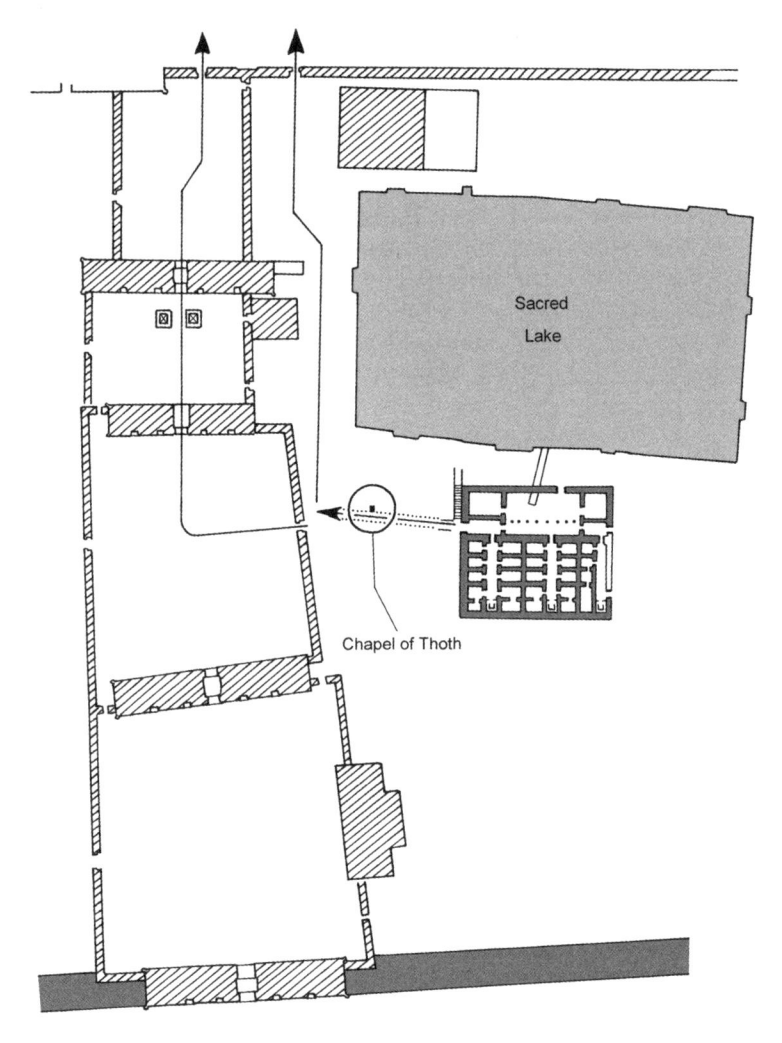

Figure 15.2 Plan of the route of consecrated offerings from the storehouse of Psamut via the Chapel of Thoth into the Temple of Amun (after Goyon, J.-C. and Traunecker, C. in *Cahiers de Karnak VII*: 356).

more realistically be termed a 'turning-station' rather than a 'way-station', although in effect it was the porters who turned, not the bark. Evidence for this can be seen by studying the design of the station. The principal doorway was abnormally wide (nearly 5 m) and occupied almost the entire width of the chapel's west façade, while the doorway in the north wall measured only 2.2 m in width (Traunecker *et al.* 1981: 96). The asymmetrical size and positioning of these two doors clearly indicates the two different axes (Fig. 15.4).

The building itself comprised a kiosk at the front with six free-standing columns (three to the north, three to the south), partially joined by intercolumnar walls, while at the rear was the sanctuary, wholly enclosed on three sides, and containing the socle upon which the bark would rest. The side walls of the sanctuary entrance were

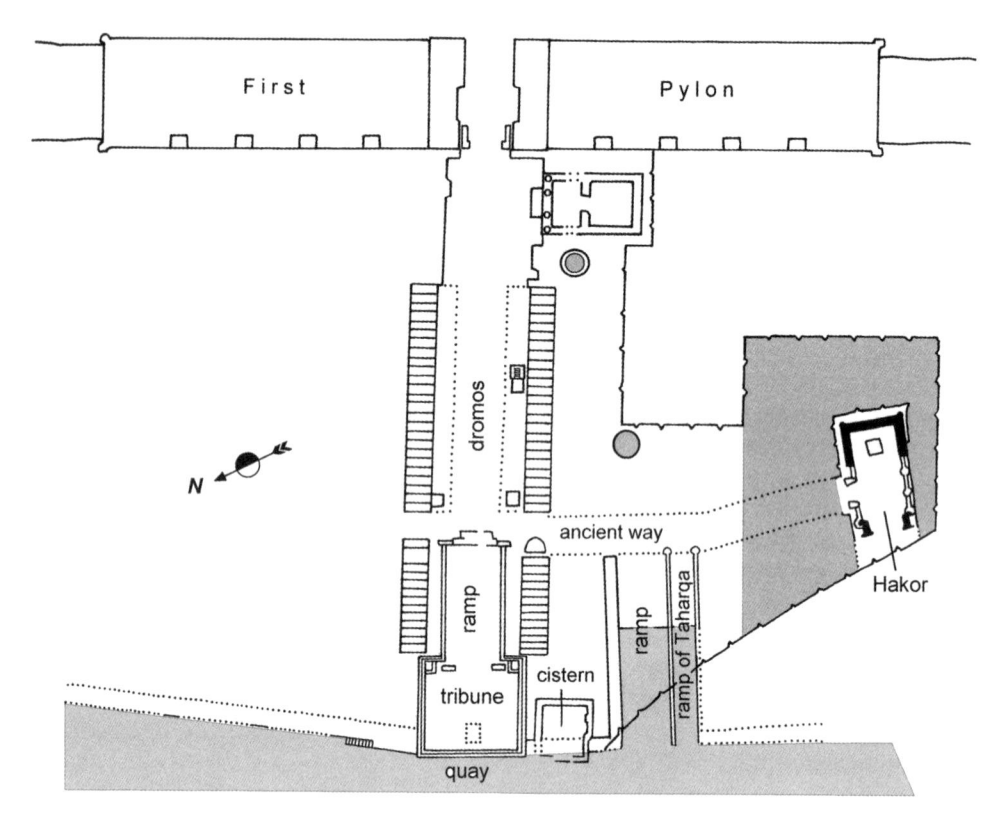

Figure 15.3 Plan showing the position of the chapel of Hakor in front of the First Pylon (after Lauffray, J., *La Chapelle d'Achôris à Karnak*, vol. I: 15).

ornamented by two pilasters, one to each side, decorated respectively with the papyrus of Lower Egypt to the north and the lotus of Upper Egypt to the south. These recall the so-called heraldic pillars of Tuthmosis III erected in front of Karnak's main bark sanctuary (Arnold 1999: 100 n. 6): the similarity cannot be coincidental (Fig. 15.5).

The six columns in the front section of the chapel are not original to the monument, but come from an earlier Kushite construction. It is significant that a formula in the name of Taharqa was carved upon the west doorway. Was it because this bark shrine replaced an earlier Kushite one (Traunecker *et al.* 1981: 17)? Taharqa is known to have erected a building in this area, as we have already seen. Or did the new dynasty wish to be associated with the last great constructor at Karnak, namely Taharqa?

The shrine's decor had two themes: that of a temporary sanctuary of Amun, to which the king, as officiant, processed; and the depiction of various rites and solemn liturgies enacted there and on the West Bank. Of especial interest are the scenes pertaining to the Ten-Year Festival, a celebration held at the start of each decade, which apparently assumed considerable importance during the reign of Hakor (Traunecker *et al.* 1981: 120). There is little evidence from the reliefs that the barks of Mut and Khonsu also used this way-station. One is left wondering whether they embarked on their barges somewhere along this western quay, or whether they had quays more adjacent to their

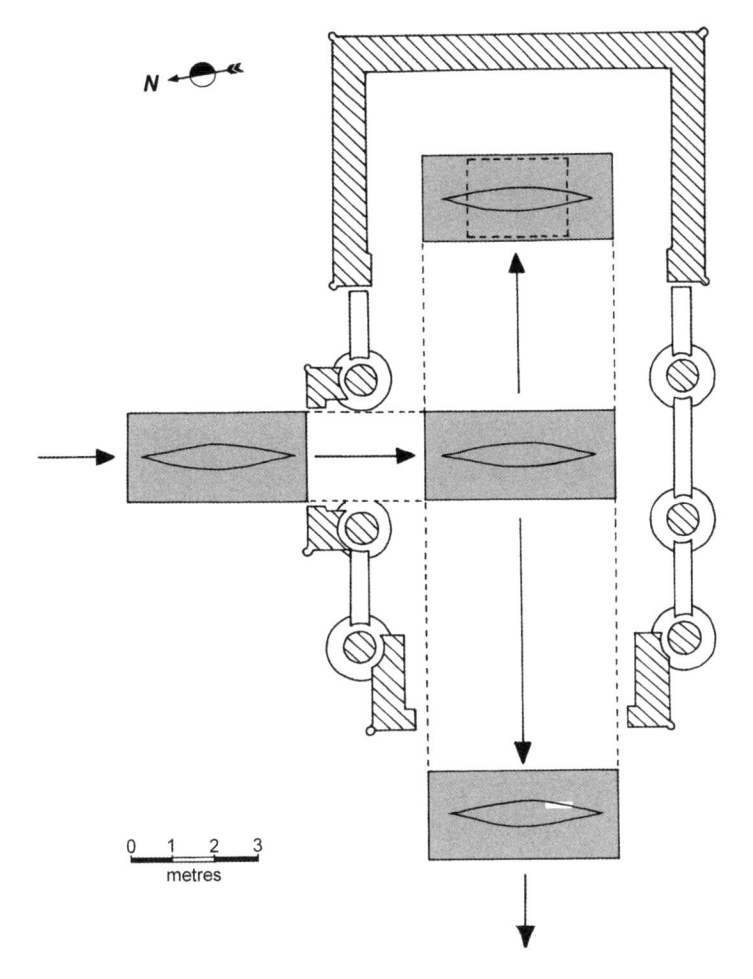

Figure 15.4 Plan showing the movement of the sacred bark into and out of the chapel of Hakor (after Traunecker, C., *La Chapelle d'Achôris à Karnak*, vol. *II*: 94).

own temples. It is known that the Khonsu temple did indeed have a separate canal, basin and quay, and now recent excavation work around the Mut precinct has found evidence that the goddess might also have had a similar arrangement of her own (Traunecker *et al.* 1981: 100 and n. 52).

Hakor had ruled for fourteen years, but Egypt's internal struggles still persisted and, although succeeded by his son Nepherites II, that new king's reign lasted a mere four months before he was ousted by the powerful ruler of Sebennytos, Nectanebo (Nakhtnebef), who declared himself king, the first of Dynasty XXX.

Dynasty XXX

Despite constant threats from a reinvigorated Persia, Nectanebo I managed to maintain stability, and was able during his eighteen-year reign to construct new monuments throughout Egypt, as well as to restore virtually all its temples: in particular he took

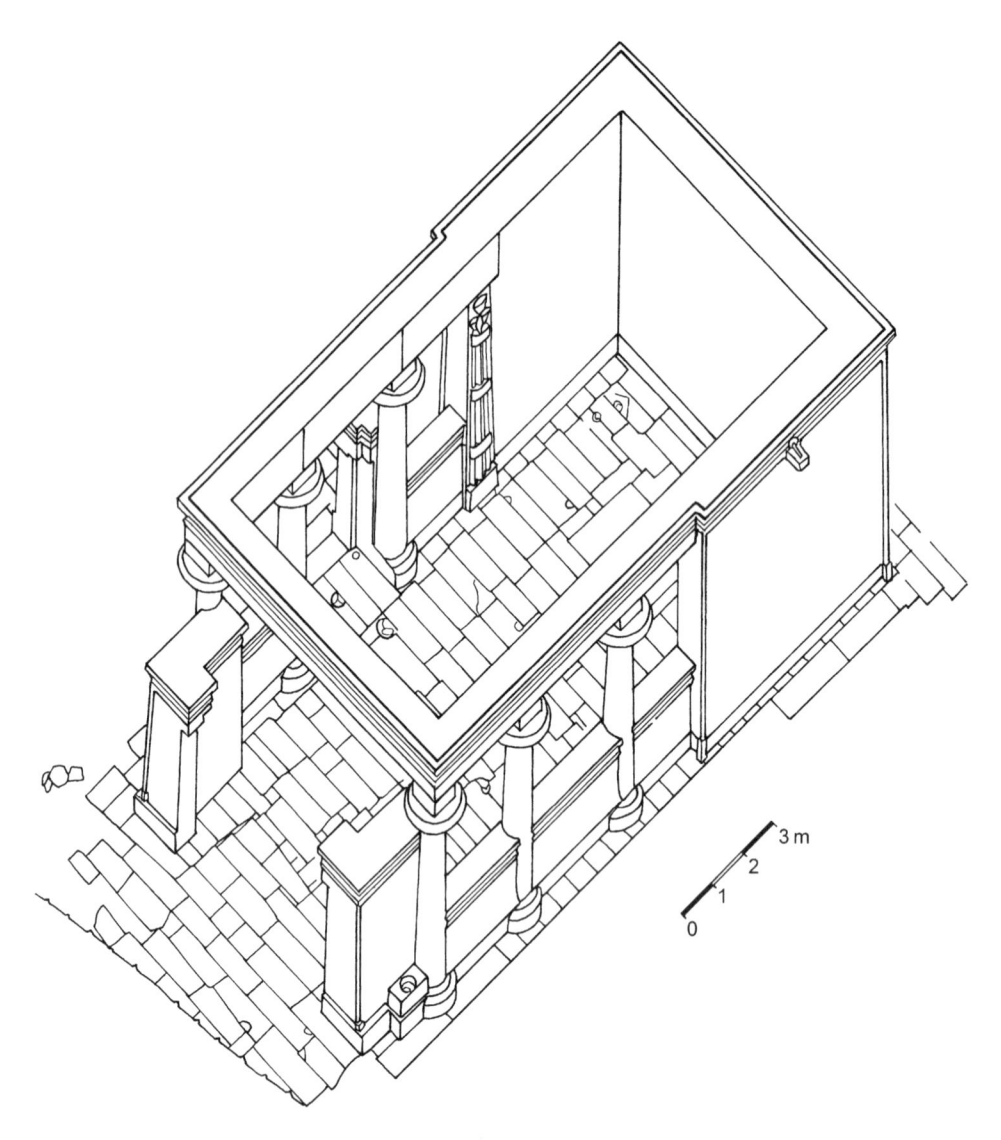

Figure 15.5 Artist's impression of the chapel of Hakor (after Lauffray, J., *La Chapelle d'Achôris à Karnak*, vol. I: 60).

pride in the restoration and embellishment of Karnak, and it is significant that he took as his throne name 'Kheperkare', the name of Karnak's founder, Senusret I.

Because of the Persian threat and because of Egypt's past experiences of repeated plunder and destruction, the kings of Dynasty XXX thought it expedient to erect huge enclosure walls in order to protect the temples from desecration (Arnold 1999: 105) and, on a more mundane level, to keep the ever-growing city of Thebes at bay as its houses encroached more and more upon Karnak's precincts. These massive constructions, which dwarfed all earlier ones, were more reminiscent of military fortifications than of the walls of sacred enclosures. Consequently, at Karnak, Nectanebo I's name is remembered above all for the colossal perimeter walls, 21 m high and 12 m thick, which extend for 2 km around Amun's domain: a prodigious undertaking. In addition, he likewise enclosed the temples of Montu and Mut at Karnak, and also that of Luxor.

These walls surrounding Amun's temple were, or course, by no means the first. There had been from the very outset an enclosure wall around the Middle Kingdom temple and, in fact, the foundations of part of its western section have recently come to light, as has been mentioned above. An impressive stretch of the girdle wall dating to Tuthmosis III has also been unearthed east of the Sacred Lake; in turn, this wall was founded upon the remains of a more ancient one. The wall of Tuthmosis III was over 6 m thick and had bastions at 17 m intervals along its outer face (Lauffray 1979: 202–3). It seems from various contemporary representations that these walls were castellated (e.g. a scene showing part of Karnak's wall and a portal can be seen depicted on the walls of the Temple of Khonsu (OI *Khonsu* I 1979: pl. 53)). It is quite apparent that the wall had been altered, strengthened and renewed many times over its history: the final complete restoration having been undertaken during the reign of Taharqa by Montuemhat, about which he informs us in a text engraved within the temple of Mut: 'I have restored the walls of the temple of Amun at Karnak to good order . . .'.

For all their size, strength and continual restoration, the Dynasty XVIII walls clearly did not afford Karnak the protection that was required in times of conflict. Nectanebo, therefore, undertook the construction of new walls designed to be so huge, so intimidating that no intruder would even contemplate an assault upon the sacred precinct.

The massive First Pylon and gateway, the largest ever constructed, were never fully completed and inscribed; nonetheless, they can be safely ascribed to Nectanebo I. The two towers of the pylon remain unfinished at a height of 31.65 m, but were intended to reach a colossal 40 m, with a width of 113 m. Each tower has four flagpole niches in its west façade, while on its eastern face great mud-brick construction ramps can still be seen. The gateway comprised two doors, set one within the other, a concept similar in design to that of the Second Pylon. The monumental doorway, 27.5 m in height, occupied the full width of the entrance between the pylon towers; while between its jambs was inserted a second much smaller door, only 10.85 m in height (Lauffray 1970: 101). It has been suggested that the great triumphal doorway was not equipped with huge wooden door-leaves simply because their sheer size and weight (estimated at over ten tonnes) would have made them totally unmanoeuvrable; this was probably why the second, smaller door had been provided (Lauffray 1970: 106) (Fig. 15.6).

The vast girdle walls surrounding the temple itself give the appearance of undulating quite noticeably – a deliberate feature of the construction technique, achieved by building the walls in sections with alternating concave and horizontal brick coursing. It should be noted, however, that while the tiers of brickwork undulate, the foundations do not and are perfectly level and regular. Almost certainly the undulation served a religious purpose: since the temple sanctuary represented the original mound of creation, so the surrounding walls represented Nun, the primaeval waters which encompassed that mound (Barguet 1962: 32). In addition to being castellated, Nectanebo's walls would have had a walkway along the top, as indicated by the presence of rooms near the top of the four monumental gateways that pierce the wall; these rooms would have provided access to and from the walkway.

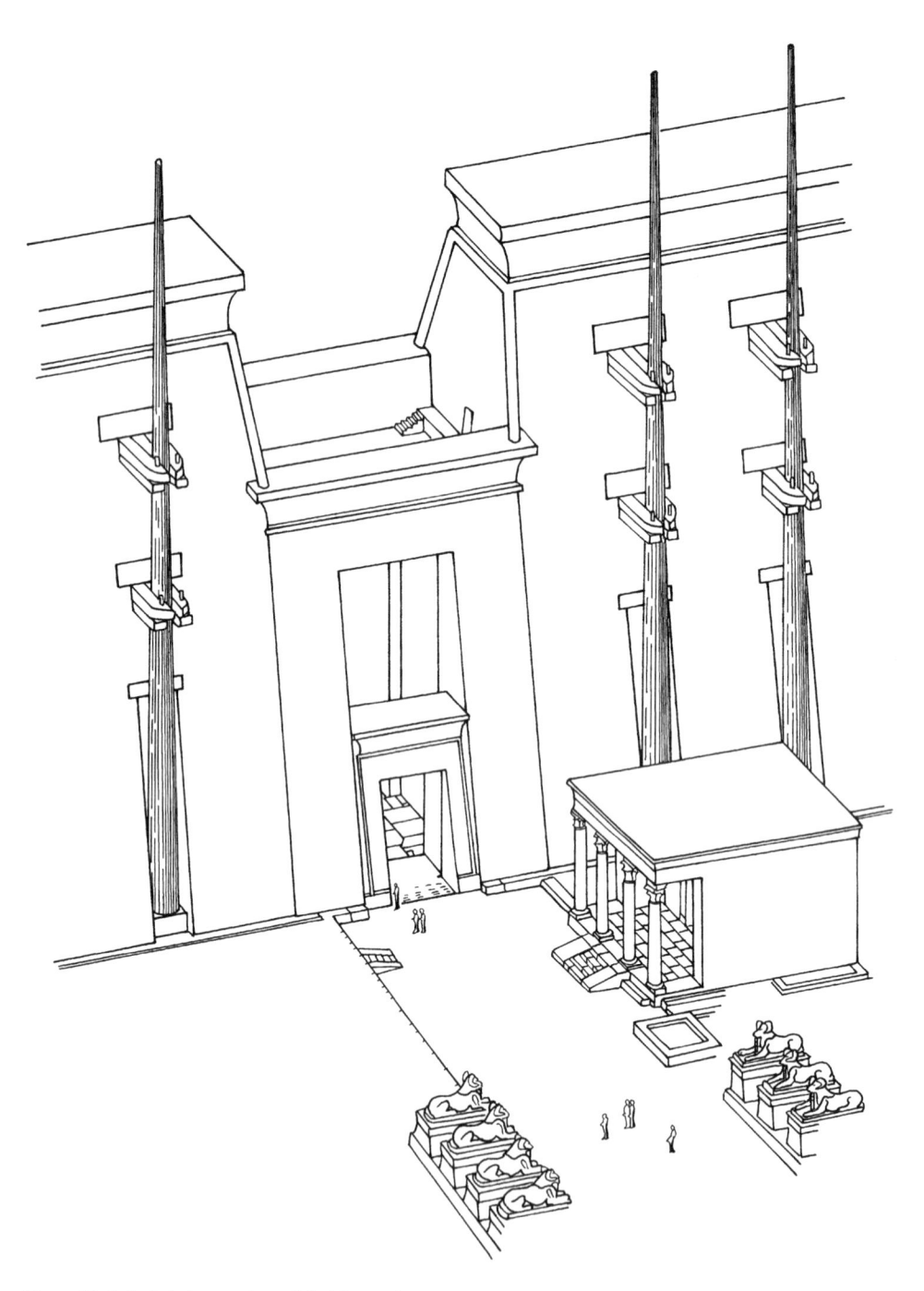

Figure 15.6 Artist's impression of the First Pylon gateway, with the later Roman temple on the right (after Lauffray, J., in *Kemi* XX: 107).

In the Cairo Museum there is an interesting sandstone stela, 80 cm in height, the exact provenance of which is unknown, although it certainly came from the Luxor area. It bears a text stating that Nectanebo had built 'for his father Amun ... who reigns at Karnak ... a new wall, completely magnificent ...'. This stela can be compared with similar ones from Karnak (Siptah) and Medinet Habu (Ramesses III), which are almost identical in size, design and wording. These stelae were sunk into the inner and/or outer faces of temple enclosure walls (Habachi 1970: 233–4). From this, it seems reasonable to assume that Karnak was, almost undoubtedly, the temple from which the Nectanebo stela derived.

Another feature of Karnak's great walls is the irregular shape of the enclosure, quite untypical of Egyptian temple construction. This can be readily explained, however, by the obvious desire of Nectanebo to enclose pre-existing monuments within Karnak's precincts. The orientation of the north wall would indicate that it was built at that angle to accommodate the Ptah temple, which had previously been independent, while the eastern wall was clearly respecting certain Ramesside constructions. The southern wall, aligned on the Tenth Pylon (which itself was not perpendicular to the main east–west axis), was extended westward in order to incorporate the temples of Khonsu and Opet, also formerly independent, and this extension made inevitable the line of Karnak's west wall with its inset main entrance (Golvin and Hegazy 1993: 146–7).

This south-west corner of the enclosure wall houses a strange feature. A tiny sandstone chapel, measuring only 1.26 m by 0.64 m, has been worked into the thickness of the masonry (Traunecker 1982b: 339). Its entrance, opening to the west, lies about 5 m from the corner and is approached by four steps up to a podium. It was recent work undertaken to restore this podium that brought to light some inscribed blocks bearing the cartouches of Nectanebo I, these obviously coming from the original construction which had been renewed later by the Ptolemies. The blocks seem to have formed part of a large 'false-door' stela. The chapel's function is uncertain, but vestiges of some scenes and an inscription on the stela suggest a connection with the processional route taken by the bark of Khonsu before crossing to the West Bank to participate in the Rites of the Mound of Djeme.

A short distance to the north of this tiny chapel, another, considerably larger, entrance gives access through the western face of the enclosure wall to the Temple of Opet. This temple had existed for many centuries before being rebuilt by Nectanebo I; later it was heavily modified by the Ptolemies. Excavation has revealed that blocks reused in the Ptolemaic foundations came from an edifice dedicated to the goddess Opet, a universal mother-goddess figure, by Taharqa, which itself replaced one of Tuthmosis III and Amenhotep II (Lauffray 1979: 218).

Little of Nectanebo's work on the Opet temple remains: a great sandstone gate in his name, opening through the enclosure wall, was approached by a ramp bordered by low walls. The gate has several scenes of the king offering to various deities; while other scenes, reworked by the Ptolemies, honour Nectanebo's cartouches. A few elements from a porch, also of the king, have survived; these preceded a stone pylon which, from its method of construction, must be dated to Taharqa, although modified later by Nectanebo (Leclant 1965: 82–3). An unusual, perhaps unique, feature of this pylon is that two flagpoles are shown cut in relief on its façade, but in reality they never existed (Azim 1987: 61). The pylon gateway gave access to an open court that had once contained a stone kiosk of Taharqa, with a second courtyard beyond. However, the main body of the existing temple is entirely Ptolemaic with some Roman decoration in the name of Augustus.

Nectanebo's provision of monumental entrances to Karnak is well illustrated by the huge gateway that gives access through the enclosure wall to the Eastern Temple of Ramesses II. This vast gate, 20 m high and 13.4 m wide, bears references to 'Amun-Re who hears prayers', testifying to the continuing use of this area by the common people as a focus for their private prayers and devotions (Barguet 1962: 225). The king had originally planned probably eleven or twelve gates through his enclosure wall, but it seems he completed four only, the rest being constructed by Nectanebo II and by the Ptolemies.

The remains of two small chapels, bearing reliefs and cartouches of Nectanebo I, can still be seen flanking the so-called contra-temple of Tuthmosis III which stands against the exterior eastern wall of Amun's temple. Both chapels are very ruinous, but the entrance to each is still obvious with two engaged columns of sandstone either side of the door; the columns of the northern chapel entrance stand on black granite bases, while those of the southern chapel are on alabaster bases.

Finally, as already referred to in Chapter 8, Nectanebo I constructed a magnificent walled avenue, paved its entire length with sandstone slabs, lined either side by more than 700 sphinxes, and planted with trees and flowers, the irrigation channels for which have recently been found. This processional way stretched from Karnak's southern gate to the main entrance of Luxor temple, a distance of some two miles. Such a truly stupendous project aptly sums up this great king's achievements.

After a stable eighteen-year reign, Nectanebo I was succeeded by his son Teos (Djedhor). However the new king, by imposing a heavy taxation burden on his subjects in order to pay his army of Greek mercenaries, became hugely unpopular quite early in his reign. This unpopularity at home was quickly exploited by his brother who, while Teos was away campaigning, declared his own son Nakhthorheb (Nectanebo II) as ruler of Egypt. The general populace approved wholeheartedly, and Nectanebo II took the throne, while the deposed Teos fled to the Persians for aid and protection. Eventually winning a resounding victory over the Persians, Nakhthorheb was acclaimed as 'Nectanebo the divine falcon' by his people, and cults were set up in his name (Arnold 1999: 124).

The king set about a programme of building that eclipsed in scale even that of Nectanebo I before him; no cult, no temple was ignored by him as construction and/or renovation was enthusiastically undertaken the length and breadth of Egypt. Such an amazing burst of energy and finance at a time when Persia was yet again threatening the whole region can perhaps only be explained as an attempt to please the gods and invoke their divine power in Egypt's defence at such a dangerous time. Perhaps on a more mundane level, it should also be viewed as a way to stimulate the country's economy since endowing, or re-endowing, the temple cults required an exploitation of all temple land to provide the necessary offerings and thus, as a consequence, work for the local labour force.

There seems little doubt that many of the early Ptolemaic monuments were actually begun by Nectanebo II, which might perhaps go some way to explain the surprising paucity of monuments bearing his name at Karnak. Dieter Arnold propounds an interesting theory (Arnold 1999: 131–2 and n. 128). He suggests that Nectanebo II initiated an ambitious scheme to renew the dilapidated remains of the Middle Kingdom temple and Tuthmosis III's bark-shrine that stood in front of it, both of which would have suffered grievously at the hands of the Assyrians and later the Persians. Arnold surmises that, having cleared the area, Nectanebo's reconstruction would have started with the bark-shrine, since he would have needed the clear access from the east to bring in the necessary stone and building materials: indeed, some blocks of Tuthmosis III's original shrine were found beneath the present granite one, which was built at a higher level. Moreover, the large granite blocks are much more typical of Nectanebo's work than of the Ptolemies whose preference for sanctuaries constructed of smaller sandstone blocks can be seen at Luxor and other temples (Arnold 1999: 138). The second Persian invasion would have put an end to this project and the completed shrine of Nectanebo II was subsequently decorated in the name of Philip Arrhidaeus, who, it should be stated, never actually visited Egypt himself. However, it is difficult to understand why, if this theory is to be believed, the Ptolemies should have tolerated the large empty space that would have been left by the dismantling of the Middle Kingdom temple remains. Moreover, it is known that the Roman emperor Tiberius attempted some restoration work in the area of the Middle Kingdom temple (Legrain 1900a: 63–4).

Certainly, it is hard to imagine that Nectanebo II, who built extensively all over Egypt, did not undertake any work at Amun's major temple but, nonetheless, this is only a hypothesis with no archaeological or textual evidence to substantiate it. It *is* true to say, however, that many of Nectanebo's projects, unfinished at his demise, were completed by the Ptolemies and attributed to them.

A similar, and equally problematic, case has been made for the great entrance gate to the south of the Khonsu temple. Decorated by Ptolemy III Euergetes I, it has been argued that the construction of this gateway should in fact be attributed to Nectanebo II. Earlier scholars pointed to Teos as its probable builder on account of that king's dedication text inscribed on the eastern exterior wall of the Khonsu temple where he declares: 'I have made a sacred gateway, which has no equal, similar to the horizon of Re' (Barguet 1962: 29 n. 2), but this text is now thought to refer to the doorway (or rather, the little contra-temple) at the rear of the said temple. Whatever the answer, it is certainly a possibility that the gateway was merely decorated by Ptolemy III, but constructed by a Dynasty XXX ruler. However, once again, this is all supposition, and only a few small buildings on the periphery of Karnak outside the enclosure walls, as well as minor works at the temples of Mut, Khonsu and Montu, can be ascribed with any confidence to Nectanebo II.

Nectanebo had ruled for about eighteen years with the threat from Persia's powerful empire constantly present; now its army was once again poised on Egypt's border ready to attack. This time the Egyptians were unable to withstand the onslaught: city after city in the Delta fell to the invaders, until Nectanebo was forced to surrender Memphis and flee to the south where, it seems, he managed to hold on to some form of independent rule for a couple of years. But it was, in effect, the end of all native Egyptian rule: a second period of Persian domination commenced, ending only when ten years later, in 332 BC, Alexander the Great crushed the Persian Empire. As a consequence, shortly after this comprehensive victory, Alexander was able to enter Egypt with ease, where he was viewed more as a liberator than as a conqueror, and in due course he was crowned in true pharaonic style as 'the son of Nectanebo II'. Anxious to add another dimension to his pharaonic credentials, Alexander undertook his celebrated trip to Amun's oracle at Siwa where he was hailed by the god as his legitimate son and heir. With this divine endorsement, Alexander took as his throne name, Meryamun Setepenre (Beloved of Amun, Chosen of Re).

16

THE FINAL PHASE

Alexander The Great and Philip Arrhidaeus

Although Alexander was Egypt's ruler for nine years, his temple building was almost non-existent. There is no surprise in this since his energies were directed initially at one mighty project, namely the founding of the great city of Alexandria on the Mediterranean, which he wished to make pre-eminent in the Greek-dominated world. But his residence in Egypt was brief. Placing the country in the hands of his two highest officials, Alexander left to continue the expansion of his empire: he was never to return, dying of a fever in Babylon in 323 BC.

Alexander's work at Karnak was, as might be expected, minimal, confined largely to a renewal of the ancient royal cult chapel of Tuthmosis III in the Akh-Menu complex. The antechamber to the sanctuary was partly renewed, some of it in Tuthmosis' name, but the sanctuary itself was a complete reworking by Alexander. He inscribed his dedication around the entire chamber:

> It is a renovation of the monument made by the King of Upper and Lower Egypt, Lord of the Two Lands, Setepenre Meryamun, son of Re, possessor of the crowns, Alexander ... after he had found it constructed under ... Menkheperre, son of Re, Tuthmosis ...

Within the sanctuary a damaged limestone statue of a falcon can still be seen, very probably dating back to Dynasty XVIII. Since the chapel is particularly dedicated to the royal cult, this statue is likely to have represented the king himself as Horus.

The name of Alexander is also attested on some blocks and architectural fragments found in the vicinity of the Opet temple; some of these almost certainly came from the tiny nearby shrine in the enclosure wall (discussed in the previous chapter) since the measurement of these various elements tallies exactly with those of the shrine. It seems relatively certain therefore that it was to Alexander that the shrine owed its later reconstruction (Traunecker 1987b: 349).

Apart from these renovations, any work undertaken by Alexander is not much in evidence: five lines of renewal text on the gateway of the Fourth Pylon and some scenes on the Khonsu temple pylon entrance bear his name. However, it should be noted that since he and his successor, Philip Arrhidaeus, shared the same throne name – Meryamun Setepenre – it is possible that where the throne name only is given, some of the work attributed to Philip might actually be that of Alexander instead.

Upon Alexander's death, power passed ostensibly to his mentally disabled half-brother, Philip Arrhidaeus, but, in effect, Egypt was governed by Alexander's trusted friend and lieutenant, Ptolemy, son of Lagos. Philip reigned for six or seven years without ever visiting Egypt. He was murdered in 316 BC and Alexander's son by his Persian wife Roxane succeeded to the throne until, some years later, he too was assassinated. Throughout this uncertain time, Ptolemy was in truth *de facto* ruler and, with no clear successor to Egypt's throne, it was he who now became pharaoh in name as well: Ptolemy I Soter. His reign ushered in a period of some two-and-a-half centuries, during which he and his successors enthusiastically embraced Egypt's gods, honouring many local cults and building extensively throughout the country. Evidence of Ptolemaic work is to be found throughout the country.

But to return to Philip Arrhidaeus and the bark-shrine at the heart of Karnak that bears his name. Built of red granite with 'doors of precious wood wrought with gold ...' (flakes of gold have indeed been found upon the door's lintel), this shrine was an exact replica, not only in size but in themes of decoration, of the shrine of Tuthmosis III which it replaced. It comprised two rooms aligned on the temple's main axis – a vestibule and a sanctuary, this latter being where the sacred bark would have been housed. It is in this second room that Philip's dedication can be seen:

> The son of Re, of his body, his beloved Philip had found the great seat of Amun fallen into ruin, which had been constructed at the time of the majesty of the King of Upper and Lower Egypt, Menkheperre ... Tuthmosis. His Majesty reconstructed it as something new in granite, as an excellent work of eternity ...

A similar dedication can be found on the shrine's exterior wall, but it is badly preserved, which is unfortunate since this version of the text had once contained the shrine's name. It has been plausibly suggested that the name could well have been 'The Favourite Place of Amun' which was, of course, the name of Hatshepsut's Chapelle Rouge, a name which Tuthmosis III chose to retain (Barguet 1962: 137). It seems logical, therefore, that since Philip had made a faithful copy of Tuthmosis' shrine, he also would have wished to keep the original name.

While the interior reliefs comprise the customary ones of the sacred bark on its socle, as well as scenes of the king offering and the dedication ceremony entitled 'giving the House to its Lord', the exterior decoration is of some interest. On the south-facing wall are four registers of scenes. The uppermost depicts the king's coronation: Philip leaving the palace, his purification at the temple entrance, the placing of the crowns upon his head within a closed and private chamber, and his ascent to the sanctuary to be enthroned by Amun. Below these royal scenes are two registers that represent events from the Beautiful Feast of the Valley. The sacred bark is depicted leaving the temple and processing from way-station to way-station; it is also shown on its return to Karnak being towed by the royal barge: 'the king is in the barge holding the rope: the return in peace from the West'. The final register shows the king performing foundation ceremony rituals. Beneath all these exterior scenes, the north and south walls of the shrine carry a list of Egypt's nomes, similar to the lists on both Hatshepsut's chapel and on the White Chapel of Senusret I: clearly an ancient tradition still being observed.

On the north side of Philip's shrine is a small independent room with its own west-facing entrance; it was destined to receive the processional statue of Amun-Kamutef, whose likeness appears on the walls.

The Ptolemaic period

With the start of the Ptolemaic era under Ptolemy I Soter, Karnak was to enjoy a period of renovation. The cartouches and reliefs of Ptolemaic kings are widely seen around the temple precincts, including those of Mut, Khonsu, Ptah and Montu, as well as several great stone gateways set in the enclosure walls.

Ptolemy I Soter himself had little time to inaugurate any building work at Karnak, and it was Ptolemy II Philadelphus who was the first of his line to commence this activity by building a propylon gate, 16.6 m high, on the approach to the temple of Mut; he also constructed, or perhaps reworked an extant contra-temple at the rear of Mut's temple. But perhaps most interesting of all from the reign of this king was the discovery of an ostracon in the area of habitation to the east of the Sacred Lake, which gives a demotic version of a royal decree that would have originally been written in Greek. This orders the officials and scribes of the Treasury to undertake a complete review, from Elephantine in the south to the Mediterranean coast in the north, of all cultivated land, field by field: the volume and area, irrigation procedures, produce and yield, as well as the type of agriculture, whether arable or livestock (Lauffray 1979: 199). This was a vast project and must undoubtedly have been part of the state's fiscal policy in relation to tax revenues.

Ptolemy III Euergetes I contributed substantially to Karnak with work on the Opet temple, Ptah temple and a monumental gate with a 120 metre-long processional approach to the Montu temple. But he is remembered above all for the magnificent stone gate to the Temple of Khonsu, known today as the 'Bab el-Amara'. As previously mentioned, it has been suggested that perhaps Nectanebo II should be credited with the construction of this elegant gate, that stands 21 m high, but the forty-eight scenes that cover its entire surface are certainly attributable to Ptolemy III. Although the gate itself was completed, the pylon towers either side were not, barely rising above foundation level.

Some of the work undertaken by Ptolemy III had its decoration completed by his successor, Ptolemy IV Philopator, who also erected a small monolithic chapel dedicated to Neferhotep on the west side of the Khonsu temple's avenue of rams, as well as a brick 'Osiris tomb' to the east of Amun's temple, adjacent to the Saite 'Osiris tomb' of Necho. This 'Osiris tomb' structure of Ptolemy IV comprised a series of underground galleries, somewhat akin to Ptolemaic catacombs, with rows of niches stacked one upon another containing Osiride figurines. The walls of these galleries were plastered and painted with scenes depicting various rituals pertaining to the cult of Osiris (Leclère 1996: 9).

Earlier structures of the same type, some dating to the New Kingdom, have also been unearthed in the area between those of Ptolemy IV and Necho (Leclère 1996: 12): it seems that this sector of eastern Karnak had become a virtual cemetery for the figurines which were interred during the course of the annual Osiris festival. A late papyrus (N3176 [S] in the Louvre Museum) refers several times to an Osirian sanctuary in this area, and this is underlined by a relief of Osiris standing before his mound (the

Mound of Djeme), which can be seen at the extreme northern end of Karnak's eastern enclosure wall (Barguet 1962: 15 n. 7).

Ptolemy IV's name can be seen all over the great colonnade of Taharqa in Karnak's first court. In addition to this usurpation, Ptolemy inserted intercolumnar walls between the existing columns: only the walls on the north side have survived to any extent, and these are decorated with figures representing the Lower Egyptian nomes being led by Ptolemy himself towards the divinity personifying Waset (or Thebes). It is evident that the southern walls once depicted the nomes of Upper Egypt in a similar fashion.

Ptolemy IV's son, Ptolemy V Epiphanes, was a mere child when he succeeded to the throne, but although he reigned about twenty-five years, his name is hardly to be seen at Karnak. The only monument of any note from his reign is a red granite stela, fragments of which were found at the temple entrance where it had once stood. Of this siting we can be certain as the text contains orders for the stela to be set up in a prominent public place upon the dromos of Karnak's entrance. The fragments that were recovered show that it was once written, as was the Rosetta Stone, in three scripts, giving an account of Ptolemy V's work in safeguarding the Theban temples and towns during certain uprisings that occurred during his reign. It also includes orders for statues of himself and his queen to be erected for the annual celebrations in honour of the royal cult, and there are instructions given concerning the sailing of the sacred bark with 'oars of gold' for the Beautiful Feast of the Valley (Lauffray 1979: 90). Thus it is clear that this ancient tradition had survived and was still being celebrated.

Following the lack of any building projects under Ptolemy V, Ptolemy VI Philometor's name, by contrast, can be seen in four of Karnak's temples: those of Ptah, Mut and Montu received additional gates or chapels, while in the temple of Amun the king restored and decorated the great gateway of the Second Pylon, recarving some of its original scenes. On the southern wall of the door embrasure, for instance, is a relief of the sacred barks of the Theban triad in their respective shrines; although the cartouches give the name of Ramesses II, they and the accompanying scenes are of Ptolemaic date (Barguet 1962: 58–9). Ptolemy VI, it seems, was not trying to usurp Ramesses' work; at the very most, he shows himself being led into the Hypostyle Hall, but in all else he defers to Ramesses, whom he obviously believed to be the Hall's original builder, and consequently a king to be much admired.

The next king to leave his mark upon Amun's temple was Ptolemy VIII Euergetes II, whose long reign produced many new temples throughout Egypt. At Karnak, he too worked upon the Second Pylon's gateway, adding a lengthy dedication text to both door jambs, each commencing with the king's names and titles (Drioton 1945: 111ff.). On the north side there is a renewal text followed by a description of the creation of the world and its organisation under Amun-Re and the king. The southern jamb describes the glory and magnificence of the renewed door, and this too is followed by accounts of Thebes' creation, its role in Egypt and the universe, its gods and festivals, and its eternal connection with the ruling king. Some considerably more modest work was also undertaken by Ptolemy VIII on the doorway of the Fourth Pylon.

The Eastern Temple of Ramesses II was an area that received considerable modification by Ptolemy VIII. The central niche which contained the stela, or false-door, at the rear of the peristyle court was knocked through to create a third doorway in that wall, flanked by the two existing doors dedicated to Mut and Khonsu respectively. This action Ptolemy VIII described with the words: 'He (Ptolemy) had unveiled that which was veiled, since his Majesty had made it open to all' (Barguet 1962: 233–4). The jambs of this new doorway show the king offering to 'Amun-Re, King of the Gods, who hears prayers', thus demonstrating that the temple's original function remained unchanged. Below these scenes, eight columns of dedication text on either side appear to be the counterpart of the lengthy mythological texts that Ptolemy VIII had inscribed on the gateway of the Second Pylon. Beyond the peristyle court, in what had been the open area containing Ramesses' colonnaded approach to the single obelisk, Ptolemy now erected side walls to north and south, thus forming an enclosed chamber with the great obelisk standing at the rear: two small rooms to either side of the obelisk were created by partition walls.

By opening a third door at the back of the temple's peristyle court, as well as other modifications, Ptolemy had provided the Eastern Temple with an east–west axis that led from its main entrance through to the single obelisk, which now stood within a holy-of-holies. In effect, he had created a sanctuary for the temple dedicated to the rising sun, Amun-Re-Horakhte (Barguet 1962: 241). Since the chamber behind the peristyle court was roofed, while the obelisk at the far end obviously was not, the effect of standing within an enclosed and darkened area while gazing up at the brilliant sunlight streaming down the towering shaft from its gilded tip to the pedestal below upon which it stood, must surely have evoked the most overwhelming sensation of being in the presence of a spiritual power.

Following on the earlier work of Ptolemy III, it was Ptolemy VIII who undertook the main task of completing the Opet temple. In this highly symbolic place, the god Amun died in the form of Osiris, entered the body of the universal mother-goddess Opet and was reborn as the rising sun. In the Late Period, this temple is known to have functioned in unison with the immediately adjacent Khonsu temple (Arnold 1999: 197), but since the god concerned here is Amun, it has been included in this work.

This mysterious temple stands markedly higher than its surroundings, having been built upon a decorated platform, 1.9 m high, which represented the primaeval mound. Within and beneath this 'mound' a series of crypts were constructed, in which is depicted an account of the death and resurrection of Osiris/Amun through the intermediary of the goddess.

The temple building itself measured 19.6 m by 22.7 m in area and was approached by a staircase from the courtyard; this gave access through the central doorway to a small hypostyle hall containing two Hathor-headed columns, behind which was the sanctuary area – a veritable network of rooms and crypts worked into the thickness of the walls and the temple substructure. The decoration of the northern crypts shows the death and regeneration of Amun as Osiris, while those to the south were of the rebirth of Amun as Horus, the rising sun (Lauffray 1979: 218), (Fig. 16.1a).

This enigmatic monument, so rarely visited today, is hugely intriguing, not least in its relationship to its much larger neighbour, the Temple of Khonsu, which, by contrast, receives a large number of visitors. That the two temples functioned in unison at this period is well known, but in what respect and how the connection developed is uncertain.

The very topography of the two temples speaks clearly of this connection (Fig. 16.1b). Their configuration resembles the letter 'T', with the Khonsu temple forming the cross-bar of that letter, and the Opet temple the upright; a narrow corridor between them just separates the two elements. With the temples' axes set at right-angles to one

Plate 16.1 Entrance to the temple of Opet.

another (north–south for Khonsu and east–west for Opet), the western side wall of the Khonsu temple faced the eastern rear wall of Opet across this narrow divide. Further, a door in that western Khonsu wall communicated directly with the doorway to a crypt which was constructed within the eastern end of the Opet temple's substructure, this crypt being immediately below the Opet sanctuary in the temple above. Consequently the Opet sanctuary was viewed as the funerary chapel of Amun-Osiris, and the crypt below as his burial chamber. This complex arrangement clearly had great significance. Whether the much earlier New Kingdom temples of Opet and Khonsu also functioned together is a fascinating question.

Apart from some reworking of the Montu temple forecourt by Ptolemy IX Soter II, work at Karnak dwindled after the death of Ptolemy VIII, until the reign of Ptolemy XII Neos Dionysos who undertook work on the Ptah temple approach and added some decoration to the pylon constructed by Nectanebo I in front of the Opet temple; to this temple he also added, or decorated, an entrance porch. A chapel dedicated to Osiris-the-Coptite-who-presides-over-the-House-of-Gold was constructed by Ptolemy XII, with further work by Tiberius many decades later. This building was sited north of Taharqa's entrance colonnade to the Eastern Temple, and was in fact built of reused blocks taken from a monument of Taharqa and the God's Wife of Amun, Amenirdis. Ptolemy recarved the blocks and enclosed the building in a complex of mud-brick walls.

Ptolemy XII was succeeded by his daughter, the famous Cleopatra VII; her history and the subsequent end of the Ptolemaic dynasty are well known. However, no chapter

THE FINAL PHASE

on the Ptolemies at Karnak is complete without mention of the spectacular finds made by Georges Legrain a century ago (Legrain 1905: 61ff.; 1906: 137ff.).

The story actually began in 1883, when Gaston Maspero, excavating to the north of the Seventh Pylon in the first court of the southern processional way, discovered parts of statues and reliefs under the soil. Later he delegated the work to Legrain who found further statues, limestone pillars and a limestone gateway – these being in the names of Senusret I and Amenhotep I; this was followed by the discovery of the dismantled limestone chapels of Amenhotep I, as well as his jubilee chapel. But it was between 1903 and 1905 that the huge, and very famous, cache of statues and other objects came to light; these were discovered in two separate pits, one going down to a depth of 14 m. Sadly however, work had to be abandoned by Legrain before the bottom of the pit had been reached, due to severe water infiltration (Barguet 1962: 277, n. 1). It is tantalising to think how much more might have been recovered. Nevertheless, over 750 statues and stelae from every period of Egypt's history, as well as 17,000 bronzes were unearthed. It was a staggering find.

Among the more unusual objects also recovered were a statue of Horemheb in 'fossilised' wood, fragments of basalt giving Nile heights from the reigns of Osorkon III and Nectanebo I, a water-clock (clepsydra) of Amenhotep III, a gold ring of Nefertiti,

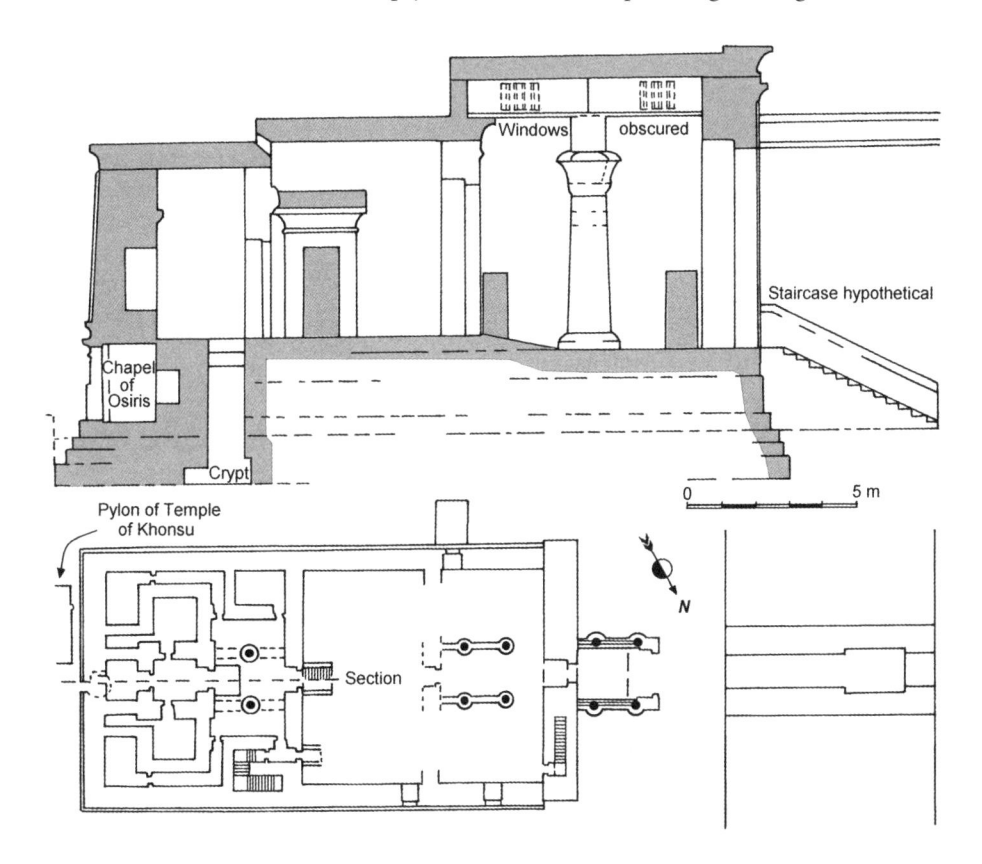

Figure 16.1 The temple of Opet under Ptolemy VIII. (a) Plan and section (after Arnold, D., *Temples of the Last Pharaohs*: 165).

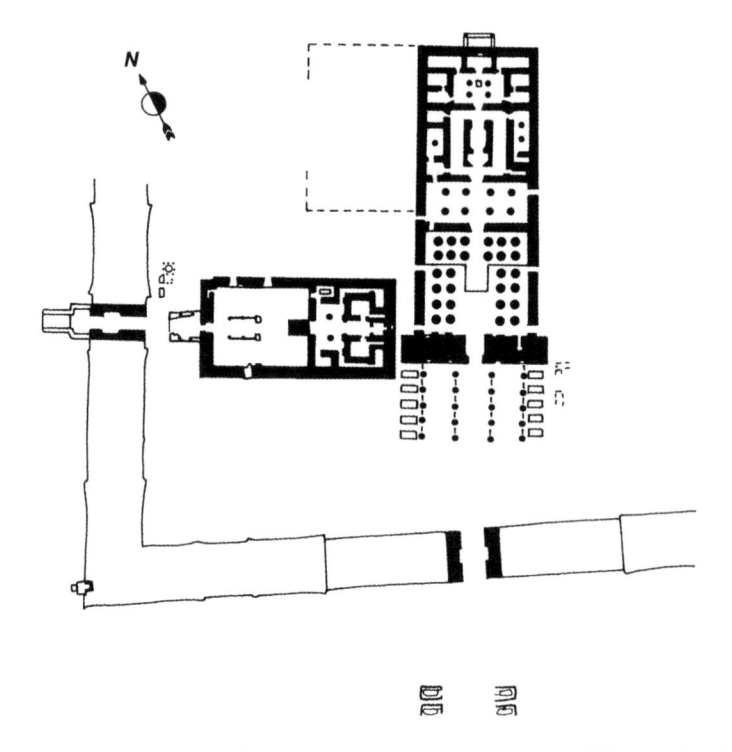

Figure 16.1 (continued) (b) Plan showing the juxtaposition of the temples of Khonsu and Opet (after Aufrère, S. *et al.*, *L'Égypte Restituée*: 115).

and some blocks of turquoise and nuggets of gold. But above all, it was the seemingly endless profusion of bronzes brought out of the ground, as well as the huge number of statues, that made this discovery so utterly astounding. Perhaps the claim made in the Great Harris Papyrus of Dynasty XX that Karnak housed at that time over 86,000 statues was no exaggeration.

The question arises as to when this great cache was buried and for what reason? And why was this particular court chosen to receive such a burial?

We can be relatively certain that, since statues in Greek draperies and copper coins bearing the head of Alexander were present in the hoard, the interment was carried out during the Ptolemaic period. It must be assumed that by this period of its history, Karnak's shrines, sanctuaries and processional ways were choked with vast quantities of statuary and votive offerings, greatly impeding all movement of the sacred barks and processional statues. In fact, the entire temple precinct must have been so heavily encumbered as to be virtually at a standstill.

But these sacred objects could not be destroyed, consequently it was necessary to find a suitable place in which to inter them. As has already been noted, this court had, from early in the New Kingdom, been used as an area in which to bury dismantled buildings and statues. One wonders whether the Ptolemaic rulers were aware of this. Was it, perhaps, recorded in the temple archives as the burial place of consecrated objects? Karnak's priests must surely have known of this tradition. Be that as it may, it was undoubtedly an area that held great significance as the point of departure of the sacred way leading out of Karnak towards the Temple of Mut and to Luxor; it was also the point of entry into the sacred heart of Karnak, Ipet-Sut.

In 31 BC, Cleopatra VII and Mark Antony were defeated by Octavian, heir to Julius Caesar, in a great sea battle at Actium. Having fled back to Egypt, Cleopatra and Mark Antony were pursued there by the victorious Octavian and the famous couple each died by their own hand. The last Ptolemy, Caesarion, Cleopatra's son by Julius Caesar, ascended the throne briefly before being ruthlessly eliminated by Octavian. Egypt thereafter became a Roman province and the personal estate of Octavian, who had declared himself the first Emperor of Rome, taking the name Caesar Augustus. Now totally under Roman domination, it was to be Roman emperors who, for the next four centuries, ruled Egypt through personally appointed prefects.

The Roman period

Throughout Egypt's history, the first ruler of a new dynasty had frequently sought to claim legitimacy to the throne and to recommend himself to his subjects by embracing the local gods and their cults and by instituting a programme of temple building. In this respect, Augustus was to be no different: Egypt saw many monuments erected in his name, and in the name of his successors. At Karnak, however, the sacred precinct was so full of shrines, hall and sanctuaries that Augustus confined his work to the extensive decoration that saw the completion of the temples of Opet and Khonsu.

Subsequent emperors contributed very little to Karnak, although other parts of the country were to receive some magnificent edifices. The only independent structure erected at Karnak by the Romans was a building that was sited in front of the First Pylon, just to the south of the main entrance gateway. It took the form of a small temple opening to the north and fronted by a portico of Corinthian columns. Measuring 14 m deep by 8.6 m wide, its walls were of mud-brick while the ramped approach, paving and parts of the single-chambered sanctuary were of sandstone. This was a temple dedicated to the imperial cult: fourteen pedestals for statues of emperors stood against the inside walls. The statues themselves are missing, but of the few legible dedications that remain on the pedestal bases, the names of Augustus, Tiberius, Claudius, and Titus, son of Vespasian, can still be deciphered (Lauffray 1971: 120).

Other than this, there is little to be seen at Karnak: Tiberius undertook some restoration work in the Court of the Middle Kingdom, some decoration within the Ptolemaic chapel of Osiris-the-Coptite and upon one of the gates to the Ptah temple; there is also a stela in his name recording the apparent rebuilding of the Mut temple enclosure wall (Traunecker and Golvin 1984: 24). Nero left a short text on the northern face of the Ninth Pylon, and Domitian's name occurs within Tuthmosis III's Eastern Temple with a very damaged text that appears to be a hymn to the rising sun.

Of more interest however, are the remains of what had once been a monumental sandstone stela erected by Domitian in front of Karnak's entrance. From the fragments recovered, the stela apparently gave financial information concerning taxes and duties to be levied upon grocers, potters, wine-sellers and other merchants (Lauffray 1979: 90). This is another instance of the placing of a stela containing decrees or public announcements in front of the temple entrance at this period of history. Does this indicate, perhaps, that during the Graeco-Roman period this area was viewed as a public zone, or was even being used as a forum or agora?

The slow decline of Karnak had begun. Certainly by the late Roman period, Karnak was no longer functioning as the sacred and secret heart of Amun's cult. Evidence points to its dwindling role, and worship of Thebes' great god was becoming focused at Luxor temple which, under Constantine the Great, the Romans had enlarged and fortified. Perhaps, as during the Amarna period, one must visualise a gradual deterioration of Karnak's courts, corridors and shrines due to decades of neglect, with just a handful of loyal priests performing the daily rites, burning incense and making offerings within a few crumbling sanctuaries, in an endeavour to keep the sacred cults alive.

But Rome itself, weakened by wars and imperial decadence, was no longer the wealthy and vigorous power it once had been. In AD 330, in an endeavour to renew imperial grandeur, the emperor Constantine ordered his engineers to lower the mighty single obelisk within Karnak's Eastern Temple and remove it to Rome, where it would stand as a symbol of power. This huge undertaking succeeded in lowering the great shaft and transporting it to Alexandria, but there it remained for many years because no ship at that time could accommodate its sheer size and weight. It took twenty-six years before the obelisk finally reached Rome, where in AD 356 it was eventually erected in the Circus Maximus (Habachi 1984: 115; Traunecker and Golvin 1984: 28–9). Possibly inspired by this success, Constantine, or his successor Theodosius, also removed one of Tuthmosis III's obelisks that stood before the Seventh Pylon, transporting it to Constantinople where it was erected in the Hippodrome in AD 391.

In AD 323, Constantine the Great had officially recognised the Christian religion, but it was not until AD 356 that the closure of all pagan temples was ordered. Finally it was the emperor Theodosius who, in AD 380, issued an edict proclaiming Christianity as the state religion. It was Karnak's death-knell.

Christian Karnak

With the closure of Egypt's temples and the banning of her gods and her religion, Karnak could no longer function. In the wake of Theodosius' edict came the Christian iconoclasts, and one can scarcely imagine the anguish of those Egyptians still faithful to the old religion as they witnessed the destruction of their sacred statues, images and reliefs.

And yet, Karnak was a holy site, hallowed ground for over two thousand years, and Man is instinctively drawn to the divine, whether he will or no. It is small wonder, therefore, that four Christian churches were established within the sacred enclosure: indeed, we can see a clear parallel in early Britain where the first Christian churches were so often founded upon sacred prehistoric sites, where standing stones still bear witness to ancient beliefs.

Today the best-known of Karnak's Christian foundations is that sited within the central hall of Tuthmosis III's Akh-Menu. Many of the columns within that hall still bear painted representations of Christian saints and other figures of veneration: apostles, martyrs, archbishops, with accompanying inscriptions in Coptic. The placement of an altar before an enclosed sanctuary can still be made out in the central area of the hall (Coquin 1972: 170).

The Temple of Khonsu also housed a Christian sanctuary, almost undoubtedly on the exact spot of the ancient Egyptian one. A cross carved beside a doorway and some Greek and Coptic graffiti, one giving the names of St Peter and St Paul, are all that remain. However, an interesting graffito carved on the wall of the staircase depicts a pilgrimage undertaken in three boats: these are represented with cabins and oars, and one with a typical pharaonic rudder, that clearly recall the divine bark processions. All three boats are surmounted by a cross (Munier and Pillet 1929: 63).

The Temple of Opet and the Edifice of Amenhotep II were similarly home to Christian sanctuaries. The somewhat ephemeral remains of three monasteries within Amun's precinct are also known. One of these was established on the high platform of mud-brick against the east face of the First Pylon, where a shell-shaped niche sculpted in the stonework can still be seen: similar niches were carved into the faces of the Eighth and Ninth Pylons. The court of the Ninth Pylon once contained a mass of Christian buildings, where many elements carved with Christian iconography have been recovered. The north face of the Eighth Pylon is interesting in that it has some fifteen deep bays cut into its stonework, each of which had once been closed by doors; this is believed to have been the monastery library, or perhaps a refectory (Munier and Pillet 1929: 76). Even a Christian cemetery for the monks was provided against the girdle wall that enclosed the Temple of Amun.

For several centuries, Karnak was to accommodate a variety of Christian monasteries, convents and churches until in AD 642, the Muslim armies invaded and conquered Egypt. Slowly, even the monasteries of Karnak became deserted, and a final silence and oblivion descended upon the ruins of the once mighty Temple of Amun.

CONCLUSION

The greatness of ancient Egypt's civilisation was rooted in its deeply felt and all-pervading religious beliefs: every facet of life was informed by these beliefs. And it was because of this that the temples of Karnak came into being and grew to be, arguably, the most complex religious site on earth. Karnak's development was to continue throughout two-and-a-half millennia, and within its sacred walls is reflected the course of Egypt's history.

The temple of Amun at Karnak began life as the shrine of an obscure local god, but was destined to become the largest and most celebrated temple in all Egypt at the height of the Empire. Similarly its god Amun, the Hidden One, rose from his humble origins to enjoy 'the most brilliant divine career ever known in all antiquity' (Drioton 1958: 39).

This book has endeavoured to discuss the chronological development of Amun's great temple and to include in that discussion the latest discoveries made by archaeologists. However, every year, thanks to the continuing and painstaking work of the CFETK (Centre Franco-Égyptien d'Étude des Temples de Karnak) and other teams, new facts are constantly coming to light, and further insights are gleaned concerning the countless constructions, reconstructions, demolitions and renovations that this mighty foundation underwent over the span of so many centuries as each king sought to leave his mark on the sacred edifice, thus demonstrating his piety and devotion.

With each new discovery, another part of Karnak's complexity is revealed, and often old theories and previously held convictions have to be discarded. It is a continual learning process. A glance through any of the recent reports on the current work being undertaken vividly illustrates the ever-changing information that is being retrieved from the discovery of yet more foundations, walls, pylons and courts, often superimposed one upon another. Each tiny snapshot that comes from a season's excavation work must be studied, analysed, understood and fitted into context. Small wonder, therefore, that our current state of knowledge is forever altering and expanding. In the coming years, more and more discoveries will without doubt be made, and our understanding of Karnak will continue to broaden and deepen with each new revelation.

Now, in the twenty-first century, as we wander amongst Karnak's tumbled halls and courts, we might justifiably say *sic transit gloria mundi*. Yet, while the glory of Karnak's past might indeed have faded, nonetheless, the temple of Amun was, is, and always will be a sacred site whose magnificent structures, steeped in countless centuries of devotion, still have the capacity to mesmerise and enthrall all who visit them. Even today, the site remains a magical, mystical place. Jean Lauffray, who has been intimately concerned with the work of the CFETK, summed it up most eloquently when he observed that the temple would always remain hallowed ground; and that consequently, despite the daily influx of hordes of tourists, with all the associated noise and confusion, when the evening comes and the tourists have gone, nightfall brings with it the return of Karnak's aura of divine mystery (Lauffray 1979: 75).

And so long as mankind draws inspiration from the past, Karnak will continue to imbue in us a sense of awe. Surely our sensations are no less intense than those of Sonnini in the eighteenth century, quoted at the opening of this book: 'not a simple adoration merely, but an ecstasy . . .'.

BIBLIOGRAPHY

Abbreviations

ASAE	*Annales du Service des Antiquités de l'Égypte*
BAR	Breasted, J.H. (1906) *Ancient Records of Egypt*, 4 vols., Chicago: University of Chicago Press
BIFAO	*Bulletin de l'Institut Français d'Archéologie Orientale*
BSEG	*Bulletin de la Société d'Égyptologie de Genève*
BSFE	*Bulletin de la Société Français d'Égyptologie*
CdE	*Chronique d'Égypte*
CRIPEL	*Cahiers de Recherches de l'Institut de Papyrologie et Égyptologie de Lille*
GM	*Göttinger Miszellen*
JAOS	*Journal of the American Oriental Society*
JARCE	*Journal of the American Research Center in Egypt*
JEA	*Journal of Egyptian Archaeology*
JNES	*Journal of Near Eastern Studies*
MDAIK	*Mitteilungen des Deutschen Archäologischen Instituts, Abteilung Kairo*
NARCE	*Newsletter of the American Research Center in Egypt*
Or (n.s.)	*Orientalia* (new series)
OI *Khonsu*	Oriental Institute, University of Chicago (1979–1981) *The Khonsu Temple*, Vols I and II, Chicago: The University of Chicago.
OI *Reliefs*	Oriental Institute, University of Chicago (1936) *Reliefs and Inscriptions at Karnak I–II. Ramesses III's temple within the Great Enclosure of Amon*, Chicago: Oriental Institute Press.
PM II	Porter, B. and Moss, R. (1972) *Topographical Bibliography of Ancient Egyptian Hieroglyphic Texts, Reliefs and Paintings. II: Theban Temples* (2nd edn), Oxford: Oxford University Press at the Clarendon Press.
RT	*Recueil de Travaux Relatifs à la Philologie et à l'Archéologie Égyptiennes et Assyriennes*
RdE	*Revue d'Égyptologie*
SAK	*Studien zur Altägyptischen Kultur*
URK IV	Sethe, K., *Urkunden der 18.Dynastie*, Heft 1–16, Leipzig 1906–1909: J.C. Hinrichs Helck, W., *Urkunden der 18.Dynastie*, Heft 17–22, Berlin 1955–1958: Akademie Verläg
VA	*Varia Aegyptiaca*
ZÄS	*Zeitschrift für Ägyptische Sprache und Altertumskunde*

Aldred, C. (1988) *Akhenaten, King of Egypt*, London: Thames & Hudson.
Amer, A. (1985) 'Reflections on the reign of Ramesses VI', *JEA* 71: 66–70.
—— (1999) *The Gateway of Ramesses IX in the Temple of Amun at Karnak*, Warminster: Aris & Phillips.
Arnold, D. (1999) *Temples of the Last Pharaohs*, Oxford: Oxford University Press.

BIBLIOGRAPHY

Azim, M. (1982a) 'Découverte de dépôts de fondation d'Horemheb au IXe pylône de Karnak', *Cahiers de Karnak VII, 1978–1981*, 93–117, Paris: Éditions Recherche sur les Civilisations.
—— (1982b) 'La structure des pylônes d'Horemheb à Karnak', *Cahiers de Karnak VII, 1978–1981*, 127–166, Paris, Éditions Recherche sur les Civilisations.
—— (1987) 'À propos du pylône du temple d'Opet à Karnak', *Cahiers de Karnak VIII, 1982–1985*, 51–80, Paris: Éditions Recherche sur les Civilisations.
Azim, M. and Traunecker, C. (1982) 'Un mât du IXe pylône au nom d'Horemheb', *Cahiers de Karnak VII, 1978–1981*, 75–92, Paris: Éditions Recherche sur les Civilisations.
Badawy, A. (1973) *A Monumental Gateway for a Temple of Sety I*, Brooklyn: The Brooklyn Museum.
Barguet, P. (1950) 'L'Obélisque de Saint-Jean-de-Latran dans le temple de Ramsès II à Karnak', *ASAE* 50, 269–80.
—— (1953) 'La structure du temple Ipet-Sout d'Amon à Karnak du Moyen Empire à Amenophis II', *BIFAO* 52, 145–55.
—— (1962) *Le Temple d'Amon-Rê à Karnak. Essai d'exégèse*, Cairo: L'Institut Français d'Archéologie Orientale.
Beckerath, J. von. (1966) 'The Nile level records at Karnak and their importance for the history of the Libyan Period (Dynasties XXII–XXIII)', *JARCE* 5, 43–55.
Bell, L. (1985) 'Luxor Temple and the cult of the Royal Ka', *JNES* 44, 251–94.
Bennett, J. (1939) 'The Restoration Inscription of Tutankhamun', *JEA* 25, 8–15.
Berg, D. (1987) 'The 29th dynasty storehouse at Karnak', *JARCE* 24, 47–52.
—— (1990) 'Some Ramesside fragments', *SAK* 17, 81–106.
Bjorkman, G. (1971) *Kings at Karnak*, Uppsala: Acta Universitatis Upsaliensis Boreas.
Blyth, E. (1999) 'Some thoughts on Seti II: "the good-looking pharaoh"', in Leahy, A. and Tait, W.J. (eds), *Studies on Ancient Egypt in honour of H.S. Smith*, 39–42, London: The Egypt Exploration Society.
Bothmer, B. (1974) 'The Karnak statue of Ny-user-ra', *MDAIK* 30, 165–70.
Brand, P. (1997) 'The "lost" obelisks and colossi of Seti I', *JARCE* 34, 101–14.
—— (1999) 'Use of the term $3\underline{h}$ in the reign of Seti I', *GM* 168, 23–33.
—— (2000) *The Monuments of Seti I: Epigraphic, historical and art historical analysis*, Leiden: E.J. Brill.
Bryan, B. (1991) *The Reign of Thutmose IV*, Baltimore: The Johns Hopkins University Press.
Cabrol, A. (1995a) 'Les criosphinx de Karnak: un nouveau dromos d'Amenhotep III', *Cahiers de Karnak X*, 1–28, Paris: Éditions Recherche sur les Civilisations.
—— (1995b) 'Une représentation de la tombe de Khâbekhenet et les dromos de Karnak-sud: nouvelles hypothèses, *Cahiers de Karnak X*, 33–57, Paris: Éditions Recherche sur les Civilisations.
Caminos, R. (1952) 'Gebel es-Silsilah No. 100', *JEA* 38, 46–61.
—— (1954) *Late Egyptian Miscellanies*, London: Oxford University Press.
—— (1958) *The Chronicle of Prince Osorkon*, Rome: Pontificium Institutum Biblicum.
—— (1964) 'The Nitocris Adoption Stela', *JEA* 50, 71–101.
Carlotti, J.-F. (1995) 'Mise au point sur les dimensions et la localisation de la chapelle d'Hatchepsout à Karnak, *Cahiers de Karnak X*, 141–57, pls. I–IX, Paris: Éditions Recherche sur les Civilisations.
—— (2001) *L'Akh-Menou de Thoutmosis III: Étude Architecturale*, Paris: Éditions Recherche sur les Civilisations.
Carlotti, J.-F. and Gabolde, L. (2003) 'Nouvelles données sur la Ouadjyt', *Cahiers de Karnak XI*, Fascicule 1, 255–319, Paris: Éditions Recherche sur les Civilisations.
Chappaz, J.-L. (1987) 'Un nouvel assemblage de *talatat*: une paroi du $Rw\underline{d}$-Mnw d'Aton', *Cahiers de Karnak VIII, 1982–1985*, 81–119, Paris: Éditions Recherche sur les Civilisations.
Chevrier, H.(1933) *Le Temple Reposoir de Ramsès III à Karnak*, Cairo: Imprimerie de l'Institut Français d'Archéologie Orientale.
—— (1949) 'Rapport sur les travaux de Karnak 1947–1948: Sanctuaire de la XIIe dynastie; Sanctuaire primitif', *ASAE* 49, 12–13 and 257–9.
—— (1950) 'Rapport sur les travaux de Karnak 1949–1950', *ASAE* 50, 429–42.
—— (1951) 'Rapport sur les travaux de Karnak 1950–1951', *ASAE* 51, 549–72.

—— (1955) 'Rapport sur les travaux de Karnak 1952–1953', *ASAE* 53, 7–19.
—— (1956) 'Chronologie des constructions de la salle Hypostyle', *ASAE* 54, 35–8.
—— (1971) 'Technique de la construction dans l'ancienne Égypte. III: Gros-oeuvre, maçonnerie', *RdE* 23, 74–8.
Chevrier, H. and Drioton, E. (1940) *Le Temple Reposoir de Séti II à Karnak*, Cairo: Imprimerie National, Boulac.
Coquin, R.-G. (1972) 'La christianization des temples de Karnak', *BIFAO* 72, 169–78.
Cotelle-Michel, L. (2003) 'Présentation préliminaire des blocs de la chapelle de Sesostris Ier découverte dans le IXe pylône de Karnak', *Cahiers de Karnak XI*, Fascicule 1, 339–63, Paris: Éditions Recherche sur les Civilisations.
Daressy, M. (1926) 'Le voyage d'inspection de M. Grébaut en 1889', *ASAE* 26, 1–22.
—— (1927) 'Sur le naos de Senusert Ier trouvé à Karnak', *Revue de l'Égypte Ancienne* I, 203–11.
Daumas, F. (1967) 'L'Origine d'Amon à Karnak', *BIFAO* 65, 201–14.
—— (1980) 'L'Interprétation des temples égyptiens anciens à la lumière des temples Gréco-Romains', *Cahiers de Karnak VI, 1973–1977*, 261–84, Cairo: Institut Français d'Archéologie Orientale.
Davies, B.G. (1995) *Egyptian Historical Records of the Later Eighteenth Dynasty*, Fascicule VI, Warminster: Aris & Phillips.
—— (1997) *Egyptian Historical Inscriptions of the Nineteenth Dynasty*, Jonsered: Paul Åströms förlag.
Davies, N. de G. (1922) *The Tomb of Puyemre at Thebes*, Vol. I, New York: Publications of the Metropolitan Museum of Art Egyptian Expedition.
—— (1923) *The Tombs of Two Officials of Tuthmosis the Fourth (nos. 75 & 90)*, London: The Egypt Exploration Society.
—— (1933a) *The Tombs of Menkheperresonb, Amenmose and Another*, London: The Egypt Exploration Society.
—— (1933b) *The Tomb of Neferhotep at Thebes*, Vol. I, New York: Publications of the Metropolitan Museum of Art Egyptian Expedition.
Desroches-Noblecourt, C. (1951) 'Deux grands obélisques précieux d'un sanctuaire à Karnak', *RdE* 8, 47–61.
Dorman, P. (1988) *The Monuments of Senenmut*, London: Kegan Paul International.
Drioton, E. (1945) 'Les dedicaces de Ptolémée Évergète II sur le deuxieme pylône de Karnak', *ASAE* 44, 111–62.
—— (1958) 'Amon avant la fondation de Thèbes', *BSFE* 26 (July), 33–41.
Eaton-Krauss, M. (1988) 'Tutankhamun at Karnak', *MDAIK* 44, 1–12.
—— (1993a) 'Toutankhamon et les monuments d'Aménophis III' in *Aménophis III: L'Égypte à son apogée. Les Dossiers d'Archéologie*, no. 180, 48–55.
—— (1993b) 'Ramesses-Re who creates the gods', in Bleiberg, E. and Freed, R. (eds), *Fragments of a Shattered Visage: Proceedings of the International Symposium on Ramesses the Great*, 15–23, Memphis: Memphis State University, Institute of Egyptian Art and Archaeology.
Ertman, E. (1993) 'A first report on the preliminary survey of unexcavated KV10 (the tomb of King Amenmesse)', *KMT, A Modern Journal of Ancient Egypt*, Vol. 4, no. 2, 38–46.
Fazzini, R. (1988) *Egypt, Dynasty XXII–XXV*, Leiden: E.J. Brill.
Gaballa, G.A. (1967) 'New evidence on the birth of Pharaoh', *Or* (n.s.), 299–304.
Gaballa, G. and Kitchen, K. (1981) 'Ramesside varia IV: the prophet Amenemope, his tomb and family', *MDAIK* 37, 161–80.
Gabolde, L. (1987) 'À propos de deux obélisques de Thoutmosis II dédiés à son père Thoutmosis I et érigés sous le règne d'Hatchepsout-pharaon à l'ouest du IVe pylône', *Cahiers de de Karnak VIII 1982–1985*, 143–58, Paris: Éditions Recherche sur les Civilisations.
—— (1993) 'La "cour de fêtes" de Thoutmosis II à Karnak', *Cahiers de Karnak IX*, 1–101, Paris: Éditions Recherche sur les Civilisations.
—— (1995) 'Le problème de l'emplacement primitif du socle de calcite de Sésostris Ier, *Cahiers de Karnak X*, 253–6, Paris: Éditions Recherche sur les Civilisations.

BIBLIOGRAPHY

—— (1998) *Le 'Grand Château d'Amon' de Sésostris Ier à Karnak*, Paris: Diffusion de Boccard.
—— (2005) *Monuments décorés en bas reliefs aux noms de Thoutmosis II et Hatchepsout à Karnak*, Cairo: Institut Français d'Archéologie Orientale.
Gabolde, M. (1998) *D'Akhenaton à Toutankhamon*, Paris: Diffusion de Boccard.
Gardiner, A. (1948) 'The founding of a new delta town in the Twentieth Dynasty', *JEA* 34, 19–22.
—— (1952) 'Tuthmosis III returns thanks to Amun', *JEA* 38, 6–23.
—— (1953) 'The coronation of King Haremhab', *JEA* 39, 13–31.
—— (1973) *Egyptian Grammar*, London: Oxford University Press.
Gauthier, H. (1912) *Le Livre des Rois*, vol. II, Cairo: L'Institut Français d'Archéologie Orientale du Caire.
Giddy, L. (Spring 2002) 'Digging Diary 2001', *Egyptian Archaeology*, no. 20, 29–33.
—— (Autumn 2002) 'Digging Diary 2001–2002', *Egyptian Archaeology*, no. 21, 27–32.
Gitton, M. (1974) 'Le palais de Karnak', *BIFAO* 74, 63–73.
Goelet Jnr, O. (1993) 'The Blessing of Ptah' in Bleiberg, E. and Freed, R. (eds), *Fragments of a Shattered Visage: Proceedings of the International Symposium on Ramesses the Great*, 28–37, Memphis: Institute of Egyptian Art and Archaeology, Memphis State University.
Gohary, J. (1979) 'Nefertiti at Karnak', in Ruffle, J., Gaballa, G. and Kitchen, K. (eds), *Glimpses of Ancient Egypt: Studies in Honour of H.W. Fairman*, 30–1, Warminster: Aris & Phillips.
—— (1992) *Akhenaten's Sed-festival at Karnak*, London: Kegan Paul International.
Golvin, J.-C. and Hegazy, E. (1993) 'Essai d'explication de la forme et des caractéristiques générales des grands enceintes de Karnak', *Cahiers de Karnak IX*, 145–60, Paris: Éditions Recherche sur les Civilisations.
Goyon, J.-C. and Traunecker, C. (1982) 'La chapelle de Thot et d'Amon au sud-ouest du lac sacré', *Cahiers de Karnak VII, 1978–1981*, 355–66, Paris: Éditions Recherche sur les Civilisations.
Graindorge, C. (1993) 'Naissance d'une chapelle reposoir de barque', in *Hatchepsout: femme pharaon. Les Dossiers d'Archéologie*, no. 187s, 42–53.
Graindorge, C. and Martinez, P. (1989) 'Karnak avant Karnak: les constructions d'Aménophis Ier et les premières liturgies amoniennes', *BSFE* 115, 36–55.
Grajetzki, W. (2005) *Ancient Egyptian Queens: a hieroglyphic dictionary*, London: Golden House Publications.
Grandet, P., (1993) *Ramsès III: Histoire d'un Règne,* Paris: Éditions Pygmalion/Gérard Watelet.
Grimal, N. and Larché, F. (1993) 'Études et fouilles: La cour de fêtes de Thoutmosis IV', *Cahiers de Karnak IX*, vii–x, Paris: Éditions Recherche sur les Civilisations.
Habachi, L. (1950) 'An inscription at Aswan referring to six obelisks', *JEA* 36, 13–18.
—— (1963) 'King Nebhepetre Menthuhotep: his monuments, place in history, deification and unusual representations in the form of gods', *MDAIK* 19, 33–6.
—— (1969) *Features of the Deification of Ramesses II*, Glückstadt: Verlag J.J. Augustin.
—— (1970) 'Le mur d'enceinte du grand temple d'Amenre à Karnak, *Kemi* 20, 229–35.
—— (1972) *The Second Stela of Kamose and his struggle against the Hyksos ruler and his capital*, Glückstadt: J.J. Augustin
—— (1974) 'A high inundation in the temple of Amenre at Karnak in the Thirteenth Dynasty', *SAK* 1, 207–14.
—— (1975) 'Building activities of Sesostris I in the area south of Thebes', *MDAIK* 31, 33–7.
—— (1984) *The Obelisks of Egypt*, Cairo: The American University in Cairo Press.
—— (1985) 'Devotion of Tuthmosis III to his predecessors: à propos a meeting of Sesostris I with his courtiers', in Posener-Krieger, P. (ed.), *Mélanges Gamal Eddin Mokhtar*, Vol. I, 349–59, Cairo: Institut Français d'Archéologie Orientale.
Hall, H.R. (1925) *Hieroglyphic texts from Egyptian Stelae etc. in the British Museum*, vol. VII, London: The Trustees of the British Museum.
Harari, I. (1959) 'Nature de la stèle de Donation de fonction du roi Ahmôsis à la reine Ahmès-Nefertari', *ASAE* 56, 139–201.

Hegazy, E.-S. (1989–90) 'The Great Processional Way of Thebes', *Journal of Ancient Chronology Forum* 3, 82–4.
Hegazy, E.-S. and Martinez, P. (1993) 'Le "Palais de Maat" et la "Place Favorite d'Amon"', in *Hatchepsout: femme pharaon. Les Dossiers d'Archéologie*, no. 187s, 54–63.
Hegazy, E.-S., Martinez, P. and Zimmer, T. (1993) 'Une vigne sous le règne d'Aménophis II', *Cahiers de Karnak IX*, 205–12, Paris: Éditions Recherche sur les Civilisations.
Hornung, E. (1983) *Conceptions of God in Ancient Egypt: The One and the Many*, London: Routledge & Kegan Paul.
Jacquet, J. (1983) *Karnak-Nord V. Le Trésor de Thoutmosis Ier: Étude Architecturale*, Cairo: L'Institut Français d'Archéologie Orientale du Caire.
—— (1987) 'Excavations at Karnak-North: observations and interpretations', in Assman, J., Burkard, G. and Davies, V. (eds), *Problems and Priorities in Egyptian Archaeology*, 105–12, London: Kegan Paul International.
Jacquet-Gordon, H. (1987) 'Excavations at Karnak-North: the utilization of minor remains', in Assman, J., Burkard, G. and Davies, V. (eds), *Problems and Priorities in Egyptian Archaeology*, 113–18, London: Kegan Paul International.
—— (1988) *Karnak-Nord VI. Le Trésor de Thoutmosis Ier: La Décoration*, Cairo: L'Institut Français d'Archéologie Orientale du Caire.
Johnson, W. Raymond (2001) 'Monuments and monumental art under Amenhotep III: evolution and meaning', in O'Connor, D. and Cline, E. (eds), *Amenhotep III: Perspectives on his Reign*, 63–94, Michigan: The University of Michigan Press.
Kees, H. (1958) 'Die weisse Kapelle Sesostris I in Karnak und das Sedfest', *MDAIK* 16, 194–213.
Kemp, B. (1989) *Ancient Egypt: Anatomy of a Civilization*, London: Routledge.
Kitchen, K. (1972) 'Ramesses VII and the Twentieth Dynasty', *JEA* 58, 182–94.
—— (1973) *The Third Intermediate Period in Egypt*, Warminster: Aris & Phillips.
—— (1982) *Pharaoh Triumphant: the Life and Times of Ramesses II*, Warminster: Aris & Phillips.
—— (1987) 'The titularies of the Ramesside kings as expression of their ideal kingship', *ASAE* 71, 131–41.
—— (1993) *Ramesside Inscriptions Translated and Annotated. Translations Vol. I: Ramesses I, Sethos I and Contemporaries*, Oxford: Blackwell.
—— (1996) *Ramesside Inscriptions Translated and Annotated. Translations Vol. II: Ramesses II, Royal Inscriptions*, Oxford: Blackwell.
—— (1999) *Ramesside Inscriptions Translated and Annotated. Notes and Comments Vol. II: Ramesses II, Royal Inscriptions*, Oxford: Blackwell.
Kozloff, A. and Bryan, B. (1992) *Egypt's Dazzling Sun: Amenhotep III and his World*, Cleveland: The Cleveland Museum of Art.
Kruchten, J.-M. (1989) *Les Annales des Prêtres de Karnak (XXI–XXIIImes dynasties) et autres textes contemporains relatifs à l'initiation des prêtres d'Amon*, Leuven: Departement Oriëntalistiek.
Lacau, P. (1954) 'Deux magasins à encens du temple de Karnak', *ASAE* 52, 185–98.
—— (1956) 'L'Or dans l'architecture égyptienne', *ASAE* 53, 221–50.
Lacau, P. and Chevrier, H. (1956) *Une Chapelle de Sésostris Ier à Karnak*, Cairo: Imprimerie de l'Institut Français d'Archéologie Orientale.
—— (1977) *Une Chapelle d'Hatchepsout à Karnak*, Cairo: Le Service des Antiquités de l'Égypte avec la collaboration de l'Institut Français d'Archéologie Orientale.
Lauffray, J. (1969) 'Le secteur nord-est du temple jubilaire de Thoutmosis III à Karnak. État des lieux et commentaire architectural', *Kemi* 19, 180–217.
—— (1970) 'Note sur les portes du Ier pylône de Karnak', *Kemi* 20, 101–10.
—— (1971) 'Abords occidentaux de premier pylône de Karnak: le dromos, la tribune et les aménagements portuaires', *Kemi* 21, 118–21.
—— (1979) *Karnak d'Égypte: Domaine du divin*, Paris: Centre National de la Recherche Scientifique.
—— (1980) 'Les travaux du Centre Franco-Égyptien d'étude des temples de Karnak de 1972 à 1977:

Cour du Moyen Empire, relevés et fouille', *Cahiers de Karnak VI, 1973–1977*, 18–26, Cairo: L'Institut Français d'Archéologie Orientale.

Lauffray, J, Sa'ad, R. and Sauneron, S. (1975) 'Rapport sur les travaux de Karnak. Activités du Centre Franco-Égyptien en 1970–1972', *Cahiers de Karnak V, 1970–1972*, 1–42, Cairo: L'Institut Français d'Archéologie Orientale.

Leclant, J. (1951) 'Les inscriptions "éthiopiennes" sur la porte du IVe pylône du grand temple d'Amon à Karnak', *RdE* 8, 101–20.

—— (1965) *Recherches sur les Monuments Thébains de la XXVe dynastie dite Éthiopienne*, Cairo: Imprimerie de l'Institut Français d'Archéologie Orientale.

Leclère, F. (1996) 'A cemetery of Osirid figures at Karnak', *Egyptian Archaeology*, no. 9, 9–12.

Lefèbvre, G. (1929) *Histoire des grands prêtres d'Amon de Karnak jusqu'à la XXIe dynastie*, Paris: Librairie Orientaliste Paul Geuthner.

Legrain, G. (1900a) 'Notes prises à Karnak', *RT* 22, 51–65.

—— (1900b) 'Le temple et les chapelles d'Osiris à Karnak. La temple d'Osiris-Hiq-Djeto', *RT* 22, 125–49.

—— (1902) 'Le temple et les chapelles d'Osiris à Karnak. La chapelle d'Osiris, Maître de la Vie', *RT* 24, 208–13.

—— (1903) 'Second rapport sur les travaux exécutés à Karnak du 31 Octobre 1901 au 15 mai 1902', *ASAE* 4, 1–40.

—— (1905) 'Renseignements sur les dernières découvertes faites à Karnak', *RT* 27, 61–82.

—— (1906) 'Nouveaux renseignements sur les dernières découvertes faites à Karnak', *RT* 28, 137–61.

—— (1929) *Les Temples de Karnak*, Brussels: Chez Vromant & Co.

Le Saout, F. and Ma'arouf, A. (1987) 'Un nouveau fragment de stèle de Toutânkhamon', *Cahiers de Karnak VIII, 1982–1985*, 285–9, Paris: Éditions Recherche sur les Civilisations.

Le Saout, F., Ma'arouf, A. and Zimmer, T. (1987) 'Le Moyen Empire à Karnak: Varia 1', *Cahiers de Karnak VIII, 1982–1985*, 293–323, Paris: Éditions Recherche sur les Civilisations.

Letellier, B. (1979) 'La cour à péristyle de Thoutmosis IV à Karnak (et la "cour de fêtes" de Thoutmosis II)', in Vercoutter, J (ed.), *Hommages à Serge Sauneron*, Vol. I, 51–72, Cairo: L'Institut Français d'Archéologie Orientale du Caire.

Loeben, C. (1987a) 'La porte sud-est de la salle *w3dyt*', *Cahiers de Karnak VIII, 1982–1985*, 207–23, Paris: Éditions Recherche sur les Civilisations.

—— (1987b) 'Amon à la place d'Aménophis I: Le relief de la porte des magasins nord de Thoutmosis III', *Cahiers de Karnak VIII, 1982–1985*, 233–43, Paris: Éditions Recherche sur les Civilisations.

—— (1994) 'Nefertiti's Pillars', in *Amarna Letters: Essays on Ancient Egypt c. 1390–1310 BC*, 41–6, San Francisco: KMT Communications.

Ma'arouf, A. and Zimmer, T. (1993) 'Le Moyen Empire à Karnak: Varia 2', *Cahiers de Karnak IX*, 223–37, Paris: Éditions Recherche sur les Civilisations.

Macadam, M. (1949) *The Temples of Kawa. I: The Inscriptions*, London: Oxford University Press for the Griffith Institute.

Manniche, L. (1982) 'The *Maru* built by Amenophis III – its significance and possible location', in Leclant, J. (ed.), *L'Égyptologie en 1979: axes prioritaires de recherches*, Tome II, 271–3, Paris: Éditions du Centre National de la Recherche Scientifique.

el-Molla, M., Hegazy, E.S. and Ma'arouf, A. (1993) 'L'Allée sacrée du temple de Khonsou', *Cahiers de Karnak IX*, 239–62, Paris: Éditions Recherche sur les Civilisations.

Munier, M. and Pillet, M. (1929) 'Les edifices Chrétiens de Karnak', *Revue de l'Égypte Ancienne II*, 58–88.

Murnane, W. (1993) 'Dans le domaine d'Amon: l'oeuvre d'Aménophis III à Karnak et à Louxor', in *Aménophis III: L'Égypte à son apogée. Les Dossiers d'Archéologie*, no. 180, 28–39.

Nelson, H.H. (1936) 'Three decrees of Ramses III from Karnak', *JAOS* 56, 232–41.

—— (1949) 'Certain reliefs at Karnak and Medinet Habu and the Ritual of Amenophis I', *JNES* 8, 201–29 and 310–45.

Nims, C.F. (1948) 'An oracle dated in "the Repeating of Births"', *JNES* 7, 157–62.

—— (1955) 'Places about Thebes', *JNES* 14, 110–23.
—— (1965) *Thebes of the Pharaohs*, London: Elek Books.
—— (1966) 'The date of the dishonoring of Hatshepsut', *ZAS* 93, 97–100.
—— (1969) 'Thutmosis III's benefactions to Amon', in *Studies in Honor of John A. Wilson*, 69–74, Chicago: University of Chicago Press.
—— (1971) 'The Eastern Temple at Karnak', in Haeny, G. (ed.), *Beiträge zur Ägyptischen Bauforschung und Altertumskunde Heft 12, Geburtstag von Herbert Ricke*, 107–11, Wiesbaden: F. Steiner.
O'Connor, D. (1995) 'Beloved of Maat, the Horizon of Re: the royal palace in New Kingdom Egypt', in O'Connor, D. and Silverman, D. (eds), *Ancient Egyptian Kingship*, 263–300, Leiden: E.J. Brill.
—— (2001) 'The City and the World: world view and built forms in the reign of Amenhotep III', in O'Connor, D. and Cline, E. (eds), *Amenhotep III: Perspectives on his Reign*, 125–72, Michigan: The University of Michigan Press.
Parker, R., Leclant, J. and Goyon, J.-C. (1979) *The Edifice of Taharqa by the Sacred Lake of Karnak*, Providence: Brown University Press.
Peden, A.J. (1994a) *Egyptian Historical Inscriptions of the Twentieth Dynasty*, Jonsered: Paul Åströms förlag.
—— (1994b) *The Reign of Ramesses IV*, Warminster: Aris & Phillips.
Petrie, W.M.F. (1896) *History of Egypt*, vol. II, London: Methuen & Sons.
—— (1909) *Qurneh*, London: British School of Archaeology in Egypt.
Pillet, M. (1922) 'Rapport sur les travaux de Karnak (1921–1922)', *ASAE* 22, 233–60.
—— (1923a) 'Le naos de Senousert Ier', *ASAE* 23, 143–58.
—— (1923b) 'Un sanctuaire-reposoir de barque sacrée d'Amenhotep Ier', *ASAE* 23, 113–17.
—— (1925) 'Rapport sur les travaux de Karnak, 1924–1925. IV: La fouille du pylône d'Amenhotep', *ASAE* 25, 1–24.
—— (1939) 'Deux représentations inédites de portes ornées de pylônes à Karnak. II: le bas-relief de Thoutmès III', *BIFAO* 38, 246–51.
Posener, G. (1962) *A Dictionary of Egyptian Civilization*, London: Methuen.
el-Razik, M. (1968) 'Study on Nectanebo I in Luxor Temple and Karnak', *MDAIK* 23, 156–9.
Redford, D. (1967) *History and Chronology of the Eighteenth Dynasty of Egypt: Seven Studies*, Toronto: University of Toronto Press.
—— (1973) 'Studies on Akhenaten at Thebes: A report on the work of the Akhenaten Temple Project of the University Museum, University of Pennsylvania', *JARCE* 10, 77–94.
—— (1980) 'The Sun-Disc in Akhenaten's Program: its worship and antecedents, II', *JARCE* 17, 21–38.
—— (1984) *Akhenaten, the Heretic King*, Cairo: The American University in Cairo Press.
—— (1986) *Pharaonic King-Lists, Annals and Day-Books*, Mississauga: Benben Books.
—— (1994) 'East Karnak and the sed-festival of Akhenaten', in Berger, C., Clerc, G. and Grimal, N. (eds), *Hommages à Jean Leclant, vol. I: Études Pharaoniques*, 485–92, Cairo: L'Institut Français d'Archéologie Orientale.
Reisner, G. (1931) *Mycerinus: The Temples of the Third Pyramid at Giza*, Cambridge, MA: Harvard University Press.
Robichon, C. and Christophe, L. (1951) *Karnak-Nord III, 1978–1981*, Cairo: Imprimerie de L'Institut Français d'Archéologie Orientale du Caire.
Robichon, C., Barguet, P. and Leclant, J.(1954) *Karnak-Nord IV (1949–1951)*, Imprimerie de L'Institut Français d'Archéologie Orientale du Caire.
Robins, R.G. (1997) *The Art of Ancient Egypt*, London: British Museum Press.
Rondot, V. (1997) *La Grande Salle Hypostyle de Karnak: Les Architraves (Texte)*, Paris: Éditions Recherche sur les Civilisations.
Roth, A.M. (1983) 'Some new texts of Herihor and Ramesses IV in the Great Hypostyle Hall at Karnak', *JNES* 42, 43–53.
Sa'ad, R. (1975) 'Fragments d'un monument de Toutânkhamon retrouvés dans le IXe pylône de Karnak', *Cahiers de Karnak V, 1970–1972*, 93–109, Cairo: L'Institut Français d'Archéologie Orientale.
el-Saghir, M. (1992) 'The Great Processional Way at Thebes (the avenue of sphinxes at Luxor)', in

Zaccone, G. and di Netro, T.R. (eds), *Sesto Congresso Internazionale di Egitologia, Atti*, Vol.I, 181–7, Turin: Tipografia Torinese.

Sauneron, S. and Vérité, J. (1969) 'Fouilles dans la zone axiale du IIIe pylône à Karnak', *Kemi* 19, 249–76.

Schaden, O. (1984) 'Report of the 1978 season at Karnak', *NARCE* 127, 44–64.

—— (1987a) 'Tutankhamun-Ay shrine at Karnak and Western Valley of the Kings Project', *NARCE* 138, 12–14.

—— (1987b) 'A Tutankhamun stela at Karnak', *Cahiers de Karnak VIII, 1982–1985*, 279–83, Paris: Éditions Recherche sur les Civilisations.

—— (1988) *The God's Father Ay*, Michigan: University Microfilms International.

Seele, K. (1940) *The coregency of Ramesses II with Seti I and the date of the Great Hypostyle Hall at Karnak*, Chicago: University of Chicago Press.

Siclen III, C. van (1982) *Two Theban Monuments from the Reign of Amenhotep II*, San Antonio: Van Siclen Books.

—— (1984) 'The date of the granite bark shrine of Tuthmosis III', *GM* 79, 53–4.

—— (1986) *The Alabaster Bark Shrine of King Amenhotep II*, San Antonio: Van Siclen Books.

—— (1990) 'Preliminary report on epigraphic work done in the Edifice of Amenhotep II: Seasons of 1988–89 and 1989–1990', *VA* 6, nos. 1–2, 75–90.

Smith, H.S. and Smith, A. (1976) 'A reconsideration of the Kamose texts', *ZAS* 103, 48–76.

Smith, R.W. and Redford, D. (1976) *The Akhenaten Temple Project. Vol. I: Initial Discoveries*, Warminster: Aris & Phillips.

Smith, W. Stevenson (with additions by W. Kelly Simpson) (1965) *The Art and Architecture of Ancient Egypt*, Harmondsworth: Penguin Books.

Sourouzian, H. (1989) *Les Monuments du roi Merenptah*, Mainz am Rhein: Verlag Philipp von Zabern.

—— (1995) 'Les colosses du IIe pylône du temple d'Amon-Rê à Karnak, remplois ramessides de la XVIIIe dynastie', *Cahiers de Karnak X, 1992–1994*, 505–43, Paris: Éditions Recherche sur les Civilisations.

Spencer, P. (1984) *The Egyptian Temple: A Lexicographical Study*, London: Kegan Paul International.

—— (2004) 'Digging Diary 2003', *Egyptian Archaeology*, no. 24 (Spring), 25–9.

Spiegelberg, W. (1900) 'Die Northamptonstele', *RT* 22, 118–21.

Swedenborg, E. (1909) *Heaven and its Wonders*, London: Dent & Sons Ltd, repr.

Traunecker, C. (1980) 'Un document nouveau sur Darius Ier à Karnak, *Cahiers de Karnak VI, 1973–1977*, 209–13, Cairo: L'Institut Français d'Archéologie Orientale.

—— (1982a) 'Rapport préliminaire sur la chapelle de Sésostris Ier découverte dans le IXe pylône', *Cahiers de Karnak VII, 1978–1981*, 121–6, Paris: Éditions Recherche sur les Civilisations.

—— (1982b) 'Un exemple de rite de substitution: une stèle de Nectanebo I', *Cahiers de Karnak VII, 1978–1981*, 339–54, Paris: Éditions Recherche sur les Civilisations.

—— (1987a) 'Les temples hauts de Basse Époque: un aspect du fonctionnement économique des temples', *RdE* 38, 147–62.

—— (1987b) 'La chapelle de Khonsou du mur d'enceinte et les travaux d'Alexandre', *Cahiers de Karnak VIII, 1982–1985*, 347–54, Paris: Éditions Recherche sur les Civilisations.

—— (1989) 'Le "Château de l'Or" de Thoutmosis III et les magasins nord de temple d'Amon', *CRIPEL* 11, 89–111.

Traunecker, C. and Golvin, J.-C. (1984) *Karnak. Résurrection d'une site*, Paris: Payot.

Traunecker, C., Le Sauot, F. and Masson, O. (1981) *La Chapelle d'Achôris à Karnak. Vol. II: Texte*, Paris: Éditions ADPF.

Vandersleyen, C. (1967) 'Une tempête sous le règne d'Amosis', *RdE* 19, 123–59.

Vandier, J. (1958) *Manuel d'archéologie égyptienne, vol. III: Les grandes époques, La Statuaire*, Paris: Picard.

Varille, A. (1950) 'Quelques notes sur le sanctuaire axial du grand temple d'Amon à Karnak', *ASAE* 50, 127–35.

Vergnieux, R. (1999) *Recherches sur les monuments thébains d'Amenhotep IV à l'aide d'outils informatiques: Méthodes de résultats. Fascicule 1: texte*, Genève: Cahiers de la Société d'Égyptologie.

Vernus, P. (1987) 'Études de philologie et de linguistique VI', *RdE* 38, 163–81.

Vörös, G and Pudleiner, R. (1997), 'The Crown of Thebes', *Egyptian Archaeology*, no. 11, 37–9.

Wallet-Lebrun, C. (1982) 'Notes sur le temple d'Amon-Rê à Karnak. 1: L'emplacement insolité des obelisques d'Hatchepsout', *BIFAO* 82, 355–62.

—— (1984) 'Notes sur le temple d'Amon-Rê à Karnak. 2: Les *w3dyt* Thoutmosides entre les IVe et Ve pylônes', *BIFAO* 84, 317–33.

Wente, E. (1967) 'On the chronology of the Twenty-First Dynasty', *JNES* 26, 155–76.

Wreszinski, W. (1923) *Atlas zur altägyptischen Kulturgeschichte*, Vol. II, Leipzig: J.C. Hinrichs.

Yoyotte, J. (1951) 'Le martelage des noms royaux éthiopiens par Psammetique II', *RdE* 8, 215–39.

—— (1953) 'Un porche doré: la porte du IVe pylône au grand temple de Karnak', *CdE* 55, 28–38.

INDEX

abattoirs 213, *214*
Abu Gurob 75
Abu Simbel 158
Abydos 77, 141, 146, 155, 158
Achoris (Hakor) *See* Hakor
Actium 233
administration 39, 98, 112, 141, 183, 187, 213
administrative buildings 26, 43
Ahhotep 28–29
Ahmes, wife of Tuthmosis I 39, 46, 51
Ahmes-Nefertari 30, 38, 53, 91, 172, 177
Ahmose 28–29, 44, 115
Ahmose II 212
Ahmose, son of Ebana 33
Akhenaten (Amenhotep IV) *See* Amenhotep IV
Akhetaten 121, 127
Akh-Menu 2–3, 8, 54, *75,* 151; Alexander 225; Christian foundations 234; Ramesses II 161; Ramesses III 176; Ramesses IV 178–79; Seti II 168; Tuthmosis II 59; Tuthmosis III 15, 54, 65, 68–77, *72,* 83, 88, 149
alabaster: bark-shrines 34–36, *35,* 40, 52, 59, 84–85, 89, 96, 100–101, 105, 181; bases/socles 11, 14, 40, 74, 197, 222; furnishings 75, 134, 140, 174, 177, 200; statues 54, 89, 129, 151, 157, 195; stelae 151, 157–58
Alexander the Great 73, 223–26
Alexandria 152, 234
alignments 26, 50, 78–79, 85, 94–95, 105, 109, 115, 121, 125, 137, 221, 229–30

altars 14, 16, 50, 59–60, 75–76, 98, 129, 197, 213, 234
Amarna period 19, 89, 94–95, 119, 123–25, 127, 129, 132, 136, 146
Amenemhab 93
Amenemhet I 10–11, 14
Amenemhet III 16
Amenemhet IV 16
Amenemope 178
Amenhotep, High Priest 23, 181
Amenhotep I 14, 33–39, *34, 37,* 40, 42, *58,* 83–84, 91, 177
Amenhotep II *2,* 45, 52, *61,* 68, 77, 93–99, *95,* 137, 146
Amenhotep III 15, 26, 28, 40, *43,* 89, *95,* 101, 103–12, *107,* 114–16, 118, *122,* 128, 137, 162
Amenhotep IV (Akhenaten) 44, 117, 119–26, *122,* 127
Amenhotep Si-se 101–2
Amenhotep, son of Hapu 110
Amenirdis I, God's Wife of Amun 192, 195–96
Amenirdis II, God's Wife of Amun 206, 209–10
Amenmesse 165–66
Amenmose 46
Ameny-Antef-Amenemhet 27
Amonhirkhopshef 178
Amun Chapel (Shabitku) 195
Amun-Kamutef *22,* 42, 54, 73–74, 76, 157, 172, 227; temple 21–23, *61,* 62, 211

247

INDEX

Amun-Re 7, 10, 12, 16, 33, 74, 76, 143, 164, 172, 203; and Akhenaten 120–21, 127–28, 132; as Horus 229; miracles 40, 52, 78; oracles 182; as Osiris 190–91, 229
Amun-Re Temple *2–4,* 10–26, *13,* 27, 34, *34,* 37, *38, 41, 58,* 77–88, *80,* 98, *116,* 162, 165, 178; entrances 160, 181, 194, 200, *215,* 228
Amun-Re-Horakhte sanctuary 229
Amyrtaeus 212
ancestors, memorials to 8, *37–38,* 38, 73, 77, 81, 83
animation of artefacts 89–91, 194–95
Ankhnesneferibre, God's Wife of Amun 210–12
Annals of Tuthmosis III 83, 86, 88, 169
Antef II 12
Apophis 28
Apries 212
archaic antiquities 7
archaic kings, statues 8
architects 36, 39–40, 42, 51, 110–11, 160, 188–89, 201
archives of the temple 175–76, 182
Arnold, Dieter 222
Aset 46–47, 51
Assurbanipal, Assyrian king 87, 207
Assyrian text, sack of Thebes 87–88
Assyrians 195, 207–9
Aswan 42, 46, 54, 111, 152, 192
Aswan stelae 152–54
Aten 119–20, 123, 125–26; temple 117, 121–22
Atum 12
Augustus 222, 233
Avaris 27
avenues *61,* 112, 114–17, 187, 189, *216,* 222
axial ways: crossing 46–47, 50, 105, 181; east-west 11, 14, 40, 55, 60, 71, 73, 76–79, 88, 102, 125, 137, 147, 149–51, 197, 203, 221, 226; north-south 62, 109, 115, 151, 174, 195 *See also* Southern Processional Way
Ay 127–32

Bab el-Amara Gate 227
baboons 174, 201
Badawy, Alexander 152

Bakenkhons, High Priest of Amun 160, 201
bakeries/kitchens 23, 26, 45, 98, 194
Bakhtan Stela 213
bandeau texts 176–77, 179
Barguet, Paul 151
bark sanctuary, central *2,* 7, 33, 37, 78–79, 83–84, 87–88, 134, 189, 216
barks 130, 136, 148, 157, 160, 168, 177, 226, 228; in reliefs *56, 57,* 88, 91, 100; of Amun 18, 20, 33–34, 40, 45, 50, 53, 59–60, 76, 85, 114, 208, 214–15; of the Theban Triad 71, 73, 105–8, 128, 140, 150–51, 166–67, 172–73, 182, 216–17, 221
bark-shrines *See also* way-stations: Amenhotep I 34–36, *35,* 40, 52, 59, 84; Amenhotep II 94, 96, 99; Hatshepsut *See* Chapelle Rouge; Philip Arrhidaeus 11, 50, 55–57, 59, 226; Ramesses II 62; Ramesses III *2, 4,* 172–73, 189; Senusret I 16, *18,* 18–20; Seti II *2,* 115, 166–68, 189; Tuthmosis I 44–45; Tuthmosis III 80–81, 84–85, 89, 101, 181; Tuthmosis IV 100–101, 105
basalt 24, 231
basins 23, 66, 85, *107,* 109, 112–13, 115, 134, 174–75, 213, 217
Bay, Chancellor 169
Beautiful Feast of the Valley 10, 20, 33, 60, 104, 150, 167, 180
Beketwerel 165
Benben of Re-Horakhte 120, 125
Birket Habu 112
Bologna Papyrus 201
Botanical Garden 70, 74
Bothmer, Bernard 8
broken lintels 123
bronze 134, 137, *138–39,* 207, 232
Bubastite Court *115,* 188–89, 213
Bubastite Gate 189–90
Buto 73

cache of statues 8, 231–33
Cachette Court *See* Court of the Cachette
Cairo Museum 12, 200, 221
calendar of religious festivals 83
Cambyses, Persian king 212
canals 62, 112–13
cartouches *46, 56, 126, 138, 138–39, 180, 184;* acknowledgement of predecessors 44,

248

INDEX

194, 221, 228; usurpation of predecessors 47, 65, 68, 80, 117, 128–29, 132, 134, 156, 165, 179, 211
cedar 29, 37, 40, 42, 70, 78, 84, 91, 106, 108, 128, 134, 148
CFETK *See* Franco-Egyptian Centre at Karnak
chambers, fourth pylon 42
Chambers of Ancestors: Amenhotep I 37–38; Tuthmosis III 8, 38, 73, 81
chaos and order 33, 38, 128, 141
Chapel of Hakor *2*, 197, 214–16, *216–18*
Chapel of the Divine Adoratrices *206*
Chapelle Rouge *3*, 36, 53, 55–60, *56*, *58*, 62, *63*, 65–66, 68–69, 80–81, 226
Chevrier, Henri 109, 136, 189
Christian period 234–35
civil war 190
Claudius 233
Cleopatra VII 230–31, 233
clepsydra 232
cliff-face stelae 152
colonnades of Taharqa *159*, 197–98, 200–202, 228, 230
colossi 12, 28, 50, 60, 71, 84, *95*, 102, 110, 122, 154, 162, 168, 172, 174, 187, 197, *199*
columns 40, 78 *See also* pillars; Corinthian 233; Hathor 206, 229; lotus 101; Osiride 89; papyrus 40, 78, 80, 97, 106, 147, 149–50, 157, 189, 197, 200, 210; sixteen-sided 14, 40, 98, 160; tent-peg 73
Constantine the Great 234
construction methods 55, 144, 219
contra-temple, Mut precinct 227
contra-temple of Tuthmosis III *72*, 222–23
copper 34, 42, 84, 93, 98, 108, 136, 176, 232
co-regencies 34, 39, 42, 51–52, 55, 59, 68, 93, 119, 191, 207
Coronation Chapel 79, 98–99
coronations 76, 79, 81, 100–101, 133, 155, 179, 202–3; inscriptions 55, 65, 133, 143, 150; reliefs 36, 58, 60, 73, 96, 148, 161, 176, 183, 200, 202–3, 226
Court of Offerings 177
Court of the Cachette *2*, 12, 36–37, 84, 96, *131*, 162–64
Court of the Great Ones (Akhenaten) 122

Court of the Second Pylon 144, 147
Court of the Seventh Pylon 12, 50
criosphinxes *61*, 114–18, 163
Crown Princes 142, 145, 163, 166, 169, 171–72, 178, 190
crowns 42, 144, 161, 164, 172
crypts, Opet Temple 229
cult images 11, 57, 103, 110, 151, 157, 162, 177, 227
cult of the divine kings 19, 37–38, 73–74, 76–77, 83, 104, 149, 151, 157, 167; Roman emperors 233

Darius I, Persian king 212
Darius II, Persian king 212
decline in temple building 178
decline in workmanship 156
decrees: Domitian 233; Horemheb 133, 140–41; Prince Osorkon 190; Psamtik I 209; Ptolemy I 227; Ptolemy II 227; Ramesses III 173–76; Tutankhamun 129
defacement of monuments 52, 95
deification 37–38, 91, 103–5, 110–11, 157, 161–62, 177 *See also* cult of the divine kings
Deir el-Bahri 8, 10, 53, 64–65, 162; Temple of Amun 53–54
Deir el-Medina 38, 45, 178
demolition 15, 36, 38, 44, 47, 50, 52–55, 66, 69, 74–75, 81, 83, 87, 92, 100, 105–6, 109, 112, 134, 136, 236
Divine Adoratrices 30, 190–92, 195–96, 203–10
Divine Father 130
divine sanction 52–53, 57 *See also* legitimization of rule; oracles
Divine Shadow 42
'Divine-of-Monuments' temples 65
division of Egypt 183
Djehuti, treasurer 54, 64, 66
Djeme, Mound of 191, 203, 221, 227–28
domestic occupation 26
Domitian 233
doors/doorways 11, 34, 42, 71, 78–81, 84, 101, 134–36, 160, 219 *See also* false-doors
Dorman, Peter 77
double peristyle court (Tuthmosis IV) 99–100

249

INDEX

double sanctuary, Akh-Menu 73–74, 76
dromos 2, *61*, 112, 114–17, 187, 189, *216*, 222
dwellings 23, 26, 181
dyads 129, 157, 160, 162, 165

east sector 54–55, 117, 121, 123, 125–26, 159, 227–28
Eastern Temple 102–3, *159*, 159–61, 187, 201, 228–29, 233
east-west axis 11, 14, 40, 55, 60, 66, 71, 73, 88, 125, 137, 151, 229
Edfu temple 42
Edifice of Amenhotep II 2, *61*, 94, *95–96*, 146, 183, 235
Edifice of the Lake (Taharqa) 2, *131*, 195, 202–6, *204–5*
El Kab, governor 29
electrum 42, 70, 79, 84, 87–88, 101–2, 106, 108, 125, 134, 136, 148, 160, 174, 194, 208
Elephantine 54, 175
Elephantine stela 171
enclosure walls: Hatshepsut 60; Nectanebo I 191, 218–21; Pinedjem I 187; Ramesses II 161–62; Ramesses III 176; Senusret I 12; Tuthmosis I 40, 42; Tuthmosis III 24–25, 36–37, 54, 69, 76–77, 88, 219
endowments 30, 145, 149, 168, 173–75, 210
Ennead of Karnak 73, 75–76
Esarhaddon, Assyrian King 207
Estate of Amun 98
eye-paint 182

faience 60, 132, 139, 151, 168–69, 177
falcons 82, 94, 160, 195, 200, 225
false-doors 82, 94, 160, 192, *193*, 195, 221, 228–29
Festal Stela 179
Festival Court (Tuthmosis II) 47–50, *48–49*, 54–55, 57, *58*, 64, 70, 89, 96, 99
Festival Hall of Tuthmosis III *See* Akh-Menu
flagstaffs 42, 84, 106, 134, 136–40, 210, 221
floods 16, 18, 27, 70, 114, 189–90, 196–97
floors 59, 74, 97, 106, 108, 144, 200; levels 10–11, 13

Forecourt of Sheshonk I *115*, 188–89, 213
fossilised wood statue 231
foundation ceremonies 100, 139, 148, 226
fowl-yards 91–92, 125, 169, 213, *214*
Franco-Egyptian Centre at Karnak 12, 236–37
funerary elements 71, 73–74, 76, 91, 130–31, 157, 167–68, 203, 230
funerary stela, (Intef II) 7

Gabolde, Luc 12, 70
Garden of Amun 98
gardens 64–65, 89, 97–98, 112, 122
Gardiner, Alan 37
gateways: enclosure walls 12, 36, 54, 62, 97, 176, 189, 221–22; pylons 42, 60, 79, 84, 120, 137, 219, 227; temples 34, 160, 172, 195, 207, 211, 221
Gebel el-Ahmar 55–57, 110
Gebel Silsileh 120, 188
Geographic Procession 65–66
gilding 33, 57, 60, 64, 74, 78, 111, 229
God's Wives of Amun 30, 190–92, 195–96, 203–10
gold 16, 19, 29, 34, 42, 54–55, 59, 73, 79–82, 84–88, 91, 97, 101–2, 104, 106, 108, 128, 132, 136, 139, 146, 148–51, 173–77, 194, 207, 226, 228, 232
gold mines 146
Golden Porch of Tuthmosis IV 101–2, *102*, 106, 194
Graeco-Roman repairs 151
graffiti 160, 234–35
granaries 98, 110–11, 175
granite 66, 79, 120, 172, 200; black *20*, 133, 152–54, 161, 207, 210; grey 152; red 11, 42, 50, 74, 80, 97, 111, 115, 117, 127, 137, 165, 176, 226, 228; rose/pink 16, 42, 81, 84–85
Great Court of Sheshonk I 115
Great Harris Papyrus 65, 171, 175, 232
Great Inscription of Merenptah 164–65
Great-of-Food offering-table 174
Gurneh 145

Hakor 2, 197, 213–14, 216–17, *216–18*
Hapi 131, 158
Hathor 24, 191

250

INDEX

Hathor facade *206,* 212
Hatshepsut 15, 40, 43–44, 46, 50–67, *58, 61, 63,* 68–69, 76, 78, 81–82, 99, 104–5, 112, 117, 124, 140, 146, 162
Hattusil 158
'hears-prayers' temples/shrines 88–89, 102–3, 160, 222, 229
Heliopolis 69, 120, 152, 179
Heliopolitan elements 12, 50, 70–71, 73, 75–77, 122 *See also* solar elements
Henen-Nesut 133
heraldic pillars 81, 194, 216
Herihor 182–83
hidden entrance, Akh-Menu 74
hieroglyphs 9, 16, 38, 44, 46, 57, 62, 82, 123, 149–50, 166, 194
'High Lookout of Kheperkare' 15
High Priest of Amun's dwelling 23
high priestesses 190–92
high priests 79, 86, 121, 160, 178, 181–83, 188, 190; increasing status 180–81, 187
Hittites 93, 157–58, 171
Holy of Holies 11, 14, 33, 52, 55, 60, 74–75, 176
homonyms 42
Horemheb 62, 94–95, 109–10, 117, 123, 127–30, 132–42, *135,* 143–44, 146
Horemsaf 188–89
Hornung, Eric 123
horticulture 98
Horus 12, 16, 50, 73, 76, 99, 133, 136, 141, 183, 225, 229
Horus Sanctuary 73
House of Gold (Shabaka) 194–95
House of Gold (Tuthmosis III) 89–91, *90,* 177
House of Maat (Hapshepsut) *See also* Palace of Maat 53, 57
House of Tiaa 100
Humen 111
Hyksos kings 27–29
hymns 114, 164, 182, 197, 233
Hypostyle Hall *2, 4,* 37, 106, 115, 136–37, 143–51, *148,* 156–57, 162–63, 177, 183

iconoclasm 19, 44, 94, 126–27, 234
imperial expansion 34, 39
incense 62–65, 81–82, 88
Ineni 36, 39–40, 42, 51

inscriptions *See also* bandeau texts; cartouches; decrees; stelae: Akhenaten 119–20, 125; Alexander 225; Amenhotep I 36; Amenhotep II 97–98; Amenhotep III 104; Amenhotep, son of Hapu 110; Darius I 212; Djehuti 54, 59; Hatshepsut 51–52, 55, 60, 64; High Priest Amenhotep 23, 181; High Priest Roy 23; Horemheb 133; Intef II 7; Menkheperreseneb 79; Merenptah 164–65; Montuemhat 208; Nectanebo I 118; Ouser 70; Piankh 183; Prince Osorkon 190; Psamut 213; Ptolemy VIII 229; Ramesses I 143; Ramesses II 155–56; Ramesses IV 179; Senenmut 53–54; Senusret I 10–11, 14; Seti I 37, 145–46, 148–51; Seti II 169; Taharqa 196–97, 203; Tutankhamun 130; Tuthmosis I 44, 46; Tuthmosis III 8, 15, 36, 40, 69, 73, 76, 78–79, 81–83, 85–87; Tuthmosis IV 101
inspection of temples 175, 187
Intef II 7–8
intercolumnar walls 84, 89, 197, 200, 211, 215, 228
inundation rites 197
inundations 16, 18, 27, 70, 114, 189–90, 196–97
invasions 163, 171, 178–80, 182, 212, 223
Ipet-Resyt 115
Ipet-Sut 8–9, 24, 42–43, 68, 73, 77, 87–88, 92, 99, 101, 134, 161, 168
ithyphallic form *See* Amun-Kamutef
irrigation 115, 222, 227
Isetnofret 163
Isis (goddess) 191
Isis, God's Wife of Amun 180
Israel 189
Israel Stela 164
Iuput 188

Jubilee Monument of Amenhotep II *See* Edifice of Amenhotep II
jubilees *See* sed-festivals
Judah 189

ka 105, 149, 157, 167
Kadesh, Battle of 147, 157–58, 163–64
Kamose 28–29

INDEX

Karomama 191
Kashta 192
Khaemwaset 163
Khonsu 140, 182, 221; precinct 33, 99, 115, 136, 172, 187; temple *2, 4, 135,* 175, 183, 213, 216–17, 223, 227, 229, 233, *321*
king-lists 38, 146
kiosks: Amenhotep I 34–36, *35,* 52, 59, 84; Ramesses III 174–75; Taharqa 115, 129, 197–200, *198–99*
kitchens/bakeries 23, 26, 45, 98, 194
Kushite period 27, 209–11, 216

lakes 16, 23, 67, 85, 112, 207 *See also* Sacred Lake
land review of Ptolemy II 227
lapis lazuli 29, 70, 82, 84, 87, 106, 108, 128, 148, 150, 206
Lateran obelisk *See* Single Obelisk
legitimization of rule 52, 68, 99, 133–34, 143, 145, 178
Legrain, Georges 167, 207, 231
Lepsius, Karl 195, 213
Libyans 163–64, 171, 178–80, 182, 188
limestone 11, 14–16, 24, 26–29, 36, 38–39, 46, 50, 53, 60, 65, 70, 129
Litany of the Sun 203
Litany of Victorious Thebes 162, 173
Luxor 20, 33, 53, 60, 62, 100, 105, 115, *116,* 121, 133, 136, 140, 154, 158, 162, 168, 234

Maat 53, 127, 132, 141; Palace of *3,* 59
Ma'at Temple *43*
Maatkare 187
magazines 44–45, 90, 131, 140, 213
Malkata 112
Mansion of the Benben 122–23
Mark Antony 233
Marriage Stela 158
Maru-Amun 112
Maspero, Gaston 231
May, High Priest of Amun 121
Medamud 121, 145
Medinet Habu 172, 174
Medinet Habu stela 143
memorials to ancestors 8, *37–38,* 38, 73, 77, 81, 83
Memphis 127, 133, 159, 165, 179, 192, 223

Mendes 212
Menkheperre, High Priest of Amun 187–88
Menkheperresoneb, High Priest of Amun 79, 83, 86
Merenptah 23, 158, 163–65, 200
Meryetre Hatshepsut 93, 95
Middle Kingdom Court 10–14, *13,* 24, 27, *58,* 71, 92, 233
Middle Kingdom Temple *3,* 11–15, *13,* 19, 23–24, 26–27, 38, 40, 43, 46, 52–53, 55, 59–60, 70–71, 76–77, 176, 219, 223
military campaigns 46, 51–52, 68, 74, 83, 91, 93, 99, 104, 130, 146–47, 157–58, 163–64, 171–73, 178, 188–89, 207–8, 211
'millions of years' temples 77, 130, 149, 155, 161, 167
Min *See* Amun-Kamutef
miracles 40, 52, 78, 179
Mitanni 93, 99
Mitrahineh 168
models of temples 152, *153*
Montu 7, 79, 117, 136; precinct 8–10, 26, 43, 98, 111, 121, 190, 195, 206, 210–11, 219, 227; temple *43,* 108, 111, 127, 133, 181, 200–201, 207, 223, 228, 230
Montuemhat 196, 208–9, 219
monument of Tutankhamun 129–31, *131, 132*
monuments of Akhenaten 125
mortuary temples 7, 33, 59, 65, 77, 116, 145, 164, 172, 175
Mound of Osiris 191, 203, 221, 227–28
mound, primaeval 114, 219, 229
mud-brick: buildings 8, 176, 195, 206–7, 213, 233; enclosing walls 8, 12, 54, 69, 84, 117, 121, 141, 176, 189, 191, 203, 230; platforms 11, 19, 36, 106, 235; pylons 12, 36, 84, 109, 137; ramps 219
Musée du Louvre 73, 191
Mut 128, 132, 158; contra-temple 227; precinct 26, 33, 53, 62, 109, 112, 115–17, *116,* 137, 187, 200, 233; shrine 10; temple 175, 207, 216–17, 228
Mutnodjmet 133
Mutnofret 46
mythological texts of Ptolemy VIII 228–29

naoi 11, 14, *20–21,* 88, 176, 195

Nebhepetre Montuhotep 10
Necho II 211
Necho of Sais 207, 209
Nectanebo I 62, 89, 117–18, 121, 160, 191, 217–22
Nectanebo II 222–23, 227
Neferhotep, tomb of 101, 106, 112, 136
Neferhotep Chapel (Ptolemy IV) 227
Nefertiti 117, 122–25
Nefertiti pillars 123, *124*, 136
Neferure 46
Nekhen 24
Nepherites I 212–13
Nepherites II 217
Nero 233
Neuserre 8, 75
New Year Festival 197
Nile: god of 131, 158; inundations 16, 18, 27, 70, 114, 189–90, 196–97; levels recorded 189–90, 231; personifications 16, 23
Nile Gate 62
nilometers *2*, 27, 203, *204*
Nine Bows 137
Nitocris, God's Wife of Amun *2*, 209–11
nomes 16, 24, 59, 226, 228
non-rectangular structure 94
north-east sector 190, 211
Northern and Southern Courts (Tuthmosis III) 81–82
Northern Lake 23, 67, 85–86
Nubia 46, 99, 146, 163, 171, 188, 192, 211
Nubian Dynasty 190–91
Nun, primaeval waters of 203, 219

obelisks *113*; Amenhotep II 98; Amenhotep III 200; Hatshepsut 43, 54–55, 77–78; Horemheb 140; Ramesses II 154, 161; Ramesses III 176; Seti I 152; Seti II 114, 166; Tuthmosis I 42; Tuthmosis II 50; Tuthmosis III 84, 86–89, 101–2, 126, *159*, 160–61, 229, 234
Octavian 222, 233
Offering Chapel (Horemheb) 140–41
Offering Chapel (Tutankhamun/Ay) 129–31, *131*, 132
offerings 88, 100; offering-chambers 40, 53, 55, 57, 60, 64, 80, 82, 131; offering-courts 177; offering-statues 173; offering-tables 10, 24, 27, 74–75, 174; offering-vases 25
officials 39, 59, 68, 85–87, 91, 125, 139–40, 149, 174–75
Old Kingdom kings 8
Open Air Museum 15, 18, 23, 55, 100
'Opening of the Mouth' 91, 194–95
Opet Festival 53, 60, 62, 104–5, 112, 133, 140, 150, 155, 167, 173
Opet Temple *2*, 99, 202, 207, 221, 225, 227, 229–30, *230–32*, 233, 235
oracles 57, 89, 108, 140, 182–83, 224
Osirian chapels *2*, 190–92, 195–96, 206–7, *208*, 210, 212, 230, *231*
Osirian forms of Re 203
Osiride columns 89, 160
Osiride figurines 211, 227
Osiride statues 12, 40, 71, 79, 172, 187
Osiris 52, 179, 190–91, 196, 211, 227, 229–30
Osiris Tombs *2*, 211, 227
Osorkon II 191
Osorkon III 141, 190–91
Osorkon, Prince 190
Ouser 70

painted decoration 1, 24, 47, 64, 73, 88, 101, 106, 109, 144, 148, 151, 174, 206, 227, 234
Palace of Maat *3*, 59–60, 64, 78, 80–81, 86 *See also* House of Maat
palaces 26, 46, 65–66; Amenhotep III 112, *122*; Akhenaten 121, *122*; Hatshepsut *63*
palanquins 125
Palermo Stone 63
Palestine 46, 163, 188
Panehsy, Viceroy of Kush 182–83
Papyrus Bologna 201
Pasaba, steward 211
'patron saints' of artisans 91
Penpato 175
peristyle courts 12, 14, 27, 45, 60, 78, 80–81, 89, 99–100, 105, 122, 160
Per-Ramesses 159
persea-tree (¡prog¿?šd)¡/prog¿ 45, 161, 179, 191
Persians 212, 218, 222–23
personifications 16, 23, 87, 162, 189

INDEX

Philip Arrhidaeus 11, 50, 55–57, 59, 223, 225–26
Piankh 183, 187
Piankhy (Piye) 192, 195
pillars *See also* columns: gold inlaid 79; heraldic 81, 194, 216; limestone 12–14, 231; monolithic 16; Nefertiti 123, *124,* 136; Osiride 12, 160; re-used 146; square 12, 79, 84, 94, 100, 122–23, 172; supporting emblems 163
Pillet, Maurice 109
Pinedjem I 114–16, 187
Piye (Piankhy) 192, 195
plaques 137, *138–39,* 168–69
pools 97–98
porches 101, *102,* 106, 119, 194, 200–202, 212, 221, 230
porticoes 12–14, 23, 34, 40, 52, 59, 71, 77, 94–96, *95,* 181, 202, 206, 213, 233
pottery 25
Pramesse 141–42 *See also* Ramesses I
predynastic antiquities 7
'Presenting the House' 152
priest-kings 114, 187
priests 23, 76, 79, 86, 121, 133, 149, 160, 167
primaeval mound 114, 219, 229
processional ramp 197
processional statues 19–20, 57, 73–74, 76, 111, 114, 208, 227
processional ways 23, 33, 47, 76–77, 112–18, *116,* 117, 166, 168, 214, *216,* 227 *See also* Southern Processional Way
processions 19–20, 50, 53, 59, 71, 125, 130, 150, 197; water-borne 33, 62, 66, 85, 100, 105, 108, 173, 182, 221
propaganda 50, 54, 60, 133, 158
prophets of Amun 70, 101, 188, 196, 208–9
propylon gate of Ptolemy II 227
provisions 64, 98
Psamtik I 190, 208–11
Psamtik II 210–11
Psamtik III 212
Psamut 213, *214–15*
Psusennes II 188
Ptah 12, 91, 158–59, 162, 164–65, 179; precinct 230; temple *2,* 45, 133, 146, 195, 221, 227–28, 233
Ptolemaic period 100, 221–23, 227–33

Ptolemy I Soter 226–27
Ptolemy II Philadelphus 227
Ptolemy III Euergetes I 223, 227
Ptolemy IV Philopator 227–28
Ptolemy V Epiphanes 228
Ptolemy VI Philomentor 228
Ptolemy VIII Euergetes II *216,* 228–30, *231*
Ptolemy IX Soter II 230
Ptolemy XII Neos Dionysos 230
public access 50, 59, 150, 157, 159–60
Punt expeditions 63–64, 140
purification 50, 100–101, 136, 213
purification kiosk 174–75
Puyemre 86–88
pylon doorway, miniature 84
pylons *2,* 46, 77–78, 123; First *4,* 113–14, 189, *216,* 219, *220,* 233, 235; Second *4,* 97, 109, 115, 123, 129, 134–37, *135,* 143–44, *148,* 151, 157, 175, 180, 183, 188–89, 197, 200, 228–29; Third *4,* 15, 27–30, 34, 46, *48,* 50, 55, 89, 101, 105–9, *107,* 119, 123, 127, *148;* Fourth *3,* 40, 42–43, *48,* 55, *58,* 101, 105, 194; Fifth *3,* 40, 42, 55, *58,* 78; Sixth 12, 42, 77, 79–80; Seventh *3,* 12, 50, 84; Eighth *3,* 23, 36–37, 53, 60, 94, 97, 137, 176, 181, 235; Ninth *4,* 16, 94–95, *95,* 109, 125, 129, 137–40, 158, 162, 168, 233, 235; Tenth *4,* 94, *95, 107,* 109–10, 117, 119–20, 137

quarries 39, 54–57, 110, 120, 152, 188
quarry-marks 109, 115, 121
quartzite 74, 102, 166; red 55–57, 69, 110, 154
quays *2,* 10, 60, 62, 66, 112, *113,* 129, 189, 197, 214, 216–17

raised relief 36, 147, 156, 177
Ramesses I 137, 143–45, 157
Ramesses II 28, 62, 65, *72, 95,* 100, 117, 129, 154–63, *159*
Ramesses III *2,* 115, 171–78
Ramesses IV 175, 178–79
Ramesses V 178–79
Ramesses VI 178–80
Ramesses VII 180
Ramesses IX 23

Ramesses X 182
Ramesses XI 182–83, 187
Ramessesnakht, High Priest of Amun 180–82
Ramesseum 158, 162, 168
ramps 10, 114, 197, *216*
rams *61,* 108, 114–16, 118, 174
Re 179, 203
rebellions 46, 93–94, 146, 163, 190, 212, 228
Red House (*pr-d¡prog¿šr*)¡/prog¿ 44
refectories 23
Re-Horakhte 99, 120, 125, 127, 160–61; lakeside temple 202–6
rekhyt-birds 59, 132, 150, 157
reliefs: Alabaster Bark-Shrine (Tuthmosis III) 181; Alabaster Bark-Shrine (Tuthmosis IV) 100; Alabaster Kiosk (Amenhotep I) 34–36; Amenmesse Tomb 165; Amun Temple, girdle wall *72,* 157; Annals of Tuthmosis III 83–84; Bark-Shrine (Philip Arrhidaeus) 226; Black Granite Naos (Senruset I) 19; Chamber of Ancestors (Tuthmosis III) 73; Chapel of Osiris Heka-Djet 191, 196; Chapel of Osiris-Ptah Neb-Ankh 207, *208*; Chapel of the Divine Adoratrices 206; Chapelle Rouge 59, *63*; Court of the Cachette 163–64; Court of the Eighth Pylon 181; Court of the First Pylon 228; Court of the Second Pylon 189; Court of the Tenth Pylon 140; Eighth Pylon 60, 176; Enclosure Wall 227–28; Granary (Amenhotep III) 110; House of Gold (Tuthmosis III) 84, 90–91; Hypostyle Hall 147–48, 157, 163; Kamose Stela 28; Khonsu Temple *135,* 183, 219; Mansion of the Benben (Akhenaten) 123–24; Middle Kingdom Temple 14, 189; Monument of Akhenaten 125; Mortuary Temple (Ramesses III) 172; Offering-Chapel (Tutankhamun) 130–31; Offering-Chapel (Tuthmosis III) 37; Palace of Maat 59–60; Panehsy tomb 183; Peristyle Court (Senruset I) 12; Pillared Court (Tuthmosis IV) 100–101; Re-Horakhte Temple (Akhenaten) 119–20; Second Pylon 136, 180; Seventh Pylon 84, 181–82; Southern Processional Way 158; Temple of Mut 200, 210; Temple of Nitocris 211; Temple of Ramesses III 172–73, 177–78; Tenth Pylon 137; Third Pylon 119; Tripartite Shrine (Seti II) 167; Wadjet Hall 111; White Chapel (Senruset I) 16, *17*
Renenutet 131
Restoration Stela 127–29
Return of the God Festival 59–60
re-use of buildings' names 36, 81, 84, 108, 149, 226
reverence for predecessors 15, 37–38, 44–46, 73, 81, 83, 134, 145, 156
Roman period 233–34
Roman Temple *220,* 233
roofing 18, 57, 78, 96, 147, 173, 175, 177, 197, 200, 203; levels 11, 13
Rosetta Stone 228
'Rowing the Deity on the Lake' 85
Roxane 226
Roy, High Priest of Amun 23
royal cult chapel of Tuthmosis III 225
Royal Progresses 173, 179

sack of Thebes 87–88
Sacred Lake 23, 66, 77, 85, 91–92, 111, 125, 131, 169, 202–3, 213
Sahure 63
Saite Dynasty 209–12, 227
sanctuaries: Hatshepsut *61,* 62; Philip Arrhidaeus 11, 50; Ptolemy VIII 229; Senusret I 71, 78–79; Tuthmosis I 44–45; Tuthmosis III 73–74
sandstone 11, 14, 27, 40, 42, 60, 65, 69, 76, 79, 84, 94, 97, 100, 106, 120, 172; *versus* limestone 39, 70
Sankhkare Montuhotep 8
Saqqara 16, 129
scarabs 98, 111, 119, 203
Schatt el-Rigal, quarries 39
Sea Peoples 163–64, 171
Sebekhotep II 115
Sebekhotep IV 27
sed-festivals 15–16, 42, 45–46, 52, 55, 60, 81, 84, 88, 94, 96, 112, 120, 122, 125, 161, 212; of God's Wives 191
Sefkhet-Abu 100
Senenmut 53–54
Seniseneb 39
Sennefer 97

255

Senusret I 8–28, *34,* 38, 45, *58,* 60, 69–71, 83, 91, 128
Seqenenre Tao I 28
Seqenenre Tao II 28
Seshat 45
Seth animals 169
Seti I *2,* 37, 44, 77, 94–95, 117, 137, 143–55, *148,* 157, 161–63
Seti II *2,* 114–15, 166–70
Seti-Merenptah 163, 165–68
Setnakhte 171
Seven Hathors 191
Shabaka 192–95
Shabitku 195–96
Shepenwepet I, God's Wife of Amun 191–92, 195–96, 206–10
Shepenwepet II, God's Wife of Amun 196
Sheshonk I 114–15, 188–90, 192
Shrine of Mut (Amenemhet I) 10
Siclen, C. van 96–97
silver 29–30, 40, 70, 79, 87, 97, 106–8, 128, 148, 158, 173–76, 194, 207
Sinai 146
Sinai stela 143
Single Obelisk 86–87, 89, 100–102, 126, *159,* 160–61, 229, 234
Sinuhe 14
Siptah 169–70
Sitre 145
Siwa 224
Smendes 114, 183, 187
Smenkhkare 127
Snofru 8
social unrest 182
Sokar 71, 73, 76
solar elements 134, 191, 197–200, 202–6
solar sanctuaries 71, 74–76, *75,* 160, 176, 200
'Son et Lumière' 24
Souls of Pe and Nekhen 173, 176
southern gateway (Bubastite) 189
Southern Lake 23, 67, 85
Southern Processional Way 21, 33, 36, 53, 60, *61,* 77, 84, 94–95, 102, 109, 115, *116,* 117–18, 129, 134, 137, 140, 163–64, 181; walls 158, 222
Sphinx Stela 99
sphinxes 62, 106, 109, 118, 123, 129, 181; ram-headed *61,* 114–18, 163

sphinx-lined avenues *61,* 112, 114–15, 117–18, 187, 189, 222
stairways 7, 11, 16, 42, 59, *75,* 76, 79, 85, 98, 114, 139–40, 151, 167, 173, 200, 203, 229, 235
state barge *See* Userhet
Stations of the King: Amenhotep II 96; Ramesses I 144
statues *See also* colossi; sphinxes: Amenemhet I 10–11; Amenhotep, High Priest 181; Amenhotep I 36, 38; Amenhotep, son of Hapu 110; Amenirdis I, God's Wife 195; Amun 54, 88–89; baboons 201; falcons 225; Hathor 24; Hatshepsut 54; Horemheb 110, 133, 231; kings 8; Mentuhotep 24; Merenptah 165; Mutnodjmet 133; Mutnofret 50; Neuserre 8; Osiride 12, 40, 71, 79, 172, 187; Pramesse 142; processional 57, 74; Ramesses I 145; Ramesses II *95,* 161–62; Ramesses III 172; Ramesses VI 180; Ramesses-who-hears-prayers 103; Senenmut 53; Senusret I 12, 24; Seti I 151–52; Seti II 168; Taharqa 207; Tutankhamun 128–29; Tuthmosis I 42, 78; Tuthmosis III 88–89; Tuthmosis IV 102–3
stelae 20, 117; Ahmose 29–30; Amenhotep IV (Akhenaten) 120; boundary of Nekhen stela 24, *25*; Djehuti (festival court) 54, 59, 64, 66; Djehuti (Northampton Stela) 54; Domitian 233; false-doors 82, 94; gold stela 144; Great Stela of Amenhotep III 111; Herihor, High Priest 182; Horemheb: on law and order 140–41; Israel Stela 164; Kamose 28; La Stèle Juridique 29; Marriage Stela of Ramesses II 140; Menkheperre 202; Nectanebo I 221; Ouser: on Akh-Menu 70; Pinedjem I 187; Psamtik I 209; Psamtik II 211; Ptolemy V 228; Ramesses I 143; Ramesses II 158; Ramesses III 171, 177; Ramesses IV 179; Ramesses IX 182; Restoration Stela 127–29; Sebekhotep IV 27; Sekhemre-Seusertawy-Sebekhotep VIII 27; Seti I 146, 152–54; Seti II 166, 169; on fowl-yard 92; Sheshonk I 188; Sphinx Stela 99; Taharqa 196; Tutankhamun

127–28, 132; Tuthmosis II 46; Tuthmosis III 45; Victory Stela 164
Step Pyramid Saqqara 16
Storehouse of Psamut 2, 213, *214–15*
storerooms 24, 63–64, 81, 128, 169, 173 *See also* granaries
strikes by workers 178
subterranean chambers 202–6, *205,* 229
subterranean galleries 227
Sun Disk *See* Aten
sun-disks 163, 168, 181
sunk relief 36, 147, 156, 177
sun-temple at Abu Gurob 75
symmetry 11, 28, 94, 125, 131, 137, 215
Syria 74, 99, 171

Tacitus 176
Taharqa 2, 85, 111, 114–15, *159,* 195–208, *198–99, 205,* 216, *216*
Takeloth II 190–91
Takeloth III 191–92
Takhat 165
talatat blocks 95, 117, 120–23, 129, 136–37
Tanutamun 207
Tauseret 169–70
temple layout, typical 11, 40
Temple of Nebhepetre Montuhotep 26
Temple of Nefertiti 125
Temple of Sankhkare Montuhotep 8–9
Temple of Seti II (triple bark-shrine) 189
Temple/bark-shrine of Ramesses III 2, 4, 172–73, 189
temporary kiosk, Hypostyle Hall 151
Ten-Year Festival 216
Teos 222–23
Tetisheri 28
Texte de la Jeunesse 82
Theban Ennead 73, 75–76
Theban Triad 73, 105, 125, 131, 147, 150, 167, 172–73, 203, 207; framed relief 177
Thebes 7, 26; personified 162, 189, 228
Theodosius 234
Thoth 45, 136, 140, 213; Chapel 140, 213, 215
Throne Room of Taharqa (Montu Temple entrance) 200–201
Tiaa 99–100
Tiberius 14, 223, 230, 233
Time of Troubles 170–71

Titus 233
Tiye 104, 110
Tod 100, 175
Tomb of Osiris (Necho II) 211
Tomb of Osiris (Ptolemy IV) 227
tombs: Amenemhab 93; Amenemope 178; Amenhotep Si-se 101–2; Amenmesse 165–66; Horemheb 129; Neferhotep 101, 106, *107,* 112, 136; Panehsy, Viceroy of Kush 183; Puyemre 86, 88; Ramesses I 145; Sennefer 97–98; Seti I 155; Sitre 145; Tuthmosis I 40
trade 104, 182 *See also* incense
transport 54, 110, 152
treasuries 44, 66, 149
Treasury of Shabaka 2, 194–95
Treasury of Tuthmosis I 26, *43–44,* 44–45, 91
treaties 93, 99, 157–58
Triad *See* Theban Triad
tribunes 85, *113,* 114, 166, *216*
triple bark-shrines: Ramesses II 62; Ramesses III 172–73; Seti II 115, 166–68, 189
turning-station 215, *216*
turquoise 70, 82, 84, 108, 128, 209, 232
turquoise mines 146
Tutankhamun (Tutankhaton) 117, 126–32, *131*
Tuthmosis I *3,* 26, 34, 39–46, *41, 43–44,* 52, *58,* 59–60, 66, 78, 86, 92
Tuthmosis II 40, 46–50, *48,* 51, 54, *58,* 86–87
Tuthmosis III *2–3,* 14–15, 23–25, 36–38, 40, 42–44, 46, 50–55, *58,* 59–60, *61,* 65–66, 68–93, *72, 80, 90,* 102, 125, *131,* 134, *159,* 160
Tuthmosis IV 86–87, 89, 99–103, 112
Tuya 162
Two Ladies names 134, 143

Unification of the Two Lands 28, 188
unification rite 81
Union with the Sun ceremony 200
Upper Gateway 54, 160, 201
Userhet 60, 100, 105, 108, 114, 200, 214
usurpation of earlier works 47, 65, 68–69, 80, 97, 117, 128–29, 132, 134, 156, 165, 179, 211, 228

257

Valley of the Queens 145
vessels 26, 83–84
Victorious Thebes 189
Victory Chapel, Wadjet Hall (Amenhotep II) 97
Victory Stela 164
vineyards 98
viziers 24, 70, 141–42, 182
votive case, bronze 207

Wadi Hammamat 63
Wadjet Hall 40–42, 47, *48–49*, 54–55, *58*, 111; Amenhotep II 97; Hatshepsut 54–55; Tuthmosis I 40–42, 54–55, 97; Tuthmosis III 77–78
Wadjmose 46
Wah-Ankh Intef II 7, 8
Wall-Chapel of Nectanebo I 221
walls *See* enclosure walls
water-borne processions 33, 62, 66, 85, 100, 105, 108, 173, 182, 216–17, 221
way-stations 60–62, *61, 63*, 89, 140, 213–16 *See* bark-shrines

Wegaf 27
West Bank *See also* mortuary temples; tombs: crossing to 10, 20, 33, 60, 214, 216, 221; palaces 112; stelae 111, 143; temples 8, 10, 12, 26, 53
western approach 33, 187
westward expansion 166
White Chapel of Senusret I 9–10, 15–16, *17*, 23, 38, 66
White House (*pr-ḥd*)(Tuthmosis I) 44
widening of entrances 168
Wilbour Papyrus 100
windows 18, 73, 125, 147, 151, 173, 176
winged solar disks 47, 134, 163 *See also* sun disks
wooden masts 200, *201*
word-play 42, 46
workshops 24, 45, 55, 91, 98, 102, 114, 151, 194

Yamu-nedjeh 86
Yoyotte, Jean 101

Related titles from Routledge

Ancient Egypt 2nd Edition
Anatomy of a Civilisation
Barry Kemp

Praise for the first edition:

'Its originality should make it required reading for all students for ancient Egypt.' – *Times Literary Supplement*

'The most provocative, thoughtful and outstanding synthesis on Ancient Egypt available in the English language.' – *Choice*

'For an Egyptologist this fine book is consistently informative, provocative and stimulating; its vision of Egypt, even without the Pharaohs in their oriental glamour, will not fail to enthral.' – *Antiquity*

Completely revised and updated to reflect the latest developments in the field, this new edition of Kemp's popular text presents a compelling reassessment of what gave ancient Egypt its distinctive and enduring characteristics.

Ranging across Ancient Egyptian material culture, social and economic experiences, and the mindset of its people, the book also includes two new chapters exploring the last ten centuries of Ancient Egyptian civilization and who, in ethnic terms, the ancients were.

Fully illustrated, the book draws on both ancient written materials and decades of excavation evidence, transforming our understanding of this remarkable civilization. Broad ranging yet impressively detailed, Kemp's work is an indispensable text for all students of Ancient Egypt.

ISBN 13: 978–0–415–23549–5 (HB)
ISBN 13: 978–0–415–23550–1 (PB)

ISBN 10: 0–415–23549–9 (HB)
ISBN 10: 0–415–23550–2 (PB)

Available at all good bookshops
For ordering and further information please visit:
www.routledge.com

Related titles from Routledge

Archaeology
The Basics
Clive Gamble

'Gamble's book provides an excellent introduction to the aims and methods of archaeology, which is by no means easy within the confines of one book. But to do so in a manner which is intellectually engaged with the subject matter and which evokes the excitement and interest of archaeological work is a considerable achievement. The best short introduction to the subject I know and one which will become a standard text for any teacher of archaeology or related subject.' – *Chris Gosden, Pitt Rivers Museum, University of Oxford, UK*

'The digger boasting the worn stub of a trowel in their right back trouser pocket should feel incomplete without a copy of *Archaeology: The Basics* in the other.' – *Current Archaeology*

From archaeological jargon to interpretation, *Archaeology: the Basics* provides an invaluable overview of a fascinating subject and probes the depths of this increasingly popular discipline, presenting critical approaches to the understanding of our past.

Lively and engaging, *Archaeology: The Basics* fires the archaeological imagination whilst tackling such questions as:

- What are the basic concepts of archaeology?
- How and what do we know about people and objects from the past?
- What makes a good explanation in archaeology?
- Why dig here?

This ultimate guide for all new and would-be archaeologists, whether they are students or interested amateurs, will prove an invaluable introduction to this wonderfully infectious discipline.

ISBN 13: 978–0–415–22803–9 (HB)
ISBN 13: 978–0–415–22153–5 (PB)

ISBN 10: 0–415–22803–4 (HB)
ISBN 10: 0–415–22153–6 (PB)

Available at all good bookshops
For ordering and further information please visit:
www.routledge.com

Related titles from Routledge

Egypt's Legacy
The Archetypes of Western Civilization: 3000 to 30 BC
Michael Rice

In *Egypt's Legcay*, Michael Rice explains the majesty and enduring appeal of Egyptian Civilization. Drawing on Jungian psychology to show why Egypt has been so important in the history of Western Civilisation. Jung claimed that there exist certain psychological drives dormant in our shared unconscious: these are the Archetypes. From the omnipotent god to the idea of the nation state, the formulation of most of these archetypes is owed to Ancient Egypt.

People of the present day continue to wonder and marvel at the majesty of Egyptian art and architecture; in this book, Michael Rice sets out to recover the sense of wonder that the Egyptians themselves felt as they contemplated the world in which they lived, and the way they expressed that wonder in the religion, art and literature. He traces the story of Egyptian civilization from its emergence in the third millennium BC to its transformation following the Macedonian conquest in 30 BC.

ISBN 13: 978–0–415–15779–X (HB)
ISBN 13: 978–0–415–26876–1 (PB)

ISBN 10: 0–415–15779–X (HB)
ISBN 10: 0–415–26876–1 (PB)

Available at all good bookshops
For ordering and further information please visit:
www.routledge.com